lonely planet

Okinawa
& the Southwest Islands

**Wendy Yanagihara, Rob Goss, Craig McLachlan,
Manami Okazaki, Benedict Walker**

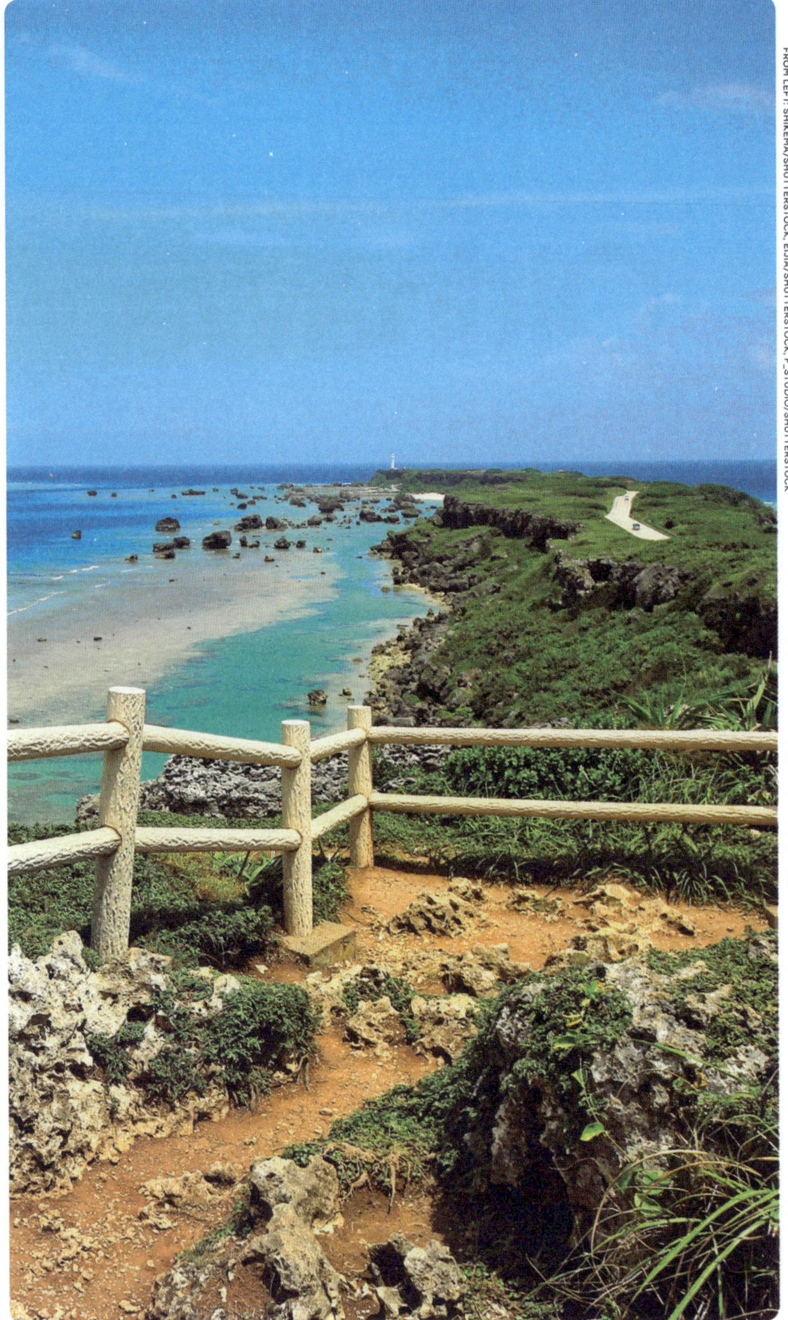

Higashi-Hennazaki (p187), Miyako-jima

CONTENTS

Ruddy kingfisher (p37)

Toolkit

Storybook

Tamagusuku ruins
(p85), Nanjō

Iriomote Island jungle (p218), Yaeyama Islands

OKINAWA & THE SOUTHERN ISLANDS

THE JOURNEY BEGINS HERE

Recently a cousin shared with me that DNA testing revealed her to be around 20% Okinawan, meaning that I too am some-per-cent Okinawan. Learning this gave me such a thrill. On my first visit to the Ryūkyū archipelago 12 years ago, island-hopping from Amami-Ōshima to Hateruma, I felt an unexpected spiritual connection to certain intriguing isles. In some ways I felt more at home in the humid jungle of Iriomote or a deserted beach on Yoron-tō than in mainland Japan, where I'd spent childhood summers.

Wendy Yanagihara

@wendy.yanagihara

Wendy is a writer and artist living in coastal California who has co-authored over 60 Lonely Planet titles. She wrote the Miyako Islands, Yaeyama Islands and introductory chapters for this book.

My favourite experience was witnessing mudskippers busting out of perfect mangrove-root camouflage (p211) and skittering across mud and water at astonishing speed – like some anime invention, but fantastically real.

WHO GOES WHERE

Our writers and experts choose the places which, for them, define Okinawa and the Southern Islands

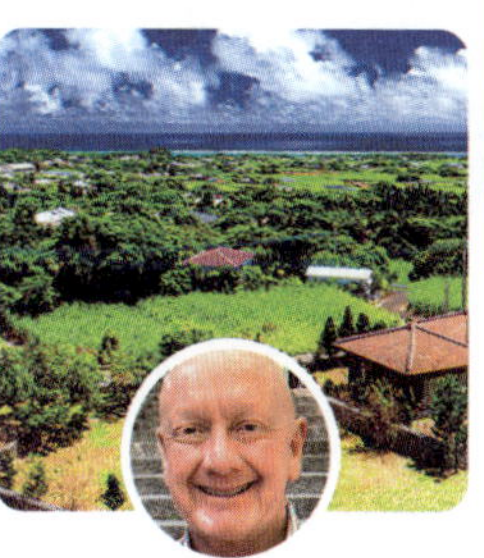

Kunigami locals' inspirational Ōgimi creative hub, on the site of the old **Kijoka Primary School** (p148), has gravitational pull for me.

Benedict Walker

@wordsandjourneys

A seasoned traveller and LP writer, Australian-born Benedict speaks fluent Japanese. He wrote the Naha, Southern Okinawa Island, Kerama Islands and Toolkit chapters.

Amami-Ōshima (p234) has a mix of everything I like: stellar scuba diving, surf beaches and exquisite textiles made with mind-boggling skill.

Manami Okazaki

@manami.tokyo

A journalist, author and producer, Manami has written several books on folk craft. She wrote the Central Okinawa Island and Northern Okinawa Island chapters, and co-wrote the Amami Islands chapter. She also wrote essays on mingei craft and sustainability.

I'm a big fan of **Yoron-tō** (p268). It's an ideal spot for pedalling in paradise, stopping off for a dip at idyllic beaches, marvelling at the turquoise hues inside the reef and just enjoying island life.

Craig McLachlan

@yuricraig

A Kiwi with wanderlust, Craig has written five books about his adventures in Japan and has been writing guidebooks for Lonely Planet for 25 years. He's a regular visitor to Okinawa. He co-wrote the Amami Islands chapter of this book.

After a trip delay from Tokyo, an evening stroll – almost alone – along the white sand of **Eef Beach** (p156) was the perfect antidote.

Rob Goss

@robgosswriter

Rob is a Tokyo-based writer and author focusing on travel and culture in Japan for media around the world. He wrote the Kume-jima chapter of this book.

CONTRIBUTING WRITERS

Helen Langford Matsui

@kamakura_by_the_sea

Rie Miyoshi

@trailmixr

Saya Tanahara

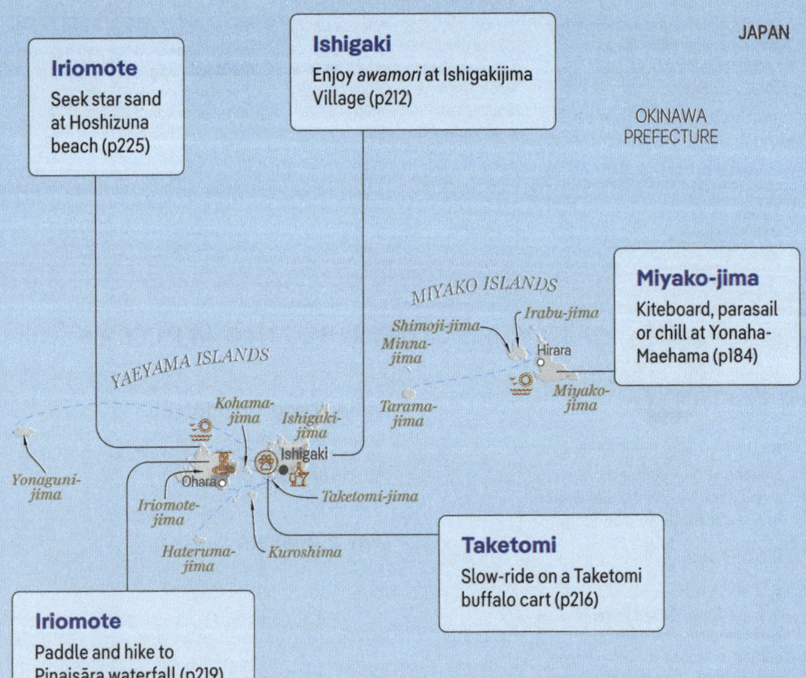
0
0
200 km
100 miles
N
Yoron-tō
Cross over to 'phantom island' Yurigahama (p268)
EAST CHINA SEA
Northern Okinawa Island
Admire ancient architecture at Nakijin-jō (p137)
JAPAN
Ishigaki
Enjoy awamori at Ishigakijima Village (p212)
OKINAWA PREFECTURE
Iriomote
Seek star sand at Hoshizuna beach (p225)
Miyako-jima
Kiteboard, parasail or chill at Yonaha-Maehama (p184)
MIYAKO ISLANDS
Irabu-jima
Shimoji-jima
Minna-jima
Hirara
YAEYAMA ISLANDS
Tarama-jima
Miyako-jima
Kohama-jima
Ishigaki-jima
Ishigaki
Yonaguni-jima
Ohara
Taketomi-jima
Iriomote-jima
Hateruma-jima
Kuroshima
Taketomi
Slow-ride on a Taketomi buffalo cart (p216)
Iriomote
Paddle and hike to Pinaisāra waterfall (p219)

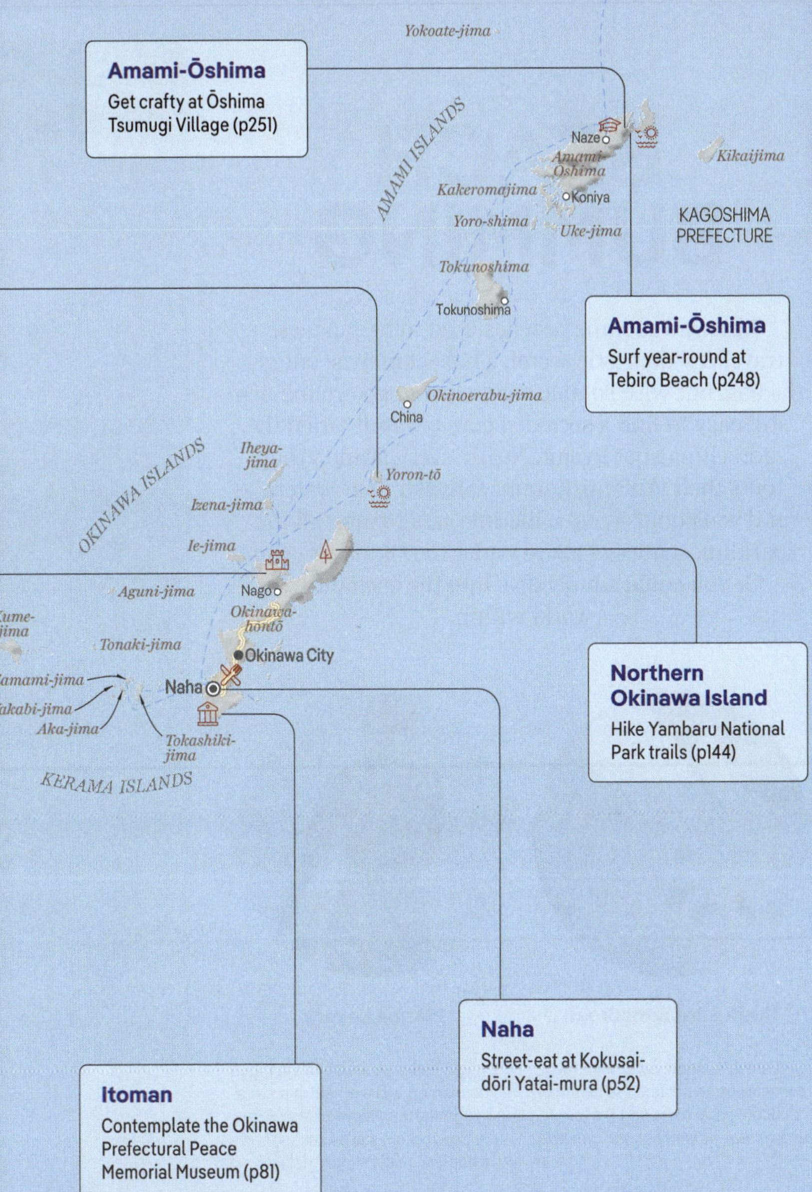
Amami-Ōshima
Get crafty at Ōshima Tsumugi Village (p251)
Amami-Ōshima
Surf year-round at Tebiro Beach (p248)
Northern Okinawa Island
Hike Yambaru National Park trails (p144)
Naha
Street-eat at Kokusai-dōri Yatai-mura (p52)
Itoman
Contemplate the Okinawa Prefectural Peace Memorial Museum (p81)
Yokoate-jima
AMAMI ISLANDS
Naze
Amami-Ōshima
Kikaijima
Kakeromajima
Koniya
Yoro-shima
Uke-jima
KAGOSHIMA PREFECTURE
Tokunoshima
Tokunoshima
Okinoerabu-jima
China
OKINAWA ISLANDS
Iheya-jima
Yoron-tō
Izena-jima
Ie-jima
Aguni-jima
Nago
Kume-jima
Okinawa-hontō
Tonaki-jima
Okinawa City
Zamami-jima
Naha
Yakabi-jima
Aka-jima
Tokashiki-jima
KERAMA ISLANDS
PACIFIC
OCEAN

BEACH BUMMING

Okinawa's sublime beaches used to be Japanese travellers' domestic secret. That cat may be out of the bag, but with so much shoreline to go around, it's still easy to find a secluded cove or family-friendly snorkelling spot to suit. Nearly every island group touts their 'Amami/Kerama/Miyako Blue' waters, and you could spend a lifetime cataloguing all the sparkling shades of azure under the Okinawan sun. Or you could simply dive into the enchanting world within.

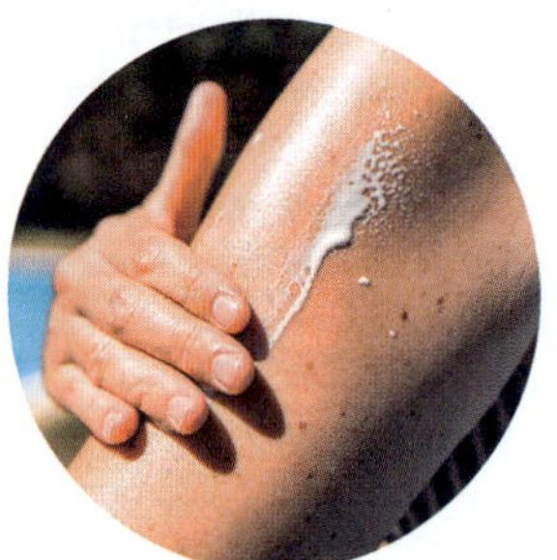

Reef-Safe Sunscreen

Always use non-nano-mineral sunscreens, to protect the health of delicate coral reefs and the larger ecosystem, as well as your own skin.

Marine Layers

It might feel counterintuitive in the sometimes oppressive heat, but swim leggings and long-sleeved rash vests provide excellent sun protection and a barrier against stinging jellies.

Open Season

Though beaches are open year-round, they are not staffed by lifeguards or strung with jellyfish nets in winter, so swim at your own risk.

BEST BEACH EXPERIENCES

Parasail over **❶ Yonaha-Maehama** (p184) and watch kiteboarders flying along below – or simply enjoy the beach's famed beauty.

Take a boat ride to visit the 'phantom island' of **❷ Yurigahama** (p268) just off the coast of Yoron-tō.

Sail on a *sabani* (traditional wooden boat) from **❸ Kondoi-hama** (p215) on Taketomi, and try your hand at paddling.

Search for star sand at **❹ Hoshizuna-no-hama** (p225) on Iriomote, bookending your beachcombing with a bit of snorkelling.

Surf year-round at **❺ Tebiro Beach** (p248) on the southern coast of Amami-Ōshima, or have a swim if there's no swell.

TERRESTRIAL ADVENTURES

Beaches and snorkelling may be Okinawa's main attractions, but the islands' interiors hold much to explore. National parklands in the Amami Islands, northern Okinawa-hontō and Iriomote form a unified UNESCO World Natural Heritage Site, filled with forest, waterfalls and rich biodiversity including the endemic Amami rabbit and Iriomote cat. Remnants of traditional life like spring-fed well systems and tidal fish traps speak of human history, and tranquil small islands retain steady agricultural rhythms.

Heat Exhaustion

Hike in the evening or early morning in hotter seasons. Okinawa's high humidity prevents perspiration from evaporating, which can lead to overheating and even heatstroke.

Hydration

Bring plenty of water and sport drinks to replenish electrolytes when adventuring. On active, sweaty days, hydrate well after drinking caffeine and before drinking alcohol.

Climate Range

Though the Ryūkyūs are considered subtropical, the Amami Islands are cooler and more temperate, while the Yaeyamas, roughly 700km south, have a tropical rainforest climate.

BEST INLAND EXPERIENCES

Hike through the lush subtropical forest of **❶ Yambaru National Park** (p144) in the far north of Okinawa-hontō.

Paddle a kayak along a mangrove-lined river to the short hike to **❷ Pinaisāra** (p219), Iriomote's tallest waterfall.

Rent a bike on **❸ Aka-jima** (p167) to ride around three of the connected Kerama Islands, looking out for Kerama deer.

Marvel at the stalactites and flowstone formations of **❹ Shōryūdō** (p264) on Okinoerabu-jima as you walk the 600m path through the cave.

Imagine hauling water at spring-fed well **❺ Sabautsu-gā** (p194) and using the tide to catch fish at stacked-stone fish traps on Irabu-jima.

OKINAWAN CULINARY DELIGHTS

Historically a trade route connecting China, Southeast Asia and Japan, the Ryūkyūs have developed culinary traditions in common while also branching out with regional differences such as *keihan* (chicken rice) in the Amami Islands, influenced by Kagoshima culture to the north. Meanwhile on Okinawa-hontō, the influence of US military-base culture led to the uniquely Okinawan inventions of taco rice and Spam *chanpurū* (stir-fry). Throughout the archipelago, the bounty of sea and soil form the foundation of culinary novelty.

Taco Rice

Okinawa's most comforting fusion food represents an unlikely harmony between multiple cultures: an American interpretation of a Mexican dish, deliciously translated Okinawa-style.

Wild Island Veggies

Gōya (bitter melon) may be Okinawa's most famous vegetable, but many other edible wild plants supply super-powered nutrition, including the striking purple-and-green *handama* (Okinawan spinach).

Sweet Treats

Must-tries include *kakigōri* (shaved ice) with brown-sugar syrup, Blue Seal ice cream, *sātā andagii* (Okinawan doughnut), and island-grown pineapple and mango.

BEST CULINARY EXPERIENCES

Follow your nose to try something you fancy at the food stalls of Naha's ❶ **Kokusai-dōri Yatai-mura** (p52).

Sip *awamori*, the rice liquor of the Ryūkyūs, preferably in the company of some local aficionados, at ❷ **Ishigakijima Village** (p212).

Feel the briny pop of wild-harvested *umibudō*, Okinawa's delicate and nutrient-rich seaweed known as green caviar, at ❸ **Poke Boo** (p196).

Screech to a stop for fresh-pressed ❹ **juice** or unbelievably sweet mango or pineapple from an Ishigaki roadside stand (p213).

Savour a bowl of *keihan*, bathed in light broth and deep cultural pride, at ❺ **Minatoya Amami Chicken Rice** (p250).

RYŪKYŪAN CULTURE

Ryūkyū culture lives vibrantly in the islands, not only in traditional festivals and ancient ruins but also in contemporary handicrafts, music, cuisine and language. Ryūkyūan languages and dialects still animate local conversations and popular music that also incorporates Okinawan instruments and singing styles. The traditional processes of weaving, pottery and art continue to be passed down, in addition to those of *sabani* (wooden boat) construction, whose new wave of younger boatwrights now counts the first woman among them.

Make Your Own

Most of the main islands have handicraft centres where you can try your hand at traditional arts and take home your own creation.

Sound of Sanshin

The three-stringed *sanshin* evolved from the Chinese *sanxian*, traditionally made with python skin to give the distinctively Okinawan sound a softer tone.

Language Islands

Among the six Ryūkyūan languages, dialects diverge from island to island and even into smaller intra-island dialects, unique linguistic islands unto themselves.

BEST CULTURAL EXPERIENCES

Taste the locally cultivated Okinawan cuisine in ❶ **Ōgimi** (p148), famous for its many inhabitants' uncommon longevity.

Dye your own textile at ❷ **Ōshima Tsumugi Village** (p251) and watch masters of the craft hand-producing luxurious *tsumugi* fabric.

Stroll through a Yaeyama community, learning about traditions, festivals and sacred sites on Iriomote's ❸ **Cultural Walk** (p224).

Learn to dye in the Okinawan style of *bingata* at ❹ **Gusuku Bingata** (p99) in Urasoe City, creating a piece of your own art.

Admire Ryūkyūan architecture on a buffalo-cart ride on traditional ❺ **Taketomi** (p214), accompanied by a live *sanshin* player for added atmosphere.

HISTORY & HERITAGE

The beginnings of the Ryūkyū Kingdom date back to the 12th century, hundreds of years before Japan annexed it. Tracing its history along the stacked limestone walls of its *gusuku* (castles) elicits a sense of awe at these resilient island kingdoms that eventually formed the larger unified archipelago. In more modern history, from the horror of war sprang the Okinawan determination to create beauty from tragedy – its war monuments persistently transmit the existential necessity of peace.

Pause for Peace

Touring war memorial sites can hit unexpectedly hard, so build in some meditation and decompression time when planning your visit.

Sacred Structure

Though *gusuku* are generally known as castles with fortified walls, their cultural origins hint that they may have begun as sacred sites.

Fossil Ruins

Because *gusuku* are made from Ryūkyūan limestone formed from ancient coral reefs, it's not unusual to find fossil remnants embedded in their painstakingly constructed walls.

BEST HISTORICAL EXPERIENCES

Take in the distinguished magnificence of the ❶ **Shuri-jō** (p65) castle grounds, rising again from the most recent ashes of 2019.

Meander the impressive, undulating, stacked-limestone ruins of 13th-century ❷ **Nakijin Castle** (p137), in size second only to Shuri-jō.

Learn the courageous stories of young women forced to make tragic wartime choices at ❸ **Himeyuri Peace Museum** (p81).

Absorb the overarching message of peace at ❹ **Okinawa Prefectural Peace Memorial Museum** (p81), near where the Battle of Okinawa ended.

Walk in the footsteps of 15th-century Miyako chieftain ❺ **Nakasone Tuyumya** (p179), whose territory was eventually subsumed into the Ryūkyū Kingdom.

REGIONS & CITIES

Find the places that tick all your boxes.

Kume-jima

SCENIC GEM ON NAHA'S DOORSTEP

Kume-jima is the kind of place you almost want to keep a secret because it's just right: an unassuming little island easily accessible from Naha with everything you need to slow down and get away from it all.

Central Okinawa Island

SERENITY, CRAFT AND FOOD GALORE

Home to US military bases, central Okinawa Island has a distinctly international flavour, especially in its cities' entertainment and shopping districts. But it's also a land of locals, where handicrafts are still made in the traditional manner and *gusuku* (Okinawan castle) ruins stand as a reminder of the people who once lived here. You'll find beach resorts and real slice-of-life Okinawa here.

Yaeyama Islands

PRISTINE SEAS AND TRADITIONAL RYŪKYŪAN CULTURE

Adventures abound in Okinawa's southernmost archipelago: dive with manta rays, SUP through mangroves, hike through subtropical forest or cycle around tiny, traditional islands. Gaze at the Southern Cross on Hateruma, dive a mysterious underwater monument off Yonaguni or trek to jungle waterfalls on wild Iriomote.

Miyako Islands

DREAMY BEACHES AND SUBLIME REEF

A picture of subtropical bliss beckons in these bucolic, low-lying isles. Swaths of powdery white-sand beaches slip into invitingly clear seas studded with offshore reefs and limestone caves. North of the islands lies the spectacular Yabiji Reef, Japan's largest coral grouping.

Amami Islands

ABUNDANT NATURE AND EXCEPTIONAL BIODIVERSITY

Comprising part of an eponymous World Heritage Site, the Amami Islands of Kagoshima Prefecture remain beautifully under the radar. Pristine beaches, vibrant coral reefs, ancient forests and vast mangroves await those seeking quiet moments with nature, as do towns and villages steeped in Ryūkyūan culture.

Northern Okinawa Island

DEEP NATURE, LONGEVITY AND CREATION ORIGINS

The focal point of northern Okinawa Island is deeply spiritual Yambaru National Park, a UNESCO-listed swath of tangled forests and endemic species that's an important site in Ryūkyūan creation mythology. Also in the northern part of the island is Ōgimi, the 'village of longevity'.

Naha

JAPAN'S CULTURAL CROSSROADS IN THE PACIFIC

The capital and largest city of Okinawa Prefecture, Naha prospered for centuries. It went on to survive invasion, occupation and all-out war to become a cosmopolitan, multicultural, accessible and fun gateway to the islands, and a centre for the revival of Ryūkyūan history and culture.

Kerama Islands

PARADISE WITHIN EASY REACH

A perfect fit for backpackers, nature lovers or learn-to-divers, the resort-free Kerama Islands have basic, relaxed accommodation, a good youth vibe, lovely reef snorkelling and a few desert-island beaches – and all just a high-speed boat ride from Naha.

Southern Okinawa Island

HISTORY, HUMANITY, CULTURE AND SPIRIT

The island's origin story begins here in this southern zone, amid *utaki* (sacred sites), spiritual pilgrimage stops and places of natural beauty. Among the region's beaches and cave systems, the atrocities of war in Okinawa's more recent history are memorialised in monuments and museums dedicated to peace.

ITINERARIES

One-Way Ferry Amami to Naha

Allow: 7 days   **Distance:** 770km

Take a slow ride through the northernmost Ryūkyūs, boarding the ferry from Kagoshima in Kyūshū Prefecture. You'll travel with locals, their cars and freight being shipped to the islands. Chug along in old-school backpacker style, at the whim of typhoons and zoning out along the ferry railings until flying fish or whale spouts break your reverie.

Tsuboya Yachimun Pottery Street (p52), Naha

① KAGOSHIMA ⏱ 1 DAY

Catch the ferry from **Kagoshima** (p270) for the 11-hour overnight journey to **Naze** (p244) on Amami-Ōshima. A basic restaurant onboard opens for the dinner hour, and the ferry has vending machines for snacks and drinks. If you've opted for the *norihōdai* (all-you-can-sail) ticket, you'll settle in on your sleeping mat for your first interisland snooze, waking bright and early for a 5am arrival.

② AMAMI-ŌSHIMA ⏱ 2 DAYS

Explore the subtropical rainforest that blankets 80% of the island, including upper-elevation cloud forest unique to these northern reaches of the Ryūkyūs. Hike **Kinsakubaru Old-Growth Forest** (p246) during the day or take a **nighttime wildlife tour** (p246). On your second day, check out the surf at **Tebiro Beach** (p248) with local surfers, or bliss out on a secluded beach.

③ TOKUNOSHIMA ⏱ 1 DAY

Land of *tōgyū*, the island sport of 'bovine sumo', Tokunoshima holds **tournaments** (p259) three times a year – in January, May and October – if you'd like to catch this wonderfully offbeat tradition. Outside the *tōgyū* tournament seasons, you may be more interested in the uncrowded dive sites, surf spots and beaches of this super-hospitable and decidedly non-touristy Amami Islands.

4 OKINOERABU-JIMA ⏱ 1 DAY

Rent a car to explore agricultural Okinoerabu-jima, where the coral uplift has created rugged limestone cliffs and a warren of cave systems. **Shōryūdō** (p264), the most famous of these caves, has 600m of public pathway showcasing its stalactites, stalagmites, flowstone formations and pools. Once you've emerged back into the sunlight, the island's undeveloped beaches and shoreline reefs invite sessions of snorkelling and sea-turtle spotting.

5 YORON-TŌ ⏱ 1 DAY

Tiny Yoron-tō feels even more like a throwback to a slower time. Embrace that pace and rent a bike to find your own, very possibly deserted, white-sand beach. The most famous is **Yurigahama** (p268), an offshore islet that only appears at low tide, when it's accessible by boat. Be sure to visit **Yoron Minzoku-mura** (p269), an outdoor cultural museum of traditionally constructed houses and vintage tools of island life.

6 NAHA ⏱ 1 DAY

You'll have plenty of time on this last leg of your ferry voyage to prepare for the mild culture shock of big-city **Naha** (p42). Fortunately, Naha's vibrancy will buoy your spirits with appealing restaurant choices, shopping arcades and lively culture at this last port of call. If you haven't had your fill of ferrying, hop onward to the nearby **Kerama Islands** (p163).

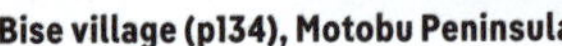

Bise village (p134), Motobu Peninsula

ITINERARIES

Okinawa Main Island & the Keramas

Allow: 6 days   **Distance:** 407km

Roam Okinawa-hontō from Naha's cultural sites, the island's southern peace memorials and the forested national park in the far north. The big island's beaches are perfectly fine, but if you seek time on the sand, go directly to the Keramas for dreamy coves and snorkelling with sea turtles.

① NAHA ⏱ 1 DAY

Find your feet in Naha, starting with a stroll along downtown drag **Kokusai-dōri** (p50), sampling local food and shopping for traditional pottery. Take the monorail further out to the expansive grounds of **Shuri-jō** (p65) and Okinawan art at the **Okinawa Prefectural Museum** (pictured; p62). End the day with dinner at **Ryūkyū Ryōri Nuchigafū** (p52), in an old teahouse at the top of a Naha hill.

② SOUTHERN OKINAWA ⏱ 1 DAY

Drive to Okinawa-hontō's southern coast to learn some of its war history from places dedicated to peace. Begin at **Okinawa Prefectural Peace Memorial Museum** (p81), taking a moment for stillness at this tranquil site, and follow it with a visit to **Himeyuri Peace Museum** (p81). Carry that peace with you on ferry to spiritual **Kudaka-jima** (pictured; p87) for a cycle tour.

③ MOTOBU PENINSULA ⏱ ½ DAY

Head northward to the Motobu Peninsula to roam the ruins of **Nakijin-jō** (p137) and get a close-up look at the mortarless stacked-stone architecture. Move on to the greener architecture of tree-lined lanes in **Bise village** (p134), where *fukugi* create attractive shady paths for strolling or cycling. Cool off with a brewery tour and tasting at **Orion Happy Park** (pictured; p136).

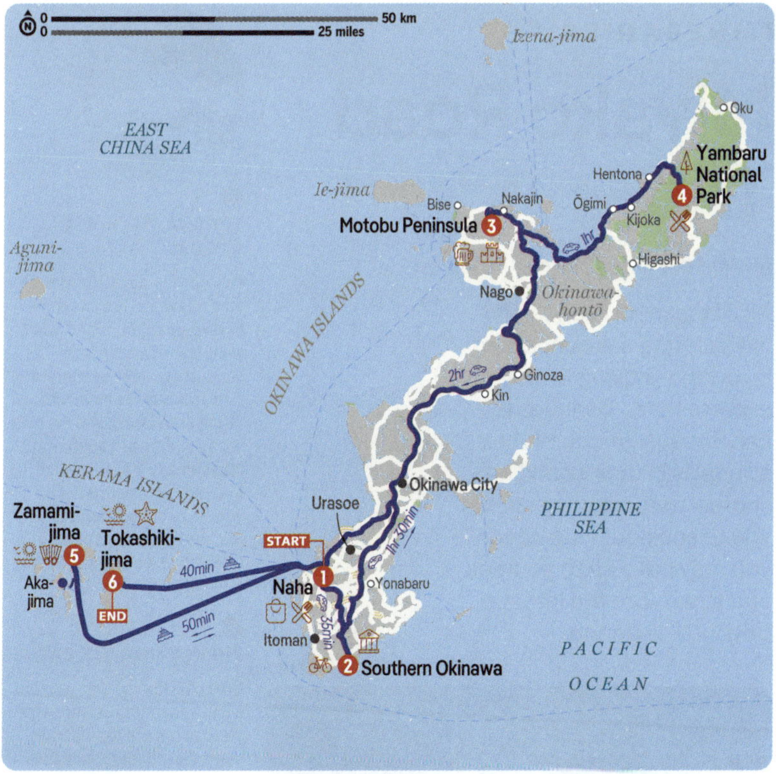

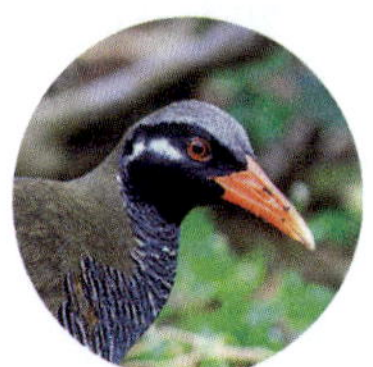

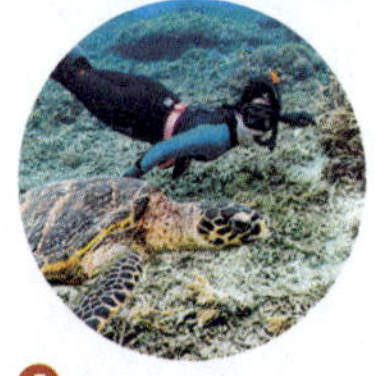

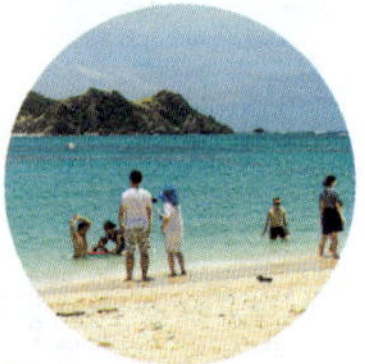

4

YAMBARU NATIONAL PARK ⏱ ½ DAY

Explore the far north of Okinawa, where **Yambaru National Park** (p144) shows off the island's wild side. Hike the trails and look out for *kuina* (Yambaru rails; pictured), the emblematic bird of the Ryūkyūs. After a day of rambling this swath of World Heritage park, savour a regionally traditional meal in **Ōgimi village** (p148) for a taste of what keeps the local centenarians kicking.

5

ZAMAMI-JIMA ⏱ 1 DAY

If you're venturing no further than Okinawa-hontō, day-tripping to the Keramas is required – first stop: **Zamami-jima** (pictured; p166), for an easy day snorkelling with sea turtles, walking the coastal road to pretty beaches and glimpsing Ryūkyū island culture and natural beauty on its smaller isles.

Detour: *Ferry to nearby* ***Aka-jima*** *(p167) and rent a bike for an additional tranquil day trip.*

6

TOKASHIKI-JIMA ⏱ 1 DAY

Drift with grazing sea turtles in a living daydream at quiet **Tokashiku Beach** (p169). Or spend the day at **Aharen Beach** (pictured; p169), one of the most beautiful in the Keramas, with beach rentals and village restaurants nearby. Tokashiki is an easy day trip, but if you're not travelling onward to more remote islands, it's worth overnighting here to soak up the dark skies and nighttime serenity.

FROM LEFT: FEATHERCOLLECTOR/SHUTTERSTOCK, D3_PLUS/SHUTTERSTOCK, BEN BRYANT/SHUTTERSTOCK

Miyako Road Trip

Allow: 4 days   **Distance:** 80km

All of the main islands off Miyako-jima are connected by bridge, making it easy to explore these beauties by car. Because much of their appeal is in their sparkling shores, road-tripping allows you to seek out little coves you may have all to yourself and to explore the intrigue beyond the beach.

17END (p196), Shimoji Island

❶ YONAHA-MAEHAMA
⏱ ½ DAY

Pick up your car at the airport for a relaxed spin around Miyako-jima. The island group's white-sand beaches are some of the most beautiful in Okinawa, like the most famous, **Sunayama** (p182), and the long, sandy stretch at **Yonaha-Maehama** (p184). If you find that they're too crowded for you, drive on to **Aragusuku** (pictured; p183) or **Yoshino** (p183) for excellent snorkelling straight off the beach.

❷ KURIMA-JIMA ⏱ ½ DAY

Cross the Kurima bridge to this small agricultural island, where you can retrace the cliffside steps the villagers once took to collect spring water at **Kurima-gā** (p197), snorkel in a high-walled **cove** (p198) or explore the coastline on an SUP at **Pacha Beach** (p198). Kurima also has its not-so-secret beaches that are worth finding.

❸ HIRARA ⏱ ½ DAY

Start your day walking around some of Miyako-jima's **historical sites** (p179), where you'll see old Ryūkyūan tomb architecture, Japan's southernmost shrine and an *utaki* (sacred site) that outside visitors are allowed to observe. The sites are a few minutes' walk from Hirara port and downtown, where you can refresh with a **coffee** (p179) or **gelato** (p185) before moving on.

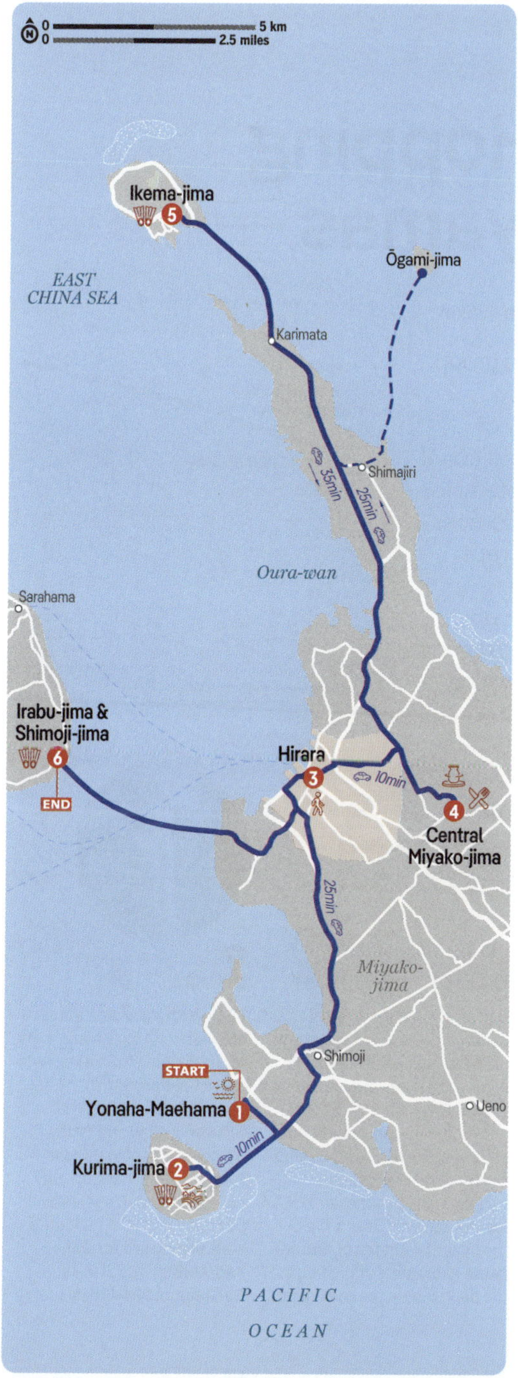

4

CENTRAL MIYAKO-JIMA
⏱ ½ DAY

Try some island mango curry for lunch at **Pari Kitchen** (p187), on the farmland where the fruit is cultivated. Afterwards, head to the nearby **Miyako Craft Workshop Village** (p184) for a lesson in weaving Miyako-*jōfu* (traditional textile) or sculpting a *shiisā* (lion-dog roof guardian) out of clay. Since the craft village is set inside the island's botanical garden, you also can wander the landscaped trails.

5

IKEMA-JIMA ⏱ 1 DAY

Ikema's best side is offshore, where **Yabiji Reef** (pictured; p182), Japan's largest coral grouping, supports a teeming ecosystem. Even if you aren't here during prime diving season, you can rent snorkelling gear for swims from Ikema's lovely beaches.

Detour: *Catch the 15-minute ferry from Shimajiri port for a serene afternoon walking around mystical* **Ōgami** *(p188), island of the gods.*

6

IRABU & SHIMOJI ⏱ 1 DAY

No one would blame you if you never strayed beyond the enticing beach of **Toguchi-no-hama** (p195). But Irabu and Shimoji also have interesting remnants of traditional, stacked-stone **fish traps** (p195) and wells, and oddball modern thrills like standing below takeoffs and landings at **17END** (p196). Peer into jewel-coloured **pools** (p182) in seaside limestone bluffs and snorkel shockingly clear waters on these closely connected isles.

Island-Hopping the Yaeyamas

Allow: 6 days   **Distance:** 425km

The southernmost island group in the Ryūkyū archipelago represents a stellar array of experiences, from the traditional architecture across Taketomi to the deep, expansive wilderness of Iriomote to the windswept remoteness of Yonaguni. Throughout, find spectacular coral reefs and abundant marine life in the Yaeyamas' sparkling clear waters.

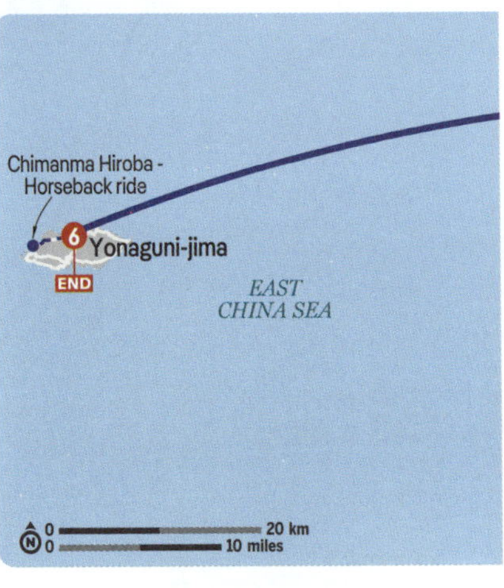

❶ ISHIGAKI ⏱ 1 DAY

Get your bearings in **Ishigaki** (p206) city with a stroll around the downtown area that fans out from the ferry terminal. Check out the shopping arcades of **Euglena Mall** (pictured), browse for handmade ceramic *shiisā* and sea salt, then choose a lunch spot at the market hall. In the evening, head to the adjoining alleys for a drink at a locals **hole-in-the-wall bar** (p212).

❷ TAKETOMI-JIMA ⏱ 1 DAY

Hop off the ferry and rent a bike for a spin around tiny **Taketomi** (p214). As you negotiate the coral-sand roads around the village, admire the traditional red-roofed houses, their walls of Ryūkyū limestone festooned with bougainvillea, before cycling to the beaches to look for star sand and take a dip at the beautiful stretch of **Kondoi-hama** (pictured; p215). Stargaze the dark skies in the calm night.

❸ UEHARA ⏱ 1 DAY

Begin with a paddle through the still waters of thick mangroves, forest-bathing from a kayak, to reach the trailhead for hiking up to **Pinaisāra waterfall** (pictured; p219) and taking a dip in the pool at its base. After paddling back the way you came, change gears by boarding a boat to Iriomote's surrounding sea for some **snorkelling** (p222) at its thriving, colourful reefs.

4 IRIOMOTE EAST ⏱ 1 DAY

Drive south along Iriomote's lush east coast, visiting the **Iriomote Wildlife Conservation Centre** (p223) to learn more about the rare Iriomote wildcat (pictured) and the island's ecology. Follow by soaking up some cultural insight on the Iriomote **Cultural Walk** (p224).

🐃 *Detour: Take a buffalo-drawn cart across the shallows to **Yubu Island** (p226) for a stroll in the botanical garden and to admire views of Iriomote.*

5 NORTHERN ISHIGAKI ⏱ 1 DAY

On your return to Ishigaki, get behind the wheel to explore the **northern section** (p213) of the island, stopping briefly to take in views of **Kabira Bay** (pictured; p210). Along the way, stretch your legs on short trails to waterfalls and local peaks, and commit to some beach time at one of Ishigaki's beautiful sandy shores and beach-accessible reefs.

6 YONAGUNI-JIMA ⏱ 1 DAY

Fly out to **Yonaguni** (p230) as a day trip. Drive the coastal road in either direction to find bluff-top lighthouses, offshore rock formations and wild seas on Japan's westernmost island. Four hours gives you plenty of time to circumnavigate the island and explore the sights at a leisurely pace.

🐎 *Detour: Build in time for a **horse ride** (p230) on the beach astride a Yonaguni pony.*

WHEN TO GO

Okinawa's best weather window is from May to October, with a few conditions to consider.

Winter requires a wetsuit for diving or snorkelling, when the air temps are cooler than the water. But winter diving remains excellent at many sites, with clear water and fewer crowds. Humpback whales migrate through the Amami and Kerama Islands from January to March.

Japan's Golden Week holiday, falling in late April and early May, is a huge domestic travel weekend, translating to higher prices and possible rental-car shortages on some islands. As May moves in, so does rainy season (*baiu* or *tsuyu*), but the weather and water are warm and the summer rush hasn't kicked in yet. The intermittent rain of *baiu* lingers through June, when summer steams up.

Heavy humidity and sweltering temps crank up in July, for stretches of sunny beach days and peak summer rates and crowding. The end of July usually ushers in typhoon season, which can stretch into September, though typhoons are famously unpredictable. Autumn sees fewer visitors and pleasantly warm temps.

⊛ I LIVE HERE

DIVING IN ALL SEASONS

Tomoko Weirauch, co-owner of Piranha Divers, takes joy in diving when she can. @piranha_divers_okinawa

Diving conditions in Okinawa are great year-round. Most divers come from June to October, when the water is warmest, around 29°C, and because the wind from November to March can make it hard to access some dive sites. I'm usually too busy working to dive in summer, but I got out the other day, and I really loved seeing so many turtles and fish, including my favourite, the titan triggerfish.

KUROSHIO CURRENT

Flowing northward through the Okinawa Trough, the 2000m-deep basin between China's continental shelf and the Ryūkyūs, the Kuroshio Current brings warm equatorial water to the island chain. The Okinawa Trough's depth keeps the current's water uncommonly clear and highly saline, nourishing Okinawa's coral reefs.

Coral reef, Zamami-jima (p166)

Weather through the Year [Naha]

JANUARY	FEBRUARY	MARCH	APRIL	MAY	JUNE
Avg. daytime max: **20°C**	Avg. daytime max: **20.6°C**	Avg. daytime max: **21.7°C**	Avg. daytime max: **24.4°C**	Avg. daytime max: **27.2°C**	Avg. daytime max: **30°C**
Days of rainfall: **24**	Days of rainfall: **22**	Days of rainfall: **22**	Days of rainfall: **18**	Days of rainfall: **21**	Days of rainfall: **20**

CORAL CRISIS

Warming water temperatures have contributed to several massive coral bleaching events in Sekisei Lagoon, once Japan's largest reef. An estimated 84% of its corals experienced bleaching in a 2024 event. When water temperatures remain too high, corals cannot recover and their ecosystems risk collapse.

Major Ryūkyū Festivals

Umibiraki (p176) marks the official opening of the beach, which in Okinawa can arrive as early as late March. Once jellyfish nets and lifeguard stations have been set up, a Shintō priest offers prayers for safety, and beach festivities begin. **April**

Japan's **O-Bon** (p64) holiday honours ancestral spirits, with families gathering for festivities over several days. In Okinawa, O-Bon is celebrated according to the lunar calendar, with *eisā* dancing, music, and food and drink. **July–September**

The traditional festival of **Hōnensai** (p224) gives thanks for abundant harvests and offers prayers for continued prosperity. Parades, folk dance, musical performances and group tug-of-war are part of the fun throughout the Ryūkyūs. **August**

Following O-Bon weekend, the **Okinawa Zentō Eisā Matsuri** (p105) takes over Okinawa City with a massive festival of *eisā* performances, music, fireworks and parades. **September**

AUTUMN FESTIVALS

Junta Ezaki, co-owner of Minshuku Sango Beach on Amami-Ōshima, muses on why autumn is Amami's best festival season. *@sangobeachi*

I'll often participate in the Hachigatsu Odori (August Dance) that's celebrated throughout the season. While the singing requires skill and lyrical knowledge, anyone can join in the dancing, even just by waving their hands or swaying to the music. When dancing brings everyone together, it reminds me of Amami's most famous saying, *kyūnu hokorashaya* (loosely, 'May today's happiness be part of every day').

Smaller Celebrations

Cherry blossoms pop earliest in sunny Okinawa, where you can view and celebrate the sea of frothy pink blooms at Motobu's **Yaedake Sakura no Mori Park** (p128) on Okinawa-hontō. **Mid-January–early February**

Join the revelry and tradition of dragon boat racing at the **Naha Hāri Matsuri** (p81), replete with races, live music and port-side festivities during Golden Week. **May**

For a smaller-scale but hugely popular country fair, travel to rural Tarama Island in the Miyakos for **Pinda Aasu Taikai** (p190), the tournament of goat-on-goat 'sumo'. **May, October**

Hyper-local **Paantu Satuupunaha** (p187) carries on the indigenous Miyako tradition of blessings by three mud-slathered masked deities appearing in the village. **October**

Naha Hāri Matsuri (p81)

TYPHOONS

Okinawa averages around seven typhoons per year from June to September. These powerful tropical cyclones bring heavy rains, strong winds and big waves, and can shut down flights and ferries for days at a time. Pay close attention to typhoon warnings and follow local advice.

 JULY	 AUGUST	 SEPTEMBER	 OCTOBER	 NOVEMBER	 DECEMBER
Avg. daytime max: **31.7°C**	Avg. daytime max: **31.7°C**	Avg. daytime max: **30.6°C**	Avg. daytime max: **28.3°C**	Avg. daytime max: **25°C**	Avg. daytime max: **21.7°C**
Days of rainfall: **20**	Days of rainfall: **23**	Days of rainfall: **20**	Days of rainfall: **19**	Days of rainfall: **20**	Days of rainfall: **21**

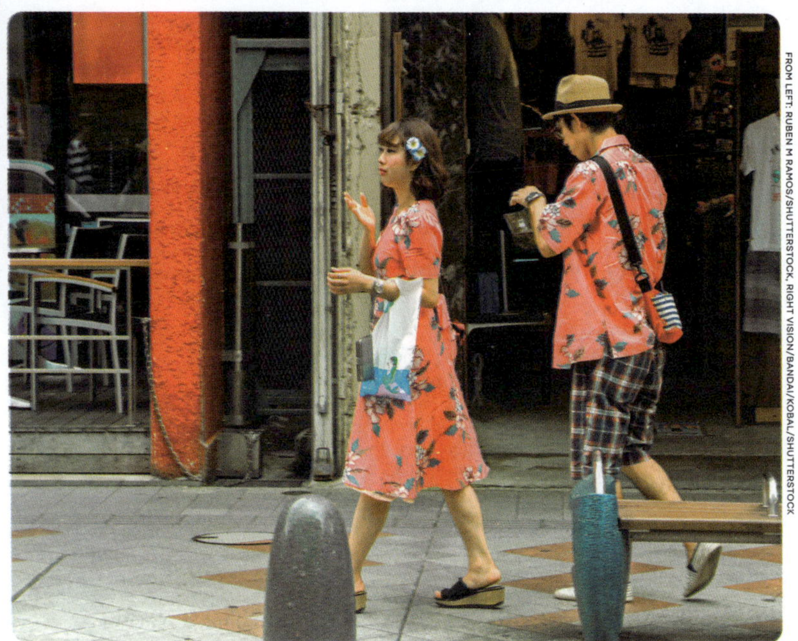

Naha (p42)

GET PREPARED FOR OKINAWA

Useful things to load in your bag, your ears and your brain.

Clothes

Lightweight layers In Okinawa's steamy climate, temperatures range from hot to hotter, with warm days and cooler nights in the winter. Loose and lightweight natural fibres are coolest for daytime, while a warmer layer will come in handy for AC and plane rides. A rain shell is also recommended.

Swimwear Quick-drying rash vests and leggings provide sun protection and a barrier against stinging jellies, but visitors accustomed to colder waters may feel much happier in minimal swimwear in the region's bathtub-warm seas.

Footwear Okinawa is laid-back, so flip-flops plus sturdier footwear for long walks and hikes may be all you need. If you plan to spend a lot of time snorkelling, water shoes or booties are a good idea for protection from coral beaches, prickly reef creatures and razor-sharp Ryūkyūan limestone.

Manners

Respect people's privacy, especially on smaller and more rural islands that aren't as accustomed to visitors. Ask for permission to photograph people and respect private property boundaries.

Utaki are sacred places that are generally off-limits to non-islanders; do not intrude on these spiritual sites.

When leaving the beach, **rinse sand from your feet and cover up** over swimwear before going into a restaurant or shop.

Okinawa: The History of an Island People (George Kerr; 2000) Must-read about Okinawa's history of colonisation and annexation through to WWII.

Islands of Protest: Japanese Literature from Okinawa (Steve Rabson, ed; 2016) Anthology of Okinawan lit, including poetry, translated into English.

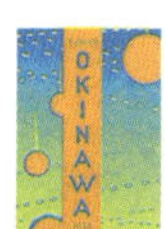

Okinawa (Higa Susumu; 2023) Short stories of WWII and postwar life told in black-and-white manga – real, but not all doom and gloom.

Okinawa: Two Postwar Novellas (Ōshiro Tatsuhiro and Higashi Mineo; 1989) Literary snapshot in time with cultural context from the translator.

Words

Below is a short list of useful words and phrases. See the p288 for more Ryūkūan language.

Hello こんにちは *konnichiwa*

Goodbye さようなら *sayōnara*

Please (general request) お願いします *onegai shimasu*

Please give/bring me... ...を下さい *kore o kudasai*. When asking for a specific thing, eg when ordering food. If you can't pronounce a food name, point to it on the menu and say *kore o kudasai* (translation: this, please).

Please (when offering) どうぞ *dōzo*

Thank you ありがとうございます *arigatō gozaimasu*

You're welcome どういたしまして *dō itashimashite*

Yes はい *hai*

No いいえ *iie*

Excuse me (to get attention) すみません *sumimasen*

Sorry ごめんなさい *gomen nasai*

I don't understand. わかりません *wakarimasen*

Do you speak English? 英語が話せますか? *eigo ga hanasemasu ka?*

Please bring the bill. お勘定をしてください *okanjō o shite kudasai*

That was delicious! おいしかった *oishikatta!*

Where are the toilets? トイレはどこですか? *toire wa doko desu ka?*

I'm lost. 道に迷いました *michi ni mayoimashita*

Help! たすけて! *tasukete!*

WATCH

Dr Coto's Clinic (Yamada Takatoshi; 2003) Engaging early-2000s TV drama following a far-flung island doctor; set on a fictionalised Yonaguni.

Sonatine (pictured above; Takeshi Kitano; 1993) Iconic *yakuza* (Japanese mafia) flick directed by and starring Japan's best known in the genre.

Okitsura (Egumi Sora; 2025) High-school rom-com anime in which a crush leads to language and culture shock; hijinks ensue.

Ruri no Shima (Nippon Television; 2005) TV series about a loner schoolgirl transplanted to pseudonymous, remote Hatoma.

LISTEN

Street Story (HY; 2003) Early album of long-running quintet of Okinawan high-school friends, fusing *sanshin*, hip-hop, punk and sunny pop.

Begin no Shimauta ~ Omototakeo 2 (Begin; 2002) Recommended especially for its love song to Okinawa, 'Shimanchu nu Takara'.

10th Anniversary Best Album Dou + Sei (Shimoji Isamu; 2012) Genre-spanning singer-songwriter who sings mostly in Miyako-jima's indigenous language.

Rimi Natsukawa Selection (Natsukawa Rimi; 2006) Ishigaki-born singer and *sanshin* player of traditional and folk-inflected contemporary Okinawan music.

Rafutē

THE FOOD SCENE

Okinawan cuisine draws from its abundant seas and soil, infusing Japanese culinary tradition and American fusion into uniquely Ryūkyūan dishes.

Okinawa is famous as a Blue Zone where centenarians abound, and the local diet is known to be an important component of healthy longevity. Staples such as *gōya* (bitter melon) help control blood sugar and lower blood pressure, while traditionally vegetable- and fish-centred meals emphasise fresh, flavourfully prepared island macronutrients. Pork also features prominently in Okinawan cuisine, with almost no parts of the pig going to waste.

In the modern day, it's not all purity and whole foods – the influence of US military bases seeped into what are now considered quintessential Okinawan dishes, such as taco rice and Spam *onigiri* (rice balls), while the pleasures of Blue Seal ice cream and *kakigōri* (shaved ice) are sweet coping mechanisms under the blazing sun. Regional foods like Okinawa soba are a pleasure to compare between the various Ryūkyūan island groups, as are the specialities unique to disparate islands, whether it be a local seaweed, seasonal mango or goat sashimi. Creative fusion rounds it all out with international flavours.

Izakaya Basics

Sharing a slew of small plates at an Okinawan *izakaya* (Japanese pub-eatery) is a delicious introduction to local culinary faves. Even when you're dining alone, ordering a few items to accompany a beer or *chūhai* (highball) gives you the opportunity

Best Okinawan Dishes

GŌYA CHANPURŪ
Bitter melon stir-fried with tofu, egg and pork belly.

OKINAWA SOBA
Chewy wheat-based noodles in broth, with fish cakes and marinated pork.

TACO RICE
Seasoned beef, shredded lettuce, tomatoes, cheese and hot sauce over rice.

to mix, match and sample as adventurously as you like – pair some vinegary, slippery *mozuku* (local seaweed) with thin strips of *mimigā* (boiled pig's ear). If there's no English menu or English-speaking staff, take a leap of faith and ask for *omakase* (chef's choice), which will keep the dishes coming until you say when.

Many of the more popular *izakaya* may require reservations, but they can sometimes find room for you at the bar if you're travelling solo or as a couple. The bar is the best seat in the house, usually face to face with the efficiently organised chaos – here you can banter with the chefs, even if via translation apps and sign language. Expect an *otoshi* (small appetiser with mandatory table fee) when you're seated. Most *izakaya* require a minimum order of one drink and one dish, so come hungry and bring your curious palate.

Vegetarians & Vegans

It can be surprisingly challenging to find strictly vegetarian or vegan offerings in Okinawa unless the venue caters to these diets. Although the Japanese monastic tradition of *shōjin-ryōri* adheres to a vegetarian regimen, outside temples 'vegetarian' is loosely interpreted. The basis for many Japanese dishes begins with *dashi* (stock) made with seaweed and fish, so even if you ask that meat or animal products not be added, *dashi* may already be incorporated into soups or sauces (and overlooked, thus undisclosed). On Okinawa-hontō (Okinawa Main Island), where tourism infrastructure and a significant foreign population are more established, it's easier not only to access vegetarian and vegan options but also to communicate dietary restrictions.

Shiikwāsā

UBIQUITOUS CITRUS

Like many foods considered medicine in Okinawa, the *shiikwāsā* occupies part of the superfood pantheon that may play a significant role in Okinawans' longevity. The tiny but mighty green-skinned citrus is rich in antioxidants and minerals, and packed with vitamin C, potassium and nobiletin, which support heart health, balanced blood sugar and immunity. *Shiikwāsā* is used in juices and desserts but also in sauces and soups for its sour and slightly bitter flavour. A tiny wedge often accompanies sashimi, grilled fish or soba to add a squeeze of bright acidity. *Shiikwāsā* trees thrive in the climate of the Ryūkyūs, with the majority of fruit grown in the northern sector of Okinawa-hontō, and you'll encounter this pleasantly tart citrus throughout the islands.

Jiimami dōfu

RAFUTĒ	**JIIMAMI DŌFU**	**SPAM ONIGIRI**	**BENI IMO**	**SĀTĀ ANDAGII**
Braised pork belly marinated in brown sugar, soy sauce and *awamori*.	Peanut-based tofu topped with sweet soy sauce and grated ginger.	Seaweed-wrapped rice balls with a slab of Spam and sometimes omelette.	Okinawan purple sweet potato made into sweet and savoury dishes.	Sweet, deep-fried egg-based dough balls – what's not to love?

Sanpin-cha **(sanpin tea)**

While vegetarian and vegan restaurants exist beyond Okinawa-hontō, do your research before arrival. As elsewhere in Japan, Indian restaurants are reliable havens for vegans and vegetarians. More remote islands may carry limited selections in their grocery stores, and most smaller islands won't have a *konbini* (convenience store). Stock up on your survival staples on bigger islands before heading off to more remote destinations; fortunately, fruits and vegetables are plentiful in these subtropical islands.

Drinks

A refreshing Okinawan brew, *sanpin-cha* (sanpin tea) is a jasmine tea made with lightly fermented oolong. Iced *sanpin-cha* has a delicate flavour and is low in caffeine, often served in tiny glasses at local restaurants but also available out of vending machines – the perfect cooling drink under the hot sun.

At the end of the day, kick back with a cold Orion, the popular rice lager brewed in Nago on Okinawa-hontō and found throughout the islands. Sipping a crisp Orion after a long snorkelling session as you sit on the beach with salty hair is pure Okinawa. In *izakaya* it's usually the *nama biiru* (draft beer) on tap. In you prefer a more complex flavour profile, do a tasting at one of the several small-scale craft breweries on Okinawa-hontō and Miyako-jima, which incorporate local ingredients in interesting styles.

Awamori, Okinawa's distilled rice liquor, is another local tradition that warrants a sip before you leave the islands. Made with long-grain indica rice from Thailand and black *koji* (rice mould), regional *awamori* shows complex flavours and can be aged for years. Production methods vary between distilleries, but *awamori* is distilled once and generally results in an 80-proof spirit. Specialities include 120-proof *hanazake*, made only on Yonaguni Island, and the *habushu* you'll see in bars and souvenir shops with a *habu* (island pit viper) coiled in the bottle – for that extra bite.

ISLAND SOBA

The Ryūkyūan soul food known as **Okinawa soba** is eaten throughout the islands, with regional and island-distinct offshoots. Though all are called 'soba', these flattish, satisfyingly chewy wheat-based noodles resemble ramen more than they do traditional Japanese soba (which is made from buckwheat). Okinawa soba is topped with slices of fish cake, marinated pork and a sprinkle of chopped scallions and pickled ginger, served in a clear, mildly sweet pork-and-bonito broth.

Delicious twists on this basic but deeply flavoured dish vary between island groups, as with **Miyako soba**, which turns everything on its head by serving the toppings at the bottom of the bowl. **Yaeyama soba** uses a round noodle topped with strips of pork, in local pepper-spiked broth. The variation called **soki soba** has fall-off-the-bone marinated spare ribs on top, while **Yonaguni soba** forgoes the pork in favour of swordfish caught in its nearby deep waters.

Local Specialities

Market Halls

Makishi Public Market (p52) Off Kokusai-dōri in Naha, shop for produce in the crammed street-level market before dining at one of the 2nd-floor stalls.

Kokusai-dōri Yatai-mura (p52) This new addition just off Kokusai-dōri brings old-timey ambience with traditional street-stall dining.

Ishigaki City Public Market (p206) The sunken middle section between Euglena Mall's two covered alleys has fish stalls and restaurant counters, while the renovated 3rd floor has a larger food hall full of tempting dining options.

Island Meat

Ishigaki beef From black cattle raised in the Yaeyamas, Ishigaki *wagyū* is famous for its light marbling and delicate texture – try it as steak, a local burger or Japanese style in *shabu-shabu* (thinly sliced beef or pork cooked with vegetables in boiling water and then dipped in sauce) or *yakiniku* (grilled meat).

Ishigaki beef

Agū Once only eaten by royalty, this island pork is uncommonly tender and is best enjoyed at its purest as *shabu-shabu*, although it might also be used in *rafutē*, *soki soba* (spare-rib soba) or *tebichi* (trotters).

Hiijā Goat meat is most often made into soup for celebrations. Braver souls can try it raw as *yagi sashimi* (goat sashimi).

Inoshishi On Iriomote, *inoshishi* (wild boar) is enjoyed as *shabu-shabu* but also as sashimi, a uniquely Yaeyama experience.

THE YEAR IN FOOD

SPRING

Discover the stone-fruit flavour of the peach pineapple – one of numerous juicy pineapple varieties grown in the Yaeyama Islands – and fresh *katsuo* (bonito; pictured) in March and April.

SUMMER

Sweet, glorious subtropical fruit ripens all summer long, with mango, pineapple, guava and dragonfruit showing up at honour stands and juice bars in the Miyakos and Yaeyamas. Bitter *gōya* (pictured) is also freshest June to August.

AUTUMN

Summer *shiikwāsā* is green and tart, while the same citrus picked in fall and winter has mellowed to a sweeter yellow. Wild *umibudō* ('sea grape' seaweed; pictured) is harvested from May, winding down in October.

WINTER

Though winters remain balmy, the wind kicks up and temps drop with blustery rain. Warm up with local island variations of Okinawa soba (pictured) in nourishing hot broth, topped with pork and spring onions.

Sea turtle (p170), Kerama Islands

THE OUTDOORS

So much of Okinawa's sunny charm comes from the siren song of its clear waters and the coves and caves of its coral limestone islands.

The dazzling main event of the Ryūkyū Islands is its alluring spectrum of aquamarine seas. Diving and snorkelling the largest coral reefs of Japan or one of the countless reefs and lagoons rewards your sense of wonder, with cartoonishly colourful nudibranchs, fish, corals and large marine fauna. Wildlife watching abounds underwater as well as on land, where hiking immerses the traveller in the islands' natural and human landscapes, and biking epitomises the joys and connections of slow travel.

Diving & Snorkelling

Regardless of where you travel in the Ryūkyūs, you'll be surrounded by enticingly warm, clear seas begging for explo-ration. Though the the wind can interfere with accessing some dive sites in winter, this happens to be the best season for humpback whale watching in the Amami and Kerama Islands (from late December to April). But even in those cooler months, when air temps can be colder than water temps, visibility remains excellent and the diving is divine.

If you're not a certified diver, most operators have discovery dive programs, and some take snorkellers on their boat trips. One of the wonderful aspects of snorkelling is that it's accessible for a range of abilities – small children who aren't comfortable in open water or adults who aren't very confident swimmers can snorkel off

More Outdoors	**CYCLING** Get around smaller rural islands like **Hateruma** (p228), passing goats and sugar cane and finding hidden beaches.	**KITEBOARDING** Catch air at **Yonaha-Maehama** (p184) on warm, crystalline seas facing a sugar-white shoreline fringed in greenery.	**SURFING** Discover there are waves to be found on **Amami-Ōshima** (p248) in the right places and conditions.

FAMILY ADVENTURES

Go whale-watching in search of spouts and breaches on a half-day boat trip from **Naha** (p60).

Snorkel among sea turtles at **Ama Beach** (p166) on Zamami Island, where they're known to gather and placidly graze.

Kayak through the mangroves of **Yambaru National Park** (p144) in the north of Okinawa-hontō.

Fish for your lunch with a local fisher from **Ikema** (p192), learning some tips from a pro.

Swim and snorkel in the protected lagoon of Miyako-jima's **Imgyā Marine Garden** (p186), with lots to explore in and out of the water.

Look for huge coconut crabs in the dark on exciting nighttime walks in the **Yaeyamas** (p212).

---

local beaches. Even in shallow reefs you can feel the thrill of finding Nemo's cousin or coming face to serene face with a green sea turtle.

Paddle Sports

With so much sea to play in, the islands offer plenty of opportunity for kayaking and stand-up paddleboarding (SUP). Some tours and rentals can send you out in a clear polycarbonate kayak, allowing you a glass-bottomed boat sort of experience. It's an ingenious invention for a place like Okinawa, where the water's amazing clarity allows you to peer at the colourful marine life passing below. You can also find SUP yoga, conducted in stiller waters on wide, stable boards.

Some islands, including Amami-Ōshima, Okinawa-hontō (Okinawa Main Island) and Iriomote, have mangrove forests in the brackish intertidal zones of river and sea that can be explored in a kayak or SUP. Paddling into mangroves gives a fascinating glimpse of these otherwise hard-to-access ecosystems that help buffer the islands from tropical storm and typhoon damage.

Hiking

Not all of the Ryūkyū Islands are great for hiking, as many of them are fairly flat. However, those blessed with some elevation, forests and waterfalls have beautiful trail systems to explore, as in the Amami-Ōshima Island, Tokunoshima Island, northern part of Okinawa Island and Iriomote Island World Natural Heritage Site. Many trails are somewhat developed in that they are paved or have a boardwalk with stairs through the thick jungle and jagged limestone substrate.

Less developed trails through national parklands include those on Amami-Ōshima and Iriomote, although trekking through their sensitive habitats requires accompaniment by a guide. These are some of the wildest places in the archipelago, where the wisdom of a local guide deepens the experience.

ACTION AREAS

See p38

Kayaking (p223), Iriomote

HORSE RIDING
Live out your horse girl (or boy) fantasies riding a rare island pony on a remote beach on **Yonaguni** (p231).

WILDLIFE WATCHING
Explore **Kinsakubaru forest** (p246) with a guide in central Amami-Ōshima, a haven where native fauna flourishes.

PARASAILING
Soar above the blues to get a higher perspective on the beaches and reefs with the warm wind in your face at **Yonaha-Maehama** (p184).

BIRDWATCHING
Keep your eyes peeled for the iconic crested serpent eagle, ruddy kingfishers and emerald doves as you explore the jungle of **Iriomote** (p219).

ACTION AREAS

Where to find Okinawa's best outdoor activities.

EAST CHINA SEA

Snorkelling/Diving

1. Kikaijima, Amami Islands (p258)
2. Tokashiki, Kerama Islands (p170)
3. Blue Cave, Okinawa (p119)
4. Yabiji Reef, Ikema (p182)
5. Manta City, Ishigaki (p206)
6. Sekisei Lagoon, Iriomote (p206)
7. Kaitei Iseki, Yonaguni (p232)

Beach

1. Asani, Amami-Ōshima (p244)
2. Nishibama, Aka-jima (p167)
3. Yonaha-Maehama, Miyako-jima (p184)
4. Yonehara, Ishigaki (p210)
5. Sukuji, Ishigaki (p210)
6. Tsuki-ga-hama, Iriomote (p225)

JAPAN

OKINAWA
PREFECTURE

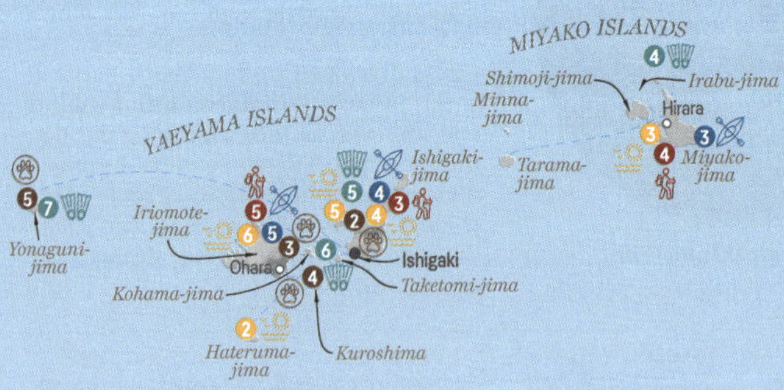

Walking/Hiking

1. Kinsakubaru Old-Growth Forest, Amami-Ōshima (p246)
2. Yambaru National Park, Okinawa (p144)
3. Tamatorizaki Observation Platform, Ishigaki (p213)
4. Ryūgūjō Observatory, Kurima (p197)
5. Cultural Walk, Iriomote (p224)

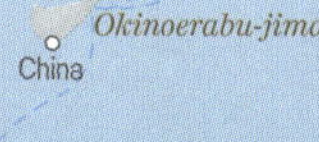

Animals/Wildlife

1. Amami Wildlife Conservation Centre, Amami-Ōshima (p252)
2. Manta Scramble, Ishigaki (p207)
3. Iriomote Wildlife Conservation Centre, Iriomote (p223)
4. Kuroshima (Sea Turtle) Research Institute, Kuroshima (p217)
5. Chimanma Hiroba, Yonaguni (p231)

Kayaking/Canoeing

1. Higashi Village Fureai Hirugi Park, northern Okinawa Island (p146)
2. Kerama Kayak Centre, Zamami-jima (p166)
3. Boraga Beach, Miyako-jima (p183)
4. Fukidogawa Mangrove Community, Ishigaki (p211)
5. Pinaisāra, Iriomote (p219)

THE GUIDE

THE GUIDE

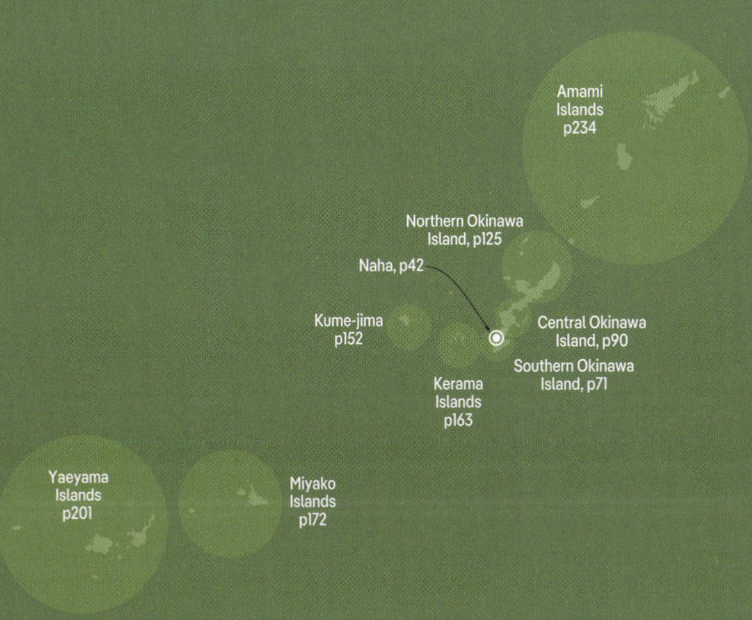

Chapters in this section are organised by hubs and their surrounding areas. We see the hub as your base in the destination, where you'll find unique experiences, local insights, insider tips and expert recommendations. It's also your gateway to the surrounding area, where you'll see what and how much you can do from there.

Southeast Botanical Gardens (p106), Okinawa City

Researched by
Benedict Walker & Manami Okazaki

Naha

JAPAN'S CULTURAL CROSSROADS IN THE PACIFIC

Poster child of the Okinawan isles, Naha delivers everything you crave from Japan and then some, with an energy and vibrancy you won't find anywhere else.

At first glance, Naha (那覇市; Naha-shi) seems like most midsize Japanese cities, until you spot the palm trees swaying in the breeze and start feeling the laid-back island vibes. The city has been the prefectural capital since Okinawa was returned to Japan following the 1945–1972 US occupation, but before that Naha was declared the prefecture's administrative hub in 1879. The largest city in Okinawa Prefecture, Naha dances to the beat of its own drum, quite literally: the city's famous *eisā* dancers keep a particular, distinctive beat on the *parankū*. Another homegrown drum, the spinning *den-den-daikō*, helps teach karate. Little drums like Naha's tap out the Ryūkyū heartbeat.

From the moment the monorail zips you from the airport to Downtown you'll sense you're in for a memorable time here. Lively main drag Kokusai-dōri, surrounded by a host of covered arcades, is a paradise for shoppers, while food trucks and Makishi market serve up eats from seafood to taco rice. There's plenty of cultural heft too, with Tsuboya Yachimun Pottery Street preserving and showcasing centuries-old techniques and NAHArt hosting world-class performances in a state-of-the-art building.

History is woven into the city's fabric. A pair of museums honour the sacrifice and suffering of the local people during WWII, and a hilltop sacred place recalls the ancient Ryūkūan religion.

Tomara Port ferry terminal offers an array of adventures from glass-bottom-boat rides to whale-watching cruises. You can also connect to the Kerama Islands and Kume-jima from here. TeamLab Okinawa's mesmerising installations make for an immersive day out, as does a trip to the imposing castle of Shuri-jō, twice destroyed and twice rebuilt in the 20th century.

Such resilience has made Naha a city of the people. Alongside a strong sense of community, individuals are valued for their unique selves. In the local Uchinaguchi language, the saying *ichariba chōdē* conveys the idea that meeting turns strangers into family, and you'll feel it in the warm welcome you're certain to receive here.

THE MAIN AREAS

KOKUSAI-DŌRI & DOWNTOWN	ASAHIBASHI & KUME	TOMARI PORT AREA	ASATO & OMOROMACHI	SHURI
Hub for shopping, entertainment and food. **p50**	Affordable base with beach and bars. **p56**	Ferry central replete with *izakaya*. **p60**	Honey pot for high-end shoppers. **p62**	Where castle ruins denote historical might. **p65**

For places to stay in Naha, see p68

TAKASHI IMAGES/SHUTTERSTOCK

Left: Prefectural Museum (p62); Above: Naminoue-gū Jinja (p58)

Find Your Way

Navigating central Naha is easy. Naha's metro, Yui-Rail, runs from the airport to most sights: Asahibashi and Makishi for Kokusai-dōri, Miebashi for Tomari Port and Omoromachi for DFS shopping mall. Beyond Shuri, a maze of hills will work your calves and test those navigation skills.

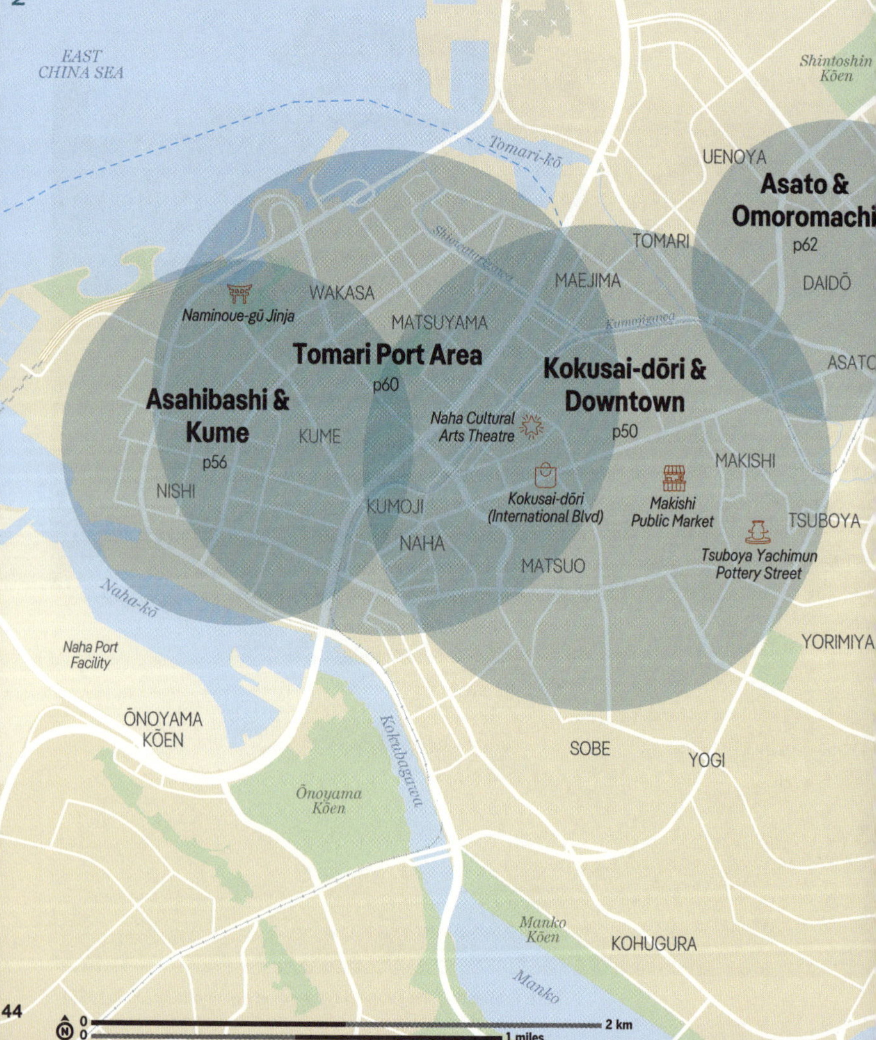

FROM THE AIRPORT

If you don't have crazy amounts of luggage, Yui-Rail is the best way into Naha. Otherwise, taxis downtown shouldn't run more than ¥2500: use Uber or the GO/Taxi app. Most rental cars are located in Akamine; shuttles leave from exits upstairs.

YUI-RAIL

Naha has a monorail! The accessible and fun Yui-Rail (*adult/child from ¥230/120, day pass ¥800/400*) runs along 17km of elevated track from Naha airport to Tedako-Uranishi; 17 intermediary stations connect to local bus routes with a new app: *busnavi-okinawa.com/top/Transit*.

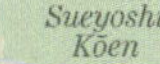

BICYCLE

Heat withstanding, Naha is easy to explore on foot or by bike. Often your accommodation will have free or cheap bikes for guests. Use apps like Klook and Rakuten to rent e-bikes and scooters from ¥5000 per day, delivered. Near Makishi station, try **e-CHARity** and **Ryukyu Rental Cycles**.

CAR

If you're sticking to the main sights in Naha, car rental can be counterproductive: parking costs and rental rates add up, and Naha's tiny-car rush hour is painfully slow.

Plan Your Days

Naha really does have something for everyone, with an array of delights to enjoy. Even if you think you know Japan, you'll be entranced by more of what you love.

BLUEHAND/SHUTTERSTOCK

Kokusai-dōri (p50)

Day 1

Morning
● From Asahibashi station, follow signs to **Okinawa Tourist Information Centre** (p52) to receive helpful advice from the wonderful multilingual staff, then walk along Kokusai-dōri, scoping out Naha's laid-back vibe.

Afternoon
● **Ichigin-dōri** marks Kokusai-dōri's halfway point. Lose hours in the **Kokusai-dōri** (p50) and **Heiwa-dōri** (p50) shopping arcades until you're ready for lively **Makishi** (p52), Naha's famous seafood market and dining area.

Evening
● Take in a show at **Urashima Dinner Theatre** (p58) or **NAHArt** (p54), or sample street food at **Kokusai-dōri Yatai-mura** (p52). Fancy an after-dinner drink? Wander the **Sakurazaka district** (p53) or hit the bars around Makishi station.

Seasonal Highlights
Try to leave your worries behind and sync your body clock to island time. In Naha there's rarely a rush to do anything.

SIP SOME TEA
Sampling frothy *bukubuku* tea at **Uchina Chaya Bukubuku** will help ease you into Ryūkyū culture and the Naha vibe.

HAVE A PICNIC
Stock up on sandwiches and convenience-store faves and head to **Onoyama-kōen** to make the most of Naha's sunshine. It's perfect if you have kids in tow.

TAKE A WALK
Local *machimai* guides *(tours from ¥1000)* are passionate about Naha's history and Ryūkyū culture. Enquire at the **Okinawa Tourist Information Centre** (p52).

Day 2

Morning
● Start the day at **Sakurazaka** (p52) bistro (inside Hyatt Regency Naha) for the city's best brunch, then loop back to the arcades for anything you missed yesterday.

Afternoon
● Stroll along **Tsuboya Yachimun Pottery Street** (p53) to learn more about Ryūkyū culture, take a pottery class or visit the **Tsuboya Pottery Museum** before walking over to check out the cool retro vibe and wares at arcade **Sakaemachi-ichiba** (p64).

Evening
● Ride Yui from Asato station to Omoromachi. Shop and dine until late at **T Galleria by DFS** (p64), then delight your kids or inner kid at **Team Lab Future Park Okinawa** (p64).

Day 3

Morning
● Stroll around **Fukushū-en** (p59) or take a stroll around **Tomari Port** (p60). Visit Naha's clifftop shrine, **Naminoue-gū Jinja** (p58), before hitting the beach below for a cleansing dip. Next stop: **Naha City Museum of History** (p58) or the **Tsushima-maru Memorial Museum** (p59) for some important perspective.

Afternoon
● Art lovers could easily spend a full day at the **Okinawa Prefectural Museum & Art Museum** (p62), but you should try to get to Shuri by mid-afternoon.

Evening
● Divide the late afternoon and evening between the **Shuri-jō** (p65) site and **Shikina-en** (p66) garden, then toast your adventures at **Zuisen Distillery** (p67) before dining locally.

MAKE ART
Try your hand at the unique art of *kintsugi* pottery work using gold leaf or learn to make jewellery and accessories at **Urushi Studio Kodemari**.

GET ON THE WATER
Whale-watching cruises and island day trips are the easiest way to get **on** the water. Head to Tomari Port to link up with **Marine Club Berry Naha** (p61).

GET IN THE WATER
Let the experts at **Marine Seasir Okinawa** gear you up and get you **in** the water, from basic snorkelling to full PADI dive certifications.

PLANE-SPOTTING
Head to **Wakasa Seaside Park** for a spectacle of takeoffs and landings. It's a short stroll from the beach and the port and even better at sunset.

HELP ME PICK:

Ryūkyū *Min'yō* Live Shows

Music is indispensable to the Okinawan lifestyle and identity. Ethnomusicologist Nathanael Ling says Ryūkyū *min'yō* (folk music) is the 'cornerstone of Ryūkyū heritage'. Ling adds, 'The people of Ryūkyū can forgo food by fasting but cannot resist the urge to sing songs each and every day'. There's hardly a person across Japan who isn't familiar with the passionate melodies of Okinawan folk songs, and no trip to Naha is complete without seeing a live show.

Where to go if you love...

Beautiful vocals

Min'yo Stage Utahime *(sunsean.co.jp/utahime.php; ¥1000 for the cover charge)* With a focus on the quality of the music, this venue on Kokusai-dōri is a fantastic place to see live performances and has less of a drinking bar feel than many other *min'yō* bars. There's dedicated stage space, and the seated area fits 150 people. The venue is owned by famed folk artist Ganeko Yoriko.

A cheerful vibe

Warayui *(warayui.owst.jp)* Also on Kokusai-dōri, this incredibly fun, vibrant *min'yō* bar is filled with raucous drinking and lots of young people clapping and cheering. There are three performances, starting at 7pm, 8pm and 9pm every night. Many acts are quite modern with the use of the guitar as well as the *shamisen*.

Spectacle and entertainment

Michi Jyune *(michijyune.com)* Family-friendly entertainment is on offer in this large food hall with lion dancers and dramatic drummer entrances. Shows start at 7pm, 8.15pm and 9.30pm. Given the venue's huge capacity, the atmosphere is more like a tourist destination, but the singers are talented.

Shabu-shabu and music

Shabu Shabu Asahiya *(@asahiya_naha)*. Ideally, all the *min'yō* live houses are experiences to be enjoyed with food and drink. Shabu Shabu Asahiya combines excellent *agu* pork *shabu-shabu* (hot pot) dishes with a less overwhelming *min'yō* live show where you can really focus on the food. It's next to Miebashi station.

Traditional food and sounds

Mion *(naha-mion.com)* Another *min'yō* bar on Kokusai-dōri, Mion serves delicious Okinawan food. The chef has 50 years' experience, so the focus is on great cooking. Dishes use ingredients like *umibudō* (an Okinawan seaweed dish), *gōyā* (bitter melon) and local fish. It's highly lauded as a restaurant as well, not just as a place to listen to music.

Min'yo Stage Utahime

Shamisen

Rimi Natsukawa

HOW TO

Go with an empty stomach The vibe at *min'yō* bars is relaxed, and people go to enjoy the food and drink as well as the music.

Listen to Okinawan *min'yō* before you go Familiarise yourself with the more popular songs such as those by Rimi Natsukawa.

Do your homework Check out the George Washington University's Okinawa Studies Research Guide *(libguides.gwu.edu/okinawa/music)* for some excellent song recommendations.

Try some *awamori* Down a glass of the island's famed spirit, drop your inhibitions and dance.

Popular Appeal

Birthplace of heart-wrenchingly poignant ballads, Okinawa produces some of Japan's most popular folk music. It's constantly changing with the times and has also enjoyed commercial success. Artists like Ishigaki island–born Rimi Natsukawa; Genji Kuniyoshi, from Miyako-jima; and Begin, a rock band that incorporates traditional folk music, are recognised and loved across Japan. According to Ling, the main characteristics of Okinawan folk are the use of the Ryūkyū scale, which has five tones (do, mi, fa, sol and ti), and the songs' structure in the form of short, lyrical poems that are sung in the local dialect, making the songs unique to each region. *Min'yō* is sung with emotional intensity and expresses joy and sadness through the beauty of the singers' voices. The use of instruments is sparse. Accompaniment is usually limited to the *sanshin* (a type of three-stringed lute), *taiko* drums and small handheld drums, and instruments called *sanba* (similar to castanets). With the popularity of stars like Begin, it's possible to see Ryūkyū artists in major concert halls across Japan and at music festivals, particularly those that focus on folk music. However, the best way to experience *min'yō* is at small live houses with copious amounts of alcohol flowing and members of the audience happily drunk-dancing.

49

Kokusai-dōri & Downtown

HUB FOR SHOPPING, ENTERTAINMENT AND FOOD

GETTING AROUND

Asahibashi and Makishi Yui-Rail stations bookend Kokusai-dōri. Walking is the way to go, as parking is prohibited along much of Kokusai-dōri and is expensive where it's permitted.

Naha's main drag, Kokusai-dōri is what might happen if the Las Vegas Strip and Tokyo's Omotesandō Blvd had a child. It's humming with energy, flavour and fun.

When people talk about Kokusai-dōri, often it's not just the street they're referring to but the maze of covered shopping arcades radiating from it and running along Ichibahon-dōri, Mutsumibashi-dōri and Heiwa-dōri. (The same goes for Makishi, which could signify the district, the market or the station.)

For accuracy, the area east of the river, from the start of Kokusai-dōri and running along the boulevard to Ichigin-dōri, then north until it hits the river, is called Kumoji; the remainder of Kokusai-dōri (which is to say most of it), including the shopping arcades and the bulk of the action, is in Makishi.

Welcome to downtown Naha: Japan, bedazzled with Americana, but Ryūkyū to its core.

Get Among it on Kokusai-dōri

Ready, set, here we go!

If you love shopping, pop culture, food and drink, you're in for a treat: **Kokusai-dōri** (International Blvd) is tourist central. Its sights are aimed squarely at your wallet, but not in a dishonest way – you're guaranteed to have fun while parting with your cash.

Despite the influence of Western pop culture and a greater diversity of humanity than you may find in more central parts of the country, Kokusai-dōri still feels like Japan.

It's fine to wander without purpose here. Closed to vehicular traffic on most Sundays, Kokusai-dōri comes alive with music, street performers, pop-up shops and photo ops galore. Let the music, your mood or your appetite lead you – it won't be long before something grabs your attention and beckons you out of the sun and into the cool. Maybe the covered shopping arcades of **Heiwa-dōri** and Mutsumi-dōri will be the first to tempt you into unplanned purchases, or perhaps the aroma of Okinawan cuisine will call to you.

☑ TOP TIP

Downtown crowds disperse at dusk. The action heads indoors as locals hit their fave *izakaya* to mingle and make *yuimāru* (important human connections). Join them!

HIGHLIGHTS
1 Kokusai-dōri (International Blvd)
2 Makishi Public Market
3 Naha Cultural Arts Theatre
4 Tsuboya Yachimun Pottery Street

SIGHTS
5 Sakurazaka

SLEEPING
6 Almont Hotel Naha Kenchomae
7 Hotel Collective
8 Hotel JAL City Naha
9 Hyatt Regency Naha
10 JR Hotel Blossom Naha
11 Tōyoko Inn Naha Asahibashi-ekimae

EATING
12 Heki Kokusai-dōri Matsuo-ten

13 Kokusai-dōri Yatai-mura
14 Lucky Tacos
15 Okinawa Soba EIBUN
16 Ryūkyū Ryōri Nuchigafū
17 Sakurazaka
18 Suitenro
19 Toritama Izumizaki
see 2 Tsubame Dining Area

DRINKING & NIGHTLIFE
20 Bar Dick
21 Cocktail Bar Daisy
22 Mandy
23 Voyager Stand Naha

SHOPPING
24 Heiwa-dōri Arcade

INFORMATION
25 Okinawa Tourist Information Centre

KOKUSAI-DŌRI & DOWNTOWN

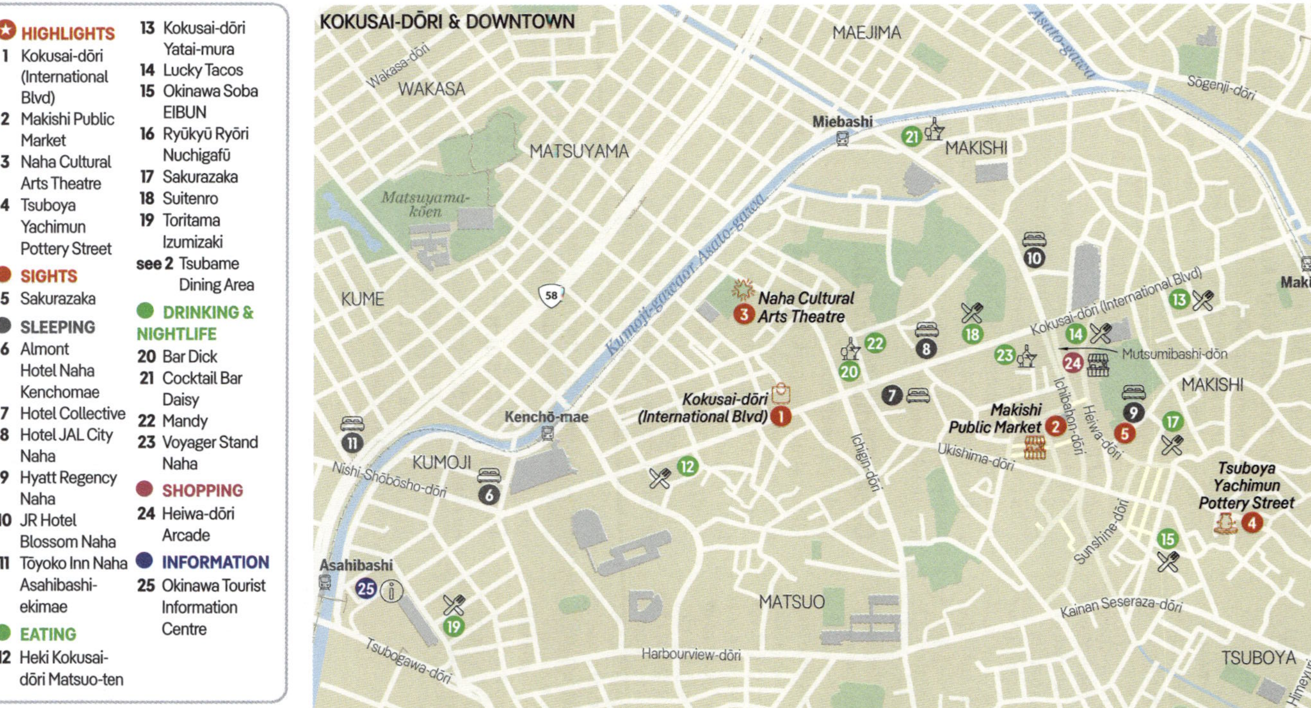

Fresh Is Best: Makishi Public Market

Okinawan cuisine, cooked to order

Since 1950 **Makishi Public Market** (*makishi-public-market.jp*) has been supplying fresh seafood (primarily) as well as meat and produce to chefs, hotels and households around the island, to the outer islands and beyond. Sushi and sashimi lovers will be hard-pressed to find the same variety, melt-in-your-mouth freshness and low prices anywhere else, which means you can go *omakase* (leave it to the chef) or *mori-awase* (I'll try it all!).

Even if you don't eat seafood or meat, a visit to the market is a fascinating and colourful experience.

On the 2nd floor, a canteen-style dining room is ringed with restaurants. Tsubame Dining Area was one of the first restaurants to cook market shoppers' fish and produce to order. Buy your protein, take it upstairs, choose a restaurant and, for a fee, they'll prepare it for you as you prefer.

Cheap Thrills for Foodies

Sizzling street food

Like a mini theme park, **Kokusai-dōri Yatai-mura** (*kokusai doori-yataimura.okinawa*) has a curated selection of around 20 food carts. Here you can indulge all your Japanese street food fantasies, like *gyōza* (dumplings), chicken *karaage* (deep fried) and Okinawan taco rice, all at once.

It would be silly not to get a decorative boxed set of reusable travel chopsticks while you're here, to aid you in your quest to sample each and every cart. Well, maybe not quite every single one – you might want to pace yourself a little, especially if you've just come from familiarising yourself with Naha's *nomi-hōdai* (all-you-can-drink) bars.

Tsuboya Yachimun Pottery Street

Revitalising Ryūkyū craft and culture

Around the corner from the crowds and commotion of Kokusai-dōri, an invisible portal transports you back through time to the cobbled streets and stone houses of old Naha's *yachimun*

EATING IN MAKISHI: OUR PICKS

Suitenro: Fusion Oki-Japanese lunches and *kaiseki* dinners in a faux-Ryūkyū villa. *11am-11pm* ¥¥

Okinawa Soba EIBUN: Queue for this wildly popular Okinawa Soba outfit made famous by NHK-TV. *11am-7.30pm* ¥¥

Lucky Tacos: Real-deal, thin and crispy Tex-Mex tacos at a nice price. *10.30am-9.30pm Fri-Wed, to 3pm Thu* ¥

Ryūkyū Ryōri Nuchigafū: Hilltop dining in a restored residence in Tsuboya. *11.30am-2pm Mon, 11.30am-2pm & 5.30-8pm Tue-Sun* ¥¥

Tsubame Dining Area: Buy fresh on the market floor and have it cooked to order upstairs. *11am-8pm* ¥¥

Toritama Izumizaki: Chicken-and-egg-themed *izakaya* behind the bus station. Juicy *nanban* chicken. *11am-10pm* ¥

Sakurazaka: Daytime dining daily at the Hyatt; best for breakfast and weekend brunch. *7am-10am & noon-3pm* ¥¥¥

Heki Kokusai-dōri Matsuo-ten: Classy but casual teppanyaki joint with an all-female staff. *11am-3.30pm & 5-8pm Fri-Wed* ¥¥¥

Kokusai-dōri Yatai-mura

pottery quarter, whose kilns have been in almost constant operation since they were first fired here in 1682, by royal decree.

Although the **Tsuboya Yachimun Pottery Street** is one of Naha's most charming areas, unfortunately, there is no magic portal: Naha was obliterated in WWII and practically rebuilt from the ground up. Today a new generation of artisans continues to produce works using techniques passed down by the generation before, ensuring the preservation of a centuries-old industry. Others draw from these influences to produce entirely new styles unique to Okinawa.

You can wander around the galleries and cafes, chat with the artists, observe the potters at work in their studios and perhaps take a pottery class. You may have the opportunity to be guided by someone who has dedicated their life to working with their imagination, using techniques and practices that have been unchanged for centuries and are only found in this part of the world. Tsuboya is testament to the determination of the Uchinanchu (Okinawans) to keep the Ryūkyū fire alive.

Cool Bars in Sakurazaka

Naha's welcoming LGBTIQ+ district

Regardless of your sexuality, the bars and *izakaya* of the **Sakurazaka** district, quietly ensconced between Makishi and Tsuboya, offer a refreshing alternative to the more touristed areas. After the war, this was the district men would come to escape their physical or mental agony. Today it's a mix of all kinds of cool bars and hangouts that cater to all comers. The district is presided over by the neighbouring Hyatt Regency (p68), whose bistro is worth a visit for brunch.

FAMILY LIFE

Keiichiro Nakamura, tourism design consultant and CEO, **Anchorring Japan** *(anchorring-japan. co.jp; @keiichiro. nakamura1976)*

I'm happiest when exploring Okinawa's amazing nature with my three kids – reef diving, hiking our unique subtropical forests and participating in local festivals. Our family's happiness is built upon a strong foundation of wellbeing that we feel, personally, with each other and nurtured by our communities. It's key to Okinawa's designation as one of earth's five precious 'Blue Zones'. I hope your family can experience this for yourselves. My trip advice? Stay for at least two weeks and try to explore the magical Miyako Islands (p172), Yaeyama Islands (p201) and Amami Islands (p234) too, if you're able.

IN A HURRY?
If you're in Naha for days only, the Downtown, Delivered walking tour (p55) will help you prioritise your time.

ICHARIBA CHŌDĒ

A combination of two Okinawan words, *ichariba* and *chōdē*, the phrase *ichariba chōdē*, transliterated into standard Japanese as *ichido aeba* (once [we] meet) and *kyōdai* (brothers and sisters), is not a clever catch-cry by a good marketing team but a philosophy deeply rooted in the Okinawan psyche: once two people meet, they're no longer strangers but family.

The Ryūkyū in ancient times felt the same way about welcoming strangers as the Uchinanchu (Okinawans) do today, which is particularly remarkable considering the centuries of foreign occupation they've endured. The persistence of this idea in Okinawan culture is likely one of the main reasons Okinawans are such a friendly and welcoming people.

Naha Culture Arts Theatre

State-of-the-Art NAHArt

Catch a show or play the piano

Even if you can't take in a performance in either of its state-of-the-art 1600-seat or 300-seat theatres, it's well worth visiting the award-winning **Naha Cultural Arts Theatre** (*NAHArt; nahart.jp*) from an architectural perspective. Known locally as Nahāto, the striking six-storey concrete structure was not without controversy. Its prime downtown site, midway between the Kenchō-mae (Prefectural Office) and Miebashi Yui-Rail stations, was formerly the location of the Kumoji Elementary School, which amalgamated with another school to make way for the behemoth performance space. Check the theatre's website for the latest listings. NAHArt's two studio spaces and exhibition hall are also frequently used for cultural events, exhibitions and conferences. The theatre's beautifully designed common areas offer respite from the Naha sun. Seek out the *minna-no-piano* (piano for everyone), located on the 1st floor.

DRINKING IN MAKISHI: OUR PICKS

Bar Dick: Cocktails galore halfway along Kokusai-dōri. *8pm-1am Tue-Sun*

Mandy: The late-night hang for when you know you should be going to bed, but hey, you're on vacation. *10pm-5am Fri-Wed*

Voyager Stand Naha: Naha branch of a popular Tokyo and Osaka nightspot chain, with DJs and all-you-can-drink deals. *9pm-2am*

Cocktail Bar Daisy: Daisy stays up late for signature cocktails, live performances and all-round good vibes. *8pm-4am*

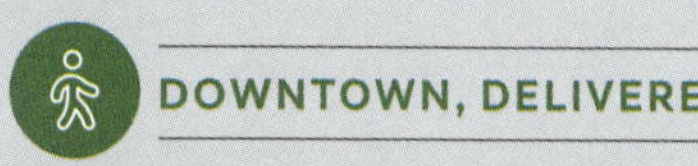

DOWNTOWN, DELIVERED

If your visit is fleeting and you're reasonably fit and full of beans, this jam-packed walking tour will get you oriented and on island time in a snap.

START	END	LENGTH
Asahibashi station	Makishi station	4.1km; 4hr

Arriving at **1 Asahibashi station**, cross the overpass and follow signs to **2 Okinawa Tourist Information Centre** (p52), where you can grab brochures and quiz the helpful staff. Exit onto Kokusai-dōri and begin your walk along the famous avenue, passing **3 Naha City Hall** and the towering prefectural offices on your right.

Cross the scramble crossing, noticing the change in vibe. Walk past the palm trees until you reach the HANDA watch shop on your right. Turn left at the intersection and follow the side street until you reach the Yui-Rail line, then turn right. You'll soon see Kumoji-bashi bridge on your left, and stunning **4 NAHArt** (p54) to the right.

Walk south on Ichigin-dōri, then take a left on any side street until your yearning for nature brings you to **5 Midorigaoka Park**. Nearby, **6 Rikkarikka-yu** is one of Naha's few public bathhouses. Drop south for a block or two and find yourself on Kokusai-dōri again. The warren of shopping arcades is well signposted and easy to explore in your own time. Enter at **7 Heiwa-dōri Arcade**, heading eventually to **8 Makishi Public Market** (p52) and **9 Tsuboya Yachimun Pottery Street** (p53). Backtrack to **10 Sakurazaka** (p53) to spend time in one of its inclusive *izakaya* before riding Yui home.

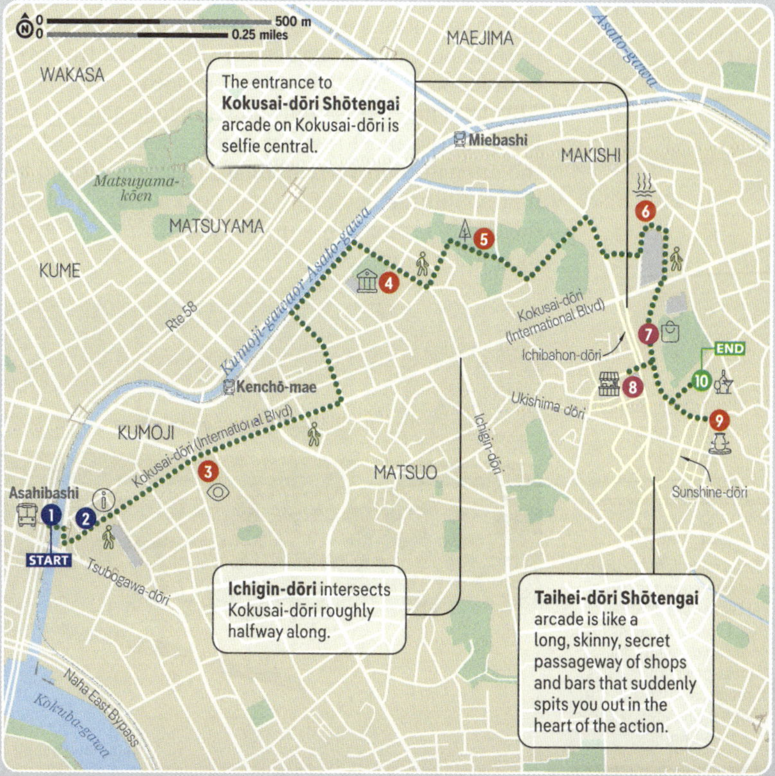

Asahibashi & Kume

AFFORDABLE BASE WITH BEACH AND BARS

GETTING AROUND

Asahibashi is just 10 minutes by monorail from Naha airport and a 20-minute walk to Tomari Port. It's also the closest Yui-Rail station to the **Naha Bus Terminal**.

Asahibashi (旭橋; Asahi Bridge) sits at the western end of Kokusai-dōri on the northwestern bank of the Kumoji river. Originally known as Kume-mura (久米村; Kume Village), Kume (久米) refers to the area west of Asahibashi all the way to the Pacific. Note: Kume is a different place entirely from Kume-jima (p152). The main reasons to find yourself in Asahibashi and Kume are value and convenience. The wide range of well-priced accommodation, dining and drinking options as well as proximity to all modes of transport and Naha's main sites make this area popular with travellers as well as locals.

By day, enjoy Naha's only downtown beach and visit Okinawa's most revered shrine, said to be where the ancient Ryūkyū religion and Japan's official religion, Shintō, meet. By night, soak up the lively atmosphere brought by sunshine, happy people, great food and Orion Beer.

☑ TOP TIP

Road rules apply to users of e-bikes and scooters in Okinawa. It's a growing local concern that visitors are increasingly riding these powered vehicles through crowded areas like shopping arcades, which is a no-no.

Naminoue beach

⭐ **HIGHLIGHTS**	5 Tsushima-maru Memorial Museum	10 LOISIR Hotel	16 Piparchi Kitchen	
1 Naminoue-gū Jinja		11 Pacific Hotel Naha	17 Urashima Dinner Theatre	
🔴 **SIGHTS**	⚫ **SLEEPING**	12 Rembrandt Style Naha		
2 Fukushū-en	6 Bibi Hotel Naha Kume	13 Resol Trinity Asahibashi	🔵 **TRANSPORT**	
3 Naha City Museum of History	7 Hotel androoms Naha Port	🟢 **EATING**	18 Naha Bus Terminal	
4 Naminoue Beach	8 Hotel Brick	14 Himalayan Curry House and Spice Center		
	9 Hotel Sansui Naha	15 Jack's Steakhouse		

Hit the Beach

Sunshine, sand and good times

Naha's only downtown swimming beach, artificial **Namino-ue** always seems to have a beautiful turquoise hue. Netted for *habukarage* (stingers) and lifeguard patrolled, it's a calm, safe place to swim, even for small children, and is frequented by tourists and locals alike. Showers, change facilities and rental lockers are available, as well as beach rentals including floats and mats. Regardless of how sunny the weather is, the beach is closed from November to April.

VISITING A SHRINE

I remember vividly when, as a high school exchange student, I visited my first Shintō shrine. My host sister taught me to remember *ni rei, ni hakushu (to) ichi rei* (two bows, two claps, then one bow). On the final bow, keep your head lowered slightly and your palms together and silently focus on your intention or request. When you feel you've expressed yourself, raise your head and walk away.

Don't worry if you forget the practice or make a mistake. It's what's in your heart that matters when you approach Japan's sacred sites. Speak openly and from your inner being, and focus on the intention behind your visit.

A Hilltop Shrine

Ryūkyū and Shintō, side by side

Perched on a little hill just above the beach, **Naminoue-gū Jinja** was originally a Ryūkyū *utaki* (sacred place of prayer). The site was transformed into a more traditional Shintō structure in the 1890s when the Japanese seized power. Its name means 'above the waves', and it's regarded as Naha's most significant shrine. You're free to wander the grounds, pay your respects or pray at any time of day or night.

Connect with Naha's Past

A city's history and the horrors of war

The **Naha City Museum of History** (*rekishi-archive.city .naha.okinawa.jp/en; adult/child ¥350/free*) provides a detailed overview of the Okinawan story, from the origins of the Ryūkyū Kingdom to the present day, with a permanent collection of artefacts and exhibits that focuses on Ryūkyūan nobility and the history of Shuri. Although English annotations are presented, the museum will be of most interest to

EATING IN KUME: OUR PICKS

Jack's Steakhouse: In business since 1953 (and it shows), but that's part of the reason people flock here. The other reason is steak. *11.30am-10.30pm Thu-Tue* ¥¥

Urashima Dinner Theatre: Showtime, Naha style! Okinawan *kaiseki* courses and traditional Ryūkyū *buyo* dancing. *6-9pm* ¥¥¥

Piparchi Kitchen: This divine little cafe-restaurant serves healthy, beautifully presented fusion cooking including set menus. *noon-3pm & 5-9pm* ¥¥

Himalayan Curry House & Spice Center: Great-value Nepali and Indian curries, dumplings and lunch and dinner sets. *11am-11pm Wed-Mon* ¥

Fukushū-en

those with Japanese ability and a deep interest in Okinawan history. It's open Friday to Wednesday.

A single event is the focus of the **Tsushima-maru Memorial Museum** (*tsushimamaru.or.jp; adult/child ¥500/300*): the sinking of the *Tsushima Maru* by torpedo in August 1944. Of the almost 1800 souls aboard the evacuation vessel, half of which were school-age children, fewer than 300 survived. Open Friday to Wednesday, the museum is a touching memorial that focuses on celebrating the short lives of the children and conveying a message of peace rather than simply denouncing war or demonising either side. Some parents might find the subject matter unsuitable for younger children.

Peaceful Green Space

Wander through Fukushū-en

Spend a pleasant hour wandering the grounds of peaceful **Fukushū-en**, opened in 1992 to celebrate Naha's sister city relationship with Fuzhou in China. A traditional Chinese walled garden, it's divided into sections and has elements such as a pond, bridges and various rock features.

When we visited, a group of women dressed in kimonos posed for photographs, as did two or three sleepy, well-fed cats lazing in the sunshine. Look for the secret passage behind the waterfall, which we climbed to find a little nook overlooking the garden. It was the perfect spot to sit and chat.

– **Benedict Walker**, Lonely Planet writer

RYŪKYŪ: FROM KINGDOM TO OUTLAW

In 1429, after centuries ruled by *aji* (local chieftains), Sho Hashi of the Chūzan Kingdom unified the Okinawan and Nansei Island groups and established what became the Ryūkyū Kingdom, a vast empire with strong trade links throughout Asia. For almost 200 years, under the protection of the Ming Dynasty, Okinawan music, dance, literature and ceramics flourished, weapons were banned, and the islanders lived in harmony with their environment.

Invasion came in 1609, when the Shimazu clan of Satsuma easily conquered the kingdom. Japan seized power in 1879 and declared that the Ryūkyū Kingdom had ceased to be. It annexed all territories, making Naha the new capital of Okinawa Prefecture and Japanese the official language. Speaking Ryūkyūan was forbidden, and teaching Ryūkyū's history and culture was outlawed.

Tomari Port Area

FERRY CENTRAL REPLETE WITH IZAKAYA

GETTING AROUND

Miebashi Yui-Rail station is a few minutes' well-signposted walk from Tomarin terminal. Avoid driving here unless you're taking a car on the ferry: the various on-ramps to the wharves can be confusing and the parking tricky.

It's more than likely that your Okinawan adventures will take you to the Kerama Islands (p163; part of Kerama-shotō National Park) or Kume-jima (p152). Both destinations are within a few hours' ferry or high-speed ferry ride from Naha. If time allows, you may even be able to venture from Naha to the further-flung Yaeyama (p201) and Miyako Islands (p172). To get to the Kerama Islands or Kume-jima you'll need to catch one of the regular scheduled passenger services, or book yourself on a day-return private tour, the majority of which depart from the Tomarin Ferry Terminal at Tomari Port (泊港).

Tomari-kō is the name of the general port area, which has been a critical piece of infrastructure for Naha and the entire island since the days of the Ryūkyū Kingdom. Along with a number of other wharves and docks, it is still used for cargo and cruise ships.

Take a Trip from Tomarin

Ride the seas to an island paradise

A variety of tour operators set sail from the Tomarin Ferry Terminal on day and half-day **diving tours**, **whale-watching cruises** and **glass-bottom boat rides**; you're really only limited by your budget and how much time you have. Perhaps the most popular options are day trips to the Kerama Islands (p163); these trips are great if you're short on time. Others will prefer travelling with the locals and exploring the freedom of getting around on interisland ferries. There's a lot to take in, and it's important to note that schedules are at the mercy of the tides and the weather. **Bus Map Okinawa** (*kotsu-okinawa .org/en/index_ferry.html*) is an excellent, locally produced, English-language information source about most interisland ferry services operating from Okinawa-hontō.

Even if you're not sure of your plans yet, it's worth a visit to the port area before you travel to get a sense of how deeply embedded the seafaring life is to the people of these islands.

☑ **TOP TIP**

A predeparture visit to the Tomarin terminal to check out the tour and ferry operators and get a sense of how it all works is a fun way to work out which other islands to visit and how to get there.

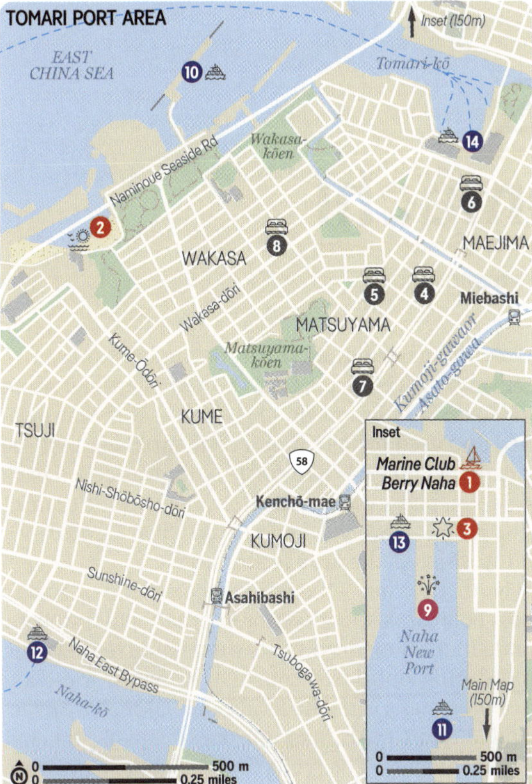

The terminal itself has an information desk, tour desks, a cafe and ticket counters. If you speak some Japanese, that will come in handy. The area between the terminal and nearby Miebashi station is a nice place for walking, with a good selection of eateries and an appealing nightlife vibe, with plenty of lively *izakaya* – though they're less frenetic than in some parts of Downtown and Kume.

Marine Club Berry Naha (*berry7.com*) operates whale-watching and Kerama Islands cruises, as does **Cerulean Blue** (*cerulean-blue.co.jp/en*), which also has a wider repertoire of tours and cruises; the trade-off is less frequent and/or less reliable departures. For ease of booking in English, real-time availability and on-the-spot discounts, the **Klook app** (*klook.com*) is gaining popularity as an Okinawan distributor.

WATERBORNE TRANSPORT

Aside from **Tomari Port**, Downtown Naha has two other port areas with marine-passenger terminals.

Naha Port, a few blocks west of Asahibashi station, has the **Naha Domestic Ferry Terminal**, with ferries to Kagoshima.

Naha New Port, north of the Tomarin terminal, is primarily used for cargo, some smaller ferries from the **Naha New Port Ferry Terminal** and some cruise ships at **Naha Cruise Terminal 2 (AJA)**.

Most cruise liners dock at **Naha Cruise Terminal 1 (Wakasa)**, located midway between Tomari Port and **Naminoue Beach** (p57).

Asato & Omoromachi

HONEY POT FOR HIGH-END SHOPPERS

GETTING AROUND

The easiest way to get to this sprawling shopper's paradise is by Yui-Rail to Asato (安里) or Omoromachi (おもろまち) stations. Once you're here, walking is the best way to get around.

After the destruction of the Battle of Okinawa in 1945 and the US occupation, the region around Asato (安里) and Omoromachi (おもろまち) was appropriated and used primarily as a residential area for the occupying forces. When governance was ceded back to Japan, plans were made to transform the district into Naha's new *(shin)* city *(toshi)* heart *(shin)* – or Shintoshin, as the area is also known.

The district has gone on to become one of Naha's most popular destinations for international travellers, lauded for its modernity, its range of luxe shopping and dining options – courtesy of two world-class shopping malls – and its focal-point Okinawa Prefectural Museum & Art Museum, one of Japan's standout establishments. The malls and the gallery-museum really are destinations in themselves. Skip the shopping if you prefer, but the gallery complex is a must-do on your Okinawan itinerary.

Okinawa Prefectural Museum & Art Museum

Culture, history and world-class art

A visit to this unique cultural vault, housing a natural history museum and an art gallery of national significance under one enormous, architecturally spectacular roof, should feature on every Okinawan itinerary.

The **Prefectural Museum** *(okimu.jp/en; adult/child ¥530/270)* hosts a vast, permanent, indoor and outdoor display entitled 'Sea and Island Life – Seeking Prosperity, Beauty and Peace', which is as expansive and insightful as it is magnificently curated, exploring life on the islands from ancient times to the present day. Excellent multilingual interpretive commentaries are easy to understand and complemented by audio guides (available for hire). The museum also hosts visiting exhibitions relating to Okinawan history and culture. Its repository holds around 94,000 artefacts, only a fraction of which are on permanent display.

The **Art Museum** *(adult/child ¥400/220)* houses an ever-expanding collection of works by local artists and artists

☑ **TOP TIP**

If you find that the baggage allowance of your onward flight isn't compatible with those few extra items you've purchased (no judgement), Japan Post is your friend.

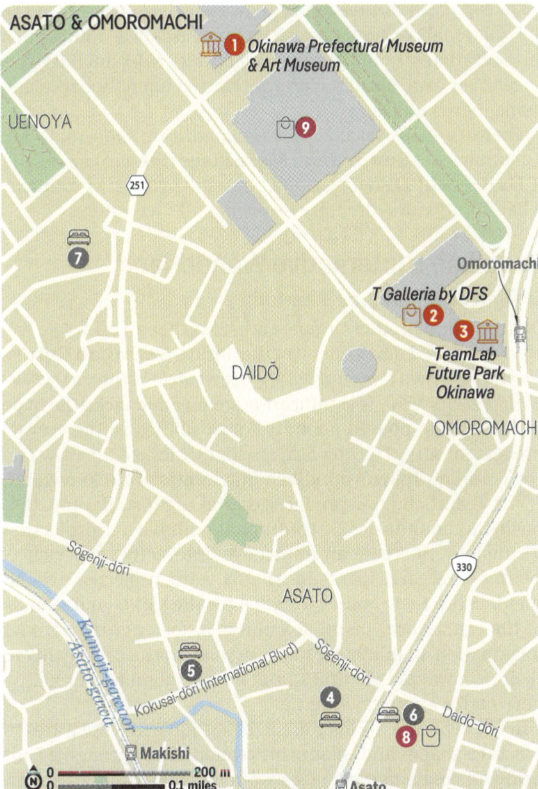

THE SANSHIN

Introduced from China in the 16th century, a precursor to the better-known *shamisen* of mainland Japan, the *sanshin* (a type of mandolin) was used for court music during the time of the Ryūkyū Kingdom and later prized by commoners for its soothing sound. Typically constructed of a wooden frame covered with python skin, the *sanshin* has a long, lacquered neck, a bamboo bridge and three strings that are struck with a plectrum, often carved from the horn of a water buffalo. In the devastation that followed WWII, *sanshin* improvised out of tin cans and nylon string cheered the exhausted survivors.

with a connection to Okinawa from pre-Ryūkyū times to the contemporary period. In total the space has around 3700 artworks. The 'Collection Exhibition' presents the most beautiful and relevant pieces in the gallery's concrete, cathedral-like halls. A visit is a must for all art lovers.

Oki-mu (or Oki-myu, as it's affectionately known), is located about 15 minutes' walk from Omoromachi station and is itself a work of art. It's a striking monolith of white-grey concrete in the style of an Okinawan *gusuku* (fortress), a building unlike any other. Both museums are closed on Monday.

Shop Till You Drop

Okinawa's megamalls

It's no secret that Okinawa has come to be regarded as one of Asia's top spots to shop. You'll find everything that consumer-oriented mainland Japan has to offer in terms of the latest tech, including Japan-only models, and all the cuteness and quirk of anime and J-pop culture. Add to that Okinawa's unique and beautiful traditional arts, crafts and textiles, plus half a century of retro Americana and military disposals galore.

NAHA'S BIGGEST FESTIVALS

Naha Sakura Festival: Thousands flock to Naha in February for Japan's favourite pastime, *hanami* (blossom viewing). Naha's cherry trees bloom two months ahead of those on the mainland.

Naha Hāri Matsuri: Okinawa's largest dragon boat races in May are part of a centuries-old tradition of praying for a prosperous harvest.

Okinawan O-bon: Okinawa's Shintō festival honouring the deceased is held at a different time to mainland Japan, roughly in July, and has different rituals.

Great Tug-of-War: This October festival involves 200m of rope weighing 43 tons, up to 15,000 competing men, women and kids, and spectators numbering around 300,000. What could go wrong?

Shuri-jō Festival: The highlight of this festival (p67), held at Shuri-jō in late October or early November, is the Ryūkyū dynasty parade.

On top of all of that are Okinawa's tax-free (waiver of the 10% national consumption tax on purchases over ¥5000 upon presentation of your passport and tourist visa) and duty-free incentives (waivers of reciprocal taxes on liquor, tobacco and some merchandise).

There to help you take advantage of this shop-topia are Omoromachi's **San-A Naha Main Place** (*san-a.co.jp/en*) and **T Galleria by DFS** (*dfs.com/en/okinawa/stores*) megamalls. There's full store directory on each mall's website.

TeamLab's Interactive Wonderland
Delight your kids (and inner kid)

Being the kid brother to global sensation TeamLab Tokyo has its upsides and downsides. On the upside, **TeamLab Future Park Okinawa** (*teamlab.art/e/futurepark-okinawa; adult/child ¥2000/1200*) is significantly smaller and lacks the hype and attention poured upon its Tokyo sibling, so the crowds are less intense. The downside is slightly less of the wow factor TeamLab Tokyo's mind-bending locations are known for.

The TeamLab crew produces digital art installations that push the boundaries of traditional audiovisual projection technology to create an immersive, interactive experience. Viewers are participants in what is being projected around them, using their bodies to influence the sights and sounds of the experience. TeamLab's aim is to foster creativity and imagination, highlighting that everyone experiences reality in their own way. A beautiful sunset for you might be a brooding horizon for another viewer.

In five separate worlds you can bring aquarium creatures to life, turn shapes and colours into sound, slide through a fruit field and create fantastical ecosystems from graffiti. You can even turn your creations into souvenirs to show your friends back home. It's geared to a young, school-age audience, but TeamLab is known for bringing out the inner kid in everyone.

TeamLab Okinawa is inside the DFS complex. Book tickets in advance online. Don't wear sandals or open-toed shoes, as you may need to change them for safety reasons; conversely, you may be asked to go barefoot for some experiences.

Sakaemachi-ichiba
Naha's coolest retro design hang

Naha's **Sakaemachi-ichiba marketplace** is a bit of a local secret. Its handful of understated bars are loved by a resident clientele, and its unique boutiques may appear to showcase the latest offerings from UTokyo College of Design graduates but are more likely the brainchild of hip Okinawans whose bilingual, multicultural upbringing has given them plenty of swagger and design smarts. Walk on over when you need to escape the crowds of Kokusai-dōri or those massive, shiny malls, but keep it on the downlow.

Shuri

WHERE CASTLE RUINS DENOTE HISTORICAL MIGHT

The original seat of the Ryūkyū Kingdom, Shuri was for centuries the birth and resting place of royalty, the economic heart of a powerful trading empire and a cosmopolitan centre that celebrated music, culture and a rich tradition of artisans and craftspeople. It lost its capital status when Okinawa was annexed by Japan and Naha was declared the prefectural capital in 1879.

Although they'd survived for several hundreds of years, Shuri's temples, shrines, tombs and majestic castle were all but destroyed in a matter of weeks during the Battle of Okinawa in 1945. From its perch above Naha, with commanding views of the town and the sea, the Shuri neighbourhood, whose historic structures were mostly rebuilt during the 1990s, is one of Naha's more exclusive residential enclaves. Deeply connected to the Okinawan story, Shuri is not only a lovely place to visit but an essential stop for anyone interested in Ryūkyū history and culture.

Shuri Castle

Naha's ultimate phoenix rises again

Built as a 13th-century fortress, **Shuri-jō** *(oki-park.jp/sp/shurijo/en)* is one of five castles in Japan to be designated a World Heritage Site. It stood sentinel above Naha until 1945, when it was levelled in US bombing raids. Rebuilt to exacting standards and reopened to the public in 1992, the castle was almost completely destroyed in 2019 by a catastrophic fire thought to have been started by an electrical fault.

Restoration and reconstruction work is ongoing and is expected to be completed in late 2026. Until then, visitors to the castle can enjoy the grounds, which have wonderful views over Naha as far as the Kerama Islands, and observe and learn about the traditional construction methods used by craftspeople in the restoration process.

Sections of the north and south halls of the main building that were not destroyed in the fire have been restored to their

---

GETTING AROUND

The quickest way to Shuri is by Yui-Rail. After that, if you're not in your own car, you'll need to rely on your own two feet. Shuri's steep, undulating hills can be killer on your calves.

☑ **TOP TIP**

If you're planning to rent a car in Naha to explore beyond the city, time your visit to Shuri – where there's some distance and change in elevation between sites – for one of your car days.

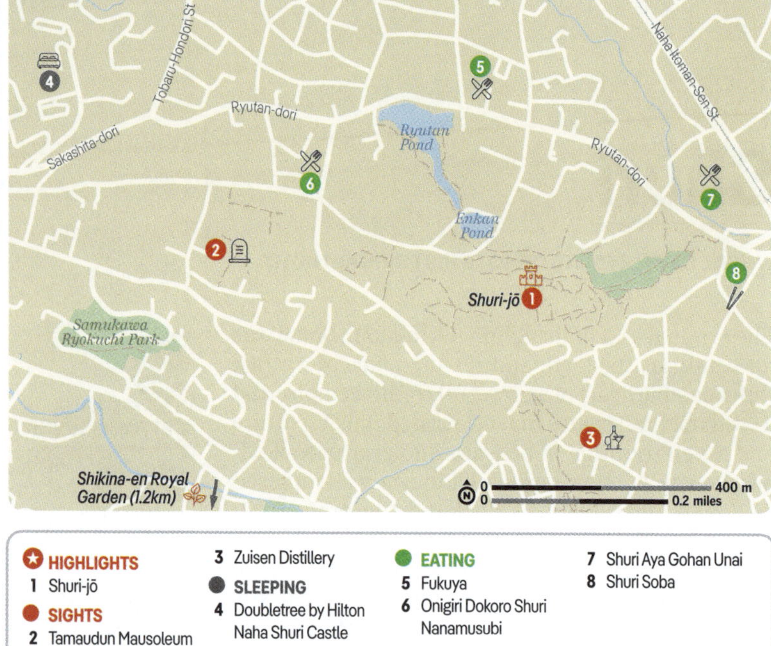

⭐ **HIGHLIGHTS**
1 Shuri-jō

🔴 **SIGHTS**
2 Tamaudun Mausoleum

3 Zuisen Distillery

⚫ **SLEEPING**
4 Doubletree by Hilton Naha Shuri Castle

🟢 **EATING**
5 Fukuya
6 Onigiri Dokoro Shuri Nanamusubi

7 Shuri Aya Gohan Unai
8 Shuri Soba

original style. Visitors can enter through the Kankai-mon gate and ascend to the Hōshin-mon, which forms the entryway to the inner sanctum of the castle. The impressive Seiden hall here has exhibits on the castle and the Okinawan royals.

The complex is 350m from Shuri's Yui-Rail station. Check the website for the latest on renovations and frequent special events.

Grand Okinawan Tombs

Resting place of kings

A few hundred metres from the castle, the imposing stone **Tamaudun Mausoleum** (*adult/child ¥350/150*) is testament to the power and influence of the Ryūkyū royal family. Its three chambers are built in the traditional manner of Okinawan tombs but in a more grandiose style befitting their occupants. There's also a small **museum**.

Historic Garden & Villa

Reimagine Ryūkyū royalty

It's hard to believe the beautiful **Shikina-en Royal Garden** (*adult/child ¥400/200*) is of modern-day construction: the original 1799 gardens and villa, built as a second residence for the Ryūkyū royal family, were destroyed in WWII. Standing by a large pond encircled by a path replete with stone

Tamaudun Mausoleum

bridges, the reconstructed villa is of Japanese design, but the gardens themselves are influenced by Chinese gardens of the period and feature endemic flora, giving the overall complex a uniquely Okinawan feel.

The site is 10 minutes' drive from Downtown Naha. Without your own wheels you'll need to catch bus 2, 4, 5 or 14 to the Shikinaen-mae stop (¥260, 20 minutes).

Touring an Awamori Distillery

Toast your travels the Okinawan way

Founded in 1887, **Zuisen Distillery** (*zuisen.co.jp*) welcomes visitors on guided tours, where you can observe how its own brand of *awamori* is made using the *shitsugi* method, passed on for generations. Free tours and tastings are available and you can purchase the smooth, potent liquor to take home. Zuisen is closed Sunday.

SHURI-JŌ FESTIVAL

Typically held towards the end of October each year on the castle grounds, along Kokusai-dōri and at various locations around Naha, the Shuri-jō Festival has grown to become one of the biggest events on the Naha cultural calendar. More in line with an international-style arts or cultural festival (with sponsors, displays and demonstrations) than a typical Japanese *matsuri*, the festival is all about evoking the spirit of the ancient Ryūkyū Kingdom. There are parades of traditional costumes, arts, crafts, musical and dance performances and historical re-enactments. If you're really interested in Ryūkyūan culture, it's worth timing your trip to Okinawa to coincide with the festival. The program is posted in advance each year on the castle's website.

EATING IN SHURI: OUR PICKS

Onigiri Dokoro Shuri Nanamusubi: This wildly popular cafe serves Okinawan-style *onigiri* with Spam. Great for Shuri garden picnics. *9.30am-5pm Thu-Tue* ¥

Shuri Soba: A short walk from Shuri station, opposite the Sairai-in Daruma shrine, this cosy soba joint has a woodsy vibe. *11am-2pm Fri-Wed* ¥

Fukuya: Charming cafe serving beautifully presented, healthy cooking in a private home. *11.30am-2.30pm & 6-9.30pm Thu-Sun* ¥¥

Shuri Aya Gohan Unai: Okinawan fine-dining experience in Japan's most laid-back city. Warm and wonderful. *noon-2.30pm & 6-10pm Wed-Sun* ¥¥¥

Places We Love to Stay

¥ Budget ¥¥ Midrange ¥¥¥ Top End

Kokusai-dōri & Downtown
MAP p51

Hotel JAL City Naha ¥¥ An oasis of comfort in the heart of the action. Its JAL affiliation is your assurance of a high standard of service and value.

JR Hotel Blossom Naha ¥¥ One of downtown Naha's best choices – design elements and old-school service make it a cut above most business hotels.

Almont Hotel Naha Kenchomae ¥¥ Good rates can be found at this well-located, simply styled boutique property. Popular with Japanese guests.

Tōyoko Inn Naha Asahibashi-ekimae ¥¥ Just a short walk north of Kokusai-dōri, this tried and true business hotel is one of many, but with extras like breakfast and paid parking, and experienced staff that make all the difference.

Hyatt Regency Naha ¥¥¥ This hotel has always been an excellent choice for location and service alone, but after full refurbishment in 2025 it's easily one of Naha's finest international hotels.

Hotel Collective ¥¥¥ Located exactly halfway along Kokusai-dōri, this luxe hotel is the premier offering if you want to be in the heart of the action. Broody blue and bronze rooms speak to refined, big-city sensibilities.

Asahibashi & Kume
MAP p57

Bibi Hotel Naha Kume ¥ Cheap, bright and airy studio-style rooms in a good location midway between the beach and the station.

Rembrandt Style Naha ¥¥ New in 2022, this 15-storey tourist-class hotel has a fresh palette and decent-sized rooms. It's handily located for both Asahibashi station and the beach.

Hotel Sansui Naha ¥¥ I love this boutique hotel near the beach for its low-key pool, rooftop bar and stylish, understated rooms. Yo-yoing rates mean bargains can be found if you book in advance – or last minute using your favourite app.

Resol Trinity Asahibashi ¥¥ Rooftop communal baths and fresh, clean styling elevate this central property popular with business travellers.

Hotel Brick ¥¥ It's showing its age, but this cool design hotel has a great penthouse apartment, if you can snag it.

Hotel androoms Naha Port ¥¥ I love this oddly named offering on Sunshine-dōri, just over from the Naha Domestic Ferry Terminal. Design smarts and a rooftop pool make it a cool choice for classy kids with cash to spend on a bit of extra comfort.

Pacific Hotel Naha ¥¥ One of Naha's older resort hotels, the Pacific is dated in a Caesar's Palace Vegas kind of way but has massive rooms with '90s decor that can be snagged at rates that give good bang for buck. Good-sized pool, too.

LOISIR Hotel ¥¥¥ This sprawling resort-style hotel has ocean views, balcony suites, big pools and dreamy sunsets. It's a little over the top, and often caters to large groups, but great rates can be found if your timing is right: sometimes it's all about luck (and travelling in low season)!

Tomari Port Area
MAP p61

Green Rich Hotel ¥ This hybrid tourist–cabin hotel is a good-value offering for the budget traveller. It's located in a neat little pocket midway between the station and Tomarin Ferry Terminal.

Randor Residence Naha Okinawa ¥¥ Formerly the hotel Pesquera, this is one of our preferred options near Tomari Port. Its stark concrete rooms are cool in both senses. Some rooms have balconies, and rates are generally reasonable. The surrounding neighbourhood is an oasis of calm just a short walk from the action.

OMO5 by Hoshino ¥¥ The droolworthy Hoshino Resorts brand has brought an equally fabulous option to a younger audience of responsible travellers. Classy and quirky, the OMO5 has exceptional staff and a wealth of Oki-centric inclusions for its low room rates. It's arguably one of Naha's best-value experiences.

Estinate Hotel ¥¥ There's a lot to love about this homely little design hotel, which could have been plucked from Tokyo's ultra-chic Omote-sandō and transplanted into Naha's up-and-coming entertainment district. Rooms are sparsely but freshly furnished with restrained bursts of colour that change the vibe from 'bed for a night' to 'home for a night'. Best of all: price.

Hotel Aqua Citta Naha

¥¥¥ One of Naha's biggest resort hotels suffers from an unenviable position right on Rte 58. You can't hear the traffic from the rooms, but you'll have a front-row seat on Naha's tiny-car traffic jams at peak hour. Rooms are luxe, but there are better offerings for the price. What's best about this hotel is its proximity to Tomarin terminal. It's the most upscale option if you have an early departure.

Asato & Omoromachi   MAP p63

Mr Kinjo in Sakaemachi ¥

There are two great things about this property: the neat, compact and very well-priced studio apartments with laundry facilities, and the great location near the fabulous Sakaemachi-ichiba shopping arcade (p64), as well as all the action of Kokusai-dōri and Omoromachi.

Hotel Okinawa with Sanrio Characters ¥¥

It's pastel and overpriced but almost always heavily booked at none-too-shabby prices. If you love Hello Kitty, you've died and gone to heaven.

Hewitt Resort ¥¥

The gargantuan Hewitt Resort has neutral, considered rooms that will appeal to those who appreciate good design and a less-is-more aesthetic. The hotel keeps rates reasonable and is in a fabulous location just shy of Asato station, a stone's throw from…everything.

Naha Terrace ¥¥¥

This aging leviathan is still one of Naha's classiest establishments, with an emphasis on service. It's popular with Japanese honeymooners. The suites are generous, but it's the service and dining options that truly stand out.

Shuri   MAP p66

Doubletree by Hilton Naha Shuri Castle ¥¥

Somewhat arbitrarily located, this property is a sunny haven of space, comfort and calm that feels like home. As long as you're not travelling in a peak period, rates are generally excellent. The only downside is the distance from transit – you'll really need a car.

Shikina-en Royal Garden (p66), Shuri

BEEBOYS/SHUTTERSTOCK

Above: Sefā Utaki (p83), Nanjō; Right: Umikaiji Terrace (p79), Tomigusuku

*Researched by
Benedict Walker*

Southern Okinawa Island

HISTORY, HUMANITY, CULTURE AND SPIRIT

Sacred sites and ancient wisdom, scenic vistas and the sombre stories of WWII memorials – southern Okinawa heralds a message of peace.

The part of Okinawa Island stretching south of the prefectural capital of Naha and the Kumoji-gawa river to neighbouring Tomigusuku, with its beaches, food, shopping and family-friendly fun, is known as southern Okinawa (沖縄本島南部, Okinawa-hontō-nanbu).

The region is bounded by an imaginary line extending from Man-kō lake's easternmost point until it reaches the coast just north of Chinen-hantō (the Chinen Peninsula). Jutting into the vast Pacific Ocean, Chinen-hantō includes a handful of tiny islands, among them Kudaka-jima, revered by the Okinawan people as the birthplace of the Ryūkyū Kingdom itself. This area belongs to Nanjō city and is where you'll find the Sefā Utaki spiritual site and a trio of castle ruins, among other draws.

During the Battle of Okinawa, it was in southern Okinawa that the Japanese army were able to hold out the longest before conceding defeat. Unsurprisingly, then, it was also here that the human costs of this terrible episode were the highest. You can put these events in context at Itoman's museums, memorial sites and land preserves. These sites unflinchingly detail the horrors of war, but their focus on a peaceful future says much about the character and outlook of the Okinawan people, who refuse to be defined by the past alone.

Southern Okinawa is today a peaceful and energising region with an abundance of natural beauty.

THE MAIN AREAS

TOMIGUSUKU	**ITOMAN**	**NANJŌ**	**KUDAKA-JIMA**
Great shopping and fun stuff for kids.	Parks and memorials dedicated to peace.	Sacred sites nestled amid forested hills.	Living classroom of nature and mythology.
p76	**p80**	**p83**	**p87**

Tomigusuku, p76

Not technically part of Naha, hilly Tomigusuku is just minutes from Downtown but feels far from the tourist crowds.

Itoman, p80

Home to war memorials and museums as well as a glassblowing village, Itoman has serious cultural credentials underpinning its urban feel.

Nanjō, p83

The location of the Uchinanchu (Okinawan) creation story, slow-paced Nanjō is home to Okinawa's most venerated *utaki* (spiritual site).

Find Your Way

Although southern Okinawa is a compact area that accounts for only a small fraction of Okinawa-hontō's total land mass, getting around it without your own wheels is both a challenge and a headache.

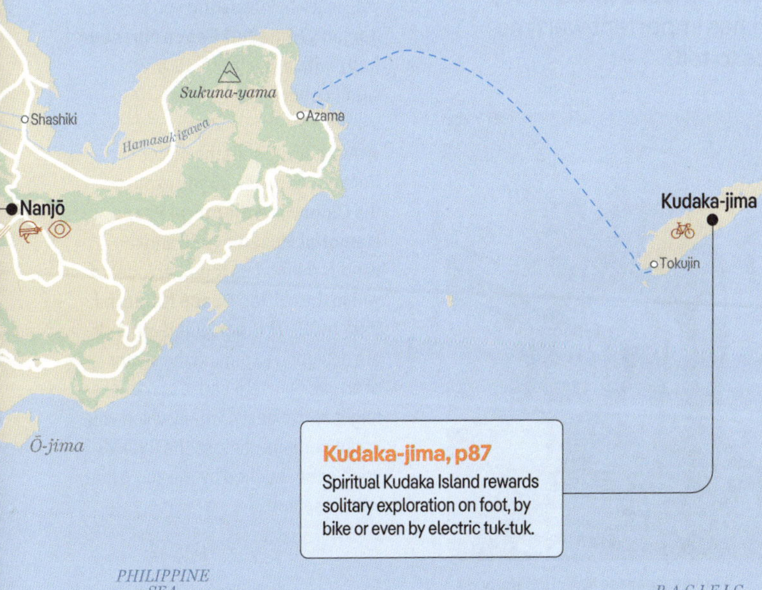

Kudaka-jima, p87
Spiritual Kudaka Island rewards solitary exploration on foot, by bike or even by electric tuk-tuk.

CAR

Renting a car at Naha airport (p45) is the only way to go. Most rental cars are located in Akamine; at the airport, wait for shuttles at numbered exits upstairs as directed by your rental company.

BUS

It's a noble but impractical idea to try to get everywhere you want to go by bus. Several **routes** (*busnavi-okinawa. com/top/Transit*) ply the hilly terrain of the south, but departures are infrequent and travel times tediously slow.

FERRY

You'll need to catch the Kudaka Line ferry *(25 minutes, ¥770/340 adult/child one way)* from Nanjō's **Azama Port** to explore sacred Kudaka Island. Fast boat departures *(from an extra ¥100)* shave 10 minutes off the journey.

Plan Your Days

It's easy to spend a few days in this lush, unhurried region. Blessed with beautiful beaches, top attractions and the Ryūkyū Kingdom's most sacred sites, it also has important wartime stories to tell.

MICHAEL GORDON/SHUTTERSTOCK

Former Japanese Navy Underground Headquarters (p77), Tomigusuku

War & Peace

● Spend a day or two exploring the museums and memorial sites of the south to deepen your understanding of Okinawa's unique history and culture. In the morning, Tomigusuku's sombre but essential **Former Japanese Navy Underground Headquarters** (p77) will surely sadden and surprise you, in a way preparing you for Itoman's **Himeyuri Peace Museum** (p81), with a similar focus and significance.

● After lunch, shift the outlook from war to peace as you explore the **Okinawa Prefectural Peace Memorial Museum** (p81) and the various memorials together located within the clifftop **Peace Memorial Park** (p80). The manicured grounds are designed to remind the visitor of an ever-present sense of nature's might and majesty, within which you might perhaps glimpse the Ryūkyū spirit or be touched by the souls that were lost here.

Seasonal Highlights

Try to leave your worries behind and sync your body clock to island time. In Naha there's rarely a rush to do anything.

FEBRUARY
Okinawa Prefecture is the first part of Japan to see cherry blossoms, with some trees blooming as early as mid-January.

MAY
May in southern Okinawa means a milder climate, fewer crowds and the beginning of festival season.

JUNE
The **Itoman Hare Matsuri** (p81), usually (but not always) in the first week of June, is a frenzied day of dragon boat racing in the name of a safe and bountiful fishing season.

Sacred Sites

● Spend a day visiting places sacred to the Ryūkyū Islands' ancient animistic culture, beginning with Okinawa's most significant spiritual site, Sefā Utaki, said to have been created by the goddess Amamikyō herself. Allow an hour to follow the stone path to the *utaki* and get a sense of the ancient atmosphere of this special place.

● Make the short drive to Azama Port, where you should aim to board the second ferry of the day, bound for little **Kudaka-jima** (p87). The Uchinanchu creation story says Amamikyō descended from Nirakanai in the heavens to Kudaka, from where she created the Ryūkyūs and all things within. Explore the island by e-bike at your own pace for the rest of the day, but don't miss the last ferry back!

Caves & Castles

● Allow a day or two for excursions back in time to Nanjo's natural world. Everything about the must-see **Valley of Gangala** (p84), from its massive caves and rushing river rapids to its mysterious *utaki* and prehistoric relics, seems unexpected and will take your senses by surprise. Across the street, theme-park-esque **Okinawa World** (p85) with its enormous 5km cave and smaller worlds celebrating Ryūkyū is a bonus that could consume the rest of the day if you're travelling with kids.

● Spend the rest of your time in slow-paced Nanjō adventuring into a trio of fabulously raw former castle sites, **Tamagusuku** (p85), **Itokazu** (p85) and **Chinen** (p85), whose enormous slabs of Okinawan granite seem to appear out of nowhere on otherwise unremarkable wooded hillsides.

SEPTEMBER

Like May, September is low season; expect fewer people, wonderful weather (but for the odd typhoon) and great prices.

OCTOBER

A lovely month to visit, with harvest season gathering pace and premier festivals (p64) enlivening Naha.

NOVEMBER

November sees the peak of the autumn harvest and is a great time to dine in local restaurants that showcase Okinawa's famed Blue Zone diet (p32).

DECEMBER

Experience Christmas in the tropics, with twinkling festive lights and balmy temps of around 22°C!

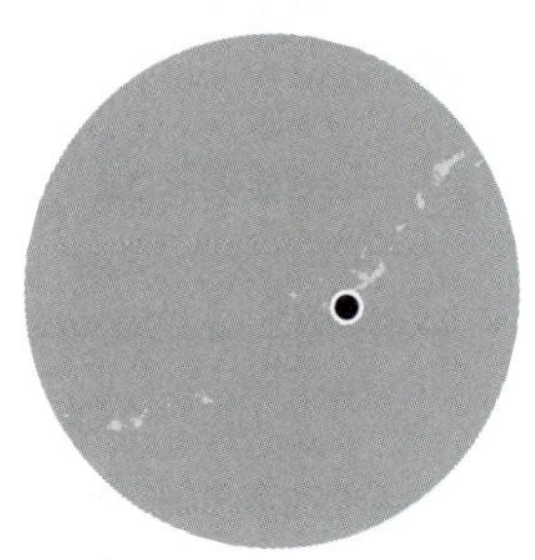

Tomigusuku

GETTING AROUND

There are bus services here, but as with most of Okinawa, you'll need to rent a car to get anywhere easily and efficiently.

Just across the river from Naha, Tomigusuku (豊見城) is Okinawa's fastest-growing urban centre. The city's variety and affordability have seen it skyrocket in popularity among young Japanese. Amid Tomigusuku's varied terrain, much of which is hilly and green, are pockets of land once tended by Ryūkyūan farmers using sustainable methods they'd employed for hundreds of years. In some places this way of farming and living, on land that's been largely undeveloped for centuries, still exists.

Density and development have progressed, and today there are many examples of how urban development and rural life can coexist efficiently and effectively in a complementary and sustainable way. Fields and farmland have found new purpose as the bucolic backdrop of chic homes that look as though they've been carved from polished concrete and dropped on hilltops, with ocean views, only half an hour from Downtown Naha.

Connect with Artisans

Ancient techniques brought to life

The new-in-2022 **Okinawa Craft Industry Promotion Centre** (*okinawa-kougeinomori.jp/en; free*) exhibits all 16 of Okinawa's traditional crafts in a permanent exhibition in the museum space. Crafts on display come not only from Okinawa-hontō but also from the Miyako and Yaeyama island groups and Kume Island. There's plenty of information in English about the range of beautiful crafts presented, particularly about how the different techniques came to be and what distinguishes one type of fabric from another.

Covering an area of over 9000 sq metres in the grounds of Tomigusuku Castle Park, the facility also rents out studios to local artisans. You can often observe and interact with them as they work – but please consult staff in advance. Workshops and special events are held throughout the year. If you're an artist or craftsperson yourself and have a particular interest in

☑ TOP TIP

Renting an apartment in Tomigusuku is a great, best-of-both-worlds alternative to staying in Naha.

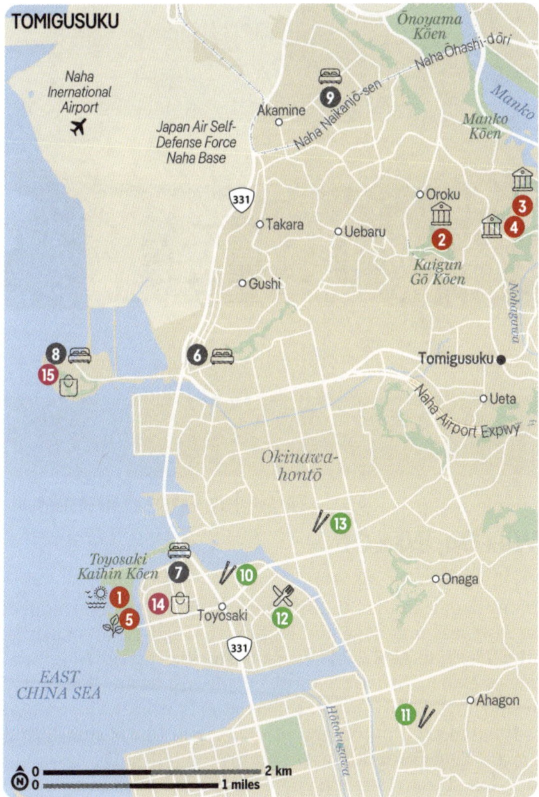

any of the traditional crafts or techniques represented at the centre, the excellent website is a great place to find out when it's best to come. It's also the best way to connect with curatorial and guide staff before your visit. The centre is open from Tuesday through Sunday, excluding public and New Year holidays.

Former Japanese Navy Underground HQ

If these walls could talk

Directly south of Naha in Kaigungo-kōen is the **Former Japanese Navy Underground Headquarters** (*kaigungou.ocvb. or.jp; adult/child ¥600/300*), where 4000 men died by suicide or were killed as the Battle of Okinawa drew to its bloody conclusion. You can walk through a few hundred metres of the hand-hewn tunnel system; wander the maze of corridors; read the commander's final words, written on the wall of his room; and inspect the holes and scars in other walls from the grenade blasts that killed many of the men stationed here.

If you don't have a car, buses 55 and 98 from Naha Bus Terminal will get you here. Get off at Uebaru Danchi-mae stop, from where it's a five-minute walk, signposted in English, to the museum entrance at the top of the hill.

OKINAWAN ARTS & CRAFTS

Of Japan's estimated 1300 types of traditional craft, the Ministry of Trade and Industry officially recognises 237 national traditional crafts as Intangible Cultural Properties, of which 16 originated in Okinawa Prefecture. These are Chibana *hanaori* textile, Kijoka *bashofu* fabric, Kumejima *tsumugi* fabric, Haebaru *hanaori* textile, Miyako *jofu* fabric, Ryūkyū *bingata* fabric dyeing, Ryūkyū *shikki* lacquerware, Ryūkyū *kasuri* fabric, the *sanshin* three-stringed instrument, Shuri *ori* textile, Tsuboya *yaki* pottery, Yaeyama *minsā* textile, Yaeyama *jofu* fabric, Yonaguni *ori* textile, Yuntanza *hanaori* textile and Yuntanza *minsā* textile. These 16 arts and crafts unique to Okinawa are particularly important from a national perspective, as they've survived by being passed down through generations, often in secret, since the time of the Ryūkyū Kingdom, despite the concerted efforts of invading parties to suppress them.

Special dojo, Okinawa Karate Museum

Wax On, Wax Off

Training with the masters

Many people in the English-speaking world were introduced to Japanese language and culture through 1980s smash hit film *The Karate Kid*. The second movie in the trilogy was set in Naha. Nowadays most people are aware that karate is one of the most popular martial arts worldwide, with an estimated 130 million practitioners, and that it comes from Japan. Some even know that it originated in Okinawa and developed from the indigenous Ryūkyūan martial arts practice known as *te*. You can learn all about the history of this branch of martial arts at the **Okinawa Karate Museum** *(Okinawa Karate Kaikan; karatekaikan.jp/en; free)*, which opened its doors in 2017.

The museum aspect is probably the smallest component of what might be more aptly named a centre for karate studies and promotion, housing not just the museum but a training dojo and a special dojo, theory classrooms and accommodation. If you've wanted to study karate or aikidō, your time is now.

A variety of training programs including residential options are available. Back in Naha's Asato area, the Ageshio group is also dedicated to the instruction and promotion of Okinawan karate. As a one-stop shop, Ageshio organises inbound karate study tours and exchanges as well as local tours and experience programs you can pick up in Naha. It also offers month-long intensives.

Beside the Seaside

Fun on and off the sand

Between **Toyosaki Seaside Park** and **Chura Sun Beach**, you're spoiled for choice when it comes to spending a day at the beach. Head down to the water's edge or spread a picnic rug on the grass to watch the sun set over the Pacific. Overhead, jetliners taking off from Naha airport soar into the vast blue beyond.

Just behind Toyosaki's park area you'll find the sizeable **IIAS Okinawa Mall**, which houses the **DMM Kariyushi Aquarium** (*en.kariyushi-aquarium.com; adult/child ¥2800/1700*) and **Little Universe** (*little-universe.com; ¥500; 3D printed figurines from ¥2500*). At Little Universe you can make a 3D mini-me of yourself, where a 3D image of you is taken and 3D printed in real time to produce a figurine in your very likeness. The popular aquarium has a petting zoo featuring four claw-footed sloths, who seem very lonely and bored, despite receiving lots of attention.

Airport Island: Senaga-jima

Shopping, dining and spa time

Naha airport's parallel runways are built on reclaimed land in the Pacific Ocean. At their southernmost extent, and squeezed in between them, is the tiny island of Senaga-jima, now forever tethered to the main runway and a Tomigusuku light-industrial park overflowing with rental cars. As bleak as this might sound, the low-density, low-rise commercial development of Senaga-jima might just be one of the best pre-flight hangs to be found anywhere.

Shopping and dining plaza **Umikaiji Terrace** has a unique pie-shaped, stepped design so that each of the more than 40 stores faces the ocean in its own direction without looking over its neighbours. From casual cafes to dress-for-dinner affairs, dining options are universally great in terms of quality, value for money, service and variety. Choose from pancakes, pizzas, taco rice, burgers, seafood and Okinawan cuisine, just to name a few.

The main draw is **Ryujin-no-yu onsen** (*umikajiterrace. com*), located in the basement of the island's **airport hotel** (p89). Onsen access is free for hotel guests and available for ¥2000 to a limited number of day-use visitors.

I visited Senaga-jima first 10 years ago, then three years later and then again seven years later, in 2025. I'm happy to report that my experience on each occasion bettered the one on the previous visit. – **Benedict Walker**, Lonely Planet writer

'NO SWIMMING' MEANS...

If you see a no-swimming sign at a beach, yup, don't swim there. If there's no lifeguard on duty or net visible, it means that the local *shiyakusho* (city hall) is responsible for you if you get stung by a *habu* (viper) or drown in the tepid shallows. Councils don't like liability for such matters, and in Japan the law is very cut and dried in this regard: even if you're injured by your own negligence, generally the local government is held liable for damages and costs. Your treatment will generally be covered by your travel health insurance, but it's the council that will ultimately foot the bill.

EATING IN TOMIGUSUKU: CHEAP EATS

Tsukemen & Curry Hidamari: There are only two things on the menu at this little lunch joint: ramen and curry. Try both! *11am-3pm Sat-Wed* ¥

Mensaku: You can't go past the spicy, sesame *tantan-men* noodles and *gyōza* at this Chinese restaurant. *noon-3pm & 6-8.30pm Tue-Thu* ¥

Yone Shokudō: An institution, this cosy diner offers great-value set menus, including Okinawa soba. *10am-5pm Fri-Wed* ¥

Hong Hu Jiao Zi Fang: You can't miss the massive red tiger signage of the Ashibinā mall branch of this popular chain restaurant. *11am-8.30pm* ¥¥

Itoman

VISTAS | PEACE PARKS | ARTS AND CRAFTS

GETTING AROUND

As with the rest of southern Okinawa, public transport is limited in Itoman. Rent a car for the freedom to explore at will.

Itoman's footprint runs south from Tomigusuku all the way to Okinawa-hontō's southernmost point and east toward Nanjō. The city is a living memorial – a place where the horrors of WWII are remembered in order to prevent such devastation from ever happening again. By the time the Battle of Okinawa ended in June 1945, most of Naha and the parts of southern Okinawa that had seen some development and infrastructure before the war, including the prefecture's short-lived first railroad, had been almost entirely destroyed.

While there's much more to Itoman than its tragic history, including plenty of quiet beaches, quirky rural cafes and bucolic scenery, its museums and memorials warrant a few hours to contemplate the past. Itoman feels like it's a city with its sights on the future. Its streets are spacious, commercial development is happening at a refreshingly smaller scale than in many other cities, and a it has a noticeably younger local population.

Contemplating War & Peace

WWII museums and memorial sites

Over 200,000 Japanese and American soldiers and Okinawan civilians lost their lives in and around Itoman in a period of weeks as the Battle of Okinawa raged to its conclusion. To remember those who were lost and share the stories of survivors, the **Peace Memorial Park** was established in 1972 above the 'suicide cliffs' where it is thought thousands of civilians leapt to their deaths rather than surrender. Within the park's 23 hectares, monuments to those lost in war are dedicated to the cause of peace. In the centre of the park, an **eternal flame** lit from the flames of peace monuments in Hiroshima and Nagasaki and on Zamami-jima in the Kerama Islands (p163) burns in the name of peace. Around the park's well-kept grounds are countless tranquil spots to sit and contemplate.

☑ TOP TIP

You might find yourself unexpectedly emotionally engaged or drawn to nature. Be gentle with yourself and keep a loose schedule so you can go with the flow.

● SIGHTS	2 Peace Memorial Park	● EATING
see 2 Cornerstone of Peace	3 Ryūkyū Glass Village	7 Itoman Gyōmin Shokudō
1 Himeyuri Peace Museum	● SLEEPING	8 Kābira
see 2 Okinawa Prefectural Peace Memorial Museum	4 Mr Kinjo in Shiozaki	9 Sentā Shokudō
	5 Ryūkyū Hotel & Resort Nashiro Beach	10 Yakiniku Goen
	6 Southern Beach Hotel & Resort	● ENTERTAINMENT
		11 Itoman Hare Matsuri

The centrepiece of the park's **Okinawa Prefectural Peace Memorial Museum** is a mausoleum holding the ashes of over 180,000 people who died during the Battle of Okinawa. The museum opened in 1975 atop Mabuni Hill, where the battle finally ended some 30 years before. It gives poignant insight into the plight of the Okinawan people as WWII approached its conclusion.

Also in the park, the clifftop **Cornerstone of Peace** (平和 の礎; *heiwa no ishiji*) was commissioned to commemorate the 50th anniversary of the end of the Battle of Okinawa. It consists of a series of 116 Okinawan granite stones on which are inscribed the names of some 240,000 men, women and children whose deaths are attributed to the impact of WWII on Okinawa. New names are added each year.

About 4km west of the park, along Rte 331, the haunting **Himeyuri Peace Museum** is located above a cave that served as an emergency field hospital during the closing days of the Battle of Okinawa. Here 240 female high-school students were pressed into service as nurses for Japanese military wounded. As American forces closed in, the students were abandoned and most perished. Driven by survivors and alumnae of the school, the monument has the promotion of peace as its mission.

DRAGON BOAT RACING

Teams from across the island practise year-round to compete in various *hāri-matsuri* (also *hari* and *hare*) maritime festivals, thought to have begun in Tomigusuku around 600 years ago. The festivals focus on a series of dragon boat races where local fishers race handmade wooden boats to pray for a safe and bountiful fishing season. The largest, **Naha Hāri Matsuri**, draws crowds of around 200,000 over three days each May. On days one and three, races are held between colourful, purpose-built boats over 14m long, replete with a dragon's head and tail and a crew of 40. In June teams race smaller handmade *sabani* boats at the **Itoman Hare Matsuri** in front of crowds that number in the tens of thousands.

THE BATTLE OF OKINAWA

Decades of Japanese colonial aggression following the Meiji restoration ignited the fire of war in the Pacific. Seconded into Japan's war, the Uchinanchu fought fiercely and loyally despite the imperial family's decades of denying their right to express their culture and speak their languages. Seeing an opportunity to end WWII, the US invaded Okinawa in March 1945. The horrific and intense Battle of Okinawa raged for 82 days in Naha and southern Okinawa, razed the capital to the ground and prepared the path for the atomic bombings of Hiroshima and Nagasaki. One in four Uchinanchu (more than 200,000 people) died – more than the death tolls of Hiroshima and Nagasaki combined.

Glassmaking, Ryūkyū Glass Village

Ryūkyū Glass Village

Watch and try glassmaking

The largest handmade-glass facility in Okinawa, **Ryūkyū Glass Village** offers a variety of glassmaking experiences and two- to three-hour glassblowing workshops (*from ¥2000*) that are suitable for adults and school-age children alike. You can also just watch the glassblowers at work, but bear in mind that it's hot in there: temperatures reach over 1300°C at the kiln. On-site are an outlet store where you can purchase all manner of colourful glassware (and have it shipped home for ¥1500) and a cafe; both are air-conditioned.

EATING IN ITOMAN: OUR PICKS

Itoman Gyōmin Shokudō: Line up for fresh seafood served any way you can imagine at this Itoman institution. *11.30am-2.30pm & 6-9pm Wed-Mon* ¥¥¥

Yakiniku Goen: The Itoman branch of this popular *yakiniku* (grilled meat) chain is best enjoyed with a group of fellow carnivores. *4-10.30pm* ¥¥¥

Sentā Shokudō: There's plenty to choose from at this no-frills lunch joint, but the *katsudon teishoku* (pork cutlet set meals) are delish and great value. *7am-5pm Tue-Sun* ¥¥

Kābira: This popular *izakaya* (pub) has live folk music most nights, great food and a lively vibe; great with friends. *3-11pm Fri-Wed* ¥¥

Nanjō

ANCIENT RUINS | SACRED SITES | BIRTHPLACE OF RYŪKYŪ

Nanjō (南城, literally, 'southern castle') is noticeably sleepier and further from the excitement of Naha than the rest of southern Okinawa. Tucked away in the southeastern corner of Okinawa-hontō on the Chinen Peninsula, where development has not yet proceeded at the rapid pace seen elsewhere on the island, Nanjō has more of a lush jungle vibe than neighbouring Tomigusuku and Itoman and is a great place to retreat to if you want to experience the slower pace of island life.

The Nanjō region is where the Ryūkyū Islands are said to have been created, and this sacred cultural backdrop is most likely why Nanjō remains largely untouched by mass tourism or large-scale urban development. It's also the most compelling reason to visit this place, where most of the treasures lie beneath the surface and require a little effort and dedication to uncover.

Sacred Sefā Utaki

A moment of reverence and gratitude

Integral to the Ryūkyūan religion (p88), an *utaki* is a special place in nature where the Uchinanchu (Okinawans) go to connect with the gods. *Utaki* are always natural features (a rock, grove, cave, tree or spring, for example) and are typically not used specifically as places of prayer. Visiting an *utaki* is about strengthening connection and communication between the people of these islands and their gods.

Of the hundreds of *utaki* around the islands, **Sefā Utaki** is regarded as the most sacred. In Ryūkyūan belief, it was created by the goddess Amamikyō after she descended to earth at Kudaka-jima and created the Ryūkyū Islands. As you walk along the stone path towards the mysterious archway known as *sangui*, observe your feelings. If you feel the awe that you might sometimes experience when you're amid nature in all its glory, focus on that feeling and allow it to build. Approach the *utaki* calmly, bow gently, and with your inner voice state your

GETTING AROUND

Steep, winding roads twist and climb from coastal crags to the highest outcrops where the Ryūkyū built their castles. That they did so without wheels is astonishing. You, however, will need a car to get around.

☑ **TOP TIP**

Nanjō is further than you think. If you're unable to spend a quiet night here, a relaxing soak in **Apeman Onsen** might also work.

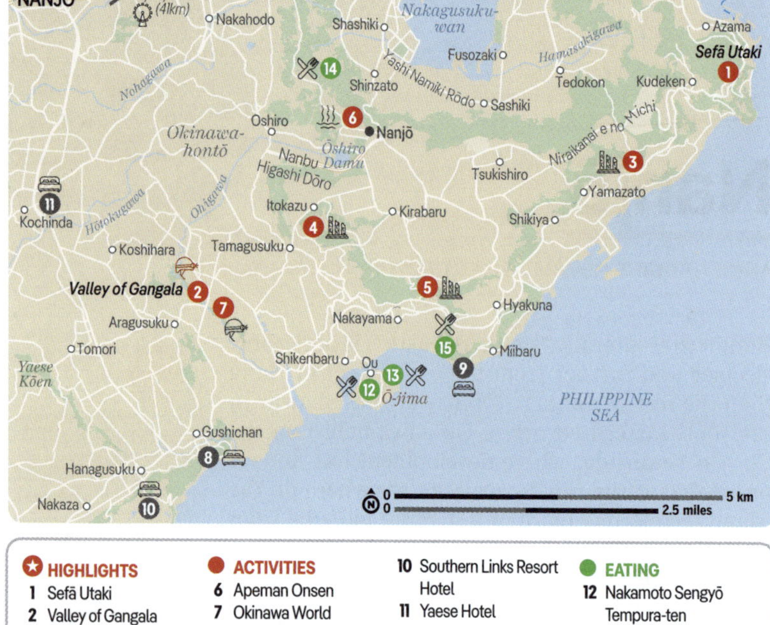

name and where you're from. Express gratitude for something that has happened for you since you connected with the spirit of the Ryūkyū. If there's something you're seeking guidance with, hold that in your mind and observe what comes. Bow again to conclude your visit.

A Prehistoric Valley

Enter a subterranean world

It's almost better to enter the **Valley of Gangala** (*gangala.com; tours per person ¥2500*) without too much information about what you're about to see. Entry is by small group tours, led by fabulous guides (in Japanese; audio guides in other languages provided free) from the Sakitari cave. You'll follow your guide along the rushing Yuhi river into the valley below, through lush subtropical rainforest with ancient banyan trees, past *utaki* from Ryūkyūan times and deeper into a subterranean world. In 2004, prehistoric ornaments, tools and human bones were found here, along with one of the earliest known fish hooks, dated to around 23,000 BCE. Your guide will detail each of the numerous points of interest this thought-provoking site holds. The course is a gentle 1km walk that is suitable for anyone with good general fitness; note there are some stairs.

If you're travelling with kids, the double act of the Valley of Gangala and Okinawa World is a good use of half a day. If I had to choose between the two, I would go for the Valley of Gangala. I've never experienced anything else quite as unique, surprising and informative in my many years of travel. – **Benedict Walker**, Lonely Planet writer

Cave & Craft Village

Okinawa World's natural and cultural attractions

The star attraction at **Okinawa World** *(en.gyokusendo.co.jp/ okinawaworld; adult/child ¥2000/1000)* is the 5km **Gyokusen-dō** (cave), where you can follow 850m of comfortable, accessible walking trails through a spectacularly lit, otherworldly landscape of ancient stalactites and stalagmites. It's the second largest cave in Japan after Akiyoshi-dō in Yamaguchi.

The replica Kingdom Village, similar to Onna's Ryūkyū-mura (p117), displays traditional Okinawan and Japanese crafts. Staff wander the site in period dress. DIY workshops are available, but check the website before you visit, as some hands-on experiences require advance reservations.

Skip Habu Park, whose resident Okinawan vipers occupy rundown quarters.

Ancient Clifftop Castles

Wander among ruined fortresses

Okinawa's oldest fortresses are perched high above the Pacific with views over Kudaka-jima. You can explore these lesser-visited sites at leisure.

Legend has it that **Tamagusuku** was built by the goddess Amamikyō herself. Much of the lower structure was removed and repurposed in US military bases, but the remaining upper ramparts give a sense of the original structure's vast scale. A large round opening in the stone walls is aligned so that sunlight shines through at sunrise on the summer solstice and at sunset on the winter solstice. In the undergrowth there's a small *utaki* marked by a sign.

Itokazu-gusuku, about 3km west, is the largest castle ruin in southern Okinawa and was built around the 14th century. Several *utaki* are dotted around the site. Just south of the Nirai-kanai bridge, on the Chinen peninsula, is one of the smallest and oldest of the prefecture's 192 castle sites, **Chinen-gusuku**. Its original level is made from Okinawan limestone, and a second level is made from refined masonry.

Kou Takahashi, Director, Valley of Gangala

I have lived in Okinawa for over 30 years since I studied at the University of the Ryūkyūs. I've been the Director of **Valley of Gangala** for the past 16 years and **ASMUI Spiritual Hikes** (p141) since 2024, serving the mission of our founder Soken Oshiro to 'pass on in order to protect' our natural, historical and cultural heritage – and particularly Okinawa's unique *utaki,* within which we feel our gods reside. My three tips for a wonderful trip are: (1) visit authentic places of nature, history and prayer; (2) knowledge matters, but try to feel each place with your senses; and (3) be sure to visit northern Okinawa to connect with our ancestors.

DINING IN NANJŌ: OUR PICKS

Yama-no-chaya Rakusui: This serene, ocean-view cafe nestled in the forest serves locally sourced, organic, vegetarian fare. *11am-3pm Fri-Wed* ¥

Ō-jima Imaiyu Market: Vendors at this squeaky-clean seaside fish market serve everything from sashimi to squid ink soup. Cheap! *9am-6pm Mon-Fri* ¥

Nakamoto Sengyō Tempura-ten: You can't miss this popular *tempura* joint by the bridge for the folks lining up to get in. Join them! *10.30am-6pm Fri-Wed* ¥¥

Pizza Kissa Mimoza-no-ki: Wonderful views and delicious, Euro-styled pizzas and Italian fare in a welcoming hideout among the trees. *10am-6pm Wed-Mon* ¥¥

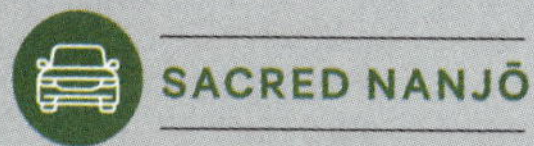

SACRED NANJŌ

This loop drive from Azama Port takes in all of Nanjō's ancient treasures. Do it in a day or stretch it over three.

START	END	LENGTH
Azama Port	Azama Port	40km; 1½hr

Before or after a ferry trip to the spiritually significant island of Kudaka-jima (p87), drive from **❶ Azama Port** ferry terminal to **❷ Sefā Utaki** (p83) to pay your respects. Head down to sea level and the tiny island of **❸ Ō-jima**, where you can stop for lunch or grab takeaway sashimi from Imayu fish market before heading up and inland to the **❹ Valley of Gangala** (p84) and **Okinawa World** (p85). Be sure to book your tickets before you arrive if you're planning to visit either attraction.

Next, spend a few hours away from the crowds, imagining what it was like to be a feudal lord on a pristine island never encroached upon by the modern world. Drive first to the **❺ Itokazu castle ruins** (p85), then compare their scale, serenity and outlook with the **❻ Tamagusuku castle ruins** (p85). On your way to the smallest and oldest of your castle conquests, stop for a soak in Nanjō town at **❼ Apeman Onsen** (p83) and stock up on supplies for the last leg of the journey, to **❽ Chinen castle ruins** (p85).

Cross the **❾ Niraikanai Bridge**, contemplating the metaphysical journey Amamikyō took from there to Kudaka-jima, as you arrive back at Azama Port. If you fancy, reward yourself with a sunset swim at adjacent Azama Sun Sun Beach.

Beyond Nanjō

Venture off the main island to explore Okinawa's spiritual home.

Long, thin Kudaka-jima lies about 5km east of Chinen-hantō in Nanjō. With an area of just 1.4 sq km, the island nonetheless has outsized importance in Okinawan mythology. Legend tells that it has been host to gods, and history shows that kings and priestesses have dwelt here. Filled with holy, historical and natural sites, Kudaka-jima is largely undeveloped for tourism, with no commercial hotels and only a handful of eateries. It has just 240 full-time residents, all descendants of families who have been here for generations, and is one of the last places on the planet where some practices of the traditional Ryūkyūan religion are still observed. A visit here is a chance to tread lightly and explore mindfully.

Kudaka-jima

Explore Okinawa's sacred island

A place of myth and legend, **Kudaka-jima** feels far removed from the 'rest of the world', yet it's only a 30-minute ferry ride from the Chinen coast in Nanjō and a 1½-hour drive from Downtown Naha. Allow yourself anywhere from half a day to a day to explore. It's said that the goddess Amamikyō descended to the island from a place called Niraikanai, far to the east, and then created the Ryūkyū Islands and people. There are many *utaki* on Kudaka-jima that are signposted as strictly off limits to anyone but one of the island's two remaining priestesses, or the local population when they are used in ceremonies and sacred rituals.

Kudaka is a special place that lends itself to quiet, solitary exploration and reflection. You can circumnavigate the island's 7km girth on foot, or by bicycle or e-tuk-tuk. When you get off the ferry you'll see the colourful bikes of Rental Kudaka (レンタル久高島) lined up waiting for you. Approach the staff directly to hire one if you didn't make an advance reservation. Only islanders are permitted to live here, so you don't need to worry too much about competing companies and better rates, although there are other rental outfitters up the hill from the wharf. Once you've secured wheels, you'll be given a map noting the island's main areas. The best way to explore is to be guided by your instincts. As a starting point, once you've ascended the slope from the wharf, turn right and

Places

Kudaka-jima p87

GETTING AROUND

The island is only accessible by **ferry** (kudakakaiun. jimdofree.com/ english); you can take the regular ferry (25 minutes; ¥770/390 adult/child one way) or a high-speed boat (15 minutes; ¥680/340 adult/ child one way) from Nanjō's Azama Port. There are six return trips per day, with the last boat leaving in each direction at 5pm, weather permitting.

THE RYŪKYŪAN RELIGION

Before it became part of Japan, Okinawa was for centuries an independent empire with complex structures of governance, its own language groups and its own religion, where women held the highest positions as priestesses called *noro* and shamans called *yuta*. Highly venerated and at risk of being lost over time, the indigenous Ryūkyūan religion is still practised by a dwindling number of initiated community members throughout the islands in the form of various rituals, cultural practices and festivals. Despite the threat of extinction, its core teachings inform an underlying belief system in Okinawan society.

Romance Road

follow the road. All of the important and interesting locations are signposted in English, and there are QR codes to direct you to more detailed information about each one.

About halfway along the island's east coast is the peaceful forest grove of **Fubo-utaki**, from where it's a short cycle to the northern tip of the island, **Cape Kaberu** (or Habyan), where it's believed the goddess Amamikyō alighted. These are two of the most sacred sites in all of Okinawa, so it's sad to see the unstoppable wave of plastic waste washing up at the cape. A cycle along **Romance Road** (said to have been paved by local women while their husbands were at sea) will take you past other restful spots into the heart of the village. Facilities on the island are limited. There are a post office, a small shop, a handful of places to eat and, happily, a place selling soft-serve ice cream.

It's also possible to visit on a half-day guided tour with **Cerulean Blue** (*per person ¥7800*). The tour price includes return ferry transportation, bicycle rental, guide and insurance. You'll need to make your own way to Azama Port. Bring your own lunch, or carry cash for a simple meal at the island's restaurant.

Places We Love to Stay

Tomigusuku
MAP p77

Y's Inn Naha Oroku-ekimae
¥ Cheery, recently renovated rooms and a great location adjacent to AEON mall and a hop, skip and jump from Oroky station make this a good-value choice.

Airport View Naha ¥ Almost in Naha, the Airport View is a good budget offering in Tomigusuku that's about as close to the airport as you can get, with Naha's attractions just a stone's throw away.

Hotel Gran View Garden Okinawa ¥¥ In an excellent location near Chura Sun Beach at Toyosaki Seaside Park and all the nearby shopping, dining and attractions, this older hotel has been recently renovated. It has a good pool, a communal Japanese-style bath, a restaurant offering buffet breakfasts, rooms with balconies and good-value rates.

Ryūkyū Onsen Senagajima Hotel ¥¥ The closest hotel to Naha's international airport is so much more than somewhere to transit, with resort-style facilities including a pool, Naha's only true onsen experience and a shopping centre with an excellent food court (p79).

Itoman
MAP p81

Mr Kinjo in Shiozaki ¥ Compact studio-style apartments with laundry facilities, kitchen and balcony in this well-located complex in central Itoman are often available at excellent rates.

Southern Beach Hotel & Resort ¥¥ An oasis from Naha's hustle and bustle while remaining within easy reach of the city. Its bright, light-filled rooms have a splash of colour and big, comfy beds, and guests enjoy the resort's pool, gym and dining facilities.

Ryūkyū Hotel & Resort Nashiro Beach ¥¥¥ In southern Itoman, this sprawling five-star resort geared to young couples and honeymooners has gorgeous, spacious rooms with ocean views, balconies and all the amenities you'd expect from a plush beachfront hotel.

Nanjō
MAP p84

Yaese Hotel ¥ This simple hotel is in a good position close to everything; it's a good option if you've been driving all day and simply need a bed for the night.

Yuinchi Hotel (& Campground) ¥¥ In the centre of Nanjō, this huge tourist hotel was once the talk of the town. While it's less so now, it's still a great choice if you're staying in the area, with a range of room types and rates, and even a campground.

Glory Island Okinawa Yabusachi Resort ¥¥ This fabulous concept resort perched high above Hyakuna Beach has funky, modular apartment-style rooms up for grabs from as low as ¥8000 per night.

Southern Links Resort Hotel ¥¥¥ Not far from the Peace Memorial Park, this sprawling golf resort has spacious rooms, an array of facilities and an idyllic location that feels far from the madding crowd.

Hyakuna Garan ¥¥¥ This exquisite ryokan is one for those who value the finer details of *kaiseki* (Japanese haute cuisine) and the concept of *wabi-sabi* (which loosely translates as 'beauty in imperfection') in architecture and design. Is this the island's best place to sleep? You'll delight in deciding.

DMM Kariyushi Aquarium (p79), Tomigusuku

*Researched by
Manami Okazaki*

Central Okinawa Island

SERENITY, CRAFT AND FOOD GALORE

Home to the former capital of the Ryūkyū Kingdom, central Okinawa-hontō has world-class ceramics, stunning beaches, impressive beginner dives and myriad food options.

Historically, Okinawa was divided into three kingdoms consisting of the island's central, northern and southern domains, and these fiefdoms were in place until the 15th century. In 1429 Shō Hashi unified these regions to create the Ryūkyū Kingdom. Urasoe was the centre of Ryūkyū both politically and culturally until Shuri became the capital.

Complex geopolitical history is manifest in almost all of the region's cultural sites, from the evidence of trade with the rest of Asia to the heavy WWII damage that annihilated much of central Okinawa Island (central Okinawa-hontō), the presence of military bases and the food and entertainment that cater to American residents and their families. The excellent Sakima Art Museum hosts nuanced exhibitions that focus on these intertwined layers of wartime history, peace and colonialism.

While Okinawa's capital is now Naha, central Okinawa-hontō offers some of the island's finest experiences. Here you can see the exquisite pottery that helped shape the *mingei* folk craft movement and visit museums and historic sites showcasing the former capital's glory. With their clear turquoise waters, the beaches around Miyagi Island are among the best in Okinawa, and you can glimpse rural life in the Ginoza area, home to farms, delicious produce and spectacular caves. The region's food offerings are varied and plentiful, from the iconic Charlie's Tacos to the unbeatable Okinawa soba at Maruchi.

THE MAIN AREAS

URASOE
Former capital with cultural offerings.
p96

CHATAN & KADENA
Leisure hub with Okinawan-American culture. **p100**

GINOWAN & OKINAWA CITY
Authentic urban experience with shopping and nightlife.
p103

YOMITAN
World-class pottery and textiles.
p107

For places to
stay in Central
Okinawa Island,
see p123

CENTRAL OKINAWA ISLAND

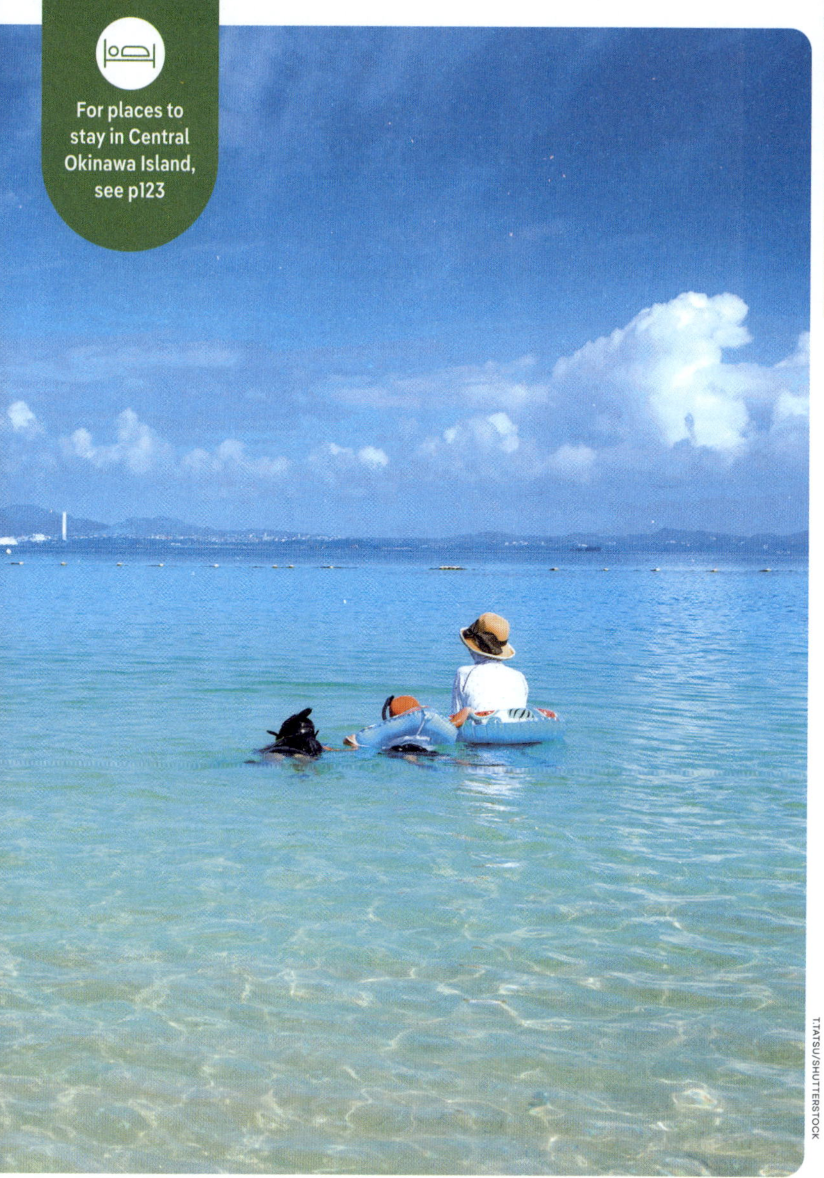

Left: *Bingata* fabric, Gusuku Bingata (p99), Urasoe; Above: Ōdomari Beach (p116), Ikei Island

URUMA
Some of Okinawa's
best island-hopping.
p114

ONNA
Lovely beaches and
great food close to
Naha. **p117**

KIN & GINOZA
Semi-rural area
with hip towns.
p120

Find Your Way

Ideal for driving, central Okinawa-hontō covers a large expanse of the island, with cultural highlights, remote peninsula beaches and the best places for inauthentic but delicious American classics.

Yomitan, p107

Atelier-hop around dozens of artisan studios in this district of crafts, taking in textiles, pottery and glass.

Chatan & Kadena, p100

Okinawan-American culture with a side of people-watching, beachside cruising and glorious sunsets.

Ginowan & Okinawa City, p103

Grungy, funky pair of towns with indie shops and an urban vibe.

Urasoe, p96

Historic centre with diversions including a ruined fortress, a US military site turned hipster town and a museum showcasing exquisite *urushi* lacquerware.

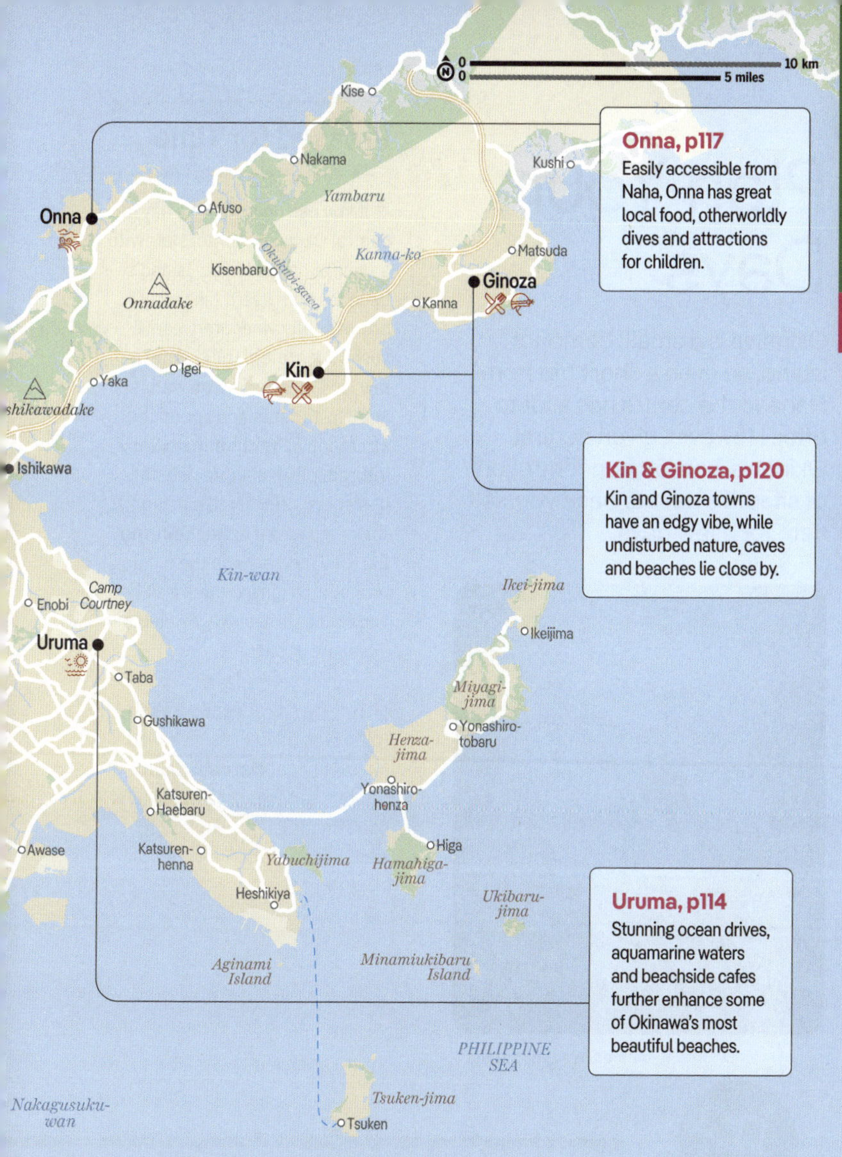

Onna, p117

Easily accessible from Naha, Onna has great local food, otherworldly dives and attractions for children.

Kin & Ginoza, p120

Kin and Ginoza towns have an edgy vibe, while undisturbed nature, caves and beaches lie close by.

Uruma, p114

Stunning ocean drives, aquamarine waters and beachside cafes further enhance some of Okinawa's most beautiful beaches.

CAR

A car is certainly the best way to travel here and is highly recommended not only as a means to reach your destination but also for the sheer fun of cruising around the island.

BUS

The central island's extensive services include community buses and services run by Ryūkyū, Toyo and Okinawa, but buses in general take an incredibly long time and are sparse.

FERRY

A fun way to get to Motobu without relying on a car is to take a 75-minute high-speed ferry ride with Daiichi Marine Service from Naha's Tomari port to Motobu's Toguchi Port.

Plan Your Days

Okinawa is a small, compact island, so even a short trip from Naha to the centre has a lot to offer. However, given central Okinawa-hontō's concentration of sites, it's best to base yourself here for a few days.

Blue Cave (p119), Onna

Pressed for Time

● If you can only spend a day in central Okinawa-hontō, start with a swim at one of Miyagi Island's beaches and grab a takeaway box of lightly vinegared *inari* sushi at **Maruichi** (p114). After a few laps in the cerulean waters, head to Yomitan and spend the afternoon at **Yachimun no Sato village** (p110) to appreciate the pottery on offer. Grab a mango *kakigori* (shaved ice) at **Onna no Eki** (p119) and browse the local produce, which includes fruit and vegetables not widely available in mainland Japan.

● End the day at **Araha Beach** (p100) watching the sunset and have dinner at **Maruchi** (p101) in Chatan, serving some of the best soba on the island with a rich, pork-based broth.

PETESPHOTOGRAPHY/GETTY IMAGES

Seasonal Highlights

Okinawa is most popular in summer, but the island's centre has many sites that can be enjoyed in winter as well.

MARCH

At the Yachimun Ceramics Fair, held at Hotel Moon Beach in Onna Village, you can pick up a variety of beautiful pottery pieces made by local craftspeople.

APRIL

The Ginowan fireworks festival offers a family-friendly festival atmosphere without the oppressive heat of summer *matsuri*.

JULY

The summer festival at Ocean Expo Park is the biggest fireworks show in Okinawa Island and can be seen at Emerald Beach at Motobu.

Two Days in the Centre

● Staying two days in the centre gives you enough time to visit more of the region's cultural offerings. On day one, book a workshop with **Gusuku Bingata** (p99) to appreciate the artistry of this complex form of textile dyeing. Afterwards, grab a coffee at one of the island's best cafes, Okinawa Cerrado Beans Store, within **Minatogawa Stateside Town** (p96), a former housing area for members of the US military.

● On the second day, peruse fine lacquerware at the **Urasoe Art Museum** (p98), then head out to the Urasoe Castle ruins at **Urasoe Dai Park** (p97) to get a feel for the Ryūkyū Kingdom's former glory. Take in the views before returning to Okinawa City for dinner at **Charlie's Tacos** (p105).

Stay Awhile

● If you can swing it, at least three days are recommended for a visit to central Okinawa-hontō. Go diving or snorkelling at the **Blue Cave** (p119) on the morning of your first day to enjoy the otherworldly light tunnels. Afterwards, get some local food at one of the many stalls and food trucks at **Onna no Eki** (p119). Browse some of the market's produce to get an understanding of what makes Okinawan food unique.

● On day two, focus on the **Sakima Art Museum** (p105), appreciating thoughtful exhibitions that deliberate on the Okinawan people's collective memory and identity.

● On your last day, browse the kitsch at **American Village** (p102) and finish by enjoying local ice cream flavours like ube and pineapple at **Blue Seal Chatan** (p102).

SEPTEMBER

The **Okinawa Zentō Eisā Matsuri** (p105) at Koza Sports Park is held over three days in mid-September.

OCTOBER

From mid-October, Okinawa City's Botanical Gardens light up and the Kin Town festival brings the fun with fireworks, *taiko* drummers, *sanshin* players and Ryūkyū dancers.

NOVEMBER

Okinawa's mild winters are a nice contrast to the humid months of summer, making the season ideal for activities that aren't centred on swimming.

DECEMBER

Illuminations across the island make for a festive atmosphere during the Christmas season. American Village goes all out with decorations and seasonal restaurant menus.

Urasoe

THRIFT SHOPS | FOOD & DRINK | CULTURE

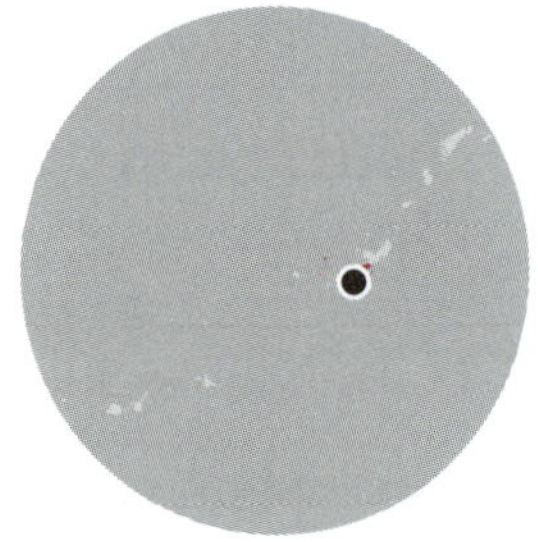

> ☑ **TOP TIP**
>
> Stroll around Minatogawa to get locally made souvenirs.

Known as the birthplace of the Ryūkyū Kingdom, Urasoe (浦添市) served as the base of the Chūzan Kingdom's domain from the late 12th to the early 15th centuries. The residence of several Ryūkyū Kingdom-era kings, Urasoe Castle was the site of important regional strategy making. While not much remains of the fortress, its ruins sit on a hill with vistas of the East China Sea. About a dozen sacred sites are found nearby.

Nowadays Urasoe is a region of only about 19 sq km on the west coast of Okinawa-hontō, but historically it also covered Ginowan, Naha Port and much of Nishihara. The city was annihilated during WWII and nearly half the population was killed. US Marine base Camp Kinser was established in 1949, and its legacy can be seen at Minatogawa, a military residence turned hipster town. Old-school shopping street Yafuso-dōri makes for an enjoyable evening stroll.

Browsing Minatogawa Village

Military residential area turned hipster town

Once a residential area for military personnel in Camp Kinser, **Minatogawa Stateside Town** was purpose built on a site cleared by dynamiting a hill. Many of the roughly 70 dwellings have since been retrofitted into shops and studios, transforming the village into a hip creator hamlet. Each of

GETTING AROUND

With its proximity to Naha, Urasoe can be navigated by public transportation. Yui Rail has three stations in Urasoe: Kyozuka, Urasoe-Maeda and Tedako Uranishi; the monorail service terminates in Urasoe. **Buses** (*busnavi-okinawa.com*) also run frequently, though you'll likely need to walk up to 1km to fill the gaps. Driving is a bit easier than in Naha, and most places have parking available; if you're continuing to road-trip north, this might be a good place to rent a car.

BEING OKINAWAN

Sakula Costar, digital creator who shares Okinawan culture online; @sakulacostar

I share unique Okinawan philosophies such as *yuuimaru* (the spirit of community and collective wellbeing); *nuchi du takara* (life is precious), a philosophy born from both hardship and appreciation of life's fragility; and *moai*, the idea of long-term community built on connection and support.

Staying connected means preserving voices that were almost lost. It means honouring our ancestors' sacrifices. And it means younger generations, especially those of mixed background like myself, have pathways to a culture that was historically marginalised and misunderstood.

To me, being Okinawan means belonging to a culture that has survived cultural erasure, war and loss while still choosing music, dance, kindness and community.

the streets is named after a US state and lined with vintage shops, clothing boutiques and craft stores. Grab a divine coffee at **Okinawa Cerrado Coffee Beans Store**, one of the numerous cafes in the district, and browse the likes of vintage clothing store **American Wave**; **Casa Machilda**, specialising in wooden toys; **Portriver Market**, with local sundries and fashion items; and **Shima Denim Works**, selling denim and upcycled fashion. Minatogawa also offers a rare chance to see inside reinforced-concrete military homes, complete with USA-style living rooms and tiled bathrooms.

History-Rich Urasoe Dai

Of conflict and kings

Expansive **Urasoe Dai Park** is home to various recreational facilities as well as cultural artefacts. Here you can play sport, clamber on a jungle gym and contemplate the lives of 13th-century monarchs, all in one place. The **Urasoe Shell Mound** contains shells, pottery and tools dating from 4000 years ago; the area is also dotted with shallow caves, although it's not possible to enter them.

The once grand **Urasoe Castle**, built in the late 13th century, predates the Ryūkyū Kingdom. It belonged to one of the kingdom's predecessors, the Chūzan Kingdom. The castle's

TRAUMA & MEMORY

Okinawa-born writer Shun Medorama writes powerful socio-political novels that speak of the Okinawan experience through the lens of war trauma, Japanese nationalism, the US military and the contested Henoko base. His book *In the Woods of Memory* has been translated into English and looks at WWII from nine points of view. As its themes include sexual assault, the book is not suitable for all readers, but it's a formidable deliberation on memory and the ethics of war. Despite several of the protagonists of Medorama's novel *Droplets* speaking in a dialect incomprehensible to most Japanese people, it won the Akutagawa Prize, one of Japan's most esteemed literary honours.

Urasoe Castle (p97)

forbidding stone walls snake up the hill, as a reminder of the imposing fortress that used to stand here. At the edge of the castle grounds is one of Okinawa's three royal mausoleums, **Urasoe Yōdore**, where several rulers and royals are entombed.

The castle grounds and ridge were used as a defensive position during the Battle of Okinawa in 1945, and several of the shallow caves on the grounds were used as dugouts by the Japanese military. The battle at the ridge, known in Okinawa as Maeda Ridge, later became the subject of a 2016 biopic directed by Mel Gibson and starring Andrew Garfield called *Hacksaw Ridge*. The battle destroyed some of the tomb's walls, and restorations were later undertaken.

Lacquer Looker

Okinawan history through lacquer art

Adjacent to ANA Field sports facility, the **Urasoe Art Museum** (*urasoe-artmuseum.jp; adult/child ¥300/free*) was Okinawa's first public art institution. The core of its permanent exhibition features Okinawan and Asian *urushi* (lacquerware), including pieces that date from the Ryūkyū Kingdom's period of prodigious international trade in the 16th century and beyond. Rotating special exhibitions feature the work of local artists and themed collections of calligraphy, sculpture and other art forms from ancient to contemporary periods. You can easily spend half a day here. Be sure to visit the garden and climb the small tower, giving a 360-degree vista of Urasoe and Naha. The museum is closed Monday.

Vibrant Bingata Textiles

A craft as resilient as Okinawa itself

While beautiful to the eye, *bingata* fabrics are more than just cloth; they exist within the context of colonialism and multicultural trade. Each narrative told through the textiles' colours and motifs is a tale of identity and perseverance. The craft's history goes back over 500 years, when *bingata* cloth was worn by Ryūkyū dancers and nobility. After WWII, *bingata* clothed commoners as well.

Urasoe-based studio **Gusuku Bingata** (城紅型染工房; *gusukubingata.com*) focuses on kimono fabric dyeing as well as contemporary souvenirs such as umbrellas and cell-phone cases. It also produces cute modern motifs such as whale sharks, hibiscuses and queen of the night cacti. Female artisan Shoko Yamashiro says, 'The characteristic of *bingata* is that it is influenced by our natural environment, like the ocean, the bright sky, the really strong sun and the year-round warm weather. One reason for the vivid colours of *bingata* is that they do not get lost in the strong sunshine. These colours enrich the heart and soul and have vibrant, healing powers. The emphasis on natural motifs such as flowers and birds is comforting to the eye.'

Yamashiro explains that there are two dye techniques: one is freehand, and the other uses dye-resistant stencils made of mulberry paper. The complexity of the stencils means they can take artisans up to a month to cut by hand. Freehand techniques make use of a culinary-style piping bag to 'draw' bold lines. Like most artisans, Yamashiro enjoys the process as much as the product and says she finds dyeing *bingata* is 'like a puzzle'. A high-end *bingata* kimono costs ¥1–2 million. The price reflects the labour that goes into their creation: each bolt of cloth takes two or three months to produce.

If you want to try a simplified version of the process, the studio hosts **workshops** (*per person from ¥2700*). Book via Facebook (*@gusukubingata.okinawa*) or WhatsApp (*+81-80-9145-1048*). English is spoken.

BINGATA HUES

While many aspects of *bingata* production overlap with mainland Japanese textile traditions, Okinawan *bingata* is distinguished by its vivid colours. The term *bingata* is derived from *bin* (meaning red) and *gata* (meaning stencil). *Bingata* isn't always dyed vermillion, but distinctive reds ranging from an intense hibiscus hue to soft, billowing pinks are a characteristic of *bingata* textiles. Ryūkyū fabrics often reference the ocean, using soft, light indigo shades rather than the concentrated blues of Edo (Tokyo) textiles. The most striking and dominant colour used in local textiles is a mustard yellow that is unique to Okinawa. In the past only royalty could wear these golden cloths, produced using the *fukugi* tree.

EATING IN URASOE: OUR PICKS

Bueno Chicken Urasoe:	**Kaisen Shokudo Tiida:**	**Ipponmatsu:** (一本松)	**Nakamura:** (お肉の店 仲村)
Famous takeaway chain selling an Argentine-inspired garlic rotisserie bird using Yambaru chicken. *10am-5.30pm Tue-Sat* ¥	Incredibly generous proportions of tempura using local produce. *11am-3.30pm Tue-Sun* ¥	Small Okinawan soba joint in an apartment complex serving firm noodles in garlicky, herby broth. *11.30am-3.30pm Fri-Tue* ¥	At this eatery in the back of a local butcher shop, enjoy soba topped with mountains of quality meat. *9am-6pm Mon-Sat* ¥

Chatan & Kadena

SHOPPING | AMERICAN CULTURE | JUNK FOOD

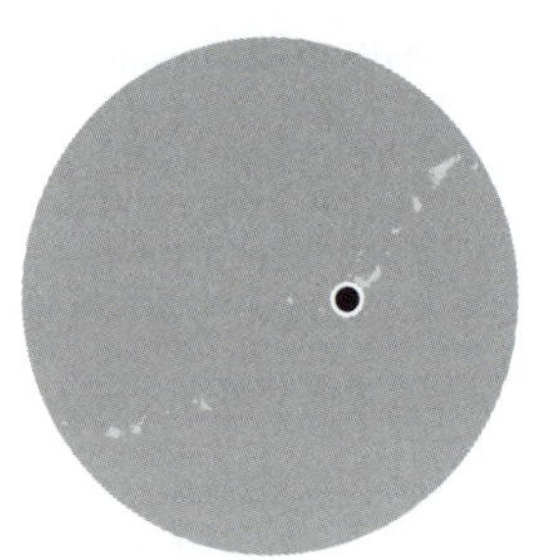

GETTING AROUND

Much of Chatan and Kadena are military sites, so the roads open to the public are quite limited. Several buses service Chatan, and there are bikes for hire at Chatan Town Tourist Information Centre. After strolling around American Village, you can ride your bike to Toguchi Beach in Kadena.

The Chatan (北谷) and Kadena (嘉手納) communities were occupied by the US military after WWII. Kadena was heavily damaged in the war, but some villagers were allowed to return to their devastated homes in October 1946. Much of the village centre became Kadena Air Base, which civilians could enter until 1948, when access was banned. As both Chatan and Kadena are still home to US infrastructure, numerous entertainment complexes, eateries and businesses cater to military personnel as well as visitors.

Downtown Chatan has the massive American Village and beaches such as Araha, which is lined with cafes. As you walk along the palm-tree-lined coast, with inline skating and jogging Americans passing by and a barrage of fighter jets roaring overhead, it can be difficult to believe you're in Japan at all. The main reasons to visit this part of Okinawa are to get some comfort food and enjoy the sunsets.

☑ TOP TIP

Catch the sunset at Chatan Beach and eat at **Flex** (p102), a Jamaican joint with lovely veranda seating.

American Village (p102)

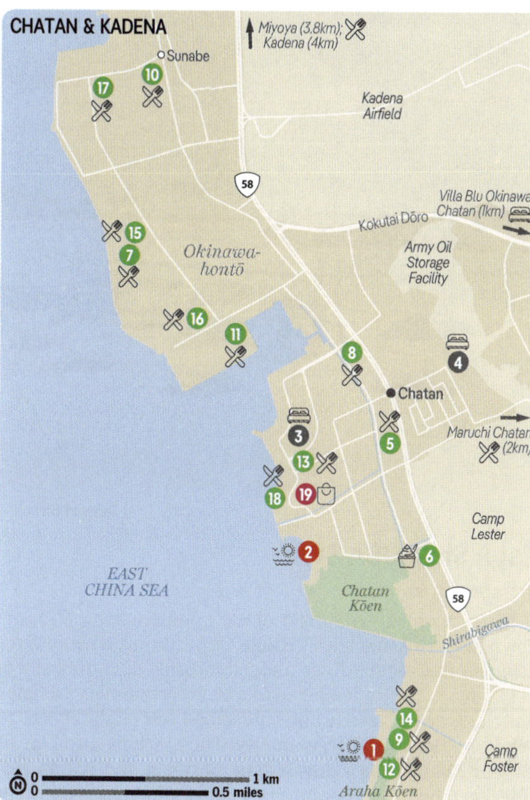

EATING IN CHATAN & KADENA: OUR PICKS

Miyoya: Okinawa soba joint in Kadena with delicious light broth and even more delicious pork on the side. *11am-2.30pm Tue-Sun* ¥

Maruchi Chatan: (沖縄 そば まるち) Umami-rich pork broth and melt-in-your-mouth spareribs served in a traditional house. *11am-7.30pm* ¥

Kinmatsu Steak: Local-favourite old-school steakhouse in Chatan with spot-on atmosphere. *11am-9.30pm* ¥¥

Timeless Chocolate: Bean-to-bar chocolate made in Chatan with Okinawan *kokuto* sugar cane. *9am-6pm* ¥

Taco Petes: Blue corn tortillas, smoky beef, slow-braised pulled pork and signature salsas. In Chatan. *hours vary Fri-Tue* ¥

Tacos-Ya Chatan: Tacos with a thick, deep-fried shell and less filling. Also has taco rice sets. *11.30am-9pm* ¥

Corners Parlor: Crispy fish tacos battered to perfection. Servings are large. In Chatan. *11.30am-5.30pm Wed-Mon* ¥

Sunrise Shack: 'Bullet coffee' (with coconut oil, butter and vanilla) and açaí bowls beachside in Chatan. *8am-4.30pm Mon-Fri, 8.30am-5.30pm Sat & Sun* ¥

ICONIC WOODEN DOLLS

While they're usually made in Tōhoku, Okinawa has its own type of contemporary *kokeshi* called Ryūkyū *miyarabi* that have been made in Naha since 1972. *Miyarabi* means 'young girl' in the local dialect, and the dolls resemble girls in traditional dress. Some are made in the likeness of Ryūkyū dancers wearing conical *hanagasa* straw hats. Other designs include dolls that resemble fisherwomen carrying baskets of fish on their heads and wearing a type of classic woven kimono called *kasuri*. The most popular type, particularly with family members of US military living on the bases, has a piece of paper wrapped around it so that people can write letters and send them to loved ones. The dolls are made by people with disabilities in a residential care facility.

Sunset Beach

Eat & Shop USA Style

A taste of Americana

If you're momentarily disoriented upon entering Mihama Town Resort's **American Village** (*okinawa-americanvillage .com/en*) in Chatan, that's understandable. Spanning several city blocks, the open-air mall and entertainment complex has the types of restaurants and shops you might expect to see in a midsize Californian city. They include an array of chain restaurants serving Indian, Mexican and Italian cuisine, seafood, burgers and pizza, plus a healthy helping of steak restaurants and Okinawan joints.

After you've stuffed yourself, browse for souvenirs, take in a film at the **Mihama 7Plex cinema** (foreign-language films are usually subtitled in Japanese but are occasionally dubbed; check before buying a ticket) or go for a stroll along the boardwalk to the adjacent **Sunset Beach**, popular for sunbathing and barbecuing.

 **EATING IN CHATAN: INTERNATIONAL FLAVOURS**

Esparza's: Funky diner with excellent tacos on house-made tortillas. Free salsa bar. *11am-9pm Mon-Fri, from 8am Sat & Sun* ¥¥

Blue Seal Chatan: Ice cream in local flavours including mango, *shikuwasa* sherbet and Okinawan brown sugar. *11am-10pm* ¥

Flex: Jerk chicken with Jamaica-sourced spices and Oki ingredients. Beachfront seating. *noon-2.30pm Fri-Mon, 4.30-11pm Thu-Tue* ¥¥

Philippines Street Food Gonta: Street snacks and colourful desserts like *halohalo* (flavoured ice and condensed milk). *hours vary* ¥

A&W Mihama: A classic drive-through option. The curly fries are a great late-night snack. *9am-midnight* ¥

Gordie's: Burgers using hand-ground beef and buns made in-house. Also serves a killer milkshake. *11-8pm* ¥

Shrimp Bus: Oily, garlicky shrimp and fish and chips. Inside American Village. *noon-9pm* ¥

Zhyvago Coffee Works: Espresso drinks, shakes and decadent sweets on the beach. *8am-8pm* ¥

Ginowan & Okinawa City

LIVE MUSIC | HISTORY | SHOPPING

Okinawa City (沖縄市; Oki City) is the second largest city in the prefecture after Naha and was formed in 1974 when two jurisdictions, Koza City and Misato Town, were merged. The city flourished due to the US military presence and has a retro vibe. During the Vietnam War, Kadena Air Base hosted US B-52s, and adjacent Koza boomed as an entertainment district. Many live music places like Café Ocean opened during this time. Today the area's dive bars, entertainment venues and shops are a draw for visitors, along with the Southeast Botanical Gardens, which are especially beautiful on winter nights when they're lit up with illuminations. The history of Ginowan, south of Okinawa City, is also intertwined with the military presence, as it's home to Futenma air station. One of eight important shrines from the Ryūkyū Kingdom era, Futenma shrine is an impressive complex that sits atop a 280m limestone cave.

Independent Shopping Haven

Hunt for souvenirs

Oki City's Gate 2 Street area is awash with quirky indie shops. You can easily spend an afternoon here strolling, browsing and stopping for snacks. The best-known restaurant in Oki City is no doubt Charlie's Tacos (p105), the place that started it all, and satisfying in every way possible. The interior of the store, dating back to 1956, is well preserved. In the same area as Charlie's Tacos, east of Kadena Base, are many independent stores. All on the same street are a few embroidery patch stores that take bespoke orders. Among them are **Tiger Patch Embroidery**, which has military-themed patches for both the US Armed Forces and the Japanese Self Defense Force, and **Tamahashi Embroidery** (玉橋ししゅう店), which sells Okinawan culture–themed patches and embroidered bomber jackets. **Tabineko Books** has resident cats and stocks many Okinawa-themed publications, many focusing on photography. **Neo Pogotown** sells vintage clothing, and **Orion** (オリオン)

GETTING AROUND

It's a 40-minute drive from Naha to Oki City. Evertrail rental company specialises in Suzuki Jimny camping vehicles with rooftop tents. The bus from Naha airport to Okinawa South interchange takes around 40 minutes; the highway bus takes 70 minutes to Goya bus stop. Community buses (¥100) run within the city areas. Find Hello Cycling bike-rental stations in Oki City and Ginowan on the company's app.

☑ TOP TIP

As Okinawa's only *sento* (public bath), Nakanoyu is an important part of Oki City community life. Go for a hot soak after a long day.

GINOWAN & OKINAWA CITY

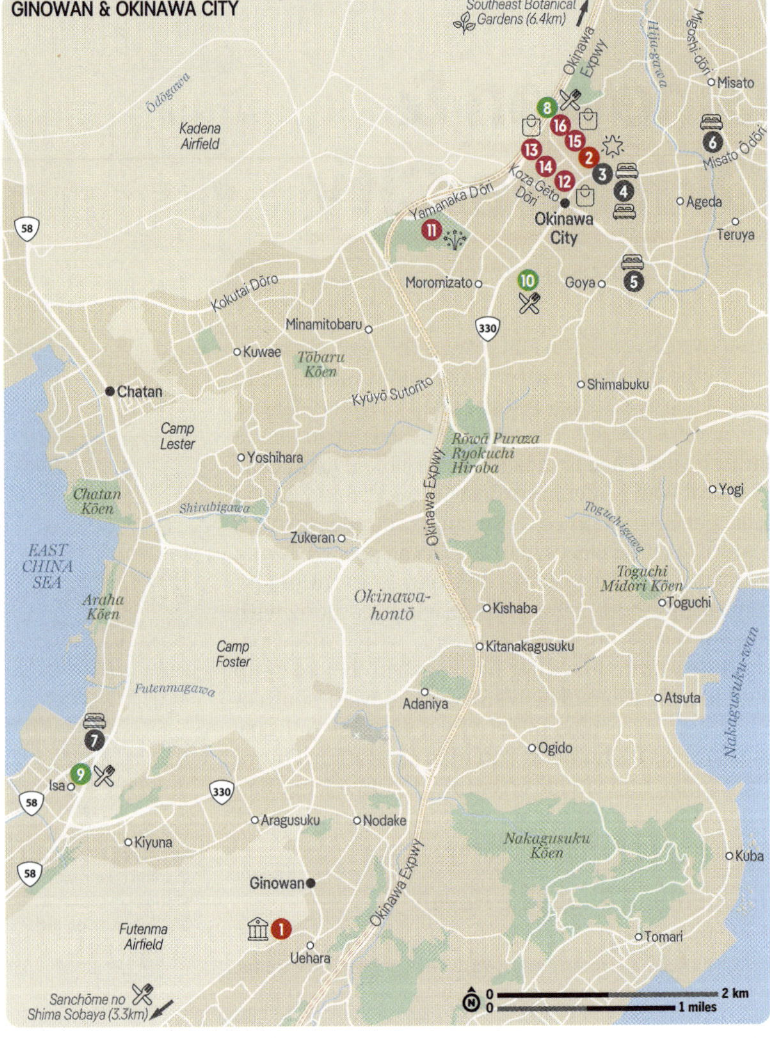

SIGHTS

1 Sakima Art Museum

ACTIVITIES

2 Orion

SLEEPING

3 Deigo Hotel
4 Goyah-so Guesthouse
5 Guesthouse Okinawa Kubotasou
6 Sazanka
7 SG Okinawa Angel House

EATING

8 Charlie's Tacos
9 Mexico Taco
10 Steak House Four Seasons

ENTERTAINMENT

11 Okinawa Zentō Eisā Matsuri

SHOPPING

12 Koza Craft Centre Fundou
13 Neo Pogotown
14 Tabineko Books
15 Tamahashi Embroidery
16 Tiger Patch Embroidery

Sakima Art Museum

is an indoor skateboarding park. Down the road, the **Koza Craft Centre Fundou** (コザ工芸館ふんどう) sells an array of craft such as pottery *shīsā* (lion dogs) and woven baskets. Refuel with cinnamon rolls at **Brown Roll** and grab a coffee from **Amber Holic**.

Socially Engaged Sakima Art Museum

A space for contemplation

Opened in 1994, **Sakima Art Museum** (佐喜眞美館; *sakima.jp*) in Ginowan holds poignant exhibitions on the themes of war and peace. Works are drawn mostly from director Michio Sakima's collection. The museum's stated aim is to exhibit art that deals with 'life and death, and anguish and salvation'. Sakima was inspired to build the museum after he saw the harrowing *Battle of Okinawa* by husband-and-wife artists Iri and Maruki Toshi. Depicting scenes from some of the bloodiest Pacific conflicts of WWII, the massive 4m by 8.5m artwork is painted with such graphic intensity that it inspired Sakima to create a space where it could be seen by everyone.

Other work in the collection of around 1000 pieces includes *bingata* textiles by Okinawan artist Yuken Teruya. Stencilled inside the classic motifs are Osprey helicopters, protestors

KOZA MUSIC CITY

During the Vietnam War, Koza flourished as an entertainment district for the US military at Kadena Base. Musical styles such as hard rock and R&B took off as a result, and eventually a new genre of Okinawan rock was born, exemplified by bands such as Murasaki and Condition Green. Dive bars and cover bands still enliven the local scene; seek out venues Gate 2 Garage, Reverse for Oldies and Club Queen. Okinawa City is also the best place to see *eisā*, a type of traditional Okinawan dance. During the **Okinawa Zentō Eisā Matsuri** at **Koza Sports Park**, dancers perform over a weekend in September in front of over 300,000 people.

EATING IN GINOWAN & OKINAWA CITY: OUR PICKS

Sanchōme Shima Sobaya: (3丁目の島そば屋) Handmade noodles swim in skipjack and kelp broth, topped with succulent pork spareribs. In Ginowan. *11am-3pm* ¥

Mexico Taco: Legendary Ginowan shop serving nothing but tacos; delicious shell and simple flavours. *10.30am-5pm Thu-Mon* ¥

Steak House Four Seasons: Teppanyaki with *wagyū*, Agū pork and lobster in Oki City. Slightly dated interior; superb food and theatrics. *11am-4pm & 5-9.30pm Mon-Fri, to 10pm Sat & Sun* ¥¥

Charlie's Tacos: Okinawa's first taco joint, Charlie's opened in Oki City in 1956 and is still the best. *11am-6pm Fri-Wed* ¥

MIXED CULTURE

YUKIKO, Okinawan tufting artist whose pieces often have Okinawan themes such as *hajichi* tattoos, Okinawan rap artists, even 1 gallon milk cartons (from occupation times); *@tufting.uptome098*

Okinawa is really strong on street culture, skaters, rappers, dancers – it's all mixed together. It's *champuru* (mixed) culture. I'm inspired by Koza City and its sense of colour. Everything is super chaotic, and it has these great embroidery stores. I don't really feel 'Japanese'; my identity is completely Okinawan. We help each other. There's a culture of everyone watching out for everyone. People are basically positive; they laugh things off, even when stuff happens. Everyone has that. The grandmas are always saying 'Eat, eat!'

Capybara, Southeast Botanical Gardens

and parachuting military (p300), all references to military base demonstrations. Other artists represented include Makoto Ueno, Käthe Kollwitz, Georges Rouault, Yayoi Kusama and Yukio Fukazawa.

Designed by Okinawan architect Makishi Yoshikazu, the building has two sets of stairs with six and 23 steps, in homage to Battle of Okinawa Memorial Day on 23 June. On this day the sun sets into the rooftop window. From the roof, visitors can see right into Marine Corps Air Station Futenma. With fighter jets roaring overhead, the juxtaposition is an abrupt reminder of the militarised space found not only on land but in the sky. The museum sits on Sakima's ancestral lands, formerly requisitioned by the US to form part of Futenma.

Exotic Botanical Gardens

Illuminated plant theme park

The sprawling **Southeast Botanical Gardens** (東南植物楽園; *southeast-botanical.jp/en; adult/child from ¥2000/800*) house over 30,000 plants representing 1300 species. The site has the feel of a botany theme park, as several sections showcase different species of plant and animal, many of which are not endemic to Okinawa. Overall the experience resembles a petting zoo, with enclosures filled with exotic birds, goats and capybaras. Half of the park has an impressive array of exotic plants, such as rows of Alexander palms, baobabs and dragon blood trees. From late October to late May, much of the park, from the lotus ponds to the palm trees, is covered in delightful nighttime illuminations.

Yomitan

SANSHIN | FARMERS MARKET | TEXTILES

During the three kingdoms, Yomitan was part of Chūzan. Later, the unified Ryūkyū Kingdom flourished as a result of the tributary system and foreign trade. Yomitan's culture reflects the Ryūkyū Islands' proximity to China in particular, which led to the exchange of customs and creative techniques. UNESCO World Heritage–designated Zakimi Castle is a famous landmark from that period.

The Battle of Okinawa started in Yomitan, which was one of the initial landing sites and suffered severe damage during the fighting. US occupation after WWII meant that Yomitan was only returned to Japan in 1972, and many aspects of its traditional culture became endangered. Despite that, Yomitan is dense with cultural heritage, and its ceramics and textiles demonstrate its artisanal excellence. The fact that these art forms still exist is testament to the local people's efforts to keep them alive. Some traditions, including Yuntanza *hanaori* textiles, were brought back from extinction.

Oki-Hawaii Sanshin Grooves

Okinawan culture in three strings

Yomitan is the birthplace of Akainko, the legendary father of *sanshin* music. A *sanshin* is a three-stringed lute used for traditional music such as Kumiodori, Ryūkyū opera, exquisite Okinawan folk songs and contemporary pop. The roots of *sanshin* lie in the Chinese *sanxian*, which was brought to the Ryūkyū Kingdom in the late 14th century. Examples of *sanshin* and a survey of its history can be seen at the **Yuntanza Museum** (*yuntanza-museum.jp; adult/child ¥500/300*), but also recommended is a visit to **Machidaya** *sanshin* store in Yomitan village. Nowadays *sanshin* are typically made of ebony and covered in snakeskin.

As Yomitan suffered great WWII damage, resources to make *sanshin* were unavailable. At that time, the bodies of the instruments were made with tin cans, while telephone wires or

GETTING AROUND

Yomitan is ideal for biking, particularly around Yachimun no Sato (p110). Cutty Jungle bike shop rents bikes and does local tours. A car is still the easiest way to cover longer distances – you can enjoy a scenic drive to Cape Zanpa lighthouse for sunset and views. A bus to Yomitan takes approximately 1½ hours from Naha. Yomitan itself has many bus routes, including a community bus.

☑ **TOP TIP**

Yachimun tableware is delicate, so pack it in your hand luggage when you fly home.

THE BEAUTY OF YACHIMUN

Terry Ellis, owner of MOGI, a folk wares store in Tokyo, and curator of several exhibitions.

Ryūkyū pottery has a tradition of rough, unglazed ware and another of glazed pottery with brushwork decoration for tableware. There are also vessels with particular forms for use in religious rituals and by aristocratic families that are not found in other parts of Japan. There's significant influence from Korea, China and Vietnam. The ware is wood fired in climbing kilns and often has a soft appearance because the slips and glazes are applied to vessels without a bisque firing. The local clay seems to favour forms that are robust or casually thrown.

● **SIGHTS**	**5** Singing Voice Pension Mamina	● **SHOPPING**
1 Yomitan Traditional Crafts Centre	● **EATING**	**10** Machidaya
2 Yuntanza Museum	**6** Blue Point	**11** Yachimun no Sato
● **SLEEPING**	**7** Kujira	**12** Yachimunya
3 Guest House Ryukyu An	**8** Sabroso!	**13** Yomitan Farmers Market Yunta Ichiba
4 Milk-ya Guest House	● **DRINKING**	**see 1** Yuntanza Hanaui Co-operative
	9 Peoples Coffee	

parachute chords were used for the strings. Machidaya also sells these tin-can versions and can craft an instrument called a *sanlele*, a sort of cross between a ukulele and a *sanshin* that's the brainchild of Peruvian Okinawan singer Alberto Shiroma.

Island Food Culture

Unique Ryūkyūan ingredients

Packed with local purveyors, **Yomitan Farmers Market Yunta Ichiba** is an opportunity to appreciate Ryūkyūan food culture. The market opened only recently, in 2011, but it already functions as a community – indeed the word *yunta* in its name is a reference to the *yuntaku* (chitchat) that takes place between purveyors and buyers. (*Yunta* is also a nod to Yuntanza, the traditional name of Yomitan village.)

The Yomitan market also has its own agricultural processing facility and serves cooked meals such as tempura and soba that use locally produced ingredients. The complex is filled with food that can't easily be found on the Japanese mainland. There's a huge variety of fresh fruit such as island bananas, staples such as *gōyā* (bitter melon) and *moui* (white cucumber), and root vegetables such as taro. There are also cuts of meat not usually used in other Japanese cuisine, such as pig's ears.

Reviving Lost Textile Traditions

Yuntanza *hanaori* cloth

Intricate and folksy, with geometric embellishments, Yuntanza *hanaori* is a type of textile technique from the Yomitan district that dates back around 600 years, to the time of the Ryūkyū Kingdom. According to Etsuko Uehara, curator of **Yuntanza Hanaui Co-operative**, 'This small kingdom looked overseas and conducted foreign trade with tributary ships. During that time there was trade with Southeast Asian countries, with the inflow of textiles from places like Burma, which influenced the weaving culture here. This became the distinct *hanaori* that continues today.' Uehara says the culture nearly went extinct and was only revived in the 1960s using fabric scraps and the memories of women in their 80s, as little remained after the war. Through the efforts of many people such as textile artisan Yonamine Sada, who was designated a Living National Treasure, the craft still exists, and there are around 100 practitioners.

The cloth is highly textured and adorned only with a few abstract motifs that resemble auspicious items like a pinwheel, which symbolises long life and happiness, or an open fan, which metaphorically spreads happiness. Visitors to the **Yomitan Traditional Crafts Centre** can try their hand at weaving a small coaster that they can take home. A prior booking is required; the course is in Japanese, but the process is simple so a translation app works fine. There are also other weavers at the centre and small items to browse and purchase.

INKED MILESTONES

Once widespread among the women of the Ryūkyū Islands, the *hajichi* tattooing tradition saw them mark their hands and wrists to denote moments in time. Some women were even tattooed as young girls. The ritual was banned after Japanese colonisation, leading to its near extinction. While Okinawan artist Moeko Heshiki is one of the only *hajichi* artists active in Okinawa now, Okinawan emigrants across the world – in places like Brazil and the United States (particularly Hawai'i) – are tattooing *hajichi* as a way of connecting to their heritage. Joining together on social media, globally dispersed Uchinānchu (Okinawans) have embraced *hajichi* as a practice and rite to make them feel close to their ancestors.

EATING IN YOMITAN: OUR PICKS

Peoples Coffee: Espresso tonic and dirty matcha lattes, plus Basque cheesecake and grilled mackerel sandwiches. *7am-5pm Sun-Fri, from 8am Sat* ¥

Blue Point: Hip cafe along the seawall serving excellent falafel sandwiches and other vegan treats. *11am-5pm Fri-Tue* ¥

¡Sabroso!: Cute Oki-Mexican joint in Yomitan selling delicious quesadillas, tacos and *horchata* (a cool rice-based drink). *11am-7pm Tue-Sun* ¥

Kujira: Casual Italian restaurant near Cape Zanpa using local ingredients to make tasty pizza, gnocchi and risotto. *11am-11pm* ¥

MANAMI OKAZAKI/LONELY PLANET

Kiln, Yachimun no Sato

Yachimun no Sato

Ryūkyū pottery made on Okinawa-hontō and the surrounding islands is known as *yachimun*. One of the best places to see the beauty of this art form is at Yachimun no Sato, established in the '70s when the Yutanza kiln relocated from Naha. Nowadays there are around 70 studios across an expansive area, as well as historic climbing kilns.

DON'T MISS

Kita Gama

Yuntanza Noborigama

Yukutaya Gama

Inamine Glass Gallery

Yachimunya

Origins

Yachimun no Sato started when Korean artisans based in the then Satsuma domain brought their techniques to Okinawa in the early 17th century. Tsuboya in Naha flourished as a pottery hamlet where artisans made ceramics for royalty and vessels for export as well as utilitarian ware. The Yachimun village in Yomitan was established in the 1970s when anti-pollution laws were brought in to curtail their use of wood-fired kilns. Famed potter Kinjo Jiro was adamant about sticking to traditional processes and moved his kiln to Yomitan in 1972.

PRACTICALITIES
● 098-958-4468 ● tabi-yachimun.jp ● hours vary by studio ● free

Characteristics

Yachimun pottery is used for plates, mugs, sake bottles, cups and flower pots. It's characterised by dense, solid forms and has a rustic and comforting appearance. Embellished with bold patterns and colours that reflect nature, the pottery is reflective of the cultural influence from various parts of Southeast Asia. Motifs include local wildlife and marine animals, and some artisans replicate the azure colours of the ocean with vivid blue glazes. Generally, Ryūkyū pottery is functional and used as tableware. The two types of Ryūkyū pottery are *joyachi* (glazed pottery), which is used for everyday wares but also made into fine-art pieces, and *arayachi* (un-glazed pottery), which is often used to make jars for storing miso and the local liquor, *awamori*.

Shopping

Give yourself a couple of hours to walk around and appreciate the diversity of wares on display at individual studios that double as shops. Most sites have artisans at work, and the entire village resembles a hamlet of potters. After you enter the village you'll see several shops on either side of the road. To reach each studio, you'll need to make your way through forested areas with large banyan trees.

Kilns

The Yuntanza Gama is the village's centrepiece, an impressive red-tiled climbing kiln used by several artisans. At the far end of the village, Kita Gama is a massive studio with an impressive tiled roof. It shows a large array of beautiful pottery pieces, some with modern touches. Yukutaya Gama (横目屋窯) is owned by potter Minoru Chibana. Some striking wares here feature cerulean glazes that reference Okinawan nature, and there are also minimalistic works with splashes of colour. Pieces are displayed outside the studios.

Shīsā

The guardian lion dog statues called *shīsā* are another major form of Yachimun pottery. *Shīsā* are found in male and female pairs on gates and house roofs all over Okinawa. First imported from China in the 14th century, they're a variant of the *komainu* found near Shintō shrines. The most impressive *shīsā* are made at **Yachimunya** (*yachimunya.uezu-design. biz*), around seven minutes by car from Yachimun no Sato. Filled with ethereal pieces, the studio specialises in expressive custom-made *shīsā*. You can also watch artisans at work here.

RYŪKYŪ GLASS

Yachimun no Sato is known for its ceramics, but the site is also home to Inamine Glass Gallery, with a wide variety of pieces by artisan Seikichi Inamine and his son Seiichiro. You can see glass workers deftly producing their delicate wares in the studio. Ryūkyū glass is known for its vibrant colours and bubbles to match the lush nature of the surrounding forests and ocean.

TOP TIPS

● There are three pottery events throughout the year. Aiming for these is a wonderful way to pick up some great sales and enjoy the general community atmosphere.

● The Yomitan Pottery Festival at Yomitan Farmers Market Yunta Ichiba (p108) takes place in February and attracts around 20,000 people.

● The Pottery Festival on the third weekend (Friday to Sunday) of December at Yachimun no Sato is one of the best times to visit the craft village.

● The Seaside Yachimun Market (dates vary; usually around November) inside Hoshino Resorts Banta Café in Yomitan village is another picturesque place to purchase *yachimun*.

HELP ME PICK:

Where to Get Tattooed in Central Okinawa

Okinawa Island has well over 75 tattoo shops, many concentrated in the centre, particularly near the military base gates. While Ryūkyū culture has its own tattooing traditions called *hajichi* (p109), the contemporary tattoo shop culture in Okinawa flourished due to the US presence. Kin-based tattoo artist MAL says, 'Okinawa has a lot of American clients, and the vibe is much more positive towards tattoos here than on the mainland. People get tattooed to commemorate or express something.'

Where to get a tattoo if you love...

Classic Japanese

The area outside the main gate of Camp Hansen has 17 tattoo shops. An apprentice of famed tattoo master Horiyasu, MAL *(@mal_esw)* is one of the few artists who is adept at Japanese-style tattoos. His shop, **Void Tattoo**, has a gallery-like atmosphere. Known for his dragons, MAL learnt *nihonga* painting at Musashino Art University, and these dynamic and rich sensibilities are something he emulates in his tattoo work. 'In Japanese painting it's about being flat but still having presence – something that exists in the space. That kind of quiet power is what I want to express.'

Japanese Americana

Cat Claw Tattoo-z *(@catclaw_tattoo_z)* in Okinawa City was formerly located in Kyoto, where it was a popular, pioneering shop specialising in Americana tattoos with a Japanese touch. The sensibilities merge the best of American traditional – such as simple forms, bold lines and solid colours – with Japanese elements to create a modern rendition of classic tattoo styles.

Americana with Okinawan themes

W-Oki *(@kenta_w_oki_tattoo)* is a Ginowan tattoo shop specialising in classic American traditional, characterised by bold lines and subdued colours in shades of yellow, red and green. Many pieces have a loose, cartoony aesthetic, and Kenta uses motifs that are Okinawa-themed, such as the Okinawa rail bird, local flowers like *gettō*, Ryūkyūan dancers and palms.

Contemporary Japanese

Dragon Tattoo *(@dragon tattoo_okinawa)* in Chatan is an all-rounder, so it can work in all styles, but its portfolio is filled with dragons, tigers, *hanya* masks and chrysanthemums. While Japanese traditional is large in scale, the studio is adept at rendering Japanese subjects with a modern look, such as without backgrounds.

Ultra-realistic black and grey

Shun Tattoo *(@shuntattoo)*, at **Monochrome Gallery** in Okinawa City, specialises in black and grey tattooing. It uses layers of black and various shades of grey ink to create pieces rich in tone and perspective. Shun also excels at realism, in particular portraits with vivid and emotional facial expressions as well as detailed skulls.

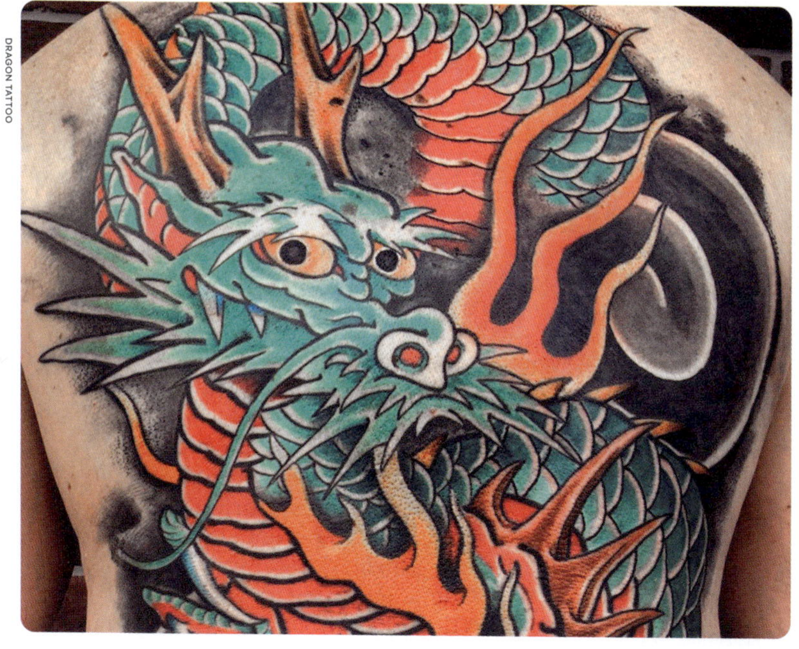

Back tattoo

─ HOW TO ─

Which style? This is a personal preference, but it's important to decide beforehand. Check the artists' portfolios and only ask for the style they're best at.

What to get? Be sure to look up the motifs' meaning before you commit. Classic Americana and Japanese images are rich in symbolism.

When? It's best to get your tattoo at the end of your trip, so you don't have to worry about whether you can swim or not.

Which shop? It's important to feel comfortable and for the shop to be impeccably clean, as tattooing carries a risk of blood-borne pathogens.

Japanese Tattooing 101

When choosing a Japanese design it's important to know that a few aspects of the composition differ from a 'sticker'-style tattoo. Japanese tattoos have a narrative, so while most people will choose a design because of its aesthetic quality, keep in mind that all motifs are rich in meaning.

Compositions are created from a few elements. The *shūdai* (central subject) is the main motif. Genres include folkloric characters, animals both mythical and real, warriors and Buddhist deities. They're all symbolic and are generally lucky or talismanic in that they're protective. Common motifs are dragons, which have snake-like bodies covered in scales and bird-like talons (usually three), and carp, which signify perseverance as they swim upstream. In Japanese the word for carp, *koi*, sounds like the word for love.

Keshōbori are the embellishments to the central motif. These can include things from nature such as flowers. *Gakubori* refers to the background, which acts as a frame; this can include clouds, waves and wind. *Nukibori* are subjects with no background, such as a tiger that is depicted 'as is'. Plenty of Okinawan motifs such as local marine life would make a lovely souvenir. Refrain from asking for *hajichi* unless you're Okinawan, though, as these are culturally specific, ritualistic designs for people of Ryūkyūan descent.

113

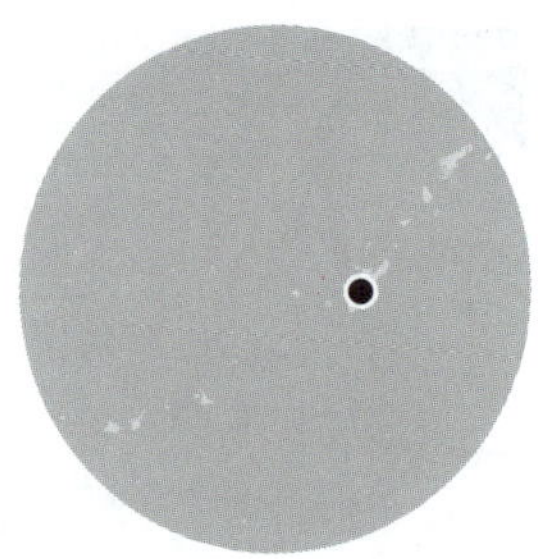

Uruma

CAVE | STUNNING BEACHES | FABULOUS DRIVES

GETTING AROUND

A car is the most convenient option for getting around. Buses from Naha Airport to Uruma take about two hours, and there is also a network of buses within Uruma itself. **Kamome no Jonathon**, on the highway going to the Yokatsu Islands, has rental bikes. By bike you can island-hop across flat terrain to visit the beaches.

Contemporary Uruma (うるま), located south of Kin and north of Nakagusuku on the east coast of Okinawa Island, was only established in 2005 with the merging of Gushikawa, Ishikawa, Katsuren and Yonashiro. It also covers the Katsuren Peninsula and the Yokatsu Islands. During the three kingdoms period, Uruma was under the jurisdiction of the Chūzan Kingdom of central Okinawa. Before WWII, Uruma had large sugar-cane fields whose yield was the highest in Okinawa. During the Battle of Okinawa, the Katsuren Peninsula and Yokatsu Islands were devastated within the first 10 days. After WWII Uruma became the site of refugee camps.

Today the main reason for visitors to come to Uruma is no doubt the spectacular beaches that tend to see fewer tourists. The water is a gorgeous shade of blue, and the beaches aren't overdeveloped. You can spend at least a day exploring, swimming and sunbathing.

☑ TOP TIP

Go all the way to Ōdomari for a great-quality beach with all the facilities but without the crowds.

A Glimpse Underground

Illuminated Cave Okinawa

With well-lit tunnels and accessible walkways and stairwells, **Cave Okinawa** *(cave.okinawa/en)* can be explored without a guide. A shelter for villagers during WWII, it's still believed to be auspicious. Parts of the 200m-long cave have dramatic coloured lighting.

✂ EATING IN URUMA: OUR PICKS

Maruichi: (丸一食品 塩屋店) Okinawan *inari* sushi with a lighter vinegar taste and whiter than the Kanto version. *9am-2pm Tue-Sun* ¥

Arakaki: (あらかき) Another Okinawan *inari* sushi joint, takeaway only; try it with garlicky *karaage* (fried chicken). *7am-4pm* ¥

Manryū Hanten: Chinese place with generous portions and standard dishes like sweet-and-sour pork and egg-drop soup. *11.30am-10pm Fri-Mon & Wed* ¥¥

Kominka Timgukuru: (沖縄古民家食堂ちむぐくる) Homely Okinawa soba restaurant with pork, goat or squid ink broth. *11am-3pm Fri-Sun* ¥

SIGHTS
1 Nakabaru Ruins
2 Ōdomari Beach
3 Tonnaha Beach

ACTIVITIES
4 Cave Okinawa

SLEEPING
5 Haberasa
6 Hideout Okinawa Uruma
7 Totono House Divine

EATING
8 Arakaki
9 Cafe Monya
10 Espacio
11 Kaichuchaya
12 Kominka Timgukuru
13 Manryū Hanten
14 Maruichi
15 raise244

SHOPPING
16 Aruhi
17 Nuchimasu

115 CENTRAL OKINAWA ISLAND URUMA THE GUIDE

OKINAWA'S UNIQUE INGREDIENTS

As chef and cookbook writer **Tim Anderson** explains, Okinawan food is entirely distinct. 'It isn't just a regional variation on Japanese food; it's really an entirely different cuisine. The techniques, ingredients and aesthetics of Okinawan food are unique.

'Goat meat is rarely seen outside the Ryūkyū Islands, where it's made into delicious sashimi, soup and gyoza. *Kokuto* is one of the most complex and aromatic types of sugar I've ever tasted. Aside from in *champurū* (stir-fry), *gōyā* (bitter melon) is also used in delicious pickles and tempura. Green papaya has an excellent, robust texture for stir-fries and pickles. And the *yomogi* (mugwort) in Okinawa has a much more intense flavour and deeper colour than what I'd had in Japan.'

KAYUMANGGI SNAPSHOT/SHUTTERSTOCK

Nakabaru Ruins

Secret Beaches

Exploring Hamahiga, Miyagi and Ikei Islands

The drive from Okinawa-hontō to the Yokatsu Islands offers spectacular views. On **Hamahiga Island** you'll find stunning beaches with clear water. Drop by **Aruhi**, a lovely bookstore with an exhibition space.

On **Miyagi Island**, **Tonnaha Beach** has a few huts with snorkels and floating devices. Salt factory **Nuchimasu**, with spectacular views of the surrounding cliffs, offers tours. Its cafe serves food using the factory's famed mineral-rich salt – try the salty-sweet ice cream.

Ōdomari Beach, further afield on **Ikei Island**, has showers, tables, umbrellas and snorkel equipment for hire. The water is calm, making it ideal for families with young children. In front of the beach are the 2000-year-old **Nakabaru Ruins**, which give a glimpse of Palaeolithic village life.

 **ISLAND CAFES: OUR PICKS**

Espacio: On the south side of Miyagi Island, this cafe serves excellent coffee in beautiful ceramics. There's a Cessna plane on its roof. *11am-7pm* ¥

raise244: Open-air terrace cafe in a wooden building right next to the beach on Hamahiga Island. *11am-6pm Mon-Fri, from 9am Sat & Sun* ¥

Kaichuchaya: Cafe on the Kaichu Dorō road to the islands, right by the beach. Light meals include Okinawa soba. *10.30am-5pm Mon-Thu, to 9pm Fri-Sun* ¥

Cafe Monya: (カフェもんやー) Ikei Island cafe next to a craft shop selling *shīsā* and turtles made of shells. Also runs workshops that kids can join. *hours vary* ¥

Onna

BLUE CAVE | RESORTS | RYŪKYŪAN VILLAGE

The village of Onna (恩納村) on Okinawa Island's west coast is where the population density of the south starts to abate. The landscape opens up to uninterrupted blue, lined with coral reefs to the west and dense forest to the east. Long and thin, Onna spans about 50 sq km, running around 27km long and 4km wide. The village is home to one of Japan's premier science and research universities, the Okinawa Institute of Science and Technology (OIST), and the graduate university is collaborating with local fishers on a coral conservation and restoration project in an attempt to alleviate the coral bleaching decimating the region's underwater ecosystems. Onna's 11,000 villagers are primarily engaged in the agriculture, fishing and tourism industries. Luxury and resort hotels have taken advantage of the area's brilliant natural setting, basing themselves along the coast, though development here is much sparser than it is further south.

Ryūkyūan Snapshot

Amble a model Okinawan village

Part museum, part theme park, **Ryūkyū-mura** (*ryukyumura.co.jp; adult/child ¥2000/800*) is an open-air exploration of Ryūkyū culture. At its heart are 10 Ryūkyūan residences brought from different corners of the archipelago. Take a free guided tour to learn the meaning of different housing elements, such as typhoon protection, open-air entranceways and places for storing clay pots where home-brewed *awamori* is fermented. There are dedicated *awamori* experiences at the on-site Sakimoto Brewery for an extra fee (advance booking required).

The park is enlivened by cultural performances, workshops and opportunities for snacking, making it kid (and adult) friendly. You might come across a performer plucking a *sanshin* and singing some of the region's haunting, soaring folk songs. In the Kijimuna Cave *eisā* dancers sing and drum in a

GETTING AROUND

Some of the area's upscale resorts offer shuttles to surrounding attractions, but most people arrive by rental car. The drive takes around 75 minutes using the tollways, but palm-tree-lined Rte 58 makes a spectacular trip, with waves sometimes breaking right over the seawall and splashing the road. Airport buses take about 1½ hours to get here.

☑ TOP TIP

The Blue Cave is one of the most accessible places to dive on Okinawa Island; go early in the morning before the crowds.

heart-pounding rhythm. There's a *shīsā* painting workshop where you can adorn your own guardian dog (p111) and a butterfly garden where you can see Okinawa's prefectural butterfly, the black-and-white *Idea leuconoe*, also known as the paper kite butterfly. With a wingspan of up to 14cm, it's the largest butterfly species in Japan.

It's easy to spend half a day here. There's a cafeteria and plenty of picnic tables next to the stage where you can enjoy island soba and top it off with a scoop of Blue Seal *shikuwasa* sherbet. The park is wheelchair and stroller accessible; loan chairs and prams are available for a small deposit.

 **EATING & DRINKING IN ONNA: DAYTIME**

Doka Doka: Ceramics studio serving coffee and elaborate toasts on house-made pottery. Ocean views. *8am-6pm Mon-Sat* ¥¥

Diamond Beach Cafe: Cute beachside spot with coffee and sweets such as fruit-slathered waffles. *9am-5pm, to 6pm Jul-Sep* ¥¥

Hakumokka: Tiny cafe featuring locally grown vegetables and homemade seasonings in dishes like vegan spring rolls and chicken *pho*. *10.30am-2.30pm Fri & Sat* ¥¥

Pallet: Shipping container turned lunch shack serving panini sandwiches with fillings like smoked duck or vegetable curry. *7am-5pm Wed-Mon* ¥¥

Into the Blue

A day at the beach

Formed by the action of the waves, the semi-submerged **Blue Cave** off Cape Maeda shimmers aqua in reflected sunlight. The maximum depth is only 6m, so it's an extremely easy dive and just as enjoyable to snorkel. You'll see fish such as butterflyfish, longfin batfish and soldierfish, and numerous underwater tunnels and cathedral-like spaces. As the light streams in, the clarity of the water makes the fish look as though they're suspended in space. Beginner divers can join without a licence. **Cerulean Blue** (*cerulean-blue.co.jp/en*) offers excellent snorkel and scuba services.

With excellent snorkelling beaches, the Cape Maeda area is one of Okinawa Island's top places to enjoy ocean activities. **Ura Maeda** is quieter, with clear water and a white sand beach ideal for sunbathing. **Zane Beach** has still, turquoise water that's perfect for secluded snorkelling.

After a dive, there is nothing more refreshing than a mango *kakigōri*. Head up to **Onna no Eki** (おんなの駅 なかゆくい市場), eight minutes away by car, for some of the island's best local snacks.

Family-Friendly Forest

An inland hike

The **Okinawa Prefectural People's Forest** (*kenminnomori-obsi.jp*) is a large park with good facilities and several kilometres of trails. Hike through tangled underbrush to lookouts over the ocean, spy birds and flowers, rent park golf equipment and admire sculptures in the landscaped areas. There's a small **Forest Mystery Museum** and a **Wood Communication Centre** with wooden toys. The park also has over a hundred tent spots for a small fee; camping equipment is available to rent. Advance bookings recommended.

CORAL RESTORATION

Of the approximately 800 types of coral in the world, Okinawa is home to around 200. Though they sometimes resemble rocks, these marine invertebrates are crucial to ocean ecosystems, attracting small marine life that in turn attracts larger predators. They also absorb carbon dioxide, produce oxygen, and act as a breakwater in the shallow, clear seas where they thrive. Unfortunately, coral are under threat worldwide from development, ocean trash and ocean warming, and Okinawan corals are also at risk. The people of Onna village, including Onna Village Fisheries Cooperative, the Okinawa Institute of Science and Technology and a number of local and domestic businesses, have partnered for coral restoration projects. Coral 'seeds' are planted and nurtured in a controlled environment before being transplanted to reefs further offshore. To learn more, visit *beokinawa.jp/coral*.

 **EATING & DRINKING IN ONNA: EVENING**

PST Okinawa by the Sea: Posh pizza place at ANA Intercontinental Resort. Cocktails, salads and thin-crust, wood-fired pizzas. *noon-3pm & 5-10pm* ¥¥

Chinuman: Lively *izakaya* (pub) featuring Okinawan food like purple sweet potato croquettes and stewed pig's feet, plus music nightly. Free hotel shuttle. *5-10.30pm* ¥¥

Gajimaru: Vegan restaurant with several types of ramen, gyoza, pasta, taco rice and more. Good for groups. *noon-10pm Sat-Thu* ¥¥

Taco Rice Cafe Kijimuna: The island's favourite fusion dish in a dozen incarnations (with avocado, teriyaki chicken, vegan, omelette-style...) *11.30am-8pm* ¥

Kin & Ginoza

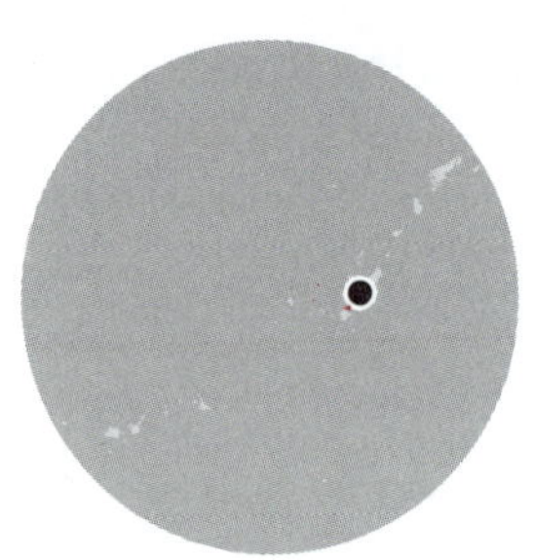

TACO RICE | CAVING | OKINAWAN TATTOOS

GETTING AROUND

A car is the best way to get around in this region, as Ginoza in particular is quite undeveloped, with no rail system. It takes around 80 minutes to get from Naha to Ginoza by bus. There are public bus services across Kin and Ginoza. Within Ginoza, a bike is a nice way to enjoy the lay of the land. The Roadside Station Tourism Centre has rental bikes.

Ginoza and Kin are adjacent towns on the east coast of Okinawa-hontō, around an hour from Naha. The region balances a bucolic atmosphere with urban comforts, so it's a great base to ensure both serenity and nightlife. Unlike much of the island, Ginoza was not a WWII battlefield. It's still predominantly rural, with excellent eateries drawing on the local produce. Beaches such as Hiipii are uncrowded, and the fantastical Matsuda Limestone Cave offers a breathtaking subterranean experience. Ginoza is also known for its distinctive performing arts, which can be seen at the local festivals.

Kin's history stretches back to the Jōmon period, but since WWII the town has hosted the US Camp Hansen. Particularly around Shinkaichi near the camp gate, the town is replete with bars, nightlife and shops filled with military personnel and English-speaking staff. Kin is also home to Taco King, at which the island's now ubiquitous taco rice was invented.

Knife Artistry

Hand-forged heritage blades

At **Kaniman Blacksmith Workshop** (カニマン鍛冶工房), close to Kin town, self-taught artisan Teijun China makes knives for a wide range of uses. The craft has been around for 800 years, and until the 1960s there were blacksmiths in every village making agricultural and fishing tools and knives. Now only three places in Okinawa still ply the trade. The handles are made from local wood types such as guava and *shikuwasa* lime as well as deer antlers. You can see China working the wood-fired furnace at his bucolic workshop, which is also inhabited by his posse of chickens. A Japanese speaker will need to call ahead to arrange a visit (+81-098-968-8459), but China has an English list of items for reference once you're there.

At beautifully designed Void Tattoo (p112), owner MAL is particularly adept at dragons. He was an apprentice of famed Tokyo tattoo master Horiyasu.

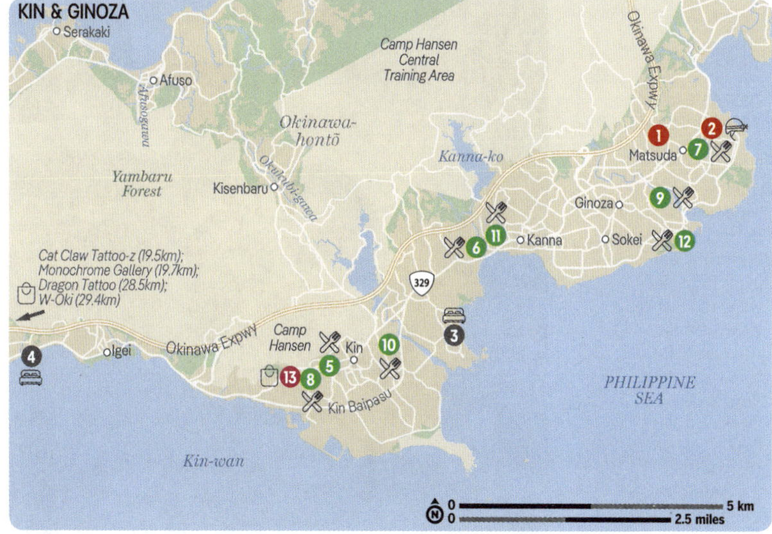

● **SIGHTS**
1 Kaniman Blacksmith Workshop

● **ACTIVITIES**
2 Matsuda Limestone Cave

● **SLEEPING**
3 ASBO Stay Hotel
4 Dot Hotel My Beach Resort

● **EATING**
5 Chingones Cantina Kin
6 Ginoza Farm Lab
7 Kanehachi 2
8 King Tacos
9 Kuruma Ebi Restaurant Tamaya

10 Namimatsu Soba
11 Parlor Kazu
12 Tempus

● **SHOPPING**
13 Void Tattoo

Limestone Labyrinth

Go batty underground

Explore the almost untouched **Matsuda Limestone Cave** (*matsuda-kucha.jimdofree.com*) on a tour guided by locals. In the pitch black, with the only light coming from your head-lamps, you'll pass rivers and rocky formations, and descend several steep ladders, learning about fantastical formations such as curtain sculptures and shimmering ridged pools along the way. The highlight of the tour is entering chambers inhabited by horseshoe bats and seeing their small, porcine faces hanging overhead. Note that there are limited English-speaking

EATING IN KIN AND GINOZA: TACOS AND OKI SOBA

King Tacos: The OG of Oki-American taco rice, with perfect texture and cheese that's a hot melted mess. In Kin. *10.30am-1pm* ¥

Chingones Cantina Kin: Wide array of Mexican dishes and margaritas plus the occasional Mariachi band appearance. *hours vary Thu-Sat* ¥

Namimatsu Soba: Worth the trip for the delicious pork belly with a nice balance between fat and tender meat. Close to Kin town. *11am-2pm Thu-Mon* ¥

Parlor Kazu: Roadside Ginoza shack that's as simple as they come, but the soba broth has a spicy punch that's delicious on a hot day. *11am-5pm Mon-Sat* ¥

OKI-AME-MEX TACO RICE

It might surprise you when you visit the 'longevity capital' that the city is packed with late-night fast-food joints brimming with food that came into existence because of the US military presence. Americanised Mexican dishes flourished across Okinawa to the degree it's synonymous with contemporary Okinawan food. The first taco joint, Charlie's Tacos, opened in Oki City in 1956. Matsuzo Gibo is credited with creating Okinawa's famed taco rice in 1984 for his two restaurants, King Tacos in Kin and the now defunct Parlor Senri. The taco filling is heaped onto Japanese white, slightly sticky rice (instead of tortilla shells) and topped with a generous amount of cheese. The flagship store is still in Kin, near one of the largest American bases, Camp Hansen.

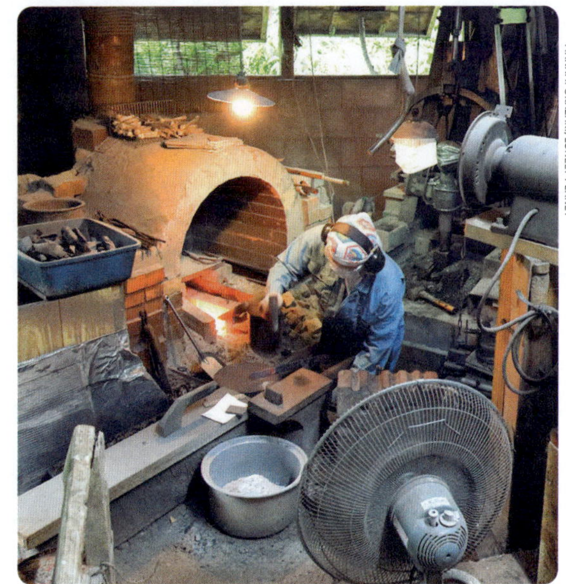

Kaniman Blacksmith Workshop (p120)

tour guides available and they may not be able to accommodate your visit.

When the torch shone on the bats, they had a collective freak-out, but the guide assured me they only have a few tours a week in order to not disturb their rest. – **Manami Okazaki**, Lonely Planet writer

EATING IN GINOZA: OUR PICKS

Kuruma Ebi Restaurant Tamaya: (車えびレストラン球屋) Specialises in shrimp locally farmed in Ginoza. Try the delicious tempura bowls. *11.30am-6pm Thu-Mon* ¥¥

Kanehachi 2: (二代目かね八) Ginormous servings of local classics. *Gōyā*, soba and pork dishes galore. *11am-2pm & 6-11pm Tue-Sun* ¥

Tempus: (炭焼家てんぷす) Low-key, unpretentious charcoal-grill restaurant using local organic vegetables, fish and pork. *6pm-midnight Wed-Mon* ¥¥

Ginoza Farm Lab: Burger joint with ocean views. Buns baked on-site, fresh ingredients and tasty fries. *11am-3pm* ¥

Places We Love to Stay

¥ Budget ¥¥ Midrange ¥¥¥ Top End

Chatan & Kadena

MAP p101

M's Stay Okinawa ¥¥ Unfussy, spartan rooms with a veranda and a washing machine inside the room. Convenient location close to American Village. Has parking.

Villa Blu Okinawa Chatan ¥¥ Not really a villa; this is apartment-style accommodation with beautiful views.

Hilton Okinawa Chatan Resort ¥¥¥ Beautiful modern hotel with an outdoor pool. It's luxurious, tattoo friendly and close to the American Village.

Ginowan & Okinawa City

MAP p104

Goyah-so Guesthouse ¥ Fantastic guesthouse in a traditional house with shared facilities. The owner plays the *sanshin,* and *min'yō* fans (p48) often stay here, so expect impromptu jams. It also serves local food.

Guesthouse Okinawa Kubotasou (久保田荘) **¥** Hostel with both single and dormitory rooms with tatami floors.

SG Okinawa Angel House ¥¥ Has a car park and spacious rooms with balcony. The top floor has a huge rooftop space.

Sazanka ¥¥ Quiet small hotel in a lovely residential area in Okinawa City. Has parking and all the basic amenities, including a shared washing machine.

Deigo Hotel ¥¥ Basic retro hotel from the '60s with a public bath. The Japanese-style tatami rooms are comfortable.

Yomitan

MAP p108

Guest House Ryukyu An (琉球庵) **¥** Bargain hostel with dormitory-style rooms inside a house in Yomitan.

Milk-ya Guest House ¥¥ Close to Senaha beach, this place caters to women only in a comfortable family-style house.

Singing Voice Pension Mamina (うたごえペンション まーみなー) **¥¥** Close to Zampa Beach in Yomitan, this super-retro pink villa is run by a lovely family. They have both tatami and futon rooms, as well as rooms with beds.

Uruma

MAP p115

Hideout Okinawa Uruma ¥¥ Spacious beachfront hotel with a nice pool. Full kitchens available.

Haberasa ¥¥ Retro boutique hotel on Ikei Island with a groovy design. The vibe is old school, but the rooms are comfortable, with a nice terrace.

Totono House Divine ¥¥¥ Traditional house that has been renovated for comfort. It has an outdoor sauna and a small garden where you can sunbathe and barbecue. Close to the coast on Hamahiga Island.

Onna

MAP p118

Hotel Miyuki Beach ¥¥ Offering great value, this family-friendly place has a private beach, a swimming pool and tatami-matted sitting areas. All rooms have balconies facing the ocean.

Surfside Bed & Breakfast ¥¥ Has old-school motel vibes, with spacious rooms, tiled bathrooms and an inner courtyard close to Nabee Beach. There are great views from the rooms' verandas.

Okinawa Kariyushi Beach Resort Ocean Spa ¥¥¥ At this huge, tattoo-friendly retro resort, the rooms have fantastic views from the verandas and the pool is massive. There's also a spa.

Kin & Ginoza

MAP p121

ASBO Stay Hotel ¥¥ Large, resort-style hotel. The rooms have a lovely view and a small veranda.

Dot Hotel My Beach Resort ¥¥ Affordable hotel with a brutalist exterior right on the oceanfront.

Above: Cape Hedo (p141), North Yambaru; Right: Nago Pineapple Park (p130), Nago City

Researched by
Manami Okazaki

Northern Okinawa Island

VAST FORESTS AND FAMILY ATTRACTIONS

You'll find an unlikely but appealing combination in the island's north: theme parks, beaches and the biodiverse haven of Yambaru National Park.

The northern part of Okinawa Island was once its most destitute district, uninhabited apart from a few villages. In the 14th-century Sanzan era it composed the Kingdom of Hokuzan, which traded with places such as Java and Sumatra despite having no major port. The largest historic landmark of the area, the UNESCO World Heritage Site of Nakijin Castle, was the administrative centre of Hokuzan, and the mighty defensive fortress is a testament to those times. The Ryūkyū Kingdom was eventually unified after Chuzan's King Sho Hashi overtook Hokuzan in 1416.

Nowadays the area's lack of development is its main attraction, with subtropical forests, waterfalls and beaches to enjoy.

Sprawling over 174 sq km, magnificent Yambaru National Park is notable for its rare diversity of landscapes, which encompass mangroves, subtropical forest and limestone formations. Tours offer insight into the endemic species that flourish in this humid climate. Many of the region's cultural attractions, such as the Oceanic Culture Museum and the Bashōfu Textiles Museum, demonstrate how local customs coexist with nature. Somewhat unexpectedly, the north also has some of Okinawa's most visited theme parks, including the Chūraumi Aquarium, the Nago Pineapple Park and the newly erected Junglia. With that in mind, traffic heading up north can be significant, so allow a lot of leeway when you make your travel plans.

THE MAIN AREAS

NAGO & THE MOTOBU PENINSULA	KUNIGAMI & NORTH YAMBARU	YAMBARU NATIONAL PARK	ŌGIMI
Theme parks and north's biggest city. **p130**	Hamlets abut impressive cape vistas. **p141**	Hikes amid diverse natural spaces. **p144**	Famed longevity village with textile heritage. **p148**

Find Your Way

There's a general paucity of public transport, so renting a car is the only efficient way to travel up north.

CAR

With the lack of public transport on the east coast and the distance between sites, a car is pretty much essential to travel efficiently up north. On Rte 58, the major north–south highway, it takes approximately two hours and forty minutes to reach the northernmost point of the island from Naha.

BUS

As you'd expect, bus travel takes significantly longer than the journey by car. From Naha airport it takes around 1¾ hours to reach Nago bus terminal and a further hour to get to Yambaru National Park.

FERRY

You can avoid significant traffic on the road heading north and go on an adventure by taking your car on the early-morning ferry from Naha to Motobu and then driving the rest of the way.

Ōgimi p148

The famed, bucolic longevity village of Ōgimi is a centre for traditional crafts.

Kunigami & North Yambaru, p141

The island's tip is a natural wonderland featuring dramatic cliffs, limestone formations, mountains and spiritual hikes.

Adaga
Island
Ada
Aha
Fukugawa
Takae
Uka-gawa
Yanbaru
National Park
Yonaha Dake
Yona
Fukugami-ko
Takazatogawa
Kunigami
Taira-wan
Higashi
Taminato
Ōgimi
Miyagi
Island
Tsuhao
Okinawa-
hontō
Genka
Genga-gawa
Arume
Mihara
PHILIPPINE
SEA
Abuoru
Island
Oura-wan
Henoko
Kōri-jima
Kouri
Sumuide
Yagaji-jima
Oijima
Island
Yohena
Haneji
Naikai
Makiya
Navaoshi
Nago
Nagodake
Yofuke
Henoko-dake
Kyoda
Matsuda
Ginoza
Nakijin
Okawa
Yabu
Motobu
Peninsula
Yaedake
Sankaku Yama
Awa
Nago-wan
Nakama
Kin
Motobu
Sakimotobu
Ohama
Sesoko
Sesoko-jima
Onmadake
Onna
Yaka
Minnajima
Ie-jima
Ie
Ishikawadake
0 10 miles
0 20 km
N
Yambaru National
Park, p144
The heart of the north, Yam-
baru's varied landscape
takes in mangroves, river
networks and subtropical
forests.
Nago & the Motobu
Peninsula, p130
Resorts, theme parks and beach-
es are the headline attractions in
Nago and its adjoining peninsula.

Plan Your Days

The family-friendly north of the island has attractions ranging from theme parks to educational hikes through the forest, plus plenty of local eats.

Yambaru National Park (p144)

HUGH LANSDOWN/SHUTTERSTOCK

Quick Visit

● Day-trip to the Motobu Peninsula, soaking up bucolic agricultural scenes, stopping in at fishing villages and sampling delicious local produce. Enjoy a mango smoothie at **Camel Sandwich & Smoothie** (p140), then take the coastal drive to **Cape Hedo** (p141), which is associated with creation myths: legend has it that the goddess Amamikyō started with Mt Hedo when forming the Ryūkyū Islands.

● Stop by the **Bashōfu Textiles Museum** (p150) in Ōgimi on the way to see the splendid textiles and watch the artisans at work, then have lunch at **Emi no Mise** (p149), a restaurant that uses local farm-to-table ingredients in 'longevity meals' (be sure to reserve in advance).

● End the day at **Ōkuma Beach** (p141) for sunset views and a relaxing swim.

Seasonal Highlights

Rain in May and June make it a good time to find deals and avoid crowds. Autumn can be gorgeous and less crowded than summer.

JANUARY

Late January to early February is cherry blossom season in tropical Okinawa. Revel in over 7000 blooming cherry blossoms in Motobu at **Yaedake Sakura no Mori Park** as well as at Nakijin Castle's **cherry blossom festival** (p137).

FEBRUARY

Yambaru Art Festival (p149) is held in Ōgimi village and venues nearby from around mid-January to mid-February.

APRIL

The **Lily Festival** (p139) sees around 100 varieties of the flower cover Ie Island from the end of April to early May.

Overnight Stay

● Follow the Quick Visit itinerary, then stay in the area overnight.

● On day two, get up bright and early for a birding tour in **Yambaru National Park** (p144) where you can see endemic species. The morning sees the most action, and no doubt the star of the show is the Okinawa rail, the icon of Okinawa. Afterwards, go on an adventure along the forest roads to have a coffee at **Bookcafe Okinawa Rail** (p146).

● Head back to Ōgimi village and go to the wonderful but now defunct **Kijoka Primary School** (Kijoka-shō for short; p148), which has been converted into an artisan village that hosts independent creators. The focus here is on local products and crafts.

A Few Days in the North

● Four days is an ideal amount of time to spend in northern Okinawa-hontō, especially if you're travelling with children. Start by following the Overnight Stay itinerary.

● On day three, spend a morning at **Nago Pineapple Park** (p130), savouring the delicious local produce. Go to the *fukugi*-tree-lined road at **Bise** (p134), where the area is rife with great beachside hangouts next to the stunning sands.

● On day four visit **Ocean Expo Park** (p131) to take in the Churaumi Aquarium and the Oceanic Culture Museum (or plump for **Junglia** (p137), opened in 2025, if the kids are really into dinosaurs), then unwind on **Emerald Beach** (p134) for the other half of the day.

JUNE

Ungami, a sea god festival for a good harvest, takes place in Shiōya Bay off Ōgimi village around the third week of June. It's designated an Important Intangible Folk Cultural Property of Japan.

JULY

Okinawa's largest pyrotechnics show, featuring 10,000 fireworks, lights up **Ocean Expo Park** (p131) in early July.

AUGUST

Summer peaks from late July to August. Expect Okinawa's hottest weather plus the risk of typhoons. Ocean activities and beaches mean August is the region's busiest tourist time.

NOVEMBER

Significantly cooler temperatures begin in November, making it ideal for hiking, walking and biking. This is a good time to enjoy the theme parks without the oppressive summer heat.

Nago City & the Motobu Peninsula

GETTING AROUND

A car is pretty much essential, but always allow for theme-park traffic when planning your trip. **Toguchi Port** (Minna Island) and **Unten Port** (Izena and Ieha) enable easy access to nearby islands; you can also take your car on board. The free Motobu sightseeing shuttle links the ports, Ocean Expo Park and many tourist sites.

The Motobu Peninsula and Nago City area was part of the Hokuzan Kingdom until the unified Ryūkyū Kingdom was established in 1416. During WWII, Motobu and Ie Island were the site of the second phase of the Battle of Okinawa. There was bloody resistance, particularly on Ie Island, where the villagers made use of underground tunnels. Ie was also where US photojournalist Ernie Pyle was killed by a sniper. Nago City was formed in 1970 when several villages were merged. It has hosted US Marine base Camp Schwab since 1956.

Motobu is an ideal place to stay, as it's the last area with creature comforts before you head further north. There are large-scale resorts and fancy beachside cafes serving up staples such as açaí bowls and burgers. The nearby theme parks can make the traffic quite intense, but Motobu is otherwise an attractive base for exploring this part of the island.

Pineapple Paradise
One for tropical fruit fans

If you have kids, or even if you don't, consider a stop at **Nago Pineapple Park** (*nagopine.com; adult/child ¥1500/800*), a kooky and kitschy amusement park dedicated to the locally grown pineapple. Pineapple-adorned carts take you on a tour of the grounds, including a pineapple farm where you can see 120 species of the fruit; the carts spout pineapple info, backed by a ridiculously catchy theme song. It's not all agricultural geekiness, though: you can taste pineapple treats (fresh bites, ice cream, taco rice, pizza – even pineapple wine and brandy), learn all about the crop and take a spin through a wacky dinosaur park populated with animatronic reptiles. You can easily spend two to three hours here on all things *Ananas comosus*.

☑ TOP TIP
If you want a bit of beach to yourself, take the ferry to Ie Island and soak up the sun.

Kuroshio tank (p136), Okinawa Churaumi Aquarium

Coral Communities

Dive in a fish metropolis

There are several opportunities to dive near Nago, and the points around **Minna Island** and **Sesoko** are popular places to start. Both are a short boat ride from **Yamakawa Port**, which is the pickup point for many dive shops. Outfitters share the boat with other companies and leave around 9am, returning around noon after visiting the two dive locations.

Minna Island has a healthy reef that offers ample opportunities to see morays, lionfish, scorpionfish, pipefish, lobsters, clownfish, garden eels and even the odd giant trevally and tuna. The maximum depth is around 25m. Sesoko's **Labyrinth** dive is shallow, making it perfect for less experienced divers. It has dramatic caves and light cathedrals, and excellent visibility. There's a psychedelic diversity of marine life here, including titan triggerfish, morays, scorpionfish, clownfish and sea snakes. **Aloha Divers** (*alohadiversokinawa.com*) and **All Blue Divers** (*allbluedivers.com*) conduct tours in English for licensed divers. Prices for two dives range from ¥20,000 to ¥30,000.

Aquatic Theme Park

All things ocean

The giant **Ocean Expo Park** (*oki-park.jp/kaiyohaku/en; adult/youth/child ¥2180/1440/710*) opened in 1975 for the Okinawa International Ocean Expo, with several museums, the enormous **Okinawa Churaumi Aquarium** and a replica of a village – which may seem like an odd attraction as there are real villages nearby. You can buy tickets just for the

continued on p136

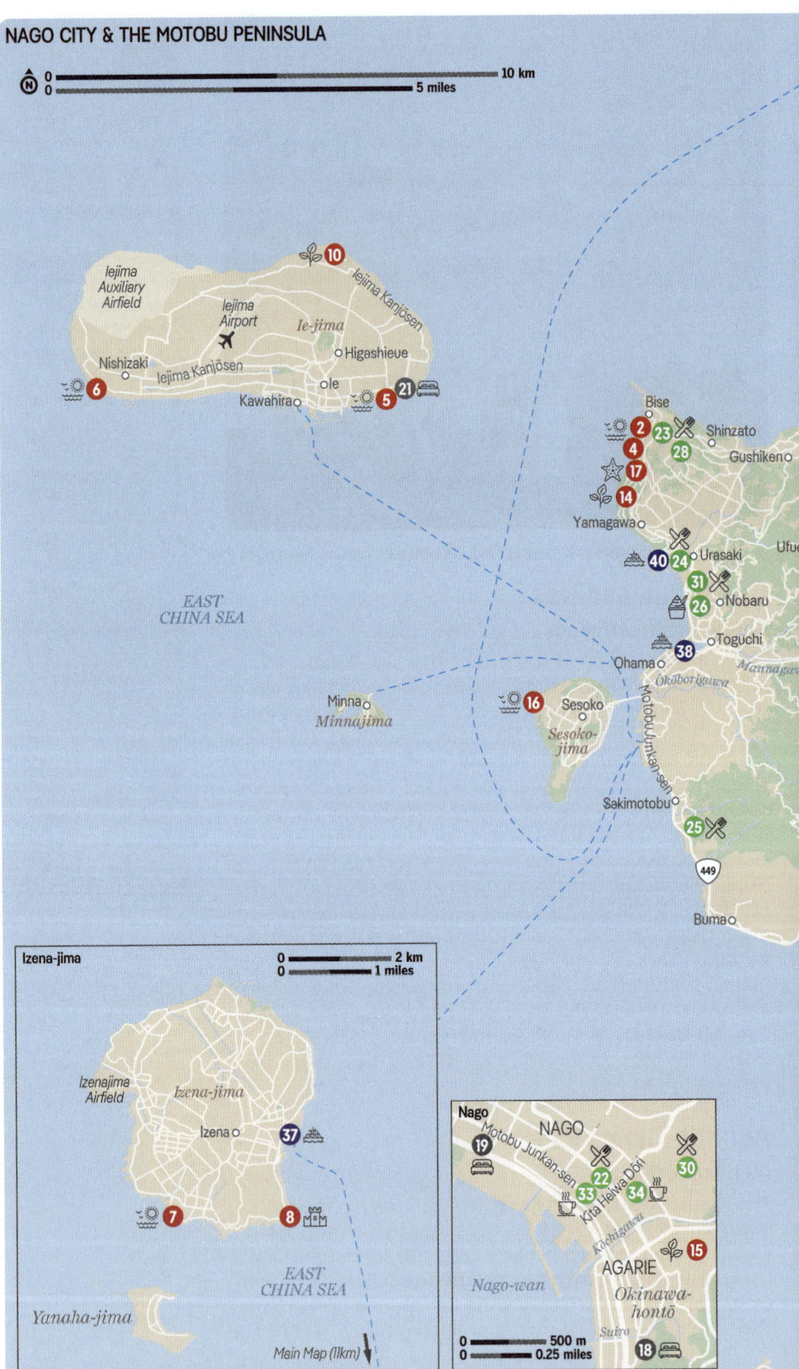
NAGO CITY & THE MOTOBU PENINSULA

N
0   10 km
0   5 miles

Iejima Auxiliary Airfield
Iejima Airport
Ie-jima
Iejima Kanjōsen
10
Nishizaki
Iejima Kanjōsen
Higashieue
6
Ole
Kawahira
5
21

Bise
2
23
Shinzato
4
28
Gushikeno
17
14
Yamagawa
Ufud
40
24
Urasaki
31
26
Nobaru
Toguchi
38
Ohama
Mannagaw
Ōkōborigawa
Motobu Junkan-sen
EAST CHINA SEA
Minna
Minnajima
16
Sesoko
Sesoko-jima
Sakimotobu
25
449
Buma

Izena-jima
0   2 km
0   1 miles
Izenajima Airfield
Izena-jima
Izena
37
7
8
EAST CHINA SEA
Yanaha-jima
Main Map (11km)

Nago
NAGO
19
Motobu Junkan-sen
30
22
33
Kita Heiwa Dōri
34
Kōchizawa
15
AGARIE
Okinawa-hontō
Nago-wan
Suira
18
0   500 m
0   0.25 miles

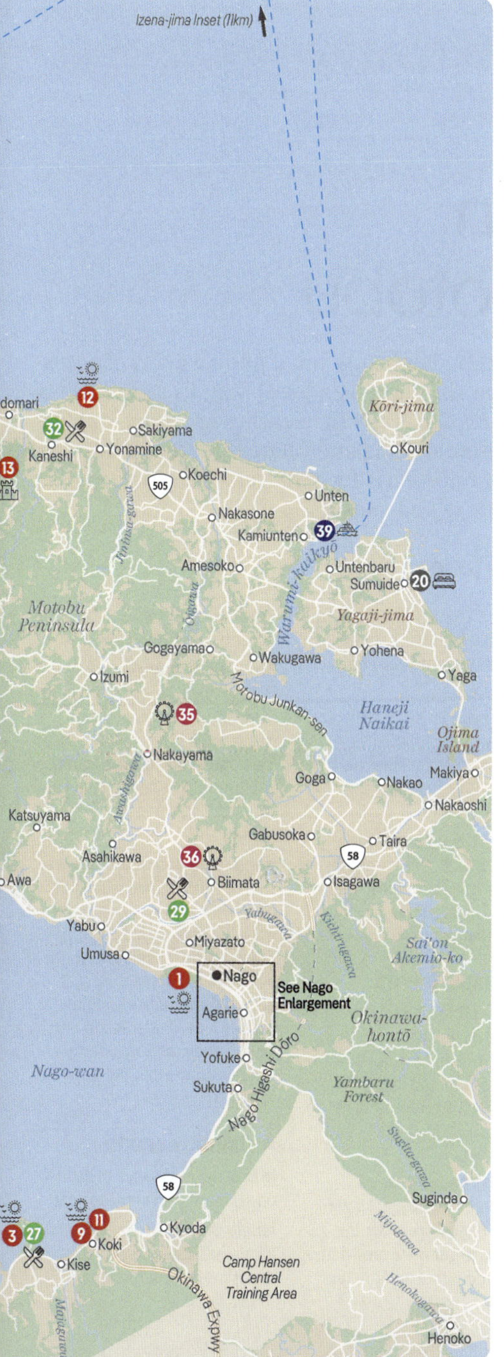

● SIGHTS

1 21 Sekinomori Beach
2 Bise Fukugi Tree Beach
3 Busena Beach
4 Emerald Beach
5 Ie Beach
6 Ishara Beach
7 Izena Beach
8 Izena Castle Ruins
9 Koki Beach
10 Lily Field Park
11 Nago Citizen Beach
12 Nagahama Beach
13 Nakijin-jō
14 Ocean Expo Park
15 Orion Happy Park
16 Sesoko Island Beach

● ACTIVITIES

17 Okinawa Churaumi Aquarium

● SLEEPING

18 Hotel Route-Inn Nago
19 Nankai Minshuku
20 Stay Hotel
21 Tsuchi no Yado

● EATING

22 Bear Kitchen
23 Beni Imoya
24 Camel Sandwich & Smoothie
25 Captain Kangaroo Hamburger
26 Ice Cream Cafe Ark
27 Maroad
28 Motobu Chicken
29 Niceness
30 Sea Living Cafe
31 Topu
32 Umi no Sachi

● DRINKING & NIGHTLIFE

33 Inno Coffee Shop
34 Lester Cafe

● ENTERTAINMENT

35 Junglia
36 Nago Pineapple Park

● TRANSPORT

37 Nakada Port
38 Toguchi Port
39 Unten Port
40 Yamakawa Port

HELP ME PICK:

Beaches in Nago & Motobu

Around Nago City and the Motobu Peninsula you'll find an array of accessible beaches. An afternoon on the shore is a great way to relax after a sweaty morning at a theme park. Generally the beaches are quiet and feel less developed than the ones around Naha and Chatan. Motobu's beaches boast still, emerald waters and are ideal for children. Take time out to cool off and watch the dramatic island sunsets.

Which beach to visit if you love...

City beaches

21 Sekinomori Beach Right in front of Enagic Stadium, Nago's city beach has perfectly still water and an adjacent park. It's a lovely place to enjoy the excellent coffees from one of Nago's premier cafes, such as **Lester Cafe** or **Inno Coffee Shop**, both around five minutes' drive away. Grab a takeaway and enjoy the sunset.

Water-borne activities

Busena Beach Located north of Onna as you enter the Nago area, well-trafficked Busena in front of Busena Terrace Beach has aqua waters and white sand. As it's a resort beach,

there's a ¥5500 fee, and there are rental facilities here for jet skis, wakeboards, tube rides and SUPs.

Koki Beach Slightly north of Busena, with a relaxed vibe, Koki has some facilities and shops with inflatables and snorkels.

Nago Citizen Beach North of Koki Beach, this is another pristine option for fun in the sun and is frequented by locals rather than tourists.

Peninsula jaunts

Sesoko Island Beach On little Sesoko Island, with stunning aqua water and pristine sand. As it's connected to the Motobu Peninsula by bridge, this beach is accessible by car (no need for a ferry).

Emerald Beach (Kokuei Okinawan Kinenkoen) Next to Ocean Expo Park (p131), this beach can get quite crowded, but it's beautiful nonetheless.

This is also the location for a fireworks festival in July.

Bise Fukugi Tree Beach Further north along the Motobu Peninsula, a tunnel of *fukugi* trees leading to the beach here is a popular social media prop. The beachfront has several chic cafes selling smoothies and curries.

Nagahama Beach On the north side of Motobu Peninsula, this beach has still, clear, emerald waters in a secluded cove. There are no facilities here, but Nagahama Beach Resort behind the beach runs guided kayak tours using transparent kayaks and stand-up boards so you can see into the waters below.

An island escape

Ie Beach This stretch of sand on Ie Island is a serene retreat.

Ishara Beach Also on Ie Island, Ishara has still, glassy water and is perfect for relaxing.

Busena Beach

HOW TO

When to go It can get oppressively hot during summer, so aim for early-morning or late-afternoon beach hangs in that season. Sunset is spectacular at all the beaches.

SUP Many beach huts rent stand-up paddleboards. These have low environmental impact and are perfect for Okinawa's still oceans.

Snorkelling Even the resort beaches have great snorkelling. Make sure you pack a snorkel and mask as there are abundant opportunities to see marine life.

Safety While the natural and undeveloped beaches are great, they're often without lifeguards. If you have children with you, it's better to go to a busier beach with facilities.

At one end of the spectrum of Okinawan beaches are the resorts, which have entrance fees, activities and private facilities. At the other end are the undeveloped beaches with no facilities whatsoever. For a really uncommercialised beach experience, Ie Island is accessible by ferry and is perfect for biking (p138). Charming traditional guesthouse Tsuchi no Yado (p151) is one of the few places that professionally cater to people with physical and mental disabilities, and it's right next to peaceful Ie Beach. For an experience with all the bells and whistles, Busena Resort offers safety nets, beach chairs, parasols and water rides.

The waters off northern Okinawa-hontō are generally extremely still, so the hazards are low. Note that some beaches don't have lifeguards, so they might not be suitable for inexperienced swimmers or small kids, although they're perfect for sunbathing. In an emergency, call 118 for the Japan Coast Guard or 119 for an ambulance.

During summer the sun is very strong, so be sure to use copious amounts of sunscreen (available at any convenience store). Between May and October sightings of venomous box jellyfish are common. For jellyfish stings, pour vinegar on the tentacles – it's always a good idea to carry a bottle of vinegar with you in the car for beach trips. Other venomous beach denizens include cone snails, blue-ringed octopuses and stonefish.

STARK BRUTALISM

While you might think of postwar Britain when you hear the term 'brutalist architecture', Okinawa is rife with brutalist concrete structures. Using thick, heavy concrete in their construction helps buildings withstand the intense typhoons and storms that frequently occur in the tropics. Only 10% of local buildings built prior to WWII remain, as most traditional wooden dwellings were annihilated in the Battle of Okinawa. Many of the iconic landmarks on the island, including Naha Prefectural Museum, are hulking concrete structures with angular shapes. Up north, be sure to check out the impressive **Churaumi Aquarium** (p131) and Nago City Hall, but even the residential and municipal buildings have a retro sci-fi look.

Nakijin-jō

continued from p131

facilities that interest you, and there's free parking. Swarming with visitors, the current aquarium was built in 2002. The highlight is without doubt the massive **Kuroshio tank**, which holds 7500 tons of water. Its resident whale sharks and manta rays nonchalantly glide past the glass walls and ranks of spectators. The aquarium also has recreations of Okinawa's reefs as well as displays dedicated to sharks and intriguing deep sea creatures.

Less well known but more informative is the Expo Park's **Oceanic Culture Museum** (¥190). It houses around 750 maritime artefacts, with the full-scale canoes among the most impressive displays. Exhibits detail the relationship between people and the ocean and cover the entirety of the Pacific. Many folk items in the collection can no longer be found in their respective countries. There's also a dedicated space for Okinawan culture, which has many parallels and relationships with the Pacific region. Displays describe the movements of marine life throughout the seasons, cultural celebrations and fisherfolk festivals, and types of traditional fishing. You can also see traditional wooden *sabani* fishing boats. The planetarium projects multilingual shows usually related to folklore.

EATING AND DRINKING IN NAGO AND MOTOBU: OUR PICKS

Niceness: Pretty vegan restaurant in what looks like a garden shed, serving curries, gluten-free bread and turmeric soy milk lattes. Cash only. *11am-3pm Thu-Sun* ¥¥

Bear Kitchen: (くまキッチン) Handmade vegan *bentōs* with brown rice and local fermented vegetables. Smoothies too. In Nago market. *10am-3pm Tue-Sat* ¥

Maroad: Posh place for a tropical afternoon tea. Petits fours have an Okinawan twist with fruit like pineapple or mango. *11.30am-10.30pm* ¥¥¥

Orion Happy Park: Beer factory where you can stop for a drink or go for a (prebooked) tour and tasting. *9.30am-4pm Tue-Sat* ¥

In early July the **Ocean Expo Fireworks Festival** (oki-park.jp/hanabi2025/en) sees 10,000 fireworks exploding over adjacent **Emerald Beach** (p134). It's Okinawa's largest-scale pyrotechnic display; it's possible to see the fireworks for free, but there are tickets for seated areas.

The Home of Kings
Bygone majesty at Nakijin

Once the seat of the Hokuzan nation, **Nakijin-jō** (nakijinjo-seki-osi.jp; adult/youth ¥1000/500) was built in the 14th century as the home of the northern kings. Today it's a beautiful ruin and a UNESCO World Heritage Site, with reconstructed limestone walls snaking over the hills and views across the glimmering sea. Volunteers lead free tours. A visit during the cherry blossom festival (late January to early February) is especially magical as the area is carpeted in stripes of bright pink, contrasting prettily with the sombre grey stone walls.

Welcome to the Junglia
Northern Okinawa's newest family attraction

Okinawan theme parks tend to replicate what's already in Okinawa, such as villages, coral reefs and, in the case of **Junglia** (junglia.jp/ adult/child ¥8000/5400), the jungle – even though it's located right next door to the actual jungle of Yambaru National Park. When the theme park opened in 2025 there were massive traffic jams all the way up the island. Across a ginormous site with dinosaur statues everywhere, the experience offers a tame bungee jump, buggy rides and suspension bridge walks. It's hardly state of the art, and it resembles an athletic park in parts, but it makes an enjoyable enough outing for young kids. Shaded areas are limited, so avoid visiting at the height of summer, when lines for rides can be 300 minutes long (yep, that's five hours).

Birthplace of a King
Time out on Izena Island

Little Izena Island, just 16.7km in circumference, is about an hour's ferry ride north of the Motobu Peninsula. It's a somewhat isolated place that sees few tourists, but the island's 1300-strong population holds on to its unspoilt nature and traditional ways.

continued on p140

SWIRLING SEA SNAKES

A familiar sight to divers in the Ryūkyū are *umi hebi* using their flattened tails like paddles to twist and turn dramatically through the water. The term *umi hebi* covers both conger eels (fish with gills) and sea snakes (a reptile with lungs). Okinawa is one of the most northern points at which sea snakes live, as they're usually found in the tropics. The most common is the *irabu* (black-banded sea krait), which is venomous but unlikely to strike. In Okinawa they're seen as having medicinal properties and traditionally used in food such as *irabu jiru* (sea snake soup) and sake. They're now a threatened species due to overfishing, which makes seeing one while diving all the more special.

CASUAL EATS ON MOTOBU PENINSULA: OUR PICKS

Topu: Tofu and soba shop in Motobu with set meals. The Okinawan *shima tofu* (island tofu) has a soft, delicious texture. *11am-3pm & 5-9pm Wed-Mon* ¥

Umi no Sachi: (海の幸) *Izakaya* (pub) in Nakijin specialising in locally caught fish served a variety of ways (fried with butter, as sashimi...). *6am-midnight* ¥¥

Captain Kangaroo Hamburger: The long waits are worth it for the yummy milkshakes and chunky, tasty burgers. *11am-5pm* ¥

Motobu Chicken: (パーラー本部チキン) Farm shack serving deep-fried chicken. Has outdoor seating. *10.30am-7.30pm Thu-Tue* ¥

Cycling Ie Island

Off northwestern Okinawa-hontō, Ie Island (伊江島) is known for beautiful beaches, dramatic coastline and historical significance. It was heavily involved in the Battle of Okinawa, and its historical sites add depth to its charm. Easily accessible by ferry, the island is only 20km around and makes for a fun, easy bike ride of two to three hours. The route is paved and has only moderate hills.

❶ Ie Port

Start at Ie Port, where four ferries from Motobu arrive each day. Grab a rental bike from **Tama Car Rentals** (*per hour/day ¥400/1000*).

The Cycle: Head towards Mt Gusuku, passing the village hall and the ruined pawn shop with a gaping hole in its side. The pawn shop was the only building not burnt down during the Battle of Okinawa.

❷ Mt Gusuku

Continue to Mt Gusuku's eastern entrance. The island is almost completely flat, so 172m-high Mt Gusuku stands out. It's also called Iejima Tacchu (*tacchu* means 'pointed' in the Okinawan language). Steep steps go all the way to the top; the climb takes 15 to 20 minutes. The summit serves up 360-degree views.

The Cycle: You'll pass the pawn shop ruins, then Shimamurayakanko Park and the Hokon

Mt Gusuku

monument, which commemorates those who died on the island during WWII.

3 Niya Thiya Cave

This large cave is also called Sennin Gama (Cave of 1000 People), a reference to the more than 1000 Okinawans who hid here and survived during WWII. Nearby is isolated GI Beach, with powdery sand and clear waters.

The Cycle: Backtrack to the intersection and continue north on Road 181 for 3km, then zigzag to Wajee Viewpoint.

4 Wajee Viewpoint

With rugged cliffs and azure waters, Wajee boasts the island's best views. The site was an important source of mineral-rich spring water that's still available today. If you look down from the viewpoint you'll see where the spring water emerges.

The Cycle: Follow the coast on the eastern side of the island for a couple of kilometres.

5 Lily Field Park & Hibiscus Garden

The 86,000-sq-metre **Lily Field Park** hosts the Ie Island Lily Festival from late April to Golden Week, with over a million Easter lilies and a view of the ocean. The **Hibiscus Garden**, 15 minutes down Road 225, is open year-round and features more than 1000 hibiscus varieties.

The Cycle: Travel 2km down Road 225 to reach Ie Island Beach Side Horse Park.

6 Ie Island Beach Side Horse Park

Before continuing south back to Ie Port, you could enjoy a leisurely **horseback ride** (*ie-horse.wixsite.com/ieuma*) along sunny Ie Beach (p134). Courses range from 20 minutes to two hours. No prior riding experience is required, but beginners must take an introductory lesson for a fee. Between May and September, when the water's warm, you can even ride and swim with your horse in the ocean.

JAPAN'S POP QUEEN

Okinawa's best-known singular person, famous across Japan, is '90s queen of pop Namie Amuro. Naha-born Amuro was loved for her outgoing fashion and her musical versatility, going from R&B to hip pop to Eurobeat. Her longevity saw her compared to Janet Jackson. She also helped popularise the sexy *gyaru* look, a youth culture rebellion against conservative gender norms that took over Tokyo's Shibuya in the '90s. When she was preparing to retire in 2018, Amuro began her final tour at Ginowan Seaside Park before continuing to Tokyo. By that point she had sold around 36 million records and was celebrated as an iconic modern woman.

Izena Tamaudun

continued from p137

You can wander Izena's rice paddies and view the coral walls of the village houses. Watch sunsets and swim on **Izena Beach**, hire a guide to show you the fishing scene (Izena is famous for squid fishing by hand at night) or stargaze dark skies at one of Izena's **free campsites**.

Izena's big claim to fame is that it was the birthplace of **King Sho En**, a 15th-century farmer turned Ryūkyū dynasty leader. There are several monuments to him here, including the small **Izena Castle Ruins** and **Izena Tamaudun**, a mausoleum for the king's family.

You won't find big chain hotels and fast food restaurants on the island. Instead, welcoming community members host homestays and family-run inns, and the village rents out basic rooms in the **community centre** *(izena-kanko.jp/charm/stay)* for as little as ¥3000 per night.

Ferries depart twice daily from **Unten Port** in Nakijin to **Nakada Port** on Izena.

EATING IN NAGO CITY AND MOTOBU: SWEET TREATS

Ice Cream Cafe Ark: Huge ocean-view ice cream parlour offering Okinawan flavours like sugar cane, *tankan* orange, and pineapple. *1-6pm* ¥

Camel Sandwich & Smoothie: Recommended combo: the *klinmitsu* mango smoothie and a Spam-and-egg sandwich. *7am-2.30pm* ¥

Sea Living Cafe: Pocket cafe inside an upscale lifestyle shop. Try an Okinawan sweet potato latte and a coconut doughnut. *2-5pm Tue-Sat, noon-5pm Sun* ¥

Beni Imoya: (べにいも屋) Small stand with takeaway sweets close to Bise Fukugi Rd. Everything has *beni imo* (Okinawan purple sweet potato). *11am-sold out Fri-Mon* ¥

Kunigami & North Yambaru

VIEWS | MOUNTAINS | WATERFALLS

Established in 1896, Kunigami is the most northerly district of the Yambaru area, stretching all the way to Cape Hedo at the northern tip of Okinawa-hontō. During WWII many people fled the south for the north and this region became a civilian refuge. The rest of the island is quite flat, but Kunigami is mountainous. Its highest peak, Mt Yonoha, stands at 503m. Around 85% of the region is covered in highly biodiverse forest, which you can explore on guided spiritual hikes. There are also accessible walks around little Kunigami village to Kunigami Forest Park and Hiji waterfall; both sites have bungalows and places to pitch tents. Most of the coast has the highway running along it, but around Tobaru there are a number of lovely beaches such as Tobaru and Ōkuma. The area in front of Okuma Private Beach & Resort has activities such as wakeboarding and banana boat rides.

GETTING AROUND

It's difficult to get anywhere in Kunigami without a car. Coastal roads flanked by little villages and the spectacular end point of Cape Hedo make for one of Japan's top drives. Sparse village buses run up and down the coast in the morning and afternoon only.

Okinawa's Northernmost Tip

Dramatic Cape Hedo

With the Pacific Ocean to the east and the East China Sea to the west, **Cape Hedo** offers majestic vistas. The seas surrounding the cape have plentiful coral life, and from above you can see the reef's spectacular gradations in colour. Historically, the cape was the site of several watchtowers. A monument built in 1976 commemorates the return of Okinawa to Japan after the US occupation ended in 1972.

Wisdom Hikes

Spirituality and animism in the forest

With a focus on traditional Ryūkyūan belief systems, animism and folklore, **ASMUI Spiritual Hikes** (アスムイハイクス; *asmui.jp*) offer hikes quite unlike any other. Your ASMUI guide will take you to sacred natural spots around the Cape Hedo area to explain the numerous *utaki* (spiritual sites)

☑ TOP TIP

Go on a night tour with a guide to see an incredible amount of wildlife with **Wanyu** (*yanbaru-guide. com*) at Yambaru Guide.

KUNIGAMI & NORTH YAMBARU

Legend

● SIGHTS
1 ASMUI Spiritual Hikes
2 Cape Hedo
3 Okuma Beach

● SLEEPING
4 Ada Garden Hotel Okinawa
5 Guest House Hechima
6 Hotel Nanmei Shinshitsu
7 Oku Yanbaru no Sato Guesthouses
8 Okuma Private Beach & Resort
9 Pension Yonoha Dake
10 Soranoma Indigo
11 Yanbaru Hostel

● EATING
12 Himawari
13 Irijoya
14 Minato Shokudo
15 OkuMasa
16 Satsuki Maru
17 Yakiniku Lion Okuma
18 Yui Yui Kunigami

and locations for prayer. In addition to providing insights into Ryūkyūan spirituality, your guide will cover topics as far ranging as the Ryūkyūan people's commitment to peace and the importance of music in retaining a culture based on reconciliation and relationships rather than war and retaliation. And the terrain you'll cover is absolutely breathtaking. You'll walk to ledges offering views of Cape Hedo and Yorontō (p268), and the landscape encompasses lush tropical vegetation, huge banyan trees and mountains covered in cycads. There are also some lunar-like areas, as the geological strata contain brown limestone and grey crystalline limestone formed from coral.

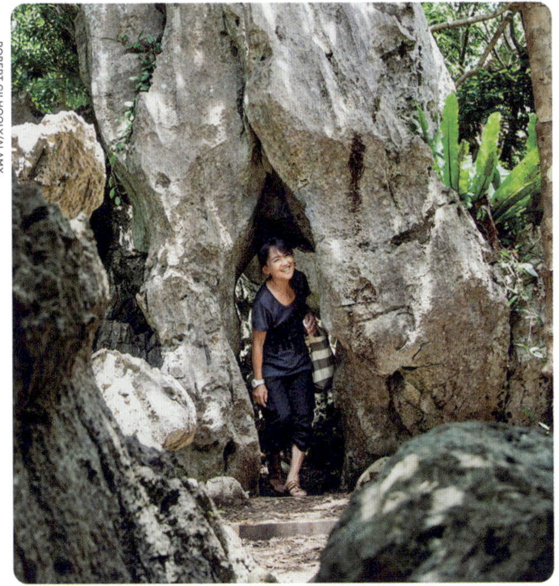

ASMUI Spiritual Hikes (p141)

The tour begins at a rock museum that explains the formation of this karst topography and gives explanations of coral reefs. ASMUI also offers some words of wisdom: 'People who run from hardship will never be happy!' The guide will activate a protective god of your own, thought to look over you and guide you through life. The experience is a fascinating window on Ryūkyūan spirituality and the ways in which the community's sense of divinity is intertwined with nature. Note that tours are in Japanese; online translation programs are your friend here.

ROADSIDE HAPPINESS

One of your best chances for a well-stocked pit stop in this region is **Yui Yui Kunigami** (*yuiyui-k.jp*). This *michi no eki* (roadside rest area) has clean public toilets, a large gift shop, half a dozen food stands and picnic tables, an outdoor playground for kids as well as an indoor play area for toddlers, and a tourist information centre with displays on the flightless *Yambaru kuina* (Okinawa rail). The rest area's **tourist information centre** (*kunigami-kanko.com/sightseeing-spots/cycling; 4hr ¥800*) has a few bicycles for rent if you're up for a side quest; the centre is within easy cycling distance of a few beaches, Kunigami village and some small museums.

TASTY EATS IN KUNIGAMI: OUR PICKS

Wow House: (わぁ〜家〜) Inside Yui Yui Kunigami rest stop, Wow House specialises in local pork. *11am-5pm Wed-Mon* ¥¥

Parlor Yumechan: Also in Yui Yui, Parlor dishes up Okinawan soul food. Okinawan *zenzai* (shaved ice with red bean) is perfect on a humid day. *11am-5pm Wed-Mon* ¥

Minato Shokudo: Set meals with local fish served a variety of ways (tempura, sashimi, fried in butter). *Mon-Wed, Fri & Sat noon-4pm* ¥¥

Himawari: (食堂ひまわり) Classic eatery with all the Okinawan comfort food. The *soki* pork is particularly delicious. *11.30am-3pm Mon-Sat* ¥

Yakiniku Lion Okuma: This popular *yakiniku* (barbecue) place hits the spot, with Okinawan *wagyū* and Yambaru Agū pork. *noon-10pm Fri-Wed* ¥¥

Irijoya: (入り門家) Soba restaurant in a traditional Okinawan house in a village setting. *11.30am-3pm Fri-Wed* ¥

OkuMasa: Simple, refined *shabu-shabu* using local vegetables and Agū pork. Book ahead. *5-9pm Thu-Tue* ¥¥¥

Satsuki Maru: (サツキ丸) In a traditional house, this soba and sashimi place has delicious soba with *mozuku* seaweed and pork. *noon-4.30pm Tue-Sat* ¥

Yambaru National Park

FOREST HIKES | BIRDING | RIVER WALKS

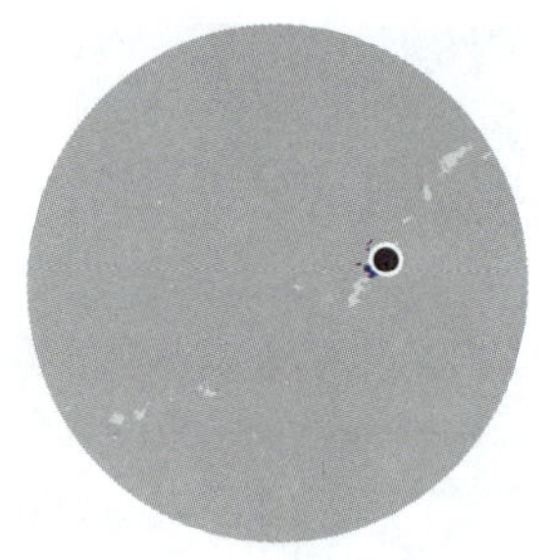

GETTING AROUND

There's really no option other than to use a car in Yambaru. The eastern side is almost devoid of public transportation, and bus stops and hiking pickup points are at remote locations such as dam car parks and roadside restaurants. The various sites are also quite far from each other.

The expansive forested area in the central part of northern Okinawa-hontō was designated as Yambaru National Park in 2016. Yambaru is the 33rd national park in Japan and the largest national park in Okinawa. The region's humid climate and abundant rainfall have supported a biodiverse ecosystem with unique endemic species, including the red-billed Okinawa rail and the Yambaru long-armed scarab beetle. The forest is punctuated by karst limestone outcrops and blooming *itajii* (Okinawa castanopsis, an evergreen species of beech) that cover a significant amount of the park's area. In southern Yambaru, the Gesashi Bay mangrove forest offers the chance to experience over 10 hectares of these unique ecosystems. Kayaking through the forest allows you to come close to these complex forests that are dense with life. Other activities including day and night hikes and traditional 'stream climbing' with its light environmental footprint allow visitors the opportunity to experience the forest in a range of ways.

Yambaru by Day & Night

Wildlife-watching hikes

The hike to **Mt Yonoha trailhead** goes through forests dense with evergreen broadleaf trees such as *itajii* (Okinawa castanopsis), which make up most of Okinawa's forest biomass, as well as giant flying spider-monkey tree ferns. Yambaru is often called a 'broccoli forest' because its treetops are voluminous while their trunks are spindly. These trees support the life of the forest, from wild boars to freshwater crabs. There are also rare endemic species to be seen, including the Okinawa woodpecker and crocodile newt. Using a knowledgable guide like **Wanyu** (*yanbaru-guide.com*) is highly recommended to understand the forest vegetation, wildlife interactions, and environmental issues such as invasive species and poaching. Quite simply, a lot of the forest's inhabitants, such as lizards perching on trees, skinks in the undergrowth and the tiny

☑ TOP TIP

While hiking during the day is pleasant, it's easier to spot critters at night. The star of the show is the Okinawa rail, but the region's snakes are also beautiful.

YAMBARU'S ICONIC BIRD

With its bright red beak, the Okinawa rail is the icon of Yambaru and a national natural monument. The bird was long recognised by locals but was only formally identified in 1981. Rails are endemic to Okinawa and only found in Yambaru, but the species is endangered due to habitat loss. Rails can't fly, which makes them easy targets for predators. In 1910, Okinawa Prefecture introduced the small Indian mongoose to eat the local *habu* (vipers) because the snakes' population was exploding on the sugar fields. However, the mongoose is awake during the day, so it completely missed the nocturnal *habu* and began eating Okinawa rail chicks instead. These days mongoose traps are set to curtail this absurd bungle.

● SIGHTS	● ACTIVITIES	5 Bookcafe Okinawa Rail
1 Higashi Village Fureai Hirugi Park	3 Mt Yonoha Trailhead	
2 Kuina no Mori museum	● EATING	6 Cafe & Zakka Banana
	4 Agachi Mui	7 Café Kurage
		8 Yui Yui Kunigami

Yambaru long-armed scarab beetle are easy to miss. Tours pick up and drop off at Yui Yui Kunigami (p143), which has a wide range of local food, including wild boar (of which there are plenty in the island's north). Wanyu speaks English, Japanese and Chinese.

Alongside the daytime tours, there are excellent **night tours** where you can look for Okinawa rails, Orii's flying foxes, brown hawk-owls, native frog species and a number of endemic and beautiful snakes such as the venomous Okinawa red-banded *habu* (viper) and *hime habu*. You can learn more about the iconic Okinawa rail at the **Kuina no Mori museum** *(ヤンバ ルクイナ生態展示学習施設; adult/child ¥700/300)* in Kuniga-mi; it's closed Wednesday. Your guide will look for animals as they slowly drive you through the forest; they'll stop when

THE POACHING THREAT

Poaching by both smugglers and tourists is a threat to wildlife in Okinawa and elsewhere in the Ryūkyūs, with some species at risk of extinction. Local wildlife tour guides lament this issue, as the animals they wish to point out are simply vanishing, to end up in pet stores or traditional medicine shops overseas. Yambaru guide **Wanyu** (*yanbaru-guide. com*) explains that Ryūkyū leaf turtles, an endemic forest species, is one of the most common targets. In 2025 four people were arrested for trying to send over a hundred of these rare turtles by post, declaring them to be toys because they would rattle in the packages. Another couple was recently arrested for trying to smuggle 682 hermit crabs.

Higashi Village Fureai Hirugi Park

they spot something. Adding greatly to the experience is the ethereal sight of the night sky with its canopy of stars.

Mysterious Mangroves

Get to know a delicate ecosystem

With their spindly exposed root systems, mangroves are the unsung heroes of the tropics and subtropics. Existing in the liminal space between the land and sea, they bridge the gap in a way that protects and enriches both sides. Hardy mangroves filter salt water to make conditions tolerable for the many plants and animals that find homes in their branches and the surrounding mudflats. They also stabilise coastal areas against erosion – crucial in an archipelago constantly battered by typhoons and tsunamis.

The largest mangrove forest on Okinawa-hontō spans over 10 hectares at the southern end of Yambaru National Park, straddling the border where the Gesashi River empties into the bay. Visit **Higashi Village Fureai Hirugi Park** to explore the improbable forest. Though the area is well equipped with wooden boardwalks for land-based exploration, a more immersive experience is paddling through the shallows by kayak or canoe. **Yambaru Experience** (*yanbaru-experience. com; adult/child ¥5000/3500*) has English-speaking guides.

CAFES AROUND YAMBARU: OUR PICKS

Café & Zakka Banana: Roadside light eats and craft beer. Cakes use local ingredients like Yambaru ginger and *gōyā* (bitter melon). *8.30am-7pm Sun-Fri* ¥

Bookcafe Okinawa Rail: Light eats and cakes, plus a large library. The car ride through the forest is an adventure. *10.30am-7pm Wed & Fri-Sun* ¥¥

Café Kurage: (海月) Very light, healthy plates and sandwiches. It's open early for breakfast and lunch. *7-10am & 11am-6pm Thu-Tue* ¥¥

Agachi Mui: (あがち 森) Beautiful mountain cafe with cakes, tarts and pizzas (all on the small side). Outdoor seating. *10am-5pm Thu-Mon* ¥

At high tide the trees' green-latticed canopy rises straight from the water, and you can glide smoothly through the channels threading the mangrove maze. Here you might see mudskippers, mud lobsters or Ryūkyū soldier crabs. If you're lucky enough to book a summer night tour, you may see fireflies winking between the branches, their reflections on the water mingling with the twinkling of the vast starry sky above.

Experience Sawanobori

Make your way upriver

Sawanobori (literally, 'stream climbing') is a type of river-tracing mountaineering where hikers follow waterways upstream towards their source. Unlike canyoning, the objective of *sawanobori* is to go against the flow of the water. Participants walk up the river and over cascading waterfalls. It's a traditional method of traversing the land without having to cut a path, as much of the mountains are covered in thick shrubs and plants.

Habu Asobi (*habu-asobi.jp/english; per person for 1-2 people/3-8 people ¥18,000/15,000*) leads beginner tours to the Nago area (and to Kunigami for experienced climbers). Making your way along the middle of the Genka Okawa River offers a completely different perspective on the landscape. You'll need a degree of dexterity to clamber up the rivers, navigate wet surfaces and traverse flowing water, and you should be prepared to wade right in. The tour crosses tranquil natural scenery and also passes 200-year-old settlements and charcoal pits. It's an energising experience, with the fresh water refreshingly cold in contrast to the stickiness of salt water. In the past *sawanobori* was done with traditional split-toe shoes, but wetsuits, grip shoes, helmets and a lifejacket are provided for this tour. Young children are welcome to join the beginner option. During the river hike there's a lunch break, with hot Okinawa soba cooked by the river on portable stoves, as well as a chance to rappel or zipline down a waterfall.

English-speaking owner Tomoya Habu says, 'In Okinawa the plant species are unique and the mountains aren't tall, and because it's warm, the water flow is just right. It's really good for beginners. Here it's warm enough to do *sawanobori* from spring to early winter. The conditions for climbing upstream gullies is ideal because there isn't too much water flow. You can also enjoy it without going to the summit. The objective is to enjoy the scenery on the way. *Sawanobori* is slower and calmer than canyoning. It's more about appreciating the moment in nature.'

THE RIVER'S ROLE

Giovanni Masucci, marine biologist at Okinawa Institute of Science and Technology, explains the part rivers play in the island's natural environment

The main ecosystem service that rivers provide is to transport sediment. Coastal erosion, storms and typhoons remove sediments, and then rivers bring them back. It's a geological transport cycle that can get disrupted if you dam a river or if you encase it in concrete. The opposite can also be true. If you're excavating at the mountain, the river can bring what you wouldn't want to reach the ocean, like red clay. Turbidity makes corals spend extra energy to clean themselves because they need sunlight for photosynthesis. If they get covered, diseases increase and can lead to bleaching.

Ōgimi

TEXTILES | BUTTERFLIES | FOOD FOR LONGEVITY

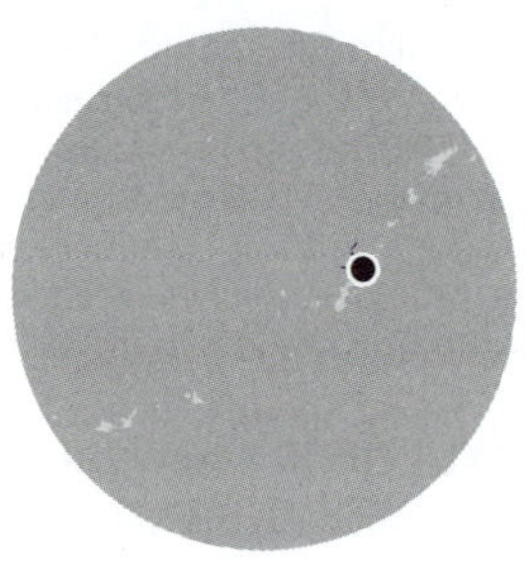

GETTING AROUND

The Ōgimi area is small, so once you're there you might not want to move at all. If you're reasonably fit and mobile, you can get away without having a car. Public transport is limited to a bus that goes up the coastal highway a few times a day.

Ōgimi is famed for three main things: the sour citrus fruit *shikuwasa*, *bashōfu* textiles and living for an exceptionally long time. The village sits northwest of Naha, facing the East China Sea, and around 76% of the surrounding area is covered in forest. The district produces 60% of Okinawa's *shikuwasa* fruit – Mt Nekumachiji is covered in *shikuwasa* trees. As you walk along the streets, don't be surprised to see the fruit rolling around on the ground. A stay in Ogimi is a wonderful opportunity to experience coastal village life. There are narrow roads that meander along the river, with a small, sacred waterfall inland and beautiful traditional houses. Ōgimi is also a haven for butterflies, with hundreds of the colourful winged insects to be seen in the local area. Among them is the distinctive great Mormon butterfly with its red accents and black-and-white striped wings.

An Island Ranch

Explore organic farm life

If you've gazed at the dense green canopy of Yambaru National Park and wondered what was out there, you might be surprised to learn that at least some of it is farmland. Run by quirky, friendly owners, **Kiyuna Farm** *(kiyunafarm1987 .wixsite.com/activity)* is a working organic dairy farm raising pasture-grazing cows. Kids will delight in meeting farm animals like cows and chickens (and barn cats). At weekends Kiyuna offers milking, butter-making and ice-cream-making experiences from ¥1000 per person; check its website for dates and reservations. Its impossibly creamy fresh-milk soft serve with Okinawan toppings such as strawberries, passionfruit and turmeric is a must-try.

Explore Ōgimi Village

Crafts and long life

In delightful Ōgimi village, the converted **Kijoka Primary School** *(kijoka-sho.jp)* is now a hip craft village featuring

☑ **TOP TIP**

At the repurposed Kijoka Primary School site, enjoy a steam at Buna Sauna and relax in a locally made Hakobune hammock afterwards.

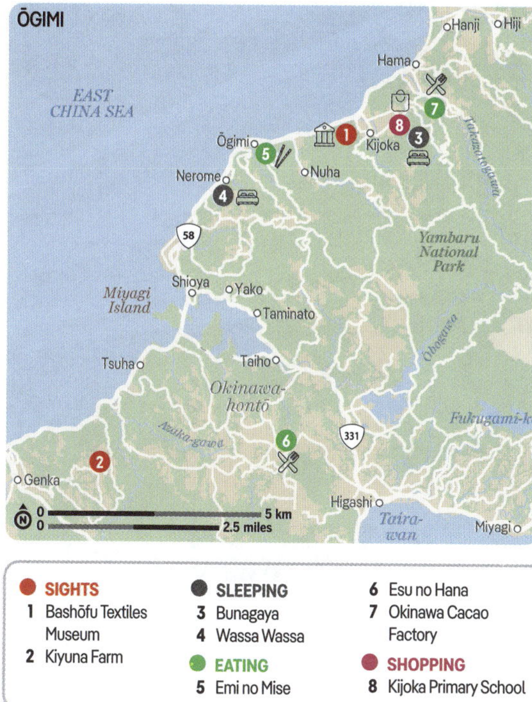

SIGHTS
1 Bashōfu Textiles Museum
2 Kiyuna Farm

SLEEPING
3 Bunagaya
4 Wassa Wassa

EATING
5 Emi no Mise

6 Esu no Hana
7 Okinawa Cacao Factory

SHOPPING
8 Kijoka Primary School

A THREATENED BLUE ZONE

Famed for its centenarians, Okinawa was listed as one of the 'Blue Zones' by Dan Buettner, author of several books about places conducive to longevity. Older Okinawan generations had traditional eating habits similar to those of other places known for long life, such as the Mediterranean. Traditional community bonds, active lifestyles, fresh food and a warm climate also supported Okinawans' healthy old age. However, the reasons for longevity in Japan at large are quite boring: they include improvements in health policy and medical accessibility. Sadly, Okinawa is going backwards of late, with a more sedentary lifestyle and diets that include a greater proportion of processed food. The prefecture currently has Japan's highest obesity rate and is tumbling down the mortality rankings.

hammock maker Hakobune, local craft shop Yambaru Crafts, bookstore Yama Books and even a great sauna, Buna Sauna. The primary school and the now defunct Ōgimi Village Kijoka Nursery School host the **Yambaru Art Festival** (*yambaru -artfes.jp/en*) from mid-January to February. Be sure to try the chocolate delights at **Okinawa Cacao Factory**. Ōgimi is also known for its longevity, with many healthy elderly living in the village. If you'd like to sample their diet, **Emi no Mise** (笑味の店; *eminomise.com*) is famed for its traditional 'longevity meals' that use its own farm-grown Okinawan vegetables that are harvested just before they're cooked. **Esu no Hana** also uses freshly picked Okinawan vegetables from its own garden, serving all-you-can-eat tempura to go with your soba. Open roughly 11am to 3pm Thursday to Tuesday, it closes when the noodles run out.

Sumptuous Bashōfu

Artisanal fabric making

The Ōgimi area offers a rare opportunity to learn all about *bashōfu*, a type of woven fabric made from the fibres of the *bashō* plant, a member of the banana family. *Bashōfu* has a light, smooth texture, making it ideal for the tropical climate. Production of the fabric is extremely labour intensive, as artisans also grow and harvest the plants; the entire process

OKINAWAN HOUSES

Traditional Okinawan homes show strong Chinese cultural influence, including features such as the *hinpun* (a wall that's placed in front of the home for privacy so the interior can't be seen from the outside). *Hinpun* are also seen as symbolically protective. Local houses' most striking aspects are the ceramic roof tiles with the omnipresent protective *shiisā* (lion dogs) on top. Long eaves called *amahaji* hang down to protect the interior from rain and sunlight. Customarily used to grow Okinawan vegetables such as radishes, carrots and potatoes for livestock feed, gardens are surrounded by coral and limestone exterior walls that create a delightful place to sit, particularly on breezy days.

Bashōfu Textiles Museum

of making a single piece of cloth takes three years. In 1974 a preservation society was established in order to pass the artisanal culture on to future generations. Manager Mieko Taira says, 'The *bashō* plant is versatile. We used it for wrapping – to wrap rice and legumes – and it was used instead of paper, for example, to line bamboo baskets to carry Ryūkyū indigo. It produces a type of food and medicine too.' Visitors to the **Bashōfu Textiles Museum** (芭蕉布会館; *bashofu.jp/in*) are greeted by the sight of *bashō* plantations as they drive up the coast and enter the village of Kijoka, around five minutes from Ōgimi village. There are 50 to 60 artisans working the looms or spinning thread, and many are still in training. According to Taira, it takes around a decade to garner the skills to make *bashōfu*. The museum also displays examples of the beautiful cloth with its subdued, billowing colours in shades of yellow, indigo and brown.

Places We Love to Stay

¥ Budget ¥¥ Midrange ¥¥¥ Top End

Nago
MAP p132

Hotel Route-Inn Nago ¥ Business hotel that's a cut above the rest, with an open-air hot spring bath on the roof and free breakfast with both Okinawan and egg-and-sausage-type options.

Nankai Minshuku (南海民宿) ¥ Old-school hostel with private rooms and shared facilities.

Stay Hotel ¥¥ Sparkling beachfront hotel in a quiet residential area with balconies, pool, hot tub, bicycle rentals and friendly, accommodating owners.

Motobu Peninsula

Isa Guesthouse ¥ This hostel next to farmland offers private rooms with shared facilities. The owner also runs a *karaage* (deep-fried) chicken joint.

Hilton Okinawa in Sesoko Island ¥¥¥ Resort hotel with a giant pool close to the aquarium. All rooms have gorgeous views. Tattoo friendly.

Orion Hotel Motobu Resort & Spa ¥¥¥ Luxurious resort with outdoor and indoor pools on the peninsula in Bise. The rooms have spectacular views.

Nakijin

Healing Village Konkimura (ヒーリングビレッジ魂喜村) ¥ With simple rooms and ocean views, this retreat also offers hypnotherapy and meditation.

Minshuku Awai (民宿 あわい) ¥ Guesthouse with home-cooked meals, private cabins and shared dining, lounge and washing facilities.

Woodpecker Nakijin ¥¥ Accommodation in modern, luxury RVs right by Oyadomari beach. Also has an on-site sauna and open-air bath.

Izena

Uchihana Community Centre ¥ Village-run centre offering basic rooms with shared bathrooms, mini-fridge and air-conditioning. Ask a Japanese speaker to call 0980-45-2435 to reserve, or try the Izena tourist association on 0980-45-2435.

Ie Island
MAP p132

Tsuchi no Yado ¥ Charming traditional guesthouse that caters to visitors with physical and mental disabilities, offering a safe space where they will be greeted with understanding and warmth.

Kunigami & North Yambaru
MAP p142

Soranoma Indigo (空の間 Indigo) ¥ This complex with many simple cottage accommodations resembles a mini village in the north of the peninsula.

Guest House Hechima ¥ Basic tatami rooms and a rooftop with beach and mountain views.

Yanbaru Hostel ¥ This fun and nicely renovated hostel has slight haunted-house vibes but is close to eateries.

Pension Yonoha Dake (ペンション与那覇岳) ¥¥ Simple log house accommodation where guests can enjoy stargazing and the surrounding nature.

Oku Yanbaru no Sato Guesthouses (奥やんばるの里) ¥¥ At these small cottages in the far north, the architecture is traditional but the inside is modern with amenities.

Ada Garden Hotel Okinawa ¥¥¥ A small oasis in the middle of the forest, this charming resort hotel is popular despite its remote location because of the likelihood of seeing Okinawa rail birds.

Hotel Nanmei Shinshitsu (やんばるホテル南溟森室) ¥¥¥ Luxurious designer inn with one-building rooms in different parts of the village and exclusive guides.

Okuma Private Beach & Resort ¥¥¥ Resort in front of Okuma with its own private beach and activities such as banana boats.

Higashi

Matayoshi Coffee Farm (又吉コーヒー園) ¥¥ Campsite and lovely cottage on a working farm. Visitors can also experience harvesting coffee beans from November to March.

Ōgimi
MAP p149

Bunagaya ¥ Stay at the former Kijo Kasho primary school, now converted into an art-and-craft village. The excellent Buna Sauna is next door.

Wassa Wassa (海と星空の小さな宿 WASSA WASSA) ¥¥¥ This small boutique hotel has only three accommodation options; the deluxe twin has a roof terrace with an outdoor bath. The sumptuous breakfasts use local ingredients.

*Researched by
Rob Goss*

Kume-jima

SCENIC GEM ON NAHA'S DOORSTEP

With unspoiled beaches, reef dives and oodles of traditional Okinawan culture, this lesser-known island delivers big experiences without the crowds.

Situated 100km west of Okinawa-hontō, from where it can be reached by ferry or a short flight, Kume-jima (久米島) is one of the easier island side trips from Naha. While it doesn't get the same level of attention as some other Okinawan islands, there are nonetheless plenty of reasons to consider adding it to your itinerary.

Firstly, with attractions like Eef Beach, the stunning Hate-no-hama sandbar and novel rock formations such as the Tatami-ishi, Kume-jima has scenic views to rival anywhere else in the archipelago. Even though it's a compact island, there are plenty of things to keep you occupied for a few days, from diving coral reefs to cycling along sugar-cane-lined roads to exploring the ruins of a pre-17th-century castle that delivers sweeping views over the East China Sea.

Perhaps more than anything, a trip to Kume-jima is an opportunity to slow down and get a feel for island life. That might take the form of spending a night at an *izakaya* (pub) trying the *kuruma ebi* (tiger prawns), *umi-no-budo* (sea grapes) and *awamori* (strong rice liquor); pottering around the local supermarkets; or trying your hand at *tsumugi* weaving. Here you can stay in comfort at a resort hotel but also step outside and instantly immerse yourself in the local culture and community.

For places to stay in Kume-jima, see p161

Left: Blue damselfish (p160); Above: Tatami-ishi (p158)

Find Your Way

With a circumference of 48km, Kume-jima is easy to get around by bicycle, bus or rental car. The airport is on the west coast, while most things to see and do are in the centre or the east.

BUS

The island has two bus routes. The Airport Line runs west-to-east from the airport to the Eef Beach area. The Isshu Line runs in a loop (clockwise and anti-clockwise), taking in most key locations other than the airport.

CAR

The roads here rarely feel busy, so a rental car is a relaxed way to explore Kume-jima. Several car-rental places are near the airport, including Orix, which takes online bookings in English.

BICYCLE

Being so compact, Kume-jima is great for cycling. You can pick up an English-language guide to cycling, including a list of rental stores, at the airport or the tourist information centre by Eef Beach.

Hate-no-hama, p156
Reached by boat, this 7km-long sandbar surrounded by emerald waters is Kume-jima's scenic highlight.

Maja, p159
A quiet little village with an older Okinawan vibe and a museum where you can learn about the island's silk-thread crafts.

Eef, p156
Home to one of Japan's '100 Most Beautiful Beaches' but also the island's largest selection of places to eat and stay.

Hate-no-hama (p156)

Plan Your Time

Two or three nights are ideal for a Kume-jima trip: you'll have time for some of the island's best experiences plus room to soak up the local vibes.

Pressed for Time

● With just a couple of days, base yourself by the stunning white sands of **Eef Beach** (p156), and then focus on a few of Kume-jima's top experiences: take a tour to the **Hate-no-hama sandbar** (p156), stop by **Yuimāru-kan** (p156) to learn about local silk weaving, and get a sweeping view of the island from the **Uegusuku** (p157) castle ruins.

A Longer Stay

● If you can stay a little longer, you can enjoy Kume-jima in a slow, unscripted way. You could have a lazy day on the **beach** (p156) or try a gentle **bike ride** (p159) to take in some of the island's everyday moments. If you do want to schedule something adventurous, a few companies offer **diving tours** (p160) in the crystal-clear surrounding waters.

Seasonal Highlights

SPRING

Warm, sunny weather is a lovely backdrop for events like the triathlon in March and April's firefly festival.

SUMMER

Hot, humid and with typhoons possible – peak tourism season is also when the Kume-jima festival and sumo tournaments take place.

AUTUMN

With fewer visitors, Kume-jima feels quieter, yet the weather is warm and sunny; conditions are ideal for cycling, boat tours and diving.

WINTER

Low season can bring discounts, but some businesses close or operate less often. Late January sees some early cherry blossoms.

155

GETTING TO KUME-JIMA

From Naha's Tomari Port, Kume Shōsen ferries leave for Kume-jima at 9am and 2pm every day, except Monday (only 9am), taking 3½ hours. Ferries in the opposite direction leave at 9am and 2pm daily (only 9am on Monday).

From Naha airport there are six to eight flights daily, taking 30 to 40 minutes, with Ryūkyū Air Commuter and Japan Transocean Air, both of which are part of the JAL group. In summer JAL also offers one daily direct flight to and from Tokyo. Buses from the airport are scheduled to leave 15 to 20 minutes after each plane arrives, but they don't wait if a flight is delayed. If that happens, you'll be in for a long wait or will need a taxi.

Beach Days
The white sands of Eef

On the eastern side of the island, **Eef Beach** (*free*) takes its name from 'white' in the local dialect, a reference to the fine white sand that, coupled with clear emerald waters, has earned this shore a place on the Japanese government's 'Top 100 Beaches' list. Stretching a couple of kilometres, Eef is big enough to avoid feeling crowded even in peak season, and with plenty of places to eat or buy picnic items nearby, it's ideal for a long, lazy beach day. The water is shallow and often calm too, so it's also great for swimming or snorkelling.

To get here, jump aboard the Isshu loop bus to **Eef Information Plaza** (where you'll also find the tourist information office) or Eef Beach Hotel. If you're driving, you'll find a large car park near the main entrance to the beach.

Maroon Yourself on a Sandbar
Take a tour to Hate-no-hama

While the scenic sands of Eef are easy to get to, the even more stunning **Hate-no-hama** (*tour prices vary*) takes a bit of effort to reach – though the effort is more than rewarded. After a 20- to 30-minute boat trip, you'll arrive at a pure-white sandbar that snakes for 7km, devoid of trees or any other features (except a Portaloo) beyond sand and sea. It almost feels as though you've been marooned here. You can only reach the sandbar as part of a tour, and they come in various configurations, ranging from half a day to a full day and often including activities such as diving and snorkelling. Some of the boats are glass bottomed, so en route you can get a glimpse of the tropical fish that inhabit Kume-jima's waters.

The best starting point is to ask about tours at the tourist information booth at the airport or the tourist information centre at Eef Information Plaza, although many hotels can also arrange tours. Whatever you go for, bear a few things in mind. There's no shade, no changing areas and nowhere to buy food and drink on Hate-no-hama, so come dressed for the beach and be sure to pack everything you'll need.

Island Threads
Silk weaving at the Yuimāru-kan

For more than 500 years, people on Kume-jima have been making a silk pongee fabric called *tsumugi*. The fabric is crafted, patterned and dyed by hand using all-natural materials. At the **Yuimāru-kan** (ユイマール館; *adult/child ¥200/100*) in Maja village, you can learn about the production process, including how some *tsumugi* items are dyed with muds to produce a reddish-black colour, and others are created using a patterning technique similar to tie-dyeing. You can also see examples of finished cloth and the products made with it.

What makes a visit here so worthwhile, though, are the workshops. From 10am to 11.30am or 1.30pm to 3.30pm every day except Wednesday, it's possible to sign up on the day for

View from Uegusuku-ato

a variety of hands-on experiences, including weaving a small coaster using a hand loom *(¥3000/2800 adult/child),* tie-dyeing a bandanna *(¥3400/3200 adult/child)* and dyeing a silk shawl *(from ¥6000, depending on the size).*

Stand Atop the Island

Visit the Uegusuku castle ruins

In the north of the island, at the summit of 310m Mt Uegusuku – Kume-jima's highest spot – are the crumbling stone remains of a castle that's believed to have been in use from around the late 14th to 16th centuries, when Kume-jima was part of the independent Ryūkyū Kingdom. While the ruins of **Uegusuku-ato** *(free)* are not the easiest place to get to on Kume-jima without a car, what with the nearest bus stop (Hiyajo Banta) being a few kilometres away on much lower ground, it's worth the effort for the views alone. From the

WHY I LOVE KUME-JIMA

Rob Goss, Lonely Planet writer
Something that always gets me about visiting Okinawa are the vibrant flowers in bloom. It's such a contrast to the grey corner of Tokyo I call home. Kume-jima is no exception. Year-round the subtropical climate is warm enough for hibiscus and bougainvillea to add colour to the island, while February and March see a variety of camellia called Kume kurenai and April to May is when white Easter lilies flower. From late September to late October, look out for golden spider lilies. From late January to early February, prepare for the gorgeous sight of the island's cherry blossoms in bloom, months before the annual pink wave of *sakura* appears in Kyoto and Tokyo.

EATING AND DRINKING BY EEF BEACH: OUR PICKS

Maruko: This bright, airy *izakaya* specialises in *yakitori* skewers but also serves local specialities like *kuruma ebi* and *awamori. 6-11pm Tue-Sun* ¥¥

Sunrise: Coffee, cocktails and dishes like taco rice are on the menu, but it's the fruity crepes that are really worth coming for. *noon-midnight Mon-Sat* ¥

Kameyoshi: A locals' favourite where you can sample classic Okinawan dishes à la carte or fill up on good-value set meals. *11.30am-2pm & 5.30-11pm Wed-Mon* ¥¥

Nijiya: With interiors heavy on Americana, Nijiya has a menu centred on juicy hamburg steaks made with Okinawan Agū pork. *11.30am-2pm & 5-10.30pm Fri-Wed* ¥¥

KUME-JIMA'S BEST LOCAL PRODUCE

Awamori: Two local distilleries, Kume-jima no Kumesen and Yoneshima Shuzo, make this strong, clear spirit, which can be drunk on ice, mixed with water or soda, or used in cocktails.

Umi-no-budō: Called sea grapes (or green caviar) in English, these tiny balls of seaweed deliver little bursts of ocean flavour on the tongue.

Kuruma ebi: Also known as Japanese tiger prawns, these are cultivated in deep sea water off Kume-jima and are renowned for their sweetness.

Jam: Try sweet-potato, mango or pineapple jam, made here without preservatives or artificial flavours.

Miso cookies: Made with locally produced miso, these sweet cookies are a classic Kume-jima souvenir.

Umi-no-budō (sea grapes)

castle's tiered levels you get a 360-degree vista over the entire island that reaches out over the East China Sea and peeks into a nearby military base.

If you're keen to discover more about Kume-jima's past, there are a total of 13 ruins scattered around the island (the tourist information centre at Eef Information Plaza has an English map with many of them marked), or you could visit the **Kume-jima Museum** in the town by the island's main port. Arguably the best old site, however, is the **former Uezu Residence**. Built in the 1750s, it's a lovely example of a traditional Ryūkyū home. At research time it was closed for renovation with no reopening date set, but keep an eye out for it when you visit.

Natural Lava Art on the Coast

See the tatami rocks

A couple of kilometres up the coast from Eef Beach (p156), the tiny island of **Ōjima** is connected to Kume-jima by a bridge that passes over strikingly clear waters. There are a few attractions here, including a small **sea turtle museum** and a swimming beach, but the reason most people stop by is to see the **Tatami-ishi** *(free)*, a natural formation of pentagonal, hexagonal and octagonal rocks along the shore that are said to resemble tatami mats – although that is a bit of a stretch of the imagination.

While they look like flat rocks, that's just the exposed top; they're actually long, columnar joints that were formed approximately 600 million years ago when andesite magma cooled and solidified near the seafloor. For the best view, come at low tide (or at least avoid high tide). If you aren't driving, the Isshu loop bus stops here, though you'll be waiting a while between buses. Alternatively, you could stop by as part of an island bike ride to combine the Tatami-ishi with some weaving

CYCLE KUME-JIMA'S EASTERN SIDE

Take an easy, flat ride that starts at the island's best beach but then delivers glimpses of everyday Kume-jima life.

START	END	LENGTH
Eef Beach	Eef Beach	12km, 2hr

From the ❶ **Eef Beach area** (p156), start by heading northeast along the main road (Rte 245), passing sugar-cane fields and the island's baseball ground, before coming to a well-signposted right turn that leads to tiny Ōjima island. Cross the bridge here and you'll soon be at the ❷ **Tatami-ishi rock formation**. From here, backtrack over the bridge, turn right and follow Rte 245 as it loops around the coast to ❸ **Maja village**, where the quiet main street will take you past several traditional homes. If you want to have a look inside one of these, stop at the modest ❹ **Nakahara's Birthplace**, then keep going up the main street to the ❺ **Yuimāru-kan** (p156) to learn about the local *tsumugi* silk weaving – or even try a workshop. Next, head back down the road until you reach a fork, where you can turn right onto Rte 89. After a few kilometres you'll be in a small town called Nakazato, where it's worth a look at the ❻ **Coop supermarket** to check out the local produce and maybe pick up a foodie souvenir (the island-made jams are great). After the Coop, take the next left and you'll soon be cycling through a swathe of sugar-cane fields that will lead you all the way back to Eef Beach.

SUGAR, SUGAR & MORE SUGAR

You can't miss the sugar cane on Kume-jima – there are vast fields of it growing all over the island, and for generations growing and processing the cane has been an important part of the local economy. The crops are harvested in the cooler winter months, before which the sugar cane (called *satōkibi* in Japanese) will have grown taller than an adult and in places gives the island a wild, overgrown look. What's it used for? Lots of it is sold and shipped as rich and malty dark sugar, which retains more minerals than white sugar, but some finds its way into sweet treats on the island like *kokutō* (brown sugar) cookies.

Mīfugā

at the Yuimāru-kan (p156) and a look at everyday island life.

You'll come across many other natural rock formations while exploring Kume-jima. On the northern coast, the **Mīfugā** (ミーフガー) rocks form an archway through which the sun sets in mid- to late July, while at the southernmost tip of the island the **Tori-no-Kuchi** (鳥の口) is said to resemble a bird's open peak pointing up to the sky. Elsewhere are rock pools, like the **Tropical Fish Pool** a few kilometres along the coast from Maja, where at low tide you can see colourful sea life such as blue damselfish and butterflyfish.

Take a Dive

Explore Kume-jima's reefs

With clear waters and a diverse underwater ecosystem that teems with tropical fish, Kume-jima has a reputation for great diving, although you can also just snorkel off beaches like Eef (p156) and Hate-no-hama (p156). Depending on the diving spot, you might come across hammerheads, whale sharks and sea turtles, see schools of barracuda, or maybe even spot a manta ray on a winter dive. There are several diving shops and tour operators, including **Shirahama Marine** (*shirahama-marine.com; prices vary*), which offers a 'snuba' course that kids can take part in. A good first stop is the tourist information centre by Eef Beach, where you can get info on diving conditions, equipment rentals and tours that do or don't require a diving licence. Expect to pay between ¥15,000 and ¥20,000 for a tour.

Places We Love to Stay

¥ **Budget** ¥¥ **Midrange** ¥¥¥ **Top End**

Eastern Kume-jima

Ōjima Campground ¥ By the Tatami-ishi (p158), this campsite is the cheapest option on Kume-jima. Facilities are basic, but it does have a few rental tents (book in advance).

Watermark Hotel ¥¥ This friendly resort hotel is by Eef Beach (though it lacks ocean views). Extra touches include poolside barbecues in summer and paid bicycle rental.

EN Resort Eef Beach Hotel ¥¥ Smart EN Resort overlooks Eef Beach and has a pool, a shop, a bar, and an activity centre that can arrange tours from July to September.

Bears Stay Kumejima Eef Beach ¥¥ A self-catering option, Bears Stay has simply designed twins and family rooms, each with their own small kitchen and laundry area.

Shinminka Villa ¥¥¥ Two sleek rental villas 1km from Eef feature gorgeous wooden interiors and fully equipped kitchens. They're ideal for self-catering in comfort.

Western Kume-jima

Kumi-no-Eki ¥ A collection of old shipping containers turned into hostel-like accommodation, Kumi-no-Eki has friendly staff who also run snorkelling tours.

Cypress Resort ¥¥ This plush resort near the airport features pools, beach access, ocean views and spacious rooms. It's inconvenient to reach without a car.

Tori-no-Kuchi

For places to stay in Kerama Islands, see p171

Above: Zamami-jima (p166); Right: Humpback whale (p169), Tokashiki-jima

Researched by
Benedict Walker

Kerama Islands

PARADISE WITHIN EASY REACH

Awe-inspiring nature at its finest, the Kerama Islands are a short ferry hop from Naha but worlds apart in every other sense.

Covering 900 sq km of ocean, Kerama-shotō National Park (慶良間諸島国立公園; Kerama-shotō Kokuritsu Kōen) also encompasses 36 tropical islands with a total land area of 35 sq km. People live on only four of the islands, Zamami-jima, Tokashiki-jima, Aka-jima and Geruma-jima, and their year-round population totals fewer than 1000.

On the archipelago's larger islands, wide arcs of coastal shore dusted with powdery white sand are punctuated by sheltered, picture-perfect coves fringed with subtropical forests that are bursting with biodiversity.

The abundance of life on land is a mere prelude to the natural bounty beneath the sea. Famed for their brilliant blue colour, affectionately referred to as 'Kerama blue', the park's pristine waters are home to more than 250 kinds of coral, among which thrive more than 350 species of reef fish. From December to May, humpback whales calve and green sea turtles hatch here. Snorkelling tours among the turtles and whale-watching cruises from Tokashiki provide an unforgettable window on these marvellous marine creatures.

Hosting a convergence of precious micro-environments teeming with life unique to this part of the Pacific Ocean, the Kerama Islands are truly something to behold – and they're just 30km from central Naha. Surrender yourself to the sea and let the beauty of Kerama-shotō National Park nurture your spirit.

THE MAIN AREAS

ZAMAMI-JIMA
Exploration, relaxation and aquatic action. **p166**

TOKASHIKI-JIMA
Accessible haven of fun. **p169**

Find Your Way

Ferries to the islands and between them run like a well-oiled machine. Most visitors get around on rental bikes and scooters, but local buses, shuttles and car rental are also options.

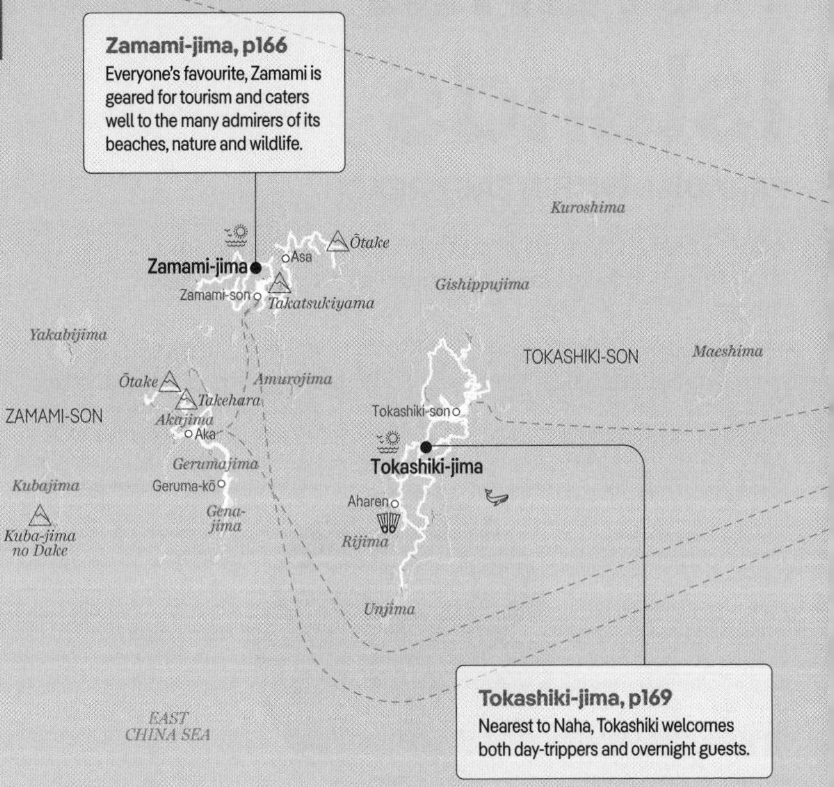

Zamami-jima, p166
Everyone's favourite, Zamami is geared for tourism and caters well to the many admirers of its beaches, nature and wildlife.

Tokashiki-jima, p169
Nearest to Naha, Tokashiki welcomes both day-trippers and overnight guests.

CAR

Cars are convenient if you're travelling in groups or planning thorough investigations of everywhere possible, but the costs of renting on island or bringing a car over on the ferry can be prohibitive.

BICYCLE

Bikes are a great way to get around the islands' low-lying areas, but stretches of hilly terrain can make traditional riding hard going. E-bikes give you a bit of extra oomph.

YOVEN/SHUTTERSTOCK

Aharen beach (p169), Tokashiki-jima

Plan Your Time

Most visitors to Okinawa come out to the Kerama Islands, whether by private vessel for a day trip or by ferry for a few days (or perhaps a lifetime) of exploring.

Get Wet

● The **Kerama Kayak Center** (p166) in Zamami will paddle you out to secret coves on uninhabited isles. On Aka-jima you can flop on a deserted shore or get PADI certified with **Marine Seasir** (p167). Tokashiki is the place for aquatic delights that include snorkelling with sea turtles. If it's high-octane water sports you crave, visit Tokashiki's **Aharen Beach** (p169).

Stay Dry

● If you prefer to enjoy the ocean from a distance, there's still plenty you can do on the islands. Join a **whale-watching cruise** (p169), island-hop by ferry, grab a bike and explore Geruma-jima's **historic buildings** (p168) or hike up any of Zamami's three **observatories** (lookouts; p168) for stunning coastal views by day and a carpet of twinkling stars at night.

Seasonal Highlights

SPRING

Spring means milder temps and fewer crowds. It's the best time to see sea turtles in their natural habitat.

SUMMER

Summer means festivals, fireworks and fun. Sunbathe, snorkel and make new friends from around the world.

AUTUMN

Rates and temps drop, but typhoons can spoil the fun. Watch weather forecasts to avoid being stranded.

WINTER

Winter makes you work for its rewards, but they're plentiful: whale watching, deserted beaches and low prices.

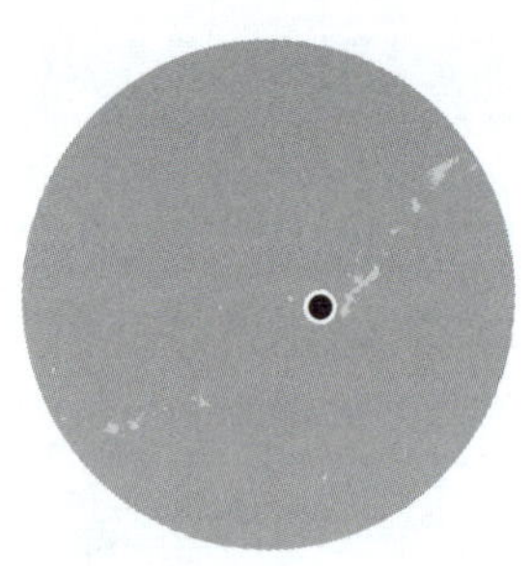

Zamami-jima

AQUATIC ACTION | EXPLORATION | RELAXATION

GETTING AROUND

Zamami has free bikes, rental e-bikes, scooters, tuk-tuks and tiny cars. For most visitors, getting to the island's three hilltop observation points or the island's more secluded beaches is an effort without motorised wheels.

The main beaches of the Keramas' most popular island, Zamami-jima (座間味島), are located within walking distance of the island's charming eponymous village, which wraps around the port and wends its way up the hillside. The village has a mix of local housing, guesthouses and visitor accommodation and most of the island's modest collection of shops, services, *shokudō* (inexpensive restaurants) and *izakaya* (pubs). The shallows around the island drop off quickly to reveal vibrant reefs perfect for swimming, snorkelling and beginner dives. There's no shortage of ways to get on the water, from SUP to kayaking, glass-bottom-boats and, from December to May, whale-watching cruises.

Neighbouring Aka-jima is best known for its gorgeous, 1km-long Nishibama beach, which is often deliciously deserted, especially in the low season. You'll be rewarded in serenity for the little extra effort required to get there. Just don't miss your ferry ride back!

Hit the Water

Go with the flow

Okinawa's islands are significantly affected by the tides, and the Keramas are no exception. When the tide is out, the wet sands are strewn with coral, but at high tide the allure of the famous Kerama blue is fully on show. Tidal variations can also cause dangerous rip currents: always check in with locals to be sure you're aware of concerns at a particular location.

Near every beach you'll find outfitters renting gear from towels to beach chairs to floaties, and there'll often be someone selling jet-boat rides, renting jet skis or running parasailing trips. Kayaking in the shallows is a great way to hit the water without getting wet. Both **Kerama Kayak Centre** and **Zamami Tour Operation** can take you to offshore Gahi-jima and Agenashiku-jima and arrange snorkelling trips.

If you're interested in diving, scuba certification or gear rental or want to enlist the services of a local guide, check in

☑ TOP TIP

Ferries and beds book up fast in the busy summer season (June to August). Book ahead if you can.

● SIGHTS
1 Marilyn Statue
2 Nishibama Beach
3 Shiro Statue
4 Takara Residence
5 World Peace Memorial

● ACTIVITIES
6 Kerama Kayak Centre
7 Marine Seasir Aka
8 Zamami Tour Operation

● SLEEPING
9 Ama Beach Youth Travel
  Village
10 Cha Villa
11 Joy Joy
12 Kerama Blue Resort
13 Minshuku Summer
   House Yū Yū
14 Zamamia International
   Guesthouse

● EATING
15 105 Grocery Store
16 Little Kitchen
17 Marumiya

with the experts at **Marine Seasir Aka**. They can also hook you up with a bed for the night.

Alternative Aka-jima

Little island, big heart

The smallest of the Keramas' inhabited islands, Aka-jima is loved by many as an alternative to the high-season crowds on Zamami and Tokashiki islands. Its beaches are equally beautiful, if not more so, but they're a little less convenient to reach. Aka's **Nishibama Beach** is about 30 minutes' walk from the port; there's one regular ferry per day to/from Naha (¥2150; *1½ hours*), up to two high-speed boats (¥3200; *50 minutes*) and, weather permitting, usually four interisland runs between Aka and Zamami (¥210 to ¥300; *10 to 15 minutes*).

WHY I LOVE ZAMAMI-JIMA

Benedict Walker, Lonely Planet writer

As an Australian who grew up enjoying regular family holidays at some of the best beaches in New South Wales, I know a good stretch of sand when I see one. When I come to Zamami-jima and dive into its famously blue waters, I get that precious feeling of being an excited kid again, in awe of the beauty of the ocean. The magic of the island lies not just in its gorgeous beaches (especially the secluded ones) but in its unique overall vibe. Here the mood is relaxed and there's a feeling of being 'away'. Stay a few days and you'll know why I'm not the only one who's fallen for Zamami.

Takara Residence

Aka is linked by road bridge to Geruma island and onwards to Fukaji island, where you'll find the tiny, disused Kerama Airport. Its runway takes up most of the island, which is otherwise uninhabited. Unless you're very fit, you'll need a car to reach Aka's other beaches, which are usually delightfully deserted, or any of its four observation decks – set high in the hills, they afford incredible views. Aka's gentle activities include a stroll around the little village by the port and swimming among myriad multicoloured corals. For a quirkier option, be sure to meet **Shiro** and learn of his enduring love for **Marilyn**. Theirs is Okinawa's most famous love story – it even made it to the silver screen in 1988 in *I Want to Meet Marilyn*.

Freedom to Roam

Explore the islands by car

Having your own wheels opens up more dining and accommodation options and is the best way to get a sense of local life away from the well-trafficked port areas. You'll be able to explore the **observatories** high in the hills above each island, which offer stunning vistas and cool respite from the summer heat and are wonderfully quiet and peaceful. A car is also the only way you'll get to Geruma-jima to visit the **Takara Residence** (Captain's House). Also on Geruma, you can wander through the forest befriending inquisitive endemic deer and deepening your understanding of Okinawa's role in WWII at the **World Peace Memorial**.

 **EATING IN THE KERAMAS**

Marumiya: Cheap, delicious, friendly and popular, this Zamami institution serves Okinawan and Japanese dishes. *11am-3pm & 6-10pm Thu-Tue* ¥

105 Grocery Store: Zamami's only 'supermarket' has *bentō* boxes, sandwiches and plentiful supplies for beach picnicking. *8am-7pm Mon-Sun* ¥

Little Kitchen: Visitors from all around the world rave about this place serving chef-standard international dishes. *6-11pm Thu-Tue* ¥¥

Sunny Coral: At Tokashiki Port, this little joint does great breakfasts and sells deli items for picnics. *8am-2pm Fri-Wed* ¥

Tokashiki-jima

BEACHES | WATER SPORTS | MARINE FRIENDS

The largest of the inhabited Kerama Islands at just over 7km long and 3km at its widest point, Tokashiki-jima (渡嘉敷島) is closest to Naha as the crow flies. The trip from Naha to Tokashiki by high-speed ferry will take you just 40 minutes. Unless you have your own boat, it's a little trickier to get between Tokashiki and the tight-knit trio of Zamami, Aka and Geruma than it is to travel among those three islands. You can get a local ferry from Tokashiki to Zamami, but officially a reservation 24 hours in advance is required. If it's a few days of sunbathing and soaking up the delights of secluded island life you want, Tokashiki is your place. Here you can also join a deep-sea snorkelling tour to swim with turtles and, from January to March, a whale-watching cruise to glimpse majestic humpbacks.

GETTING AROUND

An infrequent local bus connects the island's two settlements. Tokashiki is big enough that you'll need motorised transport if you really want to explore beyond the main sights.

Humpback Tracking

Catch whales on their world tour

Between January and March, Okinawa is a nursery for humpback whale calves. In summer the whales split their time between Russia and Alaska, where they go to feed, before heading south to Hawaii and Okinawa for breeding and raising their young. If you're lucky you'll spot a baby or juvenile humpback sticking close to its mother. It's thrilling to watch the adult whales breach (jump out of the water), spin and spout. Wear waterproof outer layers and make sure your camera is also waterproofed. **Cerulean Blue** (*cerulean-blue.co.jp/en; adult/child ¥5800/4800*) runs tours departing from Chatan and Naha on Okinawa's main island. Boats travel about an hour to the coast of the Kerama Islands, where pods are often spotted. If you get seasick, be sure to use acupressure bands or take antinausea medication. Some tour operators sell single doses at check-in for a small fee.

A Day at the Beach

Relax or get sporty

Tokashiki's two main beaches, **Tokashiku** and **Aharen**, are a little removed from the ferry terminal but can be reached by

☑ TOP TIP

If time is short but you're keen to visit Tokashiki, consider a day trip by boat from Naha.

- **SIGHTS**
  1. Aharen Beach
  2. Tokashiku Beach
- **SLEEPING**
  3. Kerama Terrace
  4. Kerama-sō
  5. Pension Sea Friend
  6. Tokashiku Marin Village
- **EATING**
  7. Sunny Coral
- **TRANSPORT**
  8. Kariyushi Rentasābisu

BOX JELLYFISH

Every swimming beach you visit will alert you to the potential dangers of marine stingers, particularly *habu kurage* (box jellyfish). The threat is real: the incredibly painful *habu kurage* venom can cause paralysis and cardiac arrest in humans, although deaths are uncommon. Wherever possible, swim in netted areas of designated swimming beaches. Sadly, this means avoiding many of the 'secret' beaches you're likely to discover as you explore the Keramas. If you're determined to swim in a non-patrolled zone, check with locals to see if jellyfish are about. If you think you've been stung, stay calm and seek immediate help: if you can, rinse the area with vinegar or sea water.

local bus or rental car, bike, e-bike or scooter. Both beaches have all manner of water-sport, kayak, SUP and equipment rentals, activities like jet boats and Jet Skis, and personalised and small-group tour operators. **Kariyushi Rentasābisu** rents cars at the ferry terminal.

Turtle Power

Deep-sea snorkelling in Tokashiki

You can have a wonderful time snorkelling off one of Tokashiki's white-sand beaches, but for a truly sublime experience book a deep-sea snorkelling tour. Outfits such as **Marine House Aharen** (*aharen.com/en; 2hr tours from ¥7000*) take guests to two mid-ocean snorkel spots where a dazzling array of rainbow fish dart and dive in shimmering turquoise waters.

Kerama-shotō National Park and Tokashiki-jima in particular are known for their large population of green sea turtles, and knowledgable guides lead you to places where you're likely to spot and even swim near them. Tours include life vest, fins and snorkel masks. They'll even photograph you (and your turtle pals) underwater using a GoPro and send you the pics as a souvenir.

Places We Love to Stay

¥ **Budget** ¥¥ **Midrange** ¥¥¥ **Top End**

Zamami-jima   MAP p167

Ama Beach Youth Travel Village ¥ This is the fancy name given to the Ama beach campground. BYO tent.

Cha Villa ¥ *'Cha-bira'* means 'I'm home!' in the local dialect. Its attached cafe serves eggy breakfasts and light meals. Japanese- and international-style rooms are available, all with private bathroom and kitchenette.

Joy Joy ¥ In the northwestern corner of the village, this little inn has international- and Japanese-style rooms surrounding a small garden. It's annexed to one of the island's favourite *izakaya*.

Minshuku Summer House Yū Yū ¥ This family-run *minshuku* (guesthouse) has whimsical marine artwork on its outer walls; quiet, comfortable Japanese- and international-style rooms with private bathrooms; and a communal rooftop deck to enjoy.

Zamamia International Guesthouse ¥ The friendly owner of this popular backpackers' place often organises barbecue dinners for guests. It's roomy, but you won't get much rest when the joint is hopping. Bathrooms are shared.

Kerama Blue Resort ¥¥ One of the better accommodation choices on Zamami, with a great location, views and updated rooms, Kerama Blue is nonetheless not really a resort. Stay at Onna (p117) on Okinawa Island if that's what you're looking for.

Aka-jima

Hanamuro Inn ¥¥ All six rooms at this cosy summer-season inn just up from the beach share bathrooms and a terrace.

Hanamuro Inter-Islander's Hotel ¥¥ Interestingly housed in a marine-biology research facility, the rooms of this private hotel set back from the village are quiet, spacious and comfortable. Each has a private balcony perfect for watching the sunrise with your morning coffee. There's a free shuttle to Nishibama Beach, and some meals are available.

Kawai Diving ¥¥ Perched just above Maehama Beach on Aka's south coast, this inn has simple rooms, a family atmosphere and a relaxed beachside location. English-speaking staff are happy to tell guests about the island and take them diving (including equipment rental one/two dives ¥7000/11,000).

Marine House Seasir ¥¥ At the western end of the main village, this property is used primarily for dive groups but has clean and spacious international- and Japanese-style rooms just a minute's amble from the beach.

Tokashiki-jima   MAP p170

Kerama-sō ¥ Set back in the village of Aharen, this raggedy, time-tested *minshuku* offers basic Japanese-style rooms.

Pension Sea Friend ¥ Simple and cheery, Sea Friend offers comfortable rooms, diving and snorkelling trips, rental cars, a good buffet breakfast at its restaurant across the street, and free shuttles to and from Tokashiki port.

Tokashiku Marin Village ¥¥ The best thing about this friendly place, popular with divers and diving groups, is its fabulous location on a beautiful, well-tended stretch of private beach. There's nothing much to do here but swim, snorkel and dive. It's dated by cutting-edge design standards but comfortable and well maintained. Both international-style and Japanese-style rooms are available.

Kerama Terrace ¥¥¥ Whilst not a luxury property by Okinawan standards, this chic boutique option in Aharen village offers arguably the island's plushest accommodation apart from private Airbnb rentals.

Researched by
Wendy Yanagihara

Miyako Islands

DREAMY BEACHES AND SUBLIME REEF

Myriad marine life, wind- and paddle-powered sports, spiritual sites and rural tranquility await the curious who venture beyond the archipelago's enticing beaches.

Considered one of the most beautiful places in Japan, the Miyako Islands (宮古列島; Miyako-rettō) are a group of eight mostly flat islands formed by coral uplift. Composed largely of Pleistocene-era reefs, this foundation of porous limestone filters rainwater and runoff before it enters the ocean, lending to the exceptionally clear waters for which Miyako-rettō is famed. Those shades of ethereal blues and emerald greens contrast with the islands' white-sand beaches, making them a popular beach holiday destination for Japanese travellers for decades. They're now on the radar of increasing numbers of international visitors.

The archipelago's main island, Miyako-jima (宮古島; Miyako Island) is the roughly triangular 'mainland' of the island group, connected by bridge to four of its neighbouring islands. North of the archipelago lies the spectacular 17km-wide Yabiji Reef, the largest coral reef system in Japan, whose waters are blessed with amazing clarity. Most of the islands are dominated by agriculture, with sugar cane the most ubiquitous crop. While their reefs and coastal lagoons are the prime draw for swimming amid colourful tropical fish, sea turtles and anemones, the islands also contain mangroves, marshy wetlands and intriguing caves. Island traditions endure in regular ceremonies and celebrations varying from island to island, as do the *hōgen* (dialects) branching off from Myakufutsu, the indigenous language of bewitching Miyako-jima.

THE MAIN AREAS

MIYAKO-JIMA
'Mainland' of
the archipelago.
p178

IKEMA ISLAND
Quiet beaches
south of Yabiji Reef.
p191

IRABU & SHIMOJI ISLANDS
Spiritual sites and
tranquil spaces. **p194**

KURIMA ISLAND
Rural outpost
for sunning and
snorkelling. **p197**

For places to stay in Miyako Islands, see p199

THE GUIDE

MIYAKO ISLANDS

MARTIN VOELLER/GETTY IMAGES

Left: Higashi-Hennazaki Lighthouse (p187), Miyako-jima; Above: Yabiji Reef (p182), Miyako-jima

173

Find Your Way

The fourth-largest island in Okinawa Prefecture, Miyako-jima represents the main island of this archipelago of dreamy white-sand beaches. Flights to the island group land here at Miyako Airport, while bridges connect Miyako-jima with several outlying islands.

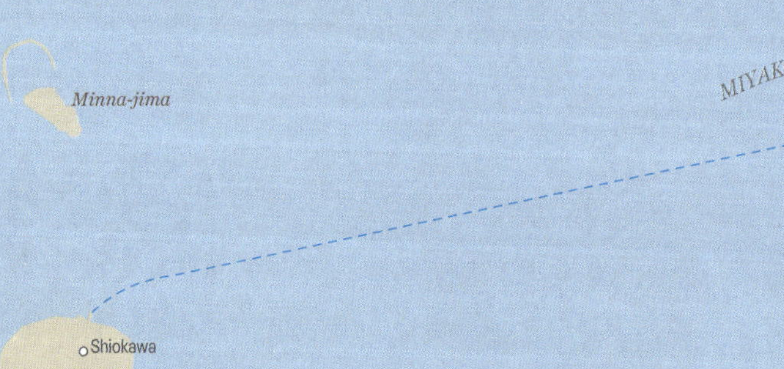

Irabu & Shimoji Islands, p194

Spiritual sites are found in limestone sinkhole pools and tsunami-tossed boulders, while the architecture of traditional living still stands amid a contemporary agricultural landscape and fishing port.

CAR

Because Miyako-jima and its connected islands are fairly large, renting a car affords maximum flexibility to explore. Reserve a car in advance, especially in high season. Multiple agencies are based near the airport.

BUS

Several bus companies serve Miyako-jima and Ikema and Irabu Islands. A loop route on Miyako-jima stops at Miyako Airport and runs into the main port town, Hirara. Buses don't extend to Shimoji or Kurima Islands.

FERRY

Small ferries make the short trip to Ōgami Island several times daily from Shimajiri Port in the northeast of Miyako-jima. To get to Tarama Island, ferries depart from Hirara Port from Monday to Saturday.

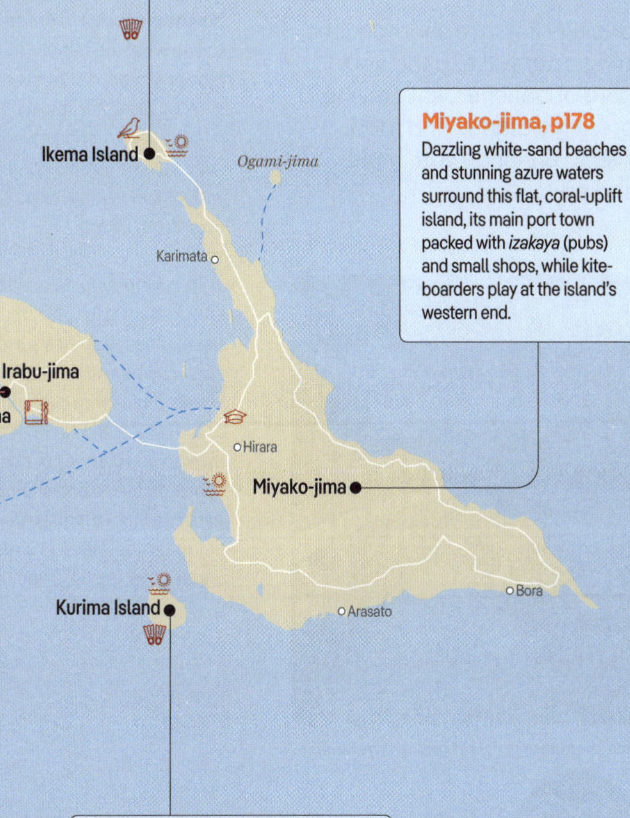

Ikema Island, p191

Yabiji, Japan's largest reef system, lies north of Ikema, where snorkelling beaches abound and Okinawa Prefecture's largest wetland provides refuge to migrating birds.

Miyako-jima, p178

Dazzling white-sand beaches and stunning azure waters surround this flat, coral-uplift island, its main port town packed with *izakaya* (pubs) and small shops, while kite-boarders play at the island's western end.

Kurima Island, p197

Tiny and tranquil, Kurima is covered with sugar cane, tobacco and sunflowers, with lovely beaches to discover for relaxed snorkelling and SUP-ing.

Plan Your Days

Especially if you're short on time, renting a car will expand your sphere of beaches, snorkelling spots, juice stands and food trucks to enhance your multi-island adventures.

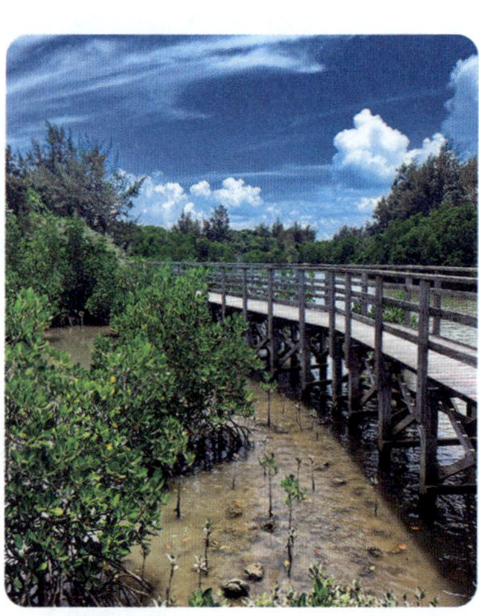

Shimajiri Mangrove Forest (p186), Miyako-jima

Two-Day Highlights

● Pick up your rental car from the airport, then pick one of Miyako-jima's iconic beaches, **Sunayama** (p182) to the north or **Yonaha-Maehama** (p184) to the south, to see what the famous Miyako blue is all about. Sun, swim and soak up the subtropical beauty at either beach, or find another that suits your mood. End your day with dinner in an alley *izakaya* in downtown Hirara.

● In the morning, take a **boat snorkelling trip** (p182) to one of the endless reef sites surrounding Miyako-jima and its nearby islands, where you'll swim over reefs of branching and table corals, diverse populations of colourful subtropical fish and anemone gardens. Cool off afterwards with a mango smoothie as you replay the underwater movie in your head.

Seasonal Highlights

The Miyako Islands are warm year-round. Typhoon season, though unpredictable, generally lasts from July through September.

APRIL

The **Miyako-jima Umibiraki** (sea opening ceremony) is held at various beaches, including **Yonaha-Maehama** (p184), on the first Sunday in April. The ceremony centres on praying for safety at sea. Festivities include traditional dance.

MAY

Goat 'sumo' tournaments called **Pinda Aasu Taikai** (p190) are held in mid-May and early October on Tarama Island. They're a local tradition on one of Miyako-rettō's most distant outposts.

JUNE

Harvest season for Miyako-jima's sweet, juicy mango peaks in June and July. Try it in everything from gelato to curry, but it's most transcendent in its purest, simplest form: sliced open and eaten off the skin.

Five Island Days

● Treat yourself to some beach time and snorkelling, with a bit of island culture to round things out. Learn how to dye, weave or cook traditional Miyako specialities at the **Miyako Craft Workshop Village** (p184), also a great option for a rainy day. Another rainy-day hit is the underwater 'aquarium' experience of **Miyakojima Marine Park** (p186), where you can look out from the fishbowl at whatever marine wildlife comes by for a look.

● Take a drive out to **Higashi-Hennazaki Lighthouse** (p187) to appreciate the coral limestone bluffs and open headland of Miyako-jima's eastern tip. Then cross one of the bridges to explore **Ikema** (p191) or **Irabu and Shimoji** (p194). Walk to spring-fed wells and fish-trap walls, and snorkel these outlying waters for more shore-accessible reef colour.

A Week Plus

● Delve deeper and spend more time lingering in the places that call to you, whether they be secluded beach coves, mysterious gem-toned pools, or dives at **Yabiji Reef** (p182), **Irabu and Shimoji** (p194) or **Kurima** (p197). Go beyond the bridges and take a ferry to **Ōgami** (p188) for a meditative walk among island gods, or truly get away to **Tarama** (p189), where goats outnumber people and agricultural island life serves as a reminder to slow way down.

● Round out your coastal adventures with what lies inland – Ikema's **wetlands** (p192) to peep geese and shorebirds, or **Shimajiri Mangrove Forest** (p186) for a walk above these protective rooted barriers against wild island weather.

JULY

The best season to dive **Yabiji Reef** (p182) and beyond lasts from May through the end of October, but the window between July and September is the ideal for calm, warm water, excellent visibility and sunny weather.

AUGUST

Though it's possible to spot sea turtles on snorkelling forays any time of year, encounters are more likely during their nesting season between May and August.

OCTOBER

In Shimajiri village the indigenous purification ritual known as **Paantu Satuupunaha** (p187) involves a trio of smelly deities muddying all souls within their reach – give it a miss if you can't go with the (mud) flow.

DECEMBER

The best season for kiteboarding is from mid-October to early March, with consistent winds making for a high percentage of rideable days, plus water temps averaging 25°C.

Miyako-jima

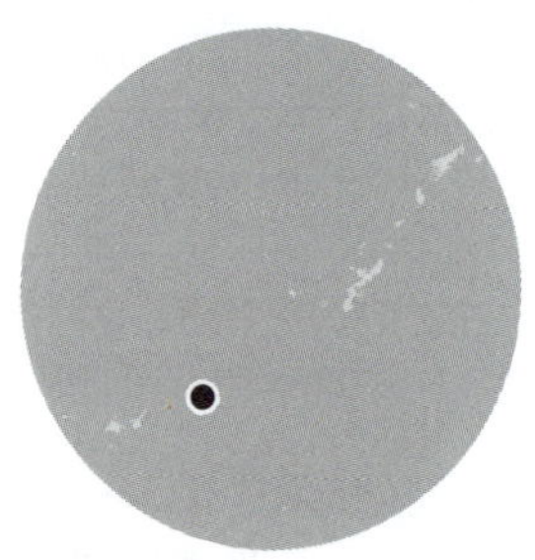

CRYSTALLINE SEAS | WHITE SANDS | WIND-POWERED PLAYGROUND

 TOP TIP

Consider buying your own gear if you plan to beach-snorkel independently. **Don Quijote** (*donki.com*) sells inexpensive snorkelling sets; water shoes are a good add-on for coral beaches and protection against hazardous sea creatures. Never snorkel alone, always stay informed of sea and site conditions, and know your own limitations.

Mellow Miyako-jima (宮古島) is a beach lover's dream. White-sand shores meet impossibly clear, aquamarine seas that stretch to the horizon, with coral reefs fanning out from the shallows. The 53,000 inhabitants of this low-lying island are concentrated in Hirara (平良港) on the west coast, only 15 minutes by car from Miyako Airport.

Divers revel in the biodiversity of Yabiji Reef in summer and in cave diving year-round, while snorkellers can find plenty to explore from beach or boat. Chasers of wind-driven pursuits such as kiteboarding and wing-foiling flock to Yonaha-Maehama Beach, whose long stretch of sand also makes it perfect for a summer beach read.

Family-friendly activities, full-service resort experiences and sites of cultural interest make Miyako-jima accessible for most. You can end your beach day in the bars and *izakaya* crammed into the alleys of downtown Hirara, but nightlife is on the tame side on this low-key isle.

GETTING AROUND

The **Miyako Island Loop Bus** (*miyakoisland bus.com*) circles from the airport to downtown Hirara through 'metropolitan' Miyako-jima. The three bus companies serving the island collectively maintain an easy-to-use website in English, complete with QR codes, timetables and fares to get you around Miyako-jima and the islands connected by bridge.

To explore the island's more remote corners in your own time, renting a car is the way to go.

Multiple companies operate near **Miyako Airport** (*miyakoap.co.jp*) and in Hirara. Even in high season it's possible to rent a car at the last minute, but your best bet is to book online ahead of arrival.

Cruise-ship arrivals portend total taxi unavailability, so if your plans involve a taxi, reserve your trip the day before to guarantee a ride.

TRACING ANCIENT PATHS IN HIRARA

Walk some of Miyako's significant spiritual and historical sites to ground yourself in island context.

START	END	LENGTH
Harimizu Utaki	Miyako Shrine	0.5km; 1hr

Begin at the sacred site **①** **Harimizu Utaki**, where it's said male deity Koitsuno and female deity Koitama descended to create Miyako-jima. Observe respectfully and absorb some of the spiritual power, but do not enter.

After paying your respects to the island's gods, walk north to the **②** **Tomb of Nakasone Tuyumya**, the powerful Miyako chieftain from the 15th to early 16th centuries. Nakasone is lauded for allowing the island to be annexed by the Ryūkyū kingdom in order to spare Miyako from the destruction the islanders' resistance would have wrought. The tomb's stepped structure incorporates design and masonry techniques from both Okinawa and Miyako, evidence of the exchange between the two cultures.

The secondary tomb nearby enshrines more of the clan's descendants. Follow the signs to the walled **③** **Atonma Tomb**, reserved for the second wives of the clan, and note its contrastingly modest design. Backtrack towards Harimizu Utaki, turning left at the **④** **cobblestone path** uphill. Built after the great earthquake of 1696, this section of the path represents only a third of what originally existed here.

At the top you'll reach the second gate and entry to **⑤** **Miyako Shrine**, established in 1590. If you wish, toss a coin into the offering box, say a prayer (there are illustrated instructions in English) and complete your spiritually minded historical stroll.

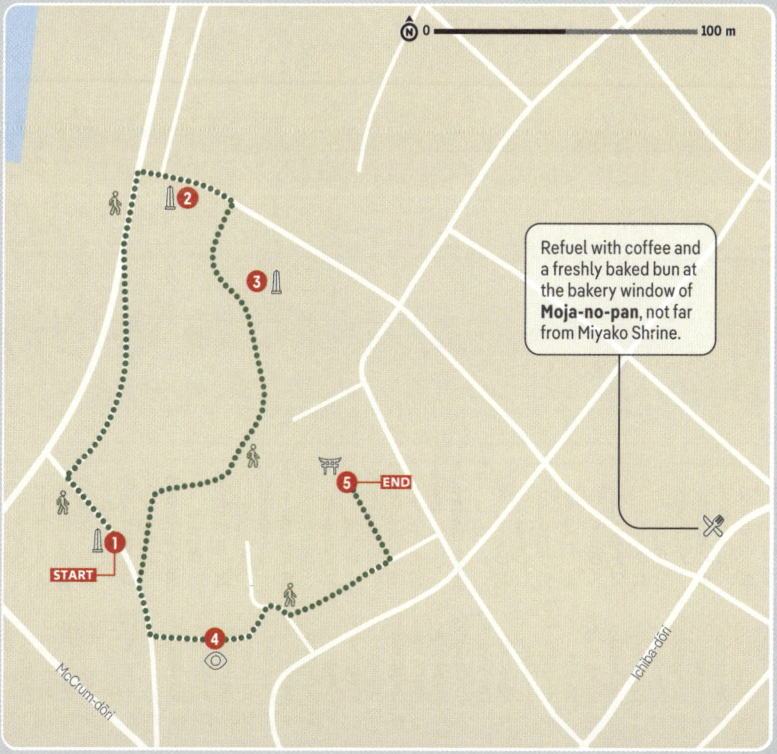

MIYAKO-JIMA

● SIGHTS
1 Aragusuku-kaigan
2 Boraga Beach
3 Higashi-Hennazaki Lighthouse
4 Imgyā Marine Garden
5 Miyakojima City Museum
6 Miyakojima City Traditional Crafts Centre
7 Miyakojima Marine Park
8 Shigira Beach
9 Shimajiri Mangrove Forest
10 Sunayama Beach
11 Yabiji Reef
12 Yonaha-Maehama
13 Yoshino Beach

● ACTIVITIES
14 Blue Honu
15 Diving Service Hekikai
16 M-air
17 Miyako Craft Workshop Village
18 Miyakojima Guide Ya-San
19 Opengate Miyakojima
20 Penguin Divers
21 Sea-One
22 Shigira Gold Onsen

● SLEEPING
23 Grand Bleu Gamin
24 Guesthouse KAZE
see 16 Guesthouse Miyakojima
25 Hotel 385
26 Hotel California Miyakojima Resort
27 Kataaki-no-Sato
28 Miyakojima Guesthouse Re-Spect
29 Zumi Terrace

● EATING
30 Asian Izakaya Kuusu
31 Harry's Garlic Shrimp Truck
32 Koja Soba-ya
33 Pari Kitchen
34 Parlor Red Dragon

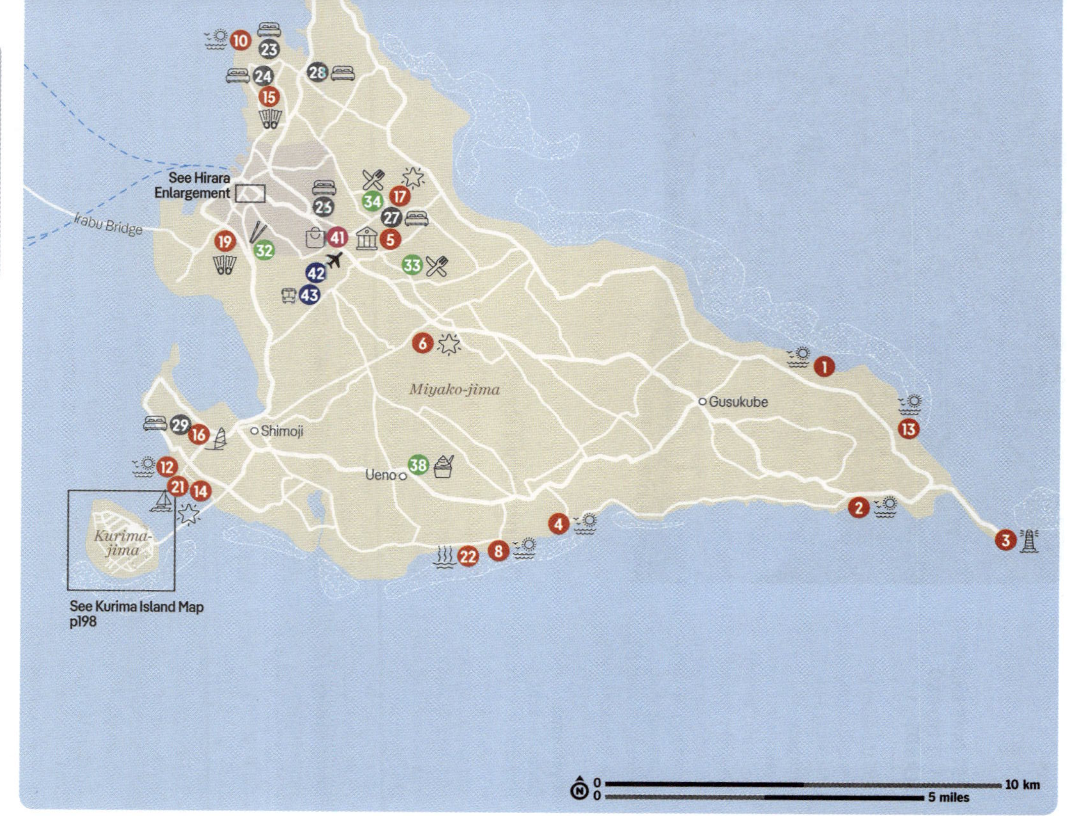

35 Pōcha Tatsuya
36 Ricco Gelato
37 Shikishima
see 6 Tida Factory
38 Utopia Farm Miyakojima
39 Yukishio

DRINKING & NIGHTLIFE
40 Island Brewing

SHOPPING
41 Don Quijote

TRANSPORT
42 Miyako Airport
43 Miyako Island Loop Bus

See Hirara Enlargement
Irabu Bridge
Miyako-jima
Gusukube
Shimoji
Ueno
Kurima-jima
See Kurima Island Map p198

0   10 km
0   5 miles

BEST DIVE SHOPS IN THE MIYAKO ISLANDS

All of these outfits offer both diving and snorkelling trips.

Opengate Miyakojima: Lots of options like night dives, introductory dive experiences and snorkelling, all with English-speaking guides and round-trip hotel transport. *open gate-miyako.com*

Miyakojima Guide Ya-San: Beginner-friendly, small-group diving and snorkelling trips (not to Yabiji Reef) with experienced and attentive English-speaking guides. *guide-ya-san.com*

Diving Service Hekikai: Very professional, friendly outfit running small-group diving and snorkelling trips. English-speaking guides; nitrox available. *hekikai-okinawa.com*

Penguin Divers: Small shop run by an English-speaking Japanese-Fijian couple offering trip options for solo travellers and all experience levels. *diving-penguin.com*

Ikemajima Diving Service: Book with plenty of notice (call 090-3790-3015) to arrange English-speaking guides with this reliable, attentive and professional shop.

Diving Yabiji Reef

Miyako-rettō's magnificent reef system

The crowning glory of the Miyako Islands, stunning **Yabiji Reef** (八重干瀬, also known as Yaebise, Yaebishi and other variations) represents the largest grouping of coral reefs in Japan. Covering around 1957 hectares several kilometres north of the Miyako archipelago, its pristine waters and robust reef systems make Yabiji one of Okinawa's marquee snorkelling destinations.

Several times annually, most dramatically in spring, low tide exposes part of the reef for a few days, creating a 'phantom island' in the shallows. While it's possible to explore some of Yabiji's hundred-plus reefs year-round, the best season for diving and snorkelling is between May and October, with the ideal window from July through September, when conditions are conducive for boats to travel to the northern reefs.

Your captain will know the best individual sites to visit on the day of your dive, but wherever you wind up, you're likely to see layers of table and branching corals in striking splashes of blue or purple, anemones and fish darting within, schools of blue damselfish and a rainbow of marine diversity in these famously crystalline waters.

Beach Blanket Miyako-jima

Miyako's big-name beaches, clockwise

Miyako's most-hyped **Sunayama Beach** is worth a stop for a snapshot of the huge dune (*sunayama* means 'sand mountain') you'll traverse to reach the greenery-backed beach and the picturesque arch at one end (off limits due to its continuing erosion). It's lovely for sunning and swimming when the water's calm. Showers and toilets are available.

Sunayama Beach

Less glamourised but great for snorkelling, **Aragusuku Beach** on the east coast has great conditions for kids and novices. Come in the mornings, when sea turtles drift in to graze, and at higher tides to lessen the risk of bumping into coral. The clear water covers lots of shallow reef, and the beach has everything you need for the day: showers, toilets, food stalls and equipment rentals.

A few kilometres south, **Yoshino Beach** is one of the island's best for snorkelling. The steep road to the beach is reserved for residents only, but during high season there's a free shuttle between the paid parking area and the beach. There are showers, toilets and gear rental.

On the south coast, there is a spring-fed pool above the cliffside **Boraga Beach**, with good snorkelling and the full-service experience. Even more interesting is the limestone cave known as **Pumpkin Hall** that you can access on a kayaking tour, which includes snorkelling offshore.

Finally, you'll pony up for parking and the convenience of the resort-style experience at **Shigira Beach**, but the beach snorkelling is fabulous: you'll see lots of fish, even in the shallows. Umbrellas, snorkelling gear, kayaks and SUPs are available to rent, and you'll find plenty to eat when you come up for air.

KNOW THINE VENOMOUS ORGANISMS

Take care not to damage reefs by touching or stepping on corals, but be sure to protect yourself against harm as well. Okinawan waters are home to venomous creatures whose stings and bites can cause severe pain; others can kill with paralysing neurotoxins. Watch for:

- lionfish
- stonefish
- black-banded sea krait (sea snake)
- *habu kurage* (box jellyfish)
- Portuguese man-of-war
- cone snail
- sea wasp anemone
- long-spined sea urchin
- crown-of-thorns sea star.

Rash vests and swim leggings offer some defence against jellyfish stings. As a rule, don't touch anything while exploring the marine environment – for your own sake as well as the sea creatures'.

EATING & DRINKING IN MIYAKO-JIMA: DOWNTOWN HIRARA

Pōcha Tatsuya: Reservations are recommended for this warm, unpretentious place serving Miyako specialities; bring a Japanese speaker or ask for *omakase* (chef's choice). *6-10pm Thu-Mon* ¥¥

Island Brewing: House-brewed beers like *shikwasā* saison, paired with Japanese-style fish tacos, jambalaya and taco rice using island-sourced ingredients. *noon-midnight Thu-Tue* ¥

Shikishima: Satisfy hankerings for *unagi* set meals at this shop in downtown Hirara. English menu; counter seating for solo walk-ins. *11.30am-2pm & 6-9.30pm Mon-Sat* ¥¥

Asian Izakaya Kuusu: Chill Southeast Asian *izakaya* with lots of Thai selections and an inclusive vibe for dinner and the evening beyond. *6pm-midnight Fri-Wed* ¥

Get Crafty at Miyako's Workshop Village

Hands-on traditional workshops

Enjoy a live glimpse of how traditional handicrafts are made – and try your hand at them – at **Miyako Craft Workshop Village** (*miyakotaiken.com; free*). Though you may happen upon demos or drop into a workshop spontaneously, it's best to make a reservation if you have your heart set on trying a specific craft. Textile experiences include weaving a Miyako-jōfu coaster on a traditional loom (¥2750) and dyeing a handkerchief using *shibori* (indigo tie-dye) technique (from ¥3300).

Each workshop is run separately, with its own phone number and opening hours – ask a Japanese speaker to call ahead to check availability. Kids as young as eight can try their hand at the loom, and even three-year-olds can participate in tie-dyeing. More contemporary crafts are also on offer: watercolour painting, making shell-bead jewellery and even cooking classes, all of which make great rainy-day activities.

Many of the makers teaching traditional skills are local elders who may not speak English, but everything is hands-on, and it's amazing what can be communicated by showing and doing.

A couple of little Miyako horses also live on-site, which is another hit with kids. The entire craft village is set within the **Miyakojima City Tropical Botanical Garden**, open from 10am to 6pm. Spend some time wandering the garden paths and taking in the view from the observation deck at the ridge line of the park. Nearby, the excellent **Miyakojima City Museum** is worth a walk-through. Along with the more usual artefacts and natural history exhibits, of particular interest are the displays on indigenous culture accompanied by detailed explanations well translated into English.

Learn more about Miyako's traditional handicrafts and see modern works at the **Miyakojima City Traditional Crafts Centre** (*miyako-kougei.com; free*), open Monday to Saturday.

When I visited the Miyako Craft Workshop Village, an experienced obāchan *(granny) patiently demonstrated how to knot a piece of tough* gettō *(shell-ginger) twine into a net water-bottle holder. My attempt looks like it was made by a small child, but it's a perfectly usable souvenir that I mostly knotted myself.*

– **Wendy Yanagihara**, Lonely Planet writer

MORE WEAVING EXPERIENCES

If you don't have the opportunity to try it here, you can learn how to work a loom and produce a small Yaeyama *minsā* (weaving) creation at **Minsā Kōgeikan** (p211) in Ishigaki.

Action-Packed Yonaha-Maehama

Adrenaline-optional beach

A 7km sweep of powdery sand facing Kurima-jima to the west across azure seas, **Yonaha-Maehama** is a classic Miyako-jima beach. The long crescent of shoreline is rightly popular for this sunlit beauty, but also for the many activities available here.

Parasailing gives you a bird's-eye view of sea, reef and maybe even a sea turtle or two – contact **Blue Honu** (*honu.jjo.cc; 1/2-person flight ¥9000/14,000*) to reserve a spot. With a rental stand on the beach, **Sea-One** (*seaonemiyako.sakura.ne.jp*) rents Jet-Skis

Yonaha-Maehama

(30min rental/ride ¥8000/4000) if you've got a licence, or you can hop on the back with one of their riders. They also tow banana boats, and rent beach chairs and umbrellas if a good beach read is more where you're at.

If you're an experienced kiteboarder, you already know about Yonaha. If you're not, but want to see how kiting feels, the veterans at **M-air** *(m-air-kite.com)* can take you on a tandem ride *(¥6000; 2-person minimum)* with an instructor. To learn to kite on your own, you'll need three to four days to build the basic skills before getting on the water. A mastery course *(¥50,000)* involves instruction over several days, though it's recommended to plan for a longer visit in case of weather interruption. The best wind kicks up in autumn and winter, the water's always warm and the vibes are buoyant.

Yonaha-Maehama has an open-air cafe, showers and toilets, and free parking in a fairly large lot.

Exploration Sans Submersion

Marine and mangrove meanders

Not all of us are water people. Fortunately, Miyako-jima's beauty can also be appreciated from dry land, like on the

I BRAKE FOR MAMORU-KUN

Hardworking traffic officer **Mamoru-kun** seems to be in multiple places at a time, silently manning intersections to monitor driving behaviour. In fact, he stands guard at various locations around Miyako 24/7, rain or shine, because he's the dummy (meant with the utmost respect) reminding drivers to follow the rules of the road.

These statues of uniformed traffic-control police, painted in clearly unnatural black and white and installed on pedestals, are collectively and affectionately known as Mamoru-kun. Fittingly, the name Mamoru means 'defend' or 'protect' in Japanese. Mamoru-kun, though initially regarded as kind of creepy, has become something of an island icon. His stern yet manga-cute face can be found on souvenir cookies and stickers.

EATING ON MIKAYO-JIMA: SWEET TREATS

Ricco Gelato: Small-batch gelato made with local milk and eggs (or without, for vegans) in flavours like *beni-imo* (purple sweet potato) and brown sugar. *11am-6pm Thu-Mon* ¥

Yukishio: Sprinkle soft-serve ice cream with flavoured, super-fine sea salts made here for a surprisingly complex result. *9am-6pm Apr-Aug, to 5pm Sep-Mar* ¥

Utopia Farm Miyakojima: Juices and seasonal soft serve made with fruit grown on the farm. Tempting flavours like mango, passionfruit and dragonfruit make for difficult choices. *10am-5pm Mon-Sat* ¥

Tida Factory: *Tida* means 'sun' in Okinawan, and the bright, fresh mango juice definitely tastes like liquid sunshine. Or cool off with a mango *kakigōri* (shaved ice). *10am-4pm* ¥

MUSIC IN THE MOTHER TONGUE

Shimoji Isamu, singer-songwriter who performs in Miyako-jima's indigenous language *@shimojiisamu*

I grew up hearing my grandparents speak Myakufutsu, but I only learned it as an adult. Twenty-three years ago I translated Eric Clapton's *San Francisco Bay Blues* into Myakufutsu and played it at the end of a show. People loved it, and that inspired me to start writing my own songs in my island language.

Around 15% of Miyako-jima's population speaks Myakufutsu, which is a UNESCO-designated endangered language. Some is now taught in elementary and junior high school, and nowadays there's increasing interest in preserving it. I'm gratified that, even if they don't understand the lyrics, when people memorise the pronunciation and sing the words in my songs, it keeps Myakufutsu living into the future.

Imgyā Marine Garden

boardwalk zigzagging through the **Shimajiri Mangrove Forest** on the northeastern coast. The path is a short 1km, going over a stone bridge, and you may observe fish swimming in the inlet and egrets amid the roots of the five species of mangrove.

If you're curious about seeing Miyako's marine life but not keen on getting wet (or if you've got small kids or accessibility issues), there's still a cool underwater experience for you. On the northern peninsula of the island, **Miyakojima Marine Park** (*miyakojima-kaichukoen.com; adult/youth/child ¥1000/800/500*) has a submerged observation room, walled with windows, where visitors roam about 5m beneath the sea's surface. Over 140 species of fish have been observed here, and you never know what will cruise by. Biological illustrations mounted on the walls help to ID the fish swimming past the windows. There's a gondola to carry wheelchairs up and down the stairs (call ahead to confirm it's in operation).

Another spot you can enjoy in either street clothes or swimwear is **Imgyā Marine Garden** (*free*) on Miyako's south coast. This marine 'garden' centres on a protected inlet where the water is always calm and the reef lively. There's also a sandy beach, plus a trail circuit along the seaward edge of the cove that leads to a greenery-covered islet with spectacular views from the peak. From much of the path you can peer down into the transparent water of the inlet.

Rent snorkelling gear, SUPs and kayaks along the road, or simply get your feet wet at the small beach and drink in the scenery.

South Coast Sunday Drive

Lighthouse lookout and hot-spring soak

If you've got a car and half a day to spend but are all beached out, make the drive to **Higashi-Hennazaki**, the narrow cape at the far southeastern corner of Miyako-jima and a National Place of Scenic Beauty. You'll quickly notice, after parking and walking briefly uphill along the cape path, the dramatic views from the cliffs of Ryūkyū limestone tumbling down to the clear turquoise waters over Miyako-jima's wide-ranging reef called **Panari**.

Along the way you'll pass impressively huge boulders deposited by the 1771 tsunami, as well as a cave gravesite for a young woman named Mamuya who, legend tells, threw herself off the cliff in a tragic tale of doomed love.

Towards the end of the cape stands **Higashi-Hennazaki Lighthouse** (*adult/child under 12yr ¥300/free*). You'll have to climb just shy of 100 steps to reach the small observation deck, but at 43m above sea level, the spectacular panoramic views of the cape and surrounding water make it worth the small price of admission. The lighthouse is usually open from 9.30am to 4.30pm, but even when it's not, the grassy, knobbly tip of the cape is lovely for a wander – watch your step, as the terrain is uneven.

After your stroll, head west along the south coast to luxuriate in a natural hot spring. Part of the sprawling Shigira Seven Miles Resort complex, **Shigira Gold Onsen** (*shigira .com/onsen; adult/child ¥2000/1000*) is the southern- and westernmost spring-fed *onsen* (hot spring) in Japan and a wonderful outdoor space to enjoy a soak, enhanced by ocean views and a garden setting. Private rooms (*per 1½hr from ¥8800)* with outdoor pools are also available for rent to soak comfortably with your own group.

Because you can linger for a few hours and end with a shower, the *onsen* is a super-relaxing way to close your visit to Miyako-jima before heading to the airport for your flight out.

HERE'S MUD IN YOUR EYE

In Shimajiri the purification event of **Paantu Satuupunaha** lives on three times a year, most dramatically in autumn, when three Paantu (gods) ramble into the village, masked and bedecked in foliage, their bodies fully coated in stinky black mud. The trio of Paantu make their way through town, blessing bystanders with good fortune by smearing all in their path with the mud – terrorising little ones whose parents offer them up for swampy benediction.

This messiness is a tradition that exorcises evil spirits from the town, and it's considered good luck to be muddied by Paantu and thus protected from illness and misfortune. Dates are determined by the lunar calendar and are only announced at the last minute.

EATING IN MIYAKO-JIMA: HIRARA AND BEYOND

Koja Soba-ya: In a traditional house, enjoy Miyako soba crammed with *soki* (pork spare rib), fish cake and *mozuku* (local seaweed). *11am-4pm Thu-Tue ¥*

Parlor Red Dragon: Outdoor seating, Hawaiian-style garlic shrimp and fresh juices outside Miyako Craft Workshop Village. *11am-5pm Sat-Wed ¥*

Pari Kitchen: Run by mango farmers east of the airport, this cute cafe serves mango curry, sublime mango pudding and delicious non-mango lunch fare. *11am-4pm Fri-Mon ¥*

Harry's Garlic Shrimp Truck: Slinging garlic shrimp out of a yellow school bus staged with an Insta-ready backdrop, Harry's land's-end lunches satisfy all senses. *11am-5pm ¥*

Beyond Miyako-jima

Islands inhabited by gods, cows, goats, and people maintaining traditional ways represent the soul of Miyako-rettō.

Places

Ōgami Island p188

Tarama Island p189

The diminutive islands unconnected by bridge to Miyako-jima are as different as they are distant from one another. One feels almost perceptibly like a sacred home for spirits, while the other embodies farm life grounded in sugar and soil. Both invite secular baptism in their cleansing seas.

Soaking up spiritual energy seems to occur by osmosis on Ōgami Island (大神島; Ōgami-jima), a place of ancient, closely guarded ways. Little exists here for seekers of external excitement, but the island is ideal for a short, silent retreat. Meanwhile, on Tarama Island (多良間島; Tarama-jima), midway between Miyako-jima and the Yaeyamas, the day-to-day of agricultural life moves with seasonal practicality.

Ōgami Island

TIME FROM MIYAKO-JIMA: **15MIN**

Perambulate and meditate among gods

The name Ōgami-jima means 'Island of the Gods', and the two dozen or so inhabitants still maintain its sacred traditions on this isle occupying less than 0.25 sq km.

After disembarking the ferry, drop your ¥100 visitor fee in the box at the port and study the island map ahead of the road. Visitors are restricted to the roads highlighted in grey; if you visit, it's imperative to respect the islanders' boundaries.

Turn left on the road, leaving the port to walk along the west coast, where the **offshore rock formations**, known locally as *nocchi*, seem to float above the clear water. After watching the wave action at the northern terminus, turn around and backtrack to the road heading uphill from the port.

Heading into the quiet village, pause at the old **well** before climbing the wooden stairway to the **Tunpara observation deck**. Just before the top, there's a stone *utaki* tucked to the right. Catch breezes from the deck as you enjoy the gorgeous views across the turquoise seas to Miyako before walking eastward through the village and descending to the island's eastern side. Along this coastal road, look for brilliant blue damselfish and larger species hunting close to the rocks, and dip your feet in the lee of *nocchi* here known as **Kamikakis**, one of Ōgami's main power spots.

End your stroll with a bite at **Opuyū Shokudō** (*10am to 5pm*), the island's only eatery. The simple menu includes curry

GETTING AROUND

Ferries (*¥710/360 adult/child return*) to Ōgami make the 15-minute round trip four times daily from Shimajiri Port. Ōgami is best navigated on foot.

Tarama Kaiun (*taramakaiun.com*) ferries from Hirara Port go to Tarama Monday through Saturday; the trip (*¥4770/2390 adult/ child return*) takes two hours each way. Alternatively, you can hop a 20-minute **RAC** flight from Miyako-jima. Exploring Tarama by bike is the best way to go.

Offshore rock formations, Ōgami Island

rice, Miyako soba and the Ōgami speciality of *kākitako-don* (smoked octopus over rice, ¥1500). Since it conveniently over-looks the port, it's the perfect spot to sip a cold drink as you await your ferry. The last boat leaves Ōgami at 4.40pm but will depart earlier if the crew doesn't see anyone else coming, so don't dawdle.

If you speak Japanese, call ahead to arrange for a **local guide** (*0980-72-5350; per person ¥2000*) to show you around, with explanations of island culture and nature.

Coral gardens of the gods

Whatever your spiritual beliefs, the coral gardens fringing the shore of Ōgami do seem fit for gods.

Ōgami embodies the kind of enchantment that appeals to those who can slow down and tune into the soul and natural minutiae of a place, so it remains the domain of its islanders and handful of daily visitors. Forest bathing up the mountain and beyond the village feels like a spiritual exhale, and if you can balance that terrestrial experience with the marine, you'll receive the full cleanse.

Locally led snorkelling tours can be arranged from around late June through September with Ōgami fisherman **Nakase-ko Manabu** (*Instagram @oogami.island; phone 090-4075-0428*), the only operator authorised by the island's municipal council. His deep knowledge of the territory and prevailing conditions will guarantee you the safest and most beautiful exploration of these pristine reefs. There's a two-person min-imum for tours, so bring a snorkelling buddy to commune with the submarine divine.

Tarama Island   TIME FROM MIYAKO-JIMA: 2HR 🚢 OR 20MIN ✈

Pinda Aasu

If you fly into Tarama, you'll get to see the lacy fringes of reef edging the coast of this agricultural patchwork island. Cat-tle, goats and sugar cane power its economy, with tourism

POWER UP

During your Okinawan travels, you may find yourself at a **power spot** (パワースポット) or wonder what the term means on a map. Though worded in English, it's a very Japanese term signifying a place of spiritual energy. The term 'power spot' appears to have emerged in the 1990s but refers to long-sacred places throughout Japan, like magnificent Meiji-jingū in Tokyo, or Mt Fuji, where a palpable sense of energy or life force has been felt for ages. Power spots also exist in small shrines (or *utaki* in Okinawa), unusual natural features or beautiful viewpoints scattered throughout the country, and are believed to refresh and rejuvenate the spirit. Embrace the opportunity to soak up the positive, soul-recharging energy when you visit a power spot.

OFF-MAP MINNA

One household short of being completely uninhabited, Minna Island (水納島; Minna-jima) – not to be confused with the Minna off Okinawa-hontō – is an appealingly remote island atop an atoll 8km north of Tarama. Aside from the shallow surrounding reefs and an ancient lookout, there are no facilities on the island and no public transport from Tarama. To roam these deserted beaches and swim the reefs in search of sea turtles, you'll need to charter a boat from Tarama. This is best arranged through your accommodation if you're overnighting on Tarama, although intrepid travellers can try their luck on day trips by asking around at the port on arrival.

Heart Rock, Ikema Island

coming in last. A visit here is a window on Ryūkyū farming life and the slow pace of island time.

You can rent a bike at **Maedomari Port** and cycle around the island as a day trip. Tarama's most notable sight is **Yaeyama Tomidai Observatory**, a 2.5m-high stacked stone tower on the highest point on the island. It dates to the 17th century. Adjacent to the historic tower is a modern observatory made of concrete, and from its 18m height you'll get a truly expansive view of the island and surrounding sea. From Tarama's central village, the roads fan out to connect with the island's ring road. Look for the routes sheltered on either side by *fukugi* trees, planted as windbreaks and now forming attractive, shady pathways. If you're on a bike, ride along the ring road looking out for the small beaches called *tuburi*, and choose one that calls to you.

Mid-May and early October are when the action fires up on Tarama with the tournaments known as **Pinda Aasu Taikai**. These goat fights are literally head-to-head matches that function similarly to *tōgyū* (bovine sumo) on Tokunoshima (p259) in the Amami Islands; that is, it's more like goat-on-goat sumo than anything. The winner is determined by which goat backs off first, thus losing the match after dramatic rearing, bouts of head-butting and sumo-like horn grappling. Goats are not forced to participate – if they don't engage, they're simply removed from the ring.

Pinda Aasu festivities are a great way to see the community gather and socialise, enjoying food and drink together as they cheer on their favourite contenders. If you're in the Miyako Islands around either event, book your island transport to Tarama as far in advance as possible. The goat ring is a 10-minute walk from Maedomari Port.

Ikema Island

YABIJI CRUISING | WETLAND BIRDWATCHING | BEACH BUMMING

Once two islands, Ikema (池間島; Ikema-jima) merged into one when a narrow strait between two islands was sealed in the 1920s and '30s. Filling in the strait created what are now the largest wetlands in Okinawa Prefecture. Small, sleepy Ikema Island is linked by a 1425m-long bridge to the northern tip of Miyako-jima. Low lying like Miyako-jima, Ikema has limestone outcroppings and white-sand shorelines rolling down to reefs just offshore, with secret pockets you might have all to yourself. North of Ikema, the great Yabiji Reef spreads out in a series of large reefs clustered together.

Ikema's action traditionally centred on the fishing port in the south. Today, fisherfolk still head to sea for bonito and sea bream but also take visitors out to fish for a meal they can enjoy at port later that day. Fish, dive and beach it to your heart's content on rural Ikema, where tranquility rules.

Beach Towels & Migrating Fowl

Ikema beaches and wetlands

While away the day searching for your preferred beach vibe on Ikema-jima. From Hirara, the drive north to the bridge takes around 25 minutes. Crossing the bridge, which rises in the middle to allow boats to travel underneath, feels like floating over the sea to Ikema.

Going clockwise, you might love getting a photo of **Heart Rock** – so named for the heart-shaped hole that appears at low tide. However, you'll have to purchase a drink or gelato at **Ninufa** (*ninufa.theshop.jp; double scoop ¥750*), which has claimed the cliffside viewpoint. Check tide times if you have your heart set on getting a photo.

A minute's drive up the road is **Ikizu Beach**, where you can snorkel from the soft, sandy shore. There are no facilities here. Looping up to the north coast, the next option along the way is **Kaginmi Beach**, if you feel confident descending and climbing back up the rope installed on the low cliff here. The payoff is fewer people, and lovely snorkelling when the tide is higher.

GETTING AROUND

While it's possible to get to Ikema on a **Yachiyo Bus** (*yachiyo-bus-taxi. jp*), you'll have to walk, cycle or drive from the two stops at the southern end of the island. As on Miyako-jima and the other islands connected by bridge, you'll give yourself the most freedom with your own wheels – since Ikema is on the smaller side, having a car will allow you to revisit beaches for better tides and get to out-of-the-way spots for a bite or sip with outstanding views.

☑ TOP TIP

Busloads of people pile out at Kaimiru (p193) for a snack and a look at the Ikema bridge from the rooftop terrace. Not as many make their way down to the pretty beach at the point below, where from underneath you get a cool bridge view stretching over the blue.

GREEN CAVIAR

Umibudō literally translates to 'sea grapes', a fruit this local seaweed resembles in miniature. The delightfully crunchy pop of *umibudō's* bright green vesicles is reminiscent of tiny fish roe, lending it the nickname 'green caviar'. Traditionally, wild *umibudō* was harvested around Miyako-rettō, but it is now also cultivated for commercial consumption. *Umibudō* appears in dishes throughout Okinawa, and can also be ordered on its own at *izakaya* when available. The seaweed is best enjoyed locally for peak freshness, so if you haven't tried it, look for it in the Miyako Islands. The saline, mineral-tasting and ever-so-sweet seaweed complements fatty fish and broths as a refreshing palate cleanser.

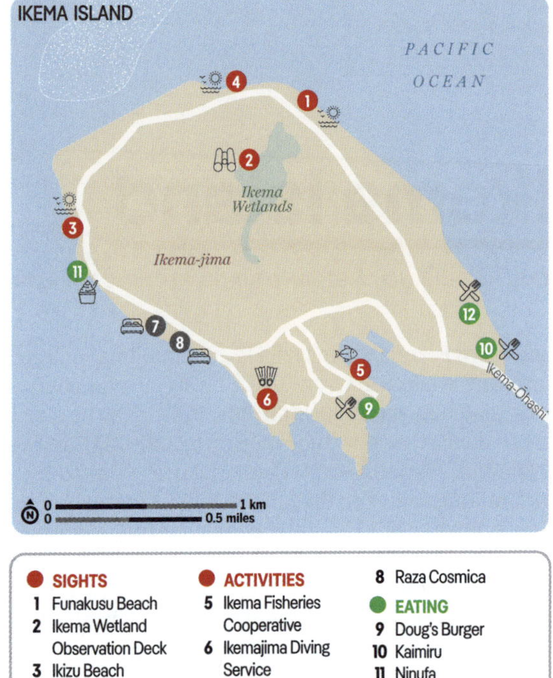

● SIGHTS	● ACTIVITIES	8 Raza Cosmica
1 Funakusu Beach	5 Ikema Fisheries	● EATING
2 Ikema Wetland	Cooperative	9 Doug's Burger
Observation Deck	6 Ikemajima Diving	10 Kaimiru
3 Ikizu Beach	Service	11 Ninufa
4 Kaginmi Beach	● SLEEPING	12 Ohama Terrace
	7 Island Terrace Neela	

Continuing down the east coast, you can rent snorkel gear near the parking area for **Funakusu Beach**. South of the parking area you'll find a pathway down to the beach through the tunnel of *kusatobera* beach shrub. It opens up to the small beach of soft sand, sheltered by pretty rock outcroppings on either side and safe for swimming and snorkelling.

Detour just inland from here for a gander from the observation deck at **Ikema Wetlands** (known locally as Yunimui), the largest wetlands in Okinawa Prefecture. Covering 38 hectares, the area is a haven for various species of migratory goose, duck and heron from October to March.

Fish with a Seasoned Pro

Fishing for your own feast

Japanese speakers might get more out of the guided experience, but any fishing enthusiast will have a blast with a local Ikema fisher on a reef tour and fishing trip. Based at the port on the island's southern end, **Ikema Fisheries Cooperative** (*miyakojima-ikemagyokyo.com*) runs boat trips out to Yabiji Reef, followed by some recreational fishing.

If you happen to visit in the spring, you may be lucky enough to see the phantom-island effect of low tides exposing the tops

Funakusu Beach

of Yabiji's reefs against the jewel-like sea of greens and blues. Because the water is so clear, you'll see lots of life from the boat while you enjoy the warm breeze and sun on your face.

After cruising around the reefs, your boat captain will take you to a fishing spot or two to drop your line. Fishing with a commercial pro with years of experience is a wonderful way to connect with an Ikema local working in a traditional trade. Plus, you're fishing to feed yourself, a pleasure for fisherfolk of any age.

When it's time to return to port, you'll hand over your catch to a restaurant run by the fisheries co-op, where you can watch your fish be cleaned before it's prepared for your lovely lunch. Depending on the type of fish you've caught, you might tuck into a spread of sashimi and fried fish with local accompaniments such as *mozuku*, rice and pickled goodies – a satisfying end to your day on the water.

TRASH TALK

Social media shows off Okinawa at its most pristine, so you might be surprised at the amount of trash cropped out of the picture. While some of it is certainly commercial fishing detritus and what the tides wash up from elsewhere, it's clear that many visitors – foreign *and* domestic – contribute to the problem by leaving trash behind on the beach.

As a responsible visitor, take your own trash back to your accommodation, where it can be sorted and disposed of properly. This is especially crucial on smaller islands that must ship recyclables and non-burnables to more developed islands with waste-processing facilities. Community organisations regularly schedule beach clean-ups, but you can help by picking up a bit of others' trash as you close out any beach day.

EATING IN IKEMA: SEA VIEWS ON THE SIDE

Ninufa: Gelato, pizza and a terrace overlooking a heart-hole rock. Gelato flavours include fresh passionfruit and brown sugar (p191). *10am-5pm Thu-Tue* ¥

Ohama Terrace: Family-run shop serving taco rice, ice cream and beer to accompany the main dish: views look across to Miyako-jima. *10am-5pm* ¥

Kaimiru: Views, and food including speciality *beni-imo* desserts. If the first parking lot is jammed, there's another up the road. *9.30am-6pm* ¥

Doug's Burger: American-style burgers catering to Japanese tastes, featuring Tarama-jima beef or yellowfin tuna; dine portside. *11am-5.30pm Fri-Wed* ¥¥

Irabu & Shimoji Islands

GETTING AROUND

Several car-rental companies have branches at **Miyako Shimojishima Airport** (*shimoji shima.jp*), including local company **Pine Rent-a-Car** (*pine-rentacar.jp*). You can fly direct to Seoul or Hong Kong from the airport.

Renting a bike is a great way to get around both islands. It's even possible to ride from Hirara across **Irabu Ōhashi** (Irabu Bridge), enjoying unparalleled views of the sea.

☑ TOP TIP

At the highest crest of Irabu Ōhashi there are very short pullouts on either side, so you can get out for a quick look or photo. If you miss them or the spots are taken, there are parking areas at either end of the bridge.

Exploring the spectacularly clear waters off of Irabu Island (伊良部島; Irabu-jima) and Shimoji Island (下地島; Shimoji-shima) is the main reason for coming here, though most boat-based diving and snorkelling trips are organised from dive shops on Miyako-jima (p178).

As rural Irabu and Shimoji are separated only by a narrow channel, they're more interconnected than not. You can easily drive around both islands as a day trip from Miyako-jima, once connected only by ferry from Hirara. The 3450m-long, upward-undulating Irabu Ōhashi was completed in 2015, making the island much more accessible to travellers. Additionally, Miyako Shimojishima Airport unveiled its tropical-chic refresh in 2019, upping the convenience of visiting these sedate Miyako isles.

Yet the chill vibes remain, and the spiritual feel of Shimoji and the traditional gathering places of Irabu make this pair an intriguing and easy escape from Miyako-jima.

Traditional Remnants, Perennial Beauty

Stone wells, walls and sandy beaches

Irabu-jima's loftiest height may be a modest 89m, but it still affords excellent views. From **Makiyama Observatory**, the highest elevation in the Miyako Islands, you can see not only Irabu Ōhashi stretching back to Miyako-jima but also Ikema and Kurima. Take in the lay of the land before heading up the eastern coast to the port town of **Sarahama** and **Sabautsu-gā**, the seaside well that sustained islanders for over 240 years.

Imagine hauling water from here three times a day, and take care descending the stairs, as the cliffs and sea create distractingly lovely views. On your ascent you can admire the masonry involved in building the stacked-stone steps.

Another remnant of traditional life exists at **Sawada-no-hama**, popular as a sunset spot with its scattered boulders contrasting with colours reflecting off the water's surface. The

IRABU & SHIMOJI ISLANDS

SIGHTS
1 17END
2 35END
3 Irabu Ōhashi
4 Makiyama Observatory
5 Nakanoshima Beach
6 Obi-iwa
7 Sabautsu-gā
8 Sawada-no-hama
9 Toguchi-no-hama

ACTIVITIES
10 Tōri-ike

SLEEPING
11 Hotel Watermark
12 Irabu Journey Inn
13 Soraniwa

EATING
14 Blue Turtle
15 Nangoku Kitchen Painmi
16 Poke Boo

TRANSPORT
17 Miyako Shimojishima Airport
18 Pine Rent-a-Car

beach isn't great for swimming but is particularly interesting for the **fish trap** (*katsu*) around the point at the western end of the beach. Built of stacked stones, the strategically laid low walls would entrap fish that swam in during high tide once the water receded.

Finally, relax on glorious **Toguchi-no-hama**, a long arc of powdery white sand and sparkling sea begging you to go for a swim. At the northwestern end, alongside the channel, there's a parking area with showers and toilets. At the southeastern end, near the Blue Turtle (p196), you have the option of popping in for refreshments. There are public toilets and showers here.

HABU IN THE RYŪKYŪS

The name *habu* refers to four species of pit viper that inhabit the Ryūkyū Islands. Though the venomous snakes are found throughout the Ryūkyūs, some islands are free of them, including Okinoerabu, Yoron and Zamami. Vipers may occasionally hitchhike on interisland boats, though – in 2013 and 2024 individual Sakishima *habu* were discovered at Hirara port on otherwise *habu*-free Miyako-jima.

Though you're likely only to see one inside a jar of *habushu* (*habu*-infused *awamori* alcohol), be aware that most bites occur in farmed fields and near residences. *Habu* are nocturnal but known to be territorial, and they have a long strike length, so keep your distance if you happen upon one. A bite could be lethal, but with highly effective treatment now available, fatalities are rare.

Spiritual Shimoji-shima

Soulful sites, land's-end liftoffs

Shimoji feels steeped in spirit, its rural pace remaining mostly unruffled by the new airport traffic.

Crossing over to the island from the south, the 3000m-long runway's southern terminus known as **35END** marks a lovely beach where you can watch jets taking off and landing. A better cove for swimming and superb snorkelling lies further north at picturesque **Nakanoshima Beach** (known locally as Kayaffa), though it's best to time your visit for the early morning or around lunch, after tour groups and boats have largely departed.

One of the more sobering sights on Shimoji is the massive boulder called **Obi-iwa** (Obi-ishi) that was washed up by the great Meiwa tsunami of 1771. Nearly 60m in circumference, it has been left unmoved by the islanders as testament to the tsunami's power. Obi-iwa became a spiritual monument where people came to pray for abundant catches and safety at sea. Walk the short path behind the boulder to see the beach below and imagine the force of the tsunami.

About 700m up the road, turn off to explore intriguing **Tōri-ike**, a pair of connected ponds fed by the sea. The pools take on deep, jewel-like blues and greens in the light; in moodier weather they look dark and impenetrable, making their ominous origin stories seem believable (takeaways: don't harm mermaids or stepchildren). Experienced divers can explore these interconnected caves from below, swimming through the tangible transition from cool to warmer water. For pedestrians, the green-blanketed limestone bluffs of this National Place of Scenic Beauty are accessible via boardwalk for a contemplative meander.

Aviation geeks can check flight info on the airport website before heading to **17END**, so named for the runway number and northern terminus. It's about a 600m walk from the parking area, but the raised path is wide and accessible. Even if you're not into this sort of thing, it's exhilarating to stand at the tip of the island with a jet touching down or taking off overhead.

EATING IN IRABU: OUR PICKS

Poke Boo: Fish from Sarahama port and locally cultivated *umibudō* adorn your poke bowl here. English menu available. *8am–4pm Thu-Tue* ¥¥

Blue Turtle: Beautifully set on Toguchi-no-hama, with a patio and good food and drink. Lunch is walk-in; reservations required for dinner. *11am–4pm & 5–10pm* ¥¥

Nangoku Kitchen Painmi: Local fish and produce, with vegan options too. Friendly English-speaking owners. Cash only. *6–10.30pm Thu-Tue, from 6.30pm Sun* ¥¥

Soraniwa: Open to nonguests for lunch only, this serene spot serves simple food drawing on quality island ingredients. *11.30am–6pm Thu-Tue* ¥¥

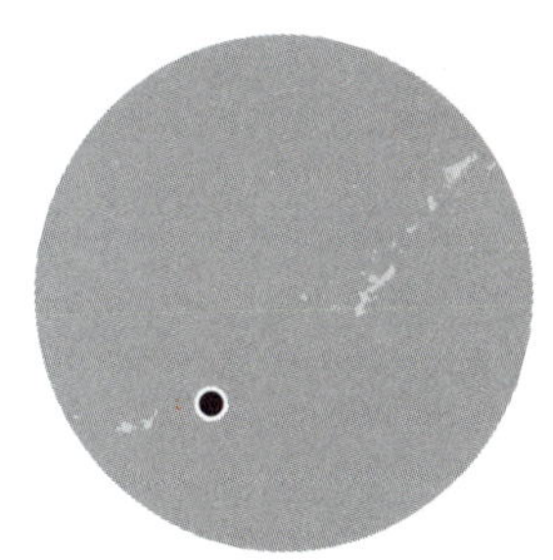

Kurima Island

SECLUDED BEACHES | SUNFLOWERS | SUP

One antidote to cruise-ship crowds and bus tours is Kurima Island (来間島; Kurima-jima), the small island across the bridge facing Miyako-jima's Yonaha-Maehama Beach (p184). Like Miyako-jima, it's relatively flat and agricultural, compact and completely rural. It's another sugar-cane-growing island with its own tranquil beaches tucked between limestone outcroppings. Kurima's quiet charm stems from positive beautification initiatives like planting empty fields with sunflowers, and adding seasonal beauty to its secluded beaches and pristine reefs. Dive shops based on Miyako-jima often bring boat divers to spots off Kurima bridge that have excellent visibility and healthy coral gardens.

You can also relax with a tropical beach lounge experience without the overly developed resort aspect – drink and dine, charter a cruise or paddle a SUP down at Pacha Beach. You'll have to head to the other side of the island to take in the sunset, but such are the simple choices Kurima presents.

See, SUP & Sip

Survey Kurima from land and sea

Start with a view of Miyako-jima from **Ryūgūjō Observatory**. Set within a shaded park, the observatory is modelled after the underwater castle of Okinawa's dragon god of the sea, with murals on that theme. From here you can walk along the path through the forested park to a set of spring-fed wells known as **Kurima-gā**. One hundred stone steps down the seaside cliff lead to the trio of descending pools, each traditionally used for a specific purpose to maximise water usage: the topmost was reserved for drinking water, the next one down for bathing and the bottom for laundry.

Next, cross over to the island's western coast and hit the beach. Of the three main beaches, **Nagamahama** is furthest north, with a gorgeous, sandy white stretch and lovely shallow water for swimming and snorkelling. Midway down

GETTING AROUND

To get to Kurima you'll have to rent a car or cycle across the Kurima bridge. No buses from Miyako-jima serve the island. As the bridge is 11km from Hirara, consider renting an e-bike if you're not an avid cyclist. Because the island has an area of less than 3 sq km, with a loop road and a basic grid within, it's impossible to get lost.

☑ TOP TIP

As on other Miyako Islands, large (harmless) spiders like giant golden orbweavers spin webs in forested areas. If you're not a fan, avoid walking the trails at Tako-kōen (p198) or exploring the park surrounding Ryūgūjō Observatory.

SUNFLOWER POWER

Since the spring of 2024, the Kurima community has run a beautification initiative and flower-planting project to help reduce littering. With fields lying fallow, trash began to accumulate and the empty patches appeared unkempt, so the idea was to fill them with sunflowers in the spring. When the flowers went to seed, they would be ploughed over to nourish the soil for the next season of sugar cane or tobacco, the main crops grown on Kurima. The big, cheery sunflowers do contrast beautifully against blue skies. If you can't resist snapping a photo, be sure to pull over so as to keep the narrow roads clear.

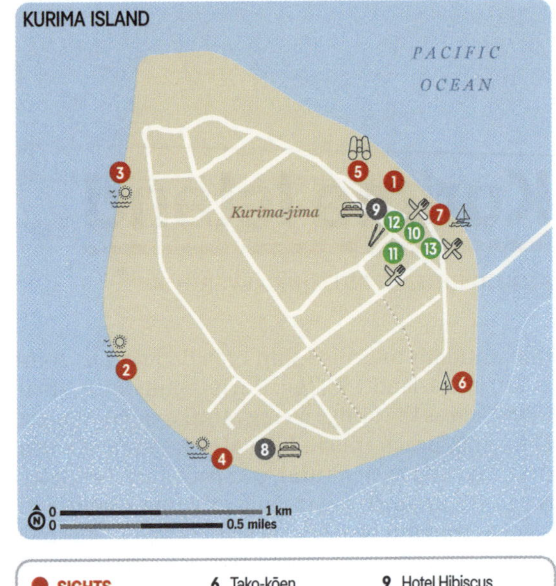

SIGHTS	6 Tako-kōen	9 Hotel Hibiscus
1 Kurima-gā	**ACTIVITIES**	**EATING**
2 Musunun Beach	7 Pacha Beach	10 Aosora Parlor
3 Nagamahama	**SLEEPING**	11 Hanafuu
4 Nagasaki Beach	8 Blanc Miyakojima	12 Marukami
5 Ryūgūjō Observatory		13 PaniPani

the coast is **Musunun Beach**, a smaller shore hemmed in by rocky coastline. It's better for sunning than swimming. Finally, there's the pocket of **Nagasaki Beach**, where you can sun and snorkel to the right of limestone bluffs.

For a walk in the park and a secluded snorkel, continue around the south to **Tako-kōen** (Octopus Park), commemorated with a huge octopus statue down the bluffside path. You can descend to a beach surrounded by rock walls for a snorkelling session in this little cove if the tide isn't too high.

If you prefer to SUP (or sip a cool drink), backtrack past the bridge and head downhill to the port, where you'll find **Pacha Beach** (*pachabeach.studio.site; cafe 11am-4pm*). Here you can charter a boat, take a guided paddle to secret beaches or set up cabana-style for snacks, sips and dips.

EATING ON KURIMA: FRESH ISLAND FARE

Hanafuu: You can walk in for lunch, but reservations are recommended at this container-housed cafe. Cash only. *11.30am-1.30pm & 6.30-9.30pm Wed-Mon* ¥

PaniPani: Old-school open-air spot serving lunch or coffee with *sātā andagi* (doughnuts) in a garden haven. Intermittently closed. *10am-4pm* ¥

Aosora Parlor: Refreshing juices and smoothies made from island fruit and hibiscus, sweetened by the fruit only. English menu. *10am-5pm* ¥

Marukami: Okinawa-soba shop famous in Japan. Sign the waitlist before they open and order at the ticket machine. *11am-3pm Mon-Sat* ¥¥

Places We Love to Stay

¥ Budget ¥¥ Midrange ¥¥¥ Top End

Miyako-jima

MAP p180

Miyakojima Guesthouse Re-Spect ¥ Friendly guesthouse with dorms, family rooms and private rooms; shared kitchen, laundry and bathrooms. Near Sunayama Beach.

Guesthouse Miyakojima ¥ A couple of cosy rooms share a bathroom plus lounge space and kitchen; one room has a private bath. Run by owners of kiteboarding shop M-air.

Hotel 385 ¥¥ Relatively roomy accommodation with a cosy urban aesthetic conveniently located in Hirara. Free parking and breakfast; walkable to downtown restaurants; has laundry facilities.

Hotel California Miyakojima Resort ¥¥ Spacious, fully equipped apartments in a residential neighbourhood, with in-unit laundry, free parking and breakfast available. Clean, quiet and great for families.

Zumi Terrace ¥¥ Sleek, solar-powered container rooms in different configurations, each with tiny private terrace, sauna, foot-rinsing station and laundry. EV-charger parking for the electric vehicle rental included with your accommodation reservation.

Guesthouse KAZE ¥¥ Clean, comfortable rooms with shared or private bathrooms and one self-contained apartment with terrace, less than 10 minutes' walk to Sunayama Beach.

Kataaki-no-Sato ¥¥¥ Immerse yourself in traditional Miyako-jima atmosphere in these unique, old-fashioned houses set within a garden. Houses are outfitted with modern comforts; some have kitchenette.

Grand Bleu Gamin ¥¥¥ The five rooms at this relaxed, elegant boutique inn have private pools, complemented by easy beach access, in-house spa, French-fusion restaurant and bar.

Tarama Island

Yume Patio Tarama ¥ Comfortable rooms in several small cottages share bathrooms and lounge spaces. Partial board can be arranged; payment for accommodations is by cash only.

Coco House ¥ Simple Western-style rooms in the original building or tatami rooms in a container structure, all of which share shower and laundry facilities; partial board available.

Ikema Island

MAP p192

Raza Cosmica ¥ Four twin rooms, three with balconies, share spotless toilets and showers at this tranquil little Indian-inflected castle by the sea with a private beach accessible at low tide.

Island Terrace Neela ¥¥¥ Ryūykūs meet the Mediterranean in free-standing villas perched above a white-sand beach, making for a romantic getaway on a quiet stretch of Ikema.

Irabu & Shimoji Islands

MAP p195

Irabu Journey Inn ¥ Founded to foster connection, this lovely guesthouse has dorms, private rooms and a rooftop terrace for sunsets and stargazing over Sawada-no-hama.

Soraniwa ¥¥ Several romantic 2nd-floor, sea-view rooms share a rooftop deck and hot tub. There are also two self-contained suites, one with private infinity pool facing the sea. Partial-board stays available.

Hotel Watermark ¥¥ Near Sawada-no-hama, this peaceful seaside hotel has a rooftop pool and direct access to the beach for quiet beach days and dark skies at night.

Kurima Island

MAP p198

Hotel Hibiscus ¥ Sociable guesthouse in a renovated island house with dorms and private rooms, all sharing bathroom, kitchen and common room. Breakfast and shuttle from Miyako Airport available.

Blanc Miyakojima ¥¥ Fully equipped, compact glamping dwellings – the two- and four-bed setups have rooftop Astroturf lawns and are steps from Nagasaki Beach. There's open-air island dining at the attached restaurant.

For places to
stay in Yaeyama
Islands, see p233

Above: Water buffalo–drawn cart (p220), Taketomi Island; Right: Yaeyama *minsā* patterns (p215)

Researched by
Wendy Yanagihara

Yaeyama Islands

PRISTINE SEAS AND TRADITIONAL RYŪKYŪAN CULTURE

Snorkel and dive flourishing coral reefs; cycle and stroll around traditional, red-roofed villages; and stargaze the darkest skies of Okinawa's southernmost archipelago.

Flying into the Yaeyama Islands (八重山諸島, Yaeyama-shotō), you'll be mesmerised from the start: the sea's transparent aquamarines deepen to ever-bluer blues and reefs sprawl from verdant coastlines. Vibrant coral reefs, virgin subtropical forest and riverside mangroves await exploration for encounters with ruddy kingfishers, coconut crabs and manta rays.

Geographically much closer to Taiwan than Japan, islanders in these southernmost of the Ryūkyūs retain a Yaima (Yaeyama) cultural pride distinct from their Okinawan and Japanese identities. So too does the Yaeyama language differ from Okinawan, diverging even further into island-specific dialects still spoken by older generations. If you're lucky enough to visit during festivals, you'll have a chance to experience these micro-cultures by witnessing traditional dances and songs sung in the *hōgen* (dialect).

But any traveller to this southern archipelago can experience relaxed Yaeyama hospitality. Walking the narrow alleys between Ryukyū limestone walls and the red-tiled roofs of old houses or riding a one-speed bike around the crushed-coral roads of outer islands, you'll discover for yourself how the analogue way of doing things contributes to the long, healthy lives of local centenarians. Tread softly and slowly, respecting the sanctity of *utaki* (sacred places), and you may be blessed with some unexpected wisdom, friendship or rowdy nights drinking *awamori* (Okinawan alcohol) along with your snorkelling, paddling, hiking and culinary adventures.

CHRIS WILLSON/ALAMY

THE MAIN AREAS

ISHIGAKI
The Yaeyamas' beachy transport hub.
p206

IRIOMOTE ISLAND
The wildest of the Yaeyamas.
p218

HATERUMA ISLAND
Southernmost inhabited isle in Japan.
p228

YONAGUNI ISLAND
Japan's far-flung westernmost island.
p230

Find Your Way

Anchored by the largest islands of Ishigaki and Iriomote, the inhabited Yaeyamas are easily reached by ferries taking 15 minutes to just under two hours. The exception is Yonaguni, a 129km, 30-minute flight from Ishigaki.

Yonaguni Island, p230
Shaggy island ponies, a mysterious underwater geological phenomenon and schools of hammerheads draw the curious to quiet, windswept Yonaguni.

FERRY

Ferries regularly connect Ishigaki with the other Yaeyama Islands. Depending on the island, there are usually multiple departures and returns daily. Ferries range in size according to their destinations – some are smaller vessels with only interior seating, while others are large catamarans with outdoor decks.

BUS

It's possible to get around on Ishigaki and Iriomote (and Yonaguni) by bus. Buses on Ishigaki conveniently depart from the bus terminal opposite the ferry port. On Iriomote, a bus travelling the length of the coastal road runs the entire route four times a day.

CAR

On the smaller islands you can easily explore on foot or by bicycle, but on the much larger Ishigaki and Iriomote it can be worth renting a car for at least a day. You'll have access to more isolated beaches, hiking trails and other sights.

Ishigaki, p206
The 'urban' centre of Ishigaki and lively transport hub has loads of dining, drinking and shopping to complement your beach lounging and reef snorkelling.

Iriomote Island, p218
Composed mostly of virgin jungle and national park land, river and sea, the island is home to the rare Iriomote cat and other endemic wildlife.

Hateruma Island, p228
A crumbling observatory, gloriously dark skies and acres of sugar cane make for a slow-travel experience way down south.

OKINAWA
PREFECTURE

Hirano

Hatoma-jima

Sotobanari-jima

Uchibanari-jima

Hoshitate
Shirahama

Kayama-jima

Ishigaki

Iriomote
Island

Kohama-jima

Taketomi-jima

Ishigaki

Ohara
Toyohara

Panari-jima

Kuroshima

Aragusuku-jima

Hateruma Island

PACIFIC
OCEAN

0
0
50 km
25 miles

Plan Your Days

Ishigaki scratches that beach-holiday itch as a long-weekend destination, but if you've got more time it's worth ferrying to the other appealing Yaeyamas for diving, paddling and cultural adventures.

Tōrin-ji (p210), Ishigaki

KLAUS-GERHARD DUMRATH/MAURITIUS IMAGES GMBH/ALAMY

One Weekend Only

● Base yourself in Ishigaki city and bus it to **Yonehara Beach** (p210) or **Kabira** (p210) for sunbathing and beach snorkelling. Even better, rent a car and embark on a **driving tour** (p213) to explore the island's more remote points, hiking trails and harder-to-reach beaches. End the evening at a tiny *izakaya* (Japanese pub-eatery) in **Ishigakijima Village** (p212) and make friends over Orion beers and *rafute* (marinated pork).

● Next day, catch a 15-minute ferry to **Taketomi** (p214), hop on a rental bike, search for star sand and take a dip in the bathtub-warm water. Relax on an oxcart while your guide plays the *sanshin* (three-stringed Okinawan guitar) as you pass the village's traditional architecture, or sail on a *sabani* (traditional Okinawan boat) before returning to Ishigaki for a multicourse dinner at **Funakura-no-Sato** (p210).

Seasonal Highlights

Island festivals occur throughout the year; ask locally for info if your travels coincide. Changing seasons and currents bring Yaeyama delights.

JANUARY

January through March is the best season for diving at **Yonaguni** (p231) to see the hammerheads migrating along the Kuroshio Current. You may luck out and encounter schooling sharks.

MARCH

Fireflies light up the night in Ishigaki and Iriomote from around late February through late May; they're at their height in mid- to late March. Several species fire up by the hundreds, including the tiny Yaeyama firefly.

APRIL

The pineapple (called 'pine' locally) harvest on Ishigaki begins in mid-April, but different varieties continue ripening through August. Small, super sweet and juicy, their varying flavour profiles are worth savouring.

Five Days to Play

● After exploring Ishigaki, spend a couple of days on **Iriomote** (p218) to kayak into the mangroves, trek to waterfalls through the jungle, and go boat snorkelling to look for sea turtles and visit teeming reefs. Visit the beautifully remodelled **Iriomote Wildlife Conservation Centre** (p223) to learn about the island's ecology and its beloved, elusive inhabitant, the *yamaneko* (Iriomote wildcat).

● You'll have to return to Ishigaki to ferry to one of the other islands, such as **Kuroshima** (p217), **Kohama** (p216) or **Hateruma** (p228) for slow bike rides to see the sights, stopping at swimming beaches and cooling off with shaved ice. If you can, spend the night on one of these smaller islands to really soak up the peace and starry nighttime skies.

A Week to Island-Hop

● Spend a bit more time in Ishigaki, walking to Okinawa's oldest wooden building, **Tōrin-ji** (p206), and getting the hang of weaving on a traditional loom at **Minsā Kōgeikan** (p211). Take a day trip to **Taketomi** (p214), move on to **Iriomote** (p218) for a few days of paddling and snorkelling, and then take your pick of other Yaeyamas to explore.

● All of the islands can be accessed by ferry from Ishigaki, except for **Yonaguni** (p230), which requires flying. But once you're on this faraway island, you could ride a native pony, dive to the mysterious underwater 'ruins' of **Kaitei Iseki** (p232) and look for giant Atlas moths.

● On returning to Ishigaki, don't forget to pick up your finished piece of *minsā* (weaving), a small souvenir of your Yaeyama adventures.

JUNE

Around mid-month the blooming season of *sagaribana* (falling flowers; p225) begins on Iriomote. Kayak tours depart before dawn to see these night-blooming flowers falling at daybreak.

JULY

Breeding season for coconut crabs (p212) is in full swing during July and August. Nighttime walks in search of these giants are cool, and seeing some is even cooler at this sweltering time of year.

AUGUST

Based on the lunar calendar, the harvest festival **Hōnensai** (p224) in July or August is marked throughout the Yaeyamas in private ceremonies involving only shamans or priestesses at *utaki*. Community celebrations follow.

SEPTEMBER

Although manta rays (p207) can be seen year-round in Ishigaki, they come to the cleaning stations around Kabira Bay from June to November, with activity peaking around September.

Ishigaki

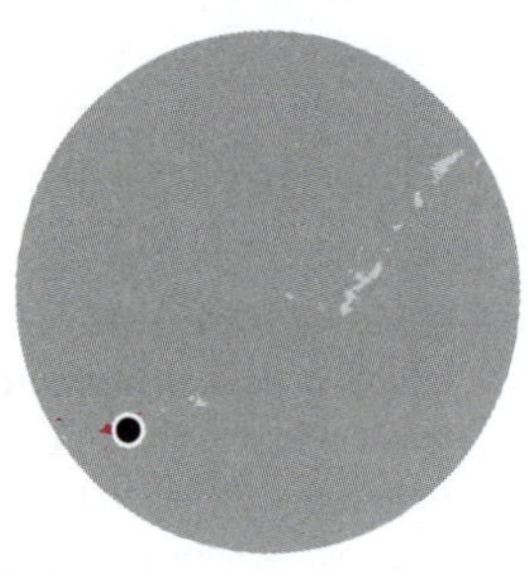

YAEYAMA SPRINGBOARD | MANTA RAYS | VACAY VIBES

 **TOP TIP**

Confusingly, the 'town' or district of **Taketomi-chō** (竹富町) spans multiple Yaeyama islands, including Iriomote-jima, Hateruma-jima and **Taketomi-jima** (竹富島; Taketomi Island). Therefore, when an address – for your lodgings, perhaps – contains the name Taketomi-chō, it doesn't necessarily mean it's on the island of Taketomi.

A beach-holiday and diving destination in its own right, Ishigaki Island (石垣島; Ishigaki-jima) is also the transport hub serving the Yaeyama Islands by air and sea. Ishigaki city (石垣市; Ishigaki-shi) officially encompasses the entire island, with its lively downtown centred on the ferry terminal. Ferries connect Ishigaki to the other inhabited Yaeyama isles, making it the most convenient base for adventures beyond. This administrative centre of the Yaeyamas is dotted with traditional red-roofed houses still standing between modern buildings, as does Okinawa's oldest temple, Tōrin-ji (桃林寺), which dates to 1614 and is guarded by its original pair of fierce wooden, tsunami-surviving deities. The island's jagged coastline offers superb opportunities for snorkelling off the beach, paddling a kayak or SUP, hiking Okinawa's highest peak and sampling some of the sweetest, juiciest locally grown pineapple you can imagine.

Diving & Snorkelling Ishigaki

Charismatic life in the corals

The Yaeyamas are one of the best diving destinations in Japan, with spectacular reefs like **Sekisei Lagoon** within Iriomote-Ishigaki National Park (p224).

GETTING AROUND

Karry Kankō (*karrykanko.com*) and **Azuma Bus** (*azumabus.co.jp*) both shuttle between the ferry terminal and Ishigaki Airport every 30 minutes or so for the 30-minute trip (*¥550*). Both buses accept cash and contactless payment on boarding. If you're not renting a car, Azuma Bus offers one-day (*¥1000/500 adult/child*) or five-day (*¥2000/1000 adult/child*) passes for unlimited rides, including the airport route.

The most convenient and flexible way to explore the island is by car, if you've brought an international driving permit. The centre of Ishigaki city is walkable, with the Euglena Mall and surrounding alleys just a couple of minutes' stroll from the port.

Manta ray

Majestic winged manta rays are one of the star attractions. Manta cleaning stations, areas where the rays glide in to receive spa treatments from fish like cleaner wrasse, are well-known spots for seeing these beauties up close. Sites like **Manta Scramble** are a 15-minute boat ride from Kabira Bay, while other cleaning stations are active in seasons when Manta Scramble is not. Further afield, the **Yonara Channel** between Iriomote and Kohama is another manta zone, with those islands also known for lots of sea turtle action.

Another fascinating phenomenon with a more precise window is the giant cuttlefish spawning season from late February to early March. Hanging out to witness these wonderfully weird creatures cooperating in a graceful dance is a rare experience.

Divers who are interested in shooting macros (photographing micro marine life) will find lots of electric-hued nudibranchs, busy shrimps, crabs, ribbon eels and fish among the anemones and corals near Yonehara Beach (p210) and off the eastern coast of Taketomi (p214). Let your dive shop know what you're into so they can show off their favourite spots.

Snorkellers will also find a spectacular variety of corals and marine life around Ishigaki, such as offshore at **Shiraho Beach** (accessed by boat only), which has over 70 species of coral, including what is believed to be the largest community of blue coral in the northern hemisphere. Beach snorkelling is easily accessible at spots like Yonehara Beach (best at high tide) and the beautiful **Blue Cave** (not to be confused with the one on Okinawa-hontō). Rent snorkelling gear as you go, or buy an inexpensive set at **Don Quijote** (*donki.com*) east of Ishigaki city for spontaneous, DIY snorkelling strikes.

ISHIGAKI'S BEST DIVE SHOPS

All of these well-established, reputable dive shops have English-speaking staff.

Prime Scuba: Located opposite the ANA Intercontinental Hotel in Maezato, just east of Ishigaki city. Offers Nitrox. *primescuba-ishigaki.com*

Sea Jack Dive Family: Based in Kabira, this family-run dive shop runs small-group dives with friendly, professional staff. *seajackdf.com*

Viking Scuba Kabira: This Japanese-Swedish husband-and-wife team operate out of Kabira, with a small boat and personal, small-group trips. *vikingscuba kabira.com*

Euro Divers: Based at Club Med Kabira, this outfit has multilingual instructors who speak English, French and Chinese. *euro-divers.jp*

Manta Holic Kabira: Another friendly shop in Kabira; can do one-dive half days as well as a full day with two dives. *mantaholic.com*

ISHIGAKI

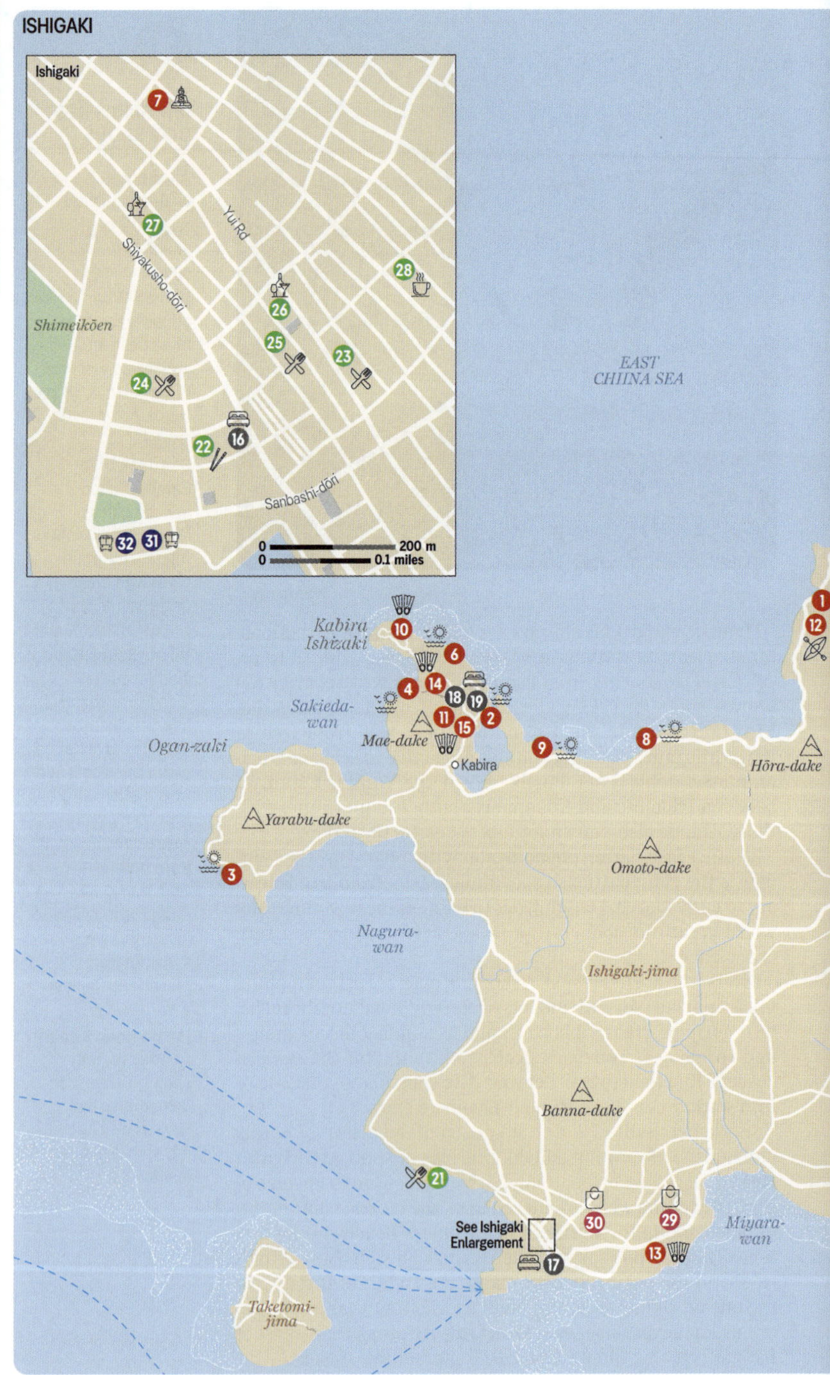

Ishigaki
Yui Rd
Shiyakusho-dōri
Shimeikōen
Sanbashi-dōri
0   200 m
0   0.1 miles
Kabira
Ishizaki
Sakieda-
wan
Ogan-zaki
Mae-dake
Kabira
Yarabu-dake
EAST
CHIINA SEA
Hōra-dake
Omoto-dake
Ishigaki-jima
Nagura-
wan
Banna-dake
Miyara-
wan
See Ishigaki
Enlargement
Taketomi-
jima

SIGHTS
1 Fukidogawa Mangroves
2 Kabira Bay
3 Ōsaki (Tachii) Beach
4 Sukuji Beach
5 Sunset Beach
6 Tabaga Beach
7 Tōrin-ji
8 Yonehara Beach
9 Yoshihara Beach

ACTIVITIES
10 Euro Divers
11 Manta Holic Kabira
12 Orion Ishigaki
13 Prime Scuba
14 Sea Jack Dive Family
15 Viking Scuba Kabira

SLEEPING
16 Hotel Cucule
17 Hotel Patina
18 Iriwa
19 Lulaliya B&B
20 Tsundara Beach Retreat

EATING
21 Funakura-no-Sato
22 Ishigakijima Village
23 Mori-no-Kokage
24 Nishiki
25 Okonomiyaki K

DRINKING & NIGHTLIFE
26 Bar Cocoзone
27 Bar Revolucion
28 Cafe Taniwha

SHOPPING
29 Don Quijote
30 Minsā Kōgeikan

TRANSPORT
31 Azuma Bus
32 Karry Kankō

ISLAND MANNERS

As tourism to the Ryūkyūs has ramped up significantly, it's more important than ever to respect island cultures and ecosystems to reduce pressure on these small, traditional communities. Many islands publish versions of 'island manners' guides in multiple languages to welcome and educate visitors while protecting their heritage.

Much of the advice is common sense, such as refraining from entering *utaki* (sacred sites), respecting the privacy of people's homes, and not walking around shirtless or in your swimwear beyond the beach. Environmental considerations include not damaging coral, not approaching wildlife, and taking all your trash back with you to your accommodation.

These are gentle cultures and delicate ecosystems, so generally adopting an attitude of deference and thoughtfulness is a solid default mode.

Sukuji Beach

Beach Time in Ishigaki

Clocking up time on the sand

Although renting a car makes the island your oyster, you can still get to a couple of choice beaches by bus. Azuma Bus (p206) makes several trips a day from Ishigaki's downtown bus terminal to popular **Yonehara Beach**, a long stretch of seashore and reef where there are showers, toilets, a campground and snorkelling-gear rentals. Check the tides, as snorkelling at high tide makes it easier to avoid stepping on or touching the coral (at low tide it's nearly impossible to swim). Along the road nearby are a couple of little places to eat.

Another favorite is **Sukuji Beach** on the opposite side of the Kabira peninsula. Take Azuma Bus 9 to the Seaside Hotel stop for the one-minute walk to the beautiful, west-facing shoreline. Alternatively, disembark at famously photogenic **Kabira Bay**, but note that Ishigaki's poster-child beach is off limits for swimming or snorkelling due to black-pearl cultivation in the bay. Most people come here to admire the view and take a **glass-bottomed boat tour**, a great way to see the marine life if you're not into snorkelling. Visitors are always stoked to see Nemo (clownfish), and you might spot a sea turtle, but the most interesting sights are pops of the gorgeous blue coral that grows in the Yaeyamas.

 **EATING IN ISHIGAKI: DOWNTOWN DINING**

Nishiki: Near the port, this fishing-centric *izakaya* (selling lures and gear) has an English menu and lots of fish dishes. *5pm-midnight Tue-Sun* ¥¥

Okonomiyaki K: Choose toppings for your *okonomiyaki* (savoury pancake), cooked for you. Some tatami seating; English menu. *11.30am-2pm & 5-10pm Wed-Mon* ¥

Mori-no-Kokage: Try very local dishes, such as tempura of *ōtaniwatari* (a wild edible plant), at this friendly *izakaya*. *5-11pm Wed-Mon* ¥¥

Funakura-no-Sato: Atmospheric spot in a traditional Okinawan house 4km west of the city. Live *sanshin* (banjo) music. Reserve. *11am-10pm Thu-Tue* ¥¥¥

If you've got a car you can explore endless options – at the western tip of the island, **Osaki (Tachii) Beach** is a dreamy slice of white sand and tranquility. In the Kabira area, **Tabaga Beach** is down an unmarked road on the way to Club Med, so finding it makes its seclusion feel even more special. A touch east of Kabira Bay, **Yoshihara Beach** is another picturesque spot with plenty of space and a bit of a wild feel. You'll find plenty of parking (for a fee), as well as snorkelling gear for rent, showers and toilets at **Sunset Beach** in the far north of the island. Consider these starting points to discovering your own secret beach.

Weaving Meaning in Yaeyama Minsā

Hands-on Yaeyama weaving

The common thread of traditional weaving varies beautifully throughout the Ryūkyū Islands. On Ishigaki, Yaeyama *minsā* patterns not only appear in traditional fabrics but are echoed in architectural designs and even the outdoor walkway tile approaching the ferry terminal. One of the most famous motifs is the alternating 5-4 pattern of squares, which is a play on words – the homonyms for certain readings of 'five' and 'four' translate into the idea of eternal love. Who knew the sidewalk spoke in such romantic code?

You can learn about the craft of Yaeyama *minsā* weaving at **Minsā Kōgeikan** (みんさー工芸館; *Minsā Crafts Museum; minsah.co.jp; free*) in Ishigaki city. On the 2nd floor is an excellent museum showing examples of *minsā* textiles and kimonos, with displays (in Japanese) on the seeds, bark and plants used for dyeing and the resulting skeins of coloured thread.

On the 1st floor, in addition to a shop selling high-quality *minsā* gifts, there's a workshop where you can try your hand at weaving. Call ahead for an appointment, though sometimes walk-ins can be accommodated. Looms are set up with the warp in place (you choose from several colour schemes), and an instructor will show you how to weave the weft, working the loom with your hands and feet. Weaving a coaster (*¥2000*) takes 20 to 30 minutes; larger pieces may take several hours. The craftswomen at the centre will finish the edges for you, usually within the next day or two.

SUP Coastal Mangroves

Paddling subtropical jungle waterways

If you aren't heading to Iriomote, you can paddle into the leaf-dappled shade of Ishigaki's own **Fukidogawa Mangroves** that make up part of Iriomote-Ishigaki National Park. Choose to kayak or SUP on a half-day tour with **Orion Ishigaki** (*orionishigaki.com; adult/child ¥8000/6000*), a local family-run outfit based a few minutes down the road from Fukidogawa – your English-speaking guide can pick you up and drop you off in Ishigaki city.

You'll begin at the river mouth, feet in the soft sand, to launch your watercraft from the beach and practise your paddle technique. On a chill glide beside the bluffs of the coastal

RYŪKYŪ ARCHITECTURE

The distinctive red-tiled roofs (*aka-gawara*) of Ryūkyūan architecture appear throughout the island chain, even on century-old houses (*kominka*) sandwiched between modern buildings in Naha and Ishigaki. But the smaller, less developed Yaeyama Islands like Taketomi and Kohama are the most appealing settings in which to see well-preserved examples of Ryūkyū *kominka* in context. While some are officially national cultural assets, many are treasured homes or lovingly restored structures that now house cafes, restaurants and *minshuku* (guesthouses).

Constructed to withstand tropical weather and typhoons, traditional houses had support posts made from naturally weather-resistant tree trunks. Tiles were plastered securely together. Walls made of stacked Ryūkyū limestone enclosed the homes for added protection and privacy. The very Okinawan finishing touch is a pair of *shiisā* atop the roof.

COCONUT CRABS

One of the fascinating critters residing on Iriomote is the massive coconut crab, the jumbo-sized version of the hermit crab. Although juveniles do don coconut shells for protection before they develop their tough adult exoskeleton, coconut crabs get their moniker from their preferred food, the green coconut. They're adept at climbing palms to snip coconuts down, which they crack open with their powerful claws. Coconut crabs are the largest terrestrial arthropods in the world, some growing to weigh over 4kg and living up to 60 years. In Okinawa their range extends from the Amami Islands to Yonaguni. If you're interested in seeing one of these nocturnal land-dwellers, you're almost guaranteed to find one on night tours in Iriomote.

KHUN TA/SHUTTERSTOCK

Fukidogawa Mangroves (p215)

limestone, keep an eye out for sea turtles surfacing for a quick breath. You might stop at a beach cove for a hydration break before heading upriver into the brackish water where salty and sweet meet.

As you navigate the wider, sunlit river, you may see fish slowly schooling below, but as you enter the narrower channels crowded by mangroves, their shade creates an air of mystique matched by the tannin-tinted water. Deep into the mangroves, which efficiently excrete salt through their leaves and roots, you'll stop amid those amazing roots and mud to look for black crabs and delightfully lightning-quick mudskippers.

Have a rinse and change into dry clothes at Orion's HQ after returning from your lovely, low-key national park foray.

DRINKING IN ISHIGAKI: DOWNTOWN BARS

Ishigakijima Village: Three-storey building packed with tiny *izakaya*, including a *senbero* (where ¥1000 gets you three drinks and a dish of the day). *hours vary*

Bar Cocosone: Vinyl and album covers deck the walls while the bartender spins eclectic selections between mixing drinks at this friendly spot. *7pm-2am*

Cafe Taniwha: This super-welcoming, cosy place, run for decades by well-travelled Kuri and Fusa, often has live jazz or ukelele. *11.30am-11pm Tue-Sat*

Bar Revolucion: Swap *awamori* for tequila at this bar, whose owner's love for Mexico and Latin America shines through in its decor, cocktails and vibe. *8pm-1am Mon-Sat*

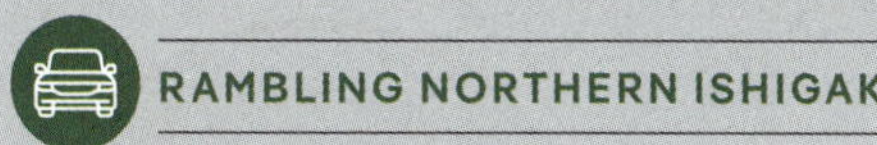

RAMBLING NORTHERN ISHIGAKI

Not in the mood for snorkelling? Choose your own alternative adventure around Ishigaki's lush land and sea.

START	END	LENGTH
Painushima Ishigaki Airport	Kabira Bay	59km; 2–3hr

Begin with a relaxed rural drive through sugarcane fields to ❶ **Tamatorizaki Observation Platform** on the northeastern coast. Boardwalks and paved paths meander to the shaded summit, where you can enjoy 360-degree views of both coastlines and the narrow isthmus into northern Ishigaki.

Next, head north to ❷ **Ibaruma Sabichi Cave** (adult/child ¥1200/600), having timed your visit for low tide. Marvel at the stalactites and stalagmites as you make your way through the cave, which opens onto the sea. If the tide is low enough, you can explore secluded beaches in both directions. Return through the cave's entrance and continue

north to ❸ **Hirakubozaki Lighthouse** to feel the breeze from Ishigaki's northern tip.

Backtrack south to log some time at ever-popular ❹ **Yonehara Beach** (p210), where you can swim, stroll and rinse off with a shower. About 1km down the road, it's only a few minutes' hike to the small ❺ **Arakawa Falls** for a quick dip before a stop at the ❻ **Kabira Park Observation Deck**. Famous for black pearl cultivation, Kabira Bay's pristine water and verdant islets are classic Ishigaki.

Before heading back to the 'big' city, pop across the peninsula to catch the sunset from west-facing ❼ **Sukuji Beach** (p210).

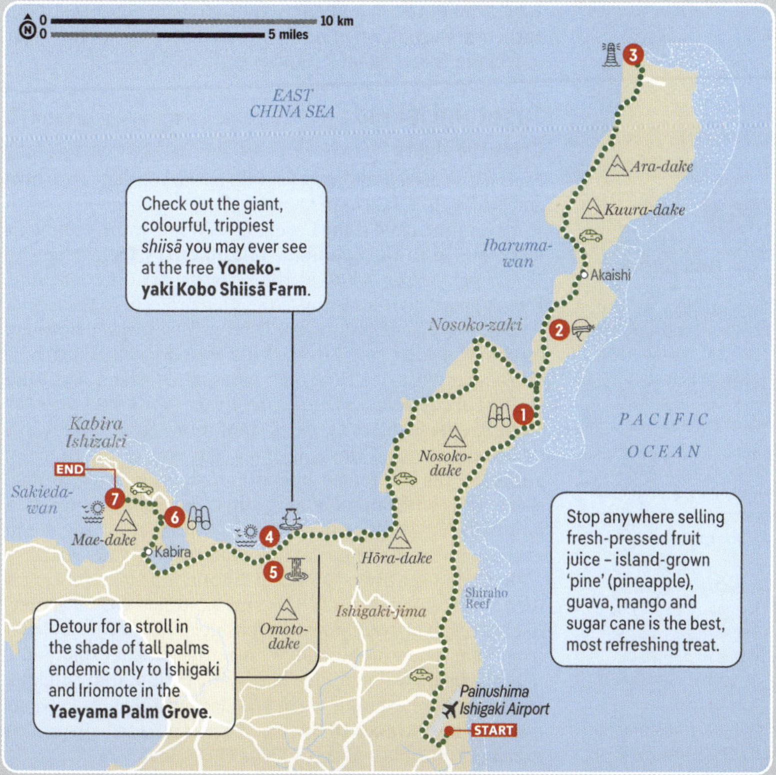

Beyond Ishigaki

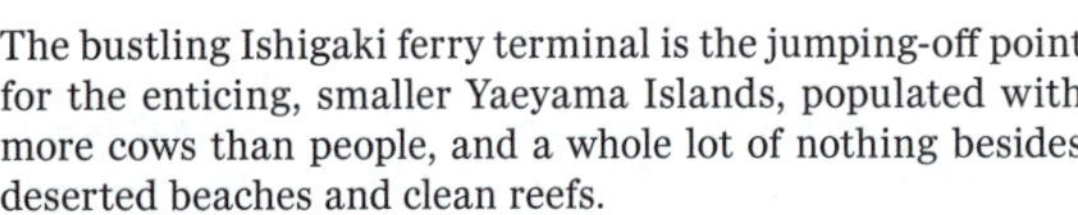

While Ishigaki has plenty to explore, ferrying to nearby islands gives a glimpse of a slower, more traditional way of Yaeyama life.

Places

Taketomi Island p214
Kohama Island p216
Kuroshima p217

The bustling Ishigaki ferry terminal is the jumping-off point for the enticing, smaller Yaeyama Islands, populated with more cows than people, and a whole lot of nothing besides deserted beaches and clean reefs.

The easy, 15-minute ferry ride to Taketomi makes this appealing island a no-brainer jaunt from Ishigaki – the island's traditional ways make it feel much removed from the 'big city'. Yet its accessibility means sharing it with a lot of visitors, and it can become slightly frantic with an amusement-park vibe. Take time to pause and enjoy your stops in what is still an authentic Yaeyama community. Even better, spend the night to feel the island exhale at the end of the day.

Taketomi Island

TIME FROM ISHIGAKI: **15MIN** 

Cycle the sights

Even with only a half-day at your disposal, you can rent a bike and cruise all of Taketomi Island (竹富島; Taketomi-jima) with stops for lunch and some beach time. While waiting for your ferry, opt in to the voluntary **island entry fee** (*utsugumi ticket; per person ¥300*) at the terminal vending machine. Fees support environmental-protection projects on the island.

Vans from bike-rental shops will be waiting to meet incoming ferries, whisking you into the village to rent bikes – they're all comparably priced and offer maps of the island. **Fat Bike Rental** (*trollfatbikes.wixsite.com/mysite; 3hr ¥1800, over 3hr ¥2400*) rents fat bikes for extra stability on coral-sand roads.

Meander through the village on your way to the beaches, admiring the red-roofed homes and stacked Ryūkyū limestone walls with sprays of bougainvillea in electric magenta and fuchsia. (Walk your bike and yield right of way if you encounter water-buffalo carts, giving them a wide berth.)

Then head southwest to **Kaiji-hama**, a beach famous for its *hoshizuna* (star sand). The star sand has gotten sparse, likely a result of overharvesting for sale; note that removing it from Kaiji is now prohibited. With a little patient exploration, beachcombers will find a few tiny stars, their scarcity making it all the more exciting when you do find some. A souvenir table at the entrance to the beach has star sand suspended in magnifying glass if you'd like a closer look.

GETTING AROUND

The islands scattered between and around Ishigaki and Iriomote are small enough to explore by bike or even on foot as a day trip. On hillier islands like Kohama you may be happier on an e-assist or fully electric bike. Many beaches, fringed by adan trees and thick foliage, may only be accessed on narrow paths through a bit of jungle, so sturdier sandals can be a boon on these pedi-powered day trips.

Taketomi Island

The rocky shore here isn't conducive to great swimming, so continue north to long, white **Kondoi-hama**, Taketomi's best swimming beach. There's bike parking at the entrance, as well as toilets, showers, and picnic tables with some shade.

Finally, stop at **Nishi-Sanbashi** on the western shore, a long, low cement pier jutting into the sea towards the horizon. Shoot an artsy pic, hop back on the bike, and return to the village to drop it off. On your way back to the ferry terminal, peek into **Taketomi Yugafu-kan** (*taketomijima.jp; free*). The small visitor centre has island folklore translated into English, natural history information and examples of folk art.

Sabani sailing

Take a different tack from the typical Taketomi day trip and book some time on a *sabani*, a traditional Okinawan sailboat. Before daily ferries plied regular interisland routes, the *sabani* served as a trading lifeline for Taketomi islanders.

Traditionally, *sabani* were carved by hollowing out tree trunks, but as the island's suitable trees were depleted, boatwrights began using *sugi* (Japanese cedar) from mainland Japan. *Sabani* are constructed without metal hardware, using dovetail joints and bamboo nails. With low-profile hulls that

HOSHIZUNA (STAR SAND)

Pressing your wet hand onto the beach to find star-shaped sand stuck to it: wondrous! If you want to be pedantic about it, no, it's not technically sand, but these impossibly teeny 'stars' make up the material beneath your feet only at certain beaches in the West and South Pacific. Specks of star sand are actually the exoskeletons of marine protists called *foraminifera*, classified as neither plant nor animal nor fungus. These particular *foraminifera* produce calciferous shells with protruding points in the shapes of stars, which, after the *foraminifera* die, are washed up onto reefs and play a key role in depositing sand onto beaches.

EATING ON TAKETOMI: OUR PICKS

Sobadokoro Takenoko: Noodle house famous for its Yaeyama soba and *sōki* soba (with pork ribs) in flavourful broth. *10.30am-3pm & 6.30-8pm Mon-Thu, 10.30am-3pm Fri* ¥

Garden Asahi: Yaeyama soba and curry sets cheerfully served in a modern dining room. English menu; cash only. *11am-2:30pm daily & 6-8pm Sun-Fri* ¥

Parlor Ganju-ya: On the road back to the terminal, end your Taketomi adventure with a *kakigōri* (shaved ice) or ice cream in this small, shaded garden. *11am-5pm* ¥

Yaaraa Cafe: Banana shakes by day, cocktails at night and great island pizza in this one-man cafe in a traditional house. *11am-4pm & 7-9pm Thu-Mon* ¥

CLUES TO ETERNAL YOUTH

Shiraho Natsuko, 93, member of 'idol' group KBG84 (Kohama Bāchan Gasshōdan – 'Kohama Granny Song Circle' – whose average age is 84)

I volunteered for KBG84 before joining because I hadn't yet turned 80, the group's minimum age! As I get older, it's so much fun to gather and talk and see everyone's faces. We only meet once a week, and I really look forward to singing and dancing together. We practise contemporary songs, but Kohama has hundreds of traditional island songs passed down from long ago that everyone learns from singing together at festivals and ceremonies.

Part of what makes Kohama special is that it's so small – everyone knows each other. We are a very close-knit community, and importantly, there is still great respect for our elders here, for the most senior on down.

allow them to glide over shallow reefs and panelled sails in the style of Chinese junks, it's dreamy to catch the tropical breezes on one of these traditional vessels.

To sail on a *sabani* off the shores of Taketomi, book ahead with **Shu-kaji** (*shukajitaketomijima.com; 1-/2-person sail ¥16,500/26,400*), established by friendly guides Uesedo Akira, a Taketomi native, and his English-speaking co-captain Funakoshi Hiroyasu.

Water buffalo carts

The classic touristy thing to do on Taketomi is bump along on a **water buffalo–drawn cart** through town, and despite how cheesy it might sound, it's charming. Rides are low commitment, lasting about half an hour, and they're a unique, accessible way to roll through the villages accompanied by live *sanshin* music on board.

Most importantly, the buffalo are very well cared for – in the hottest seasons you can wander the yard to see their pens outfitted with shade umbrellas and misters keeping them cool. When it's time to set out, they're harnessed to their cart knowing where to go, often following their route by heart and plodding along with a flower behind one ear.

Rides leave multiple times a day. Sign up on arrival at **Taketomi Kankō Center** (*high-season water buffalo rides adult/ child 6-11yr/child 3-5yr ¥3900/2900/1900*).

Kohama Island

TIME FROM ISHIGAKI: **30MIN**

Time slows on the Sugar Road

Find Blue Zone Okinawa on Kohama Island (小浜島; Kohamajima), a sugar-cane-covered isle whence sprang the world's most elderly J-pop girl group. As on other Ryūkyūan islands that still maintain traditional ways and a slower, more human pace, there's no reason to hurry here. There are no buses to catch, only farm trucks and tractors. In any case the best way to get around is by bike.

When you get off the ferry, stock up on some cold drinks, walk past the port parking lot and rent an **e-assist bike** from one of the little shops along the waterfront, such as **Rentacar Yui**, which will give you an island map and suggest a cycling route. Yui is open from 8am to the last ferry departure, and e-assist bikes cost around ¥550 per hour. You'll appreciate the e-boost, as the island's centre is hilly.

Ride up **Sugar Road** for a picturesque intro to the island, passing meadows of placid black bovines and rustling sugar cane. Meander a bit through the maze of red-roofed Taketomi houses, looking out for the not-so-traditional murals depicting cartoon *gōya* (bitter melons) playing golf and selling gifts. Leaving the village, you'll certainly want to find the base of **Ufudaki,** the highest point on the island, where you can climb the 280-odd steps to a shaded tower for wide-ranging views across the island and the sea below. The tower was originally built as a lookout for signal fires during the Satsuma colonisation of the Ryūkyū Islands, and Ufudaki's elevation made it the obvious choice of location.

Head to the island's west coast to wander alongside the Ishinagata **mangroves**, or ride north to **Coral Beach**, arguably Kohama's most beautiful shoreline of coral sand. With little tourist infrastructure, Kohama makes a lovely island for enjoying simple leisure time like reading a book on a quiet beach, sipping *awamori* as the sun sets and stargazing at night – which you can do with a stay at Pana Pana (p233), the small guesthouse at the island's far western end.

Kuroshima

TIME FROM ISHIGAKI: **30MIN**

Downshifting to Heart Island pace

A bird's-eye view of Kuroshima (黒島) reveals its heart-ish shape, earning it the nickname 'Heart Island'. One of the things we heart about it is how little tourism exists here. Like on Taketomi, renting a bike is the most fun way to explore the island, though refreshingly unlike Taketomi, far fewer visitors come here. There's no star sand, but there *are* gobs of cows and a plentitude of peace. The 3000 cattle raised for *wagyū* famously outnumber people on Kuroshima 13 to one. You're probably not here for black cows but for white-sand beaches, mesmerising blue ocean hues and low-speed Yaeyama life.

Pick up a bike at **Heart Land Cafe** (*heartland96.com; rentals 2hr/4hr/day ¥800/1300/1600*) across from the port. Since the cafe is the only eatery that's reliably open, you may wish to start with a plate of beef curry rice (*¥1000*) to fuel your ride around the flat, 10-sq-km island.

From the port, veer west along the coastal road to white-sand **Nishinohama** (no swimming) and then south past **mushroom-shaped rocks** offshore to the **Kuroshima Research Institute** (*kuroshima.org; ¥500*). The centre studies the three species of sea turtle – hawksbills, green sea turtles and loggerheads – that nest at Nishinohama from April to October. After a primer on the turtles, continue south to pause at **Puzumari**, the mound of Ryūkyū limestone formerly used as a lookout for incoming ships. It's adjacent to Kuroshima's welcoming but underwhelming **visitor centre**.

Keep pedalling south for a spot of swimming, sunning and snorkelling at **Nakamoto Beach**, soaking up the solitude before riding into Kuroshima village for a look at its traditional red-tiled roofs and Okinawan architecture. Bring your cycle tour to a close with a walk to the end of **Iko Pier** before bidding goodbye to Kuroshima, heart full.

SHIMA UTA

Iterations of 'Shima Uta' (Island Song), its familiar *sanshin* notes plinking through the soundscape throughout the islands, feel so deeply associated with Okinawa that you might assume the song to be a traditional tune. However, the original folk-pop version was debuted by Yamanashi Prefecture band The Boom in 1992. The band's singer Miyazawa Kazufumi wrote its longing, love-song lyrics, whose deeper meaning was inspired by the death and loss sustained by Okinawa in WWII.

Multiple artists have since covered 'Shima Uta'. In 2002 Okinawan singer Natsukawa Rimi reclaimed the song, in a sense, covering it in stripped-down style that showcases the *sanshin*, while in the same year Argentine musician Alfredo Casero infused the song with Latin flavour while staying true to its rock roots. Once you recognise it, you'll hear it everywhere.

EATING ON KOHAMA: ISLAND NOSHES

Bob's Cafe: Harbour views enhance your Kohama-sugar teriyaki burger. Closed arbitrarily to resupply; call ahead. *11.30am-3.30pm* ¥

Coyote: Casual portside spot to cool your heels with taco rice or shaved ice as you await your ferry. Cash only. *11am-6pm Fri-Wed* ¥

Ajidokoro Fukugi: Yaeyama soba in a friendly shop out west in Hososaki; check IG @fukugi.kohama for irregular closures; call to reserve. *5.30-11pm* ¥

Tida Shokudō: Village cafe serving satisfying island lunches including taco rice, soba and *mozuku* (local seaweed) bowls. *noon-2pm* ¥

Iriomote Island

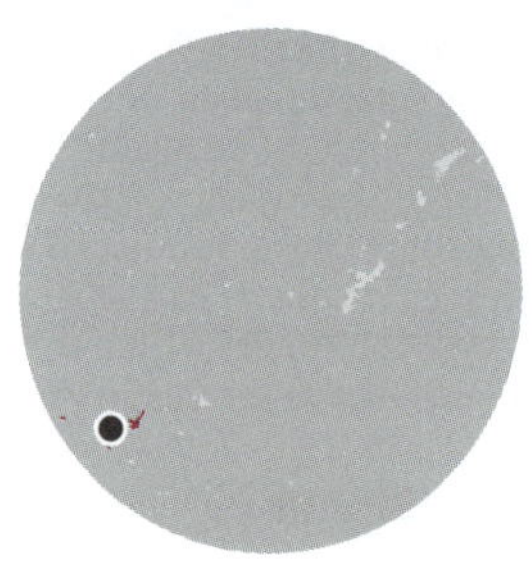

WILD YAEYAMA | MANGROVE JUNGLE | VIBRANT REEFS

 **TOP TIP**

In August 2025, Iriomote's 952-day streak of no *yamaneko* casualties ended with a vehicle strike. Though you're highly unlikely to spot one of these elusive, rare cats, observe the island's slow speed limits to help prevent an accident. Signs are posted where past sightings have occurred.

The most alluringly untamed of the Yaeyama Islands, Iriomote Island (西表島; Iriomote-jima) encompasses the greatest area of Iriomote-Ishigaki National Park. With around 90% of the island clad in virgin jungle, the largest of the Yaeyamas also represents nearly half of the Amami-Oshima Island, Tokunoshima Island, northern part of Okinawa Island, and Iriomote Island UNESCO World Natural Heritage Site designated in 2021.

Iriomote is a sanctuary for all seven species of mangrove that exist in Japan, as well as rare endemic flora and fauna including the Iriomote wildcat, known as the *yamaneko*. Rivers run through the island's subtropical jungle, its gorgeous waterfalls spilling into shaded pools, making their way to the sea and its teeming coral reefs. If you venture to enchanting Irimutii (Iriomote's indigenous name), do your best to pad into the island's wilderness with as light a footprint as its native feline.

GETTING AROUND

Ferries from Ishigaki run to Uehara port on the northeastern side of the island as well as to Ōhara port on the southeastern end of the island. The ports are 35km apart (around 45 minutes' drive), so make sure you're catching the right ferry for your activity or accommodation. **Anei Kankō** (*aneikankou. co.jp*) and **Yaeyama Kankō** (*yaeyama.co.jp*) travel to both ports several times a day.

When conditions are too rough, Uehara-bound ferries are redirected to Ōhara, in which case the ferry company provides a free **shuttle bus** onward to Uehara. In this case, check whether you need a bus ticket, which they will provide.

On Iriomote you can rent a bike to get around near your accommodation. Tour companies will pick you up directly from the ferry terminal or at your hotel, but if you want to explore further, you'll need to rent a car. **Yamaneko Rent-a-Car** (*iriomote.com/top/rentacar-2*) has branches in Uehara and Ōhara; book well ahead in high season.

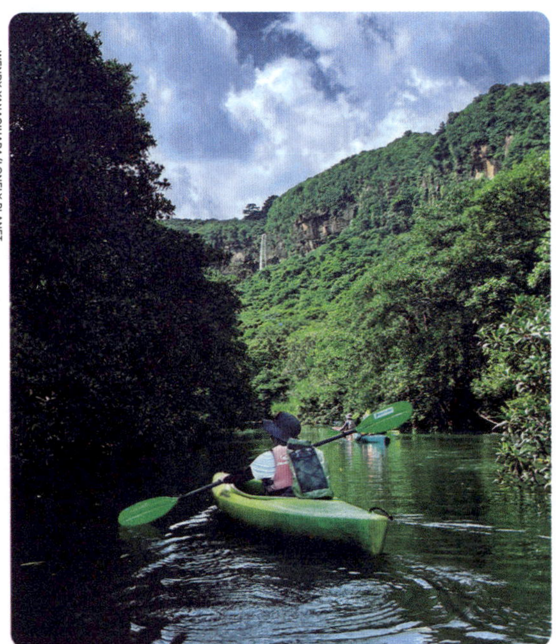

Kayaking to the Pinaisāra waterfall

Paddling to Pinaisāra

Mangrove kayaking to a waterfall

Undoubtedly the most popular tour on Iriomote, kayaking through the mangrove forest to hike up to the **Pinaisāra** waterfall draws daily visitors by the dozens for good reason.

Locally owned companies like **Iriomote Osanpo Kibun** (*iriomote-osanpo.com; adult/child ¥11,000/9000*) will pick you up at the Uehara ferry terminal and drive you to the river. After gearing up, your small flotilla will take a leisurely paddle through several species of *hirugi* (mangrove). Along the way, your guide will drop some knowledge on mangrove ecology, ID that fleeting red streak as a ruddy kingfisher or point out that 55m-high Pinaisāra is Okinawa Prefecture's tallest waterfall.

At the takeout you'll hike up a short, steep trail to Pinaisāra's boulder-ringed pool. You'll stop for a dip, some photos with the waterfall behind you and a picnic lunch in the shade. After the return hike, you'll paddle back the way you came.

Though the small groups naturally stagger their start times, it can certainly feel like a busload when multiple groups accumulate at the pool. An alternative paddle trip begins closer to Ōhara port. **Iriomote Station East** (*ise.festivalexpress.net; half-day adult/child ¥8000/6500*) runs tranquil SUP tours through the mangroves on the **Nakama River**.

For SUP and various foil-boarding adventures, contact **Waterman** (*i-waterman.com; 1½hr SUP tour per person ¥7150*).

continued on p222

LOCAL GUIDES & ISLAND STEWARDSHIP

Ojima Naoya, owner and guide at Iriomote Osanpo Kibun *@iriomote_osanpo_kibun*

When I began working here as a guide in 2004, I joined the Iriomote Island Canoe Association, established over 30 years ago. The association created rules that we follow to ensure visitor safety and minimise impact on the island's environment.

For example, there are daily visitor limits to five places in the national park, including Pinaisāra and the Mayagusuku waterfall area. Because only registered, licensed guides may bring visitors to these wilderness areas, internet searches for these specific locations will return licensed, locally run companies that are permitted to take small groups there. Local guides love our island, know it best and are invested in caring for it responsibly.

IRIOMOTE ISLAND

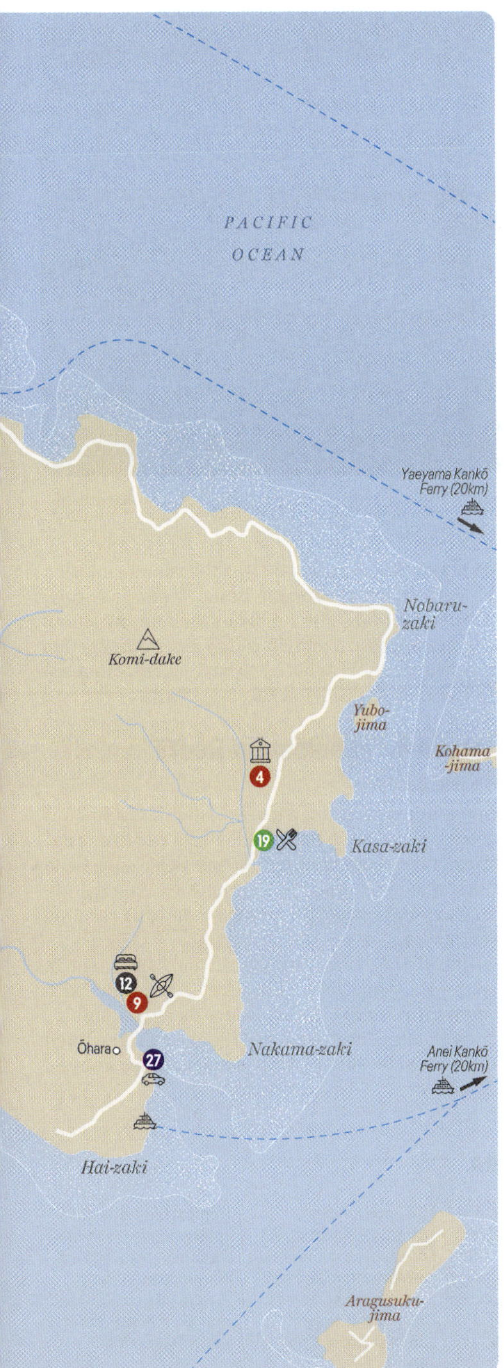

⭐ **HIGHLIGHTS**
1 Ida-no-hama

🔴 **SIGHTS**
2 Barasu-tō
3 Hoshizuna-no-hama
4 Iriomote Wildlife Conservation Centre
5 Pinaisāra
6 Tsuki-ga-hama

🔴 **ACTIVITIES**
7 Iriomote Jungle Book
8 Iriomote Osanpo Kibun
9 Iriomote Station East
10 Waterman

⚫ **SLEEPING**
11 Guesthouse Nesou
12 Guesthouse Shima Otoya
13 Irumote-sō
14 Kanpira-sō
15 Villa Hirugi
16 Villa Unarizaki

🟢 **EATING**
17 Hook
18 Ichitaka
19 Komi Dining Umikaze
20 Laugh La Garden
21 Nakayukui
22 Tamago
23 Tropical Dining Jeener
24 Umanchu

🟣 **TRANSPORT**
25 Funauki Port
26 Shirahama Port
27 Yamaneko Rent-a-Car

WHY I LOVE IRIOMOTE

Wendy Yanagihara,
Lonely Planet writer

When visiting Iriomote for the first time over a decade ago, I stopped along the road at dusk to listen to some frogs trilling in the field nearby. I love frogs, so as the light faded away, I stood listening happily as their syncopated songs rose and fell.

On my recent visit to the since remodelled **Iriomote Wildlife Conservation Centre**, I found their audio exhibit, which has buttons you can press to hear the calls of various island frogs. As soon as I heard the Yaeyama *aogaeru*, I was transported to that field on the other side of the island, listening to the frog serenade in the quotidian kind of magic that imbues Iriomote.

Barasu-tō

continued from p219

To climb **Mt Komi** (Komi-dake) and trek the island's interior, get in touch with **Iriomote Jungle Book** *(irijanbook.com; per person from ¥15,000)*. The English-speaking owners of **Hanauta** *(hugging-nature.com; half-day per 2 adults from ¥22,000)* run private tours tailored to each client, from sea kayaking to trekking to visits to other waterfalls.

Barasu Island & Technicolour Reefs

Coral above and below

Disappearing and reappearing with the tides, **Barasu-tō** is a tiny cay peeking out of the blue water like a white mirage. Boats to Barasu take about 10 minutes from Uehara port and will time the stop for maximum island exposure. You'll probably want to wear water shoes to disembark and poke around the coral fragments.

Though a lot of the coral directly off Barasu is, sadly, bleached, there are some interesting reef formations with healthy communities of fish to see. Tours usually stop here for a bit of snorkelling, as sea turtles like hanging out and feeding in this area. Be sure to keep some distance away so as not to disturb them.

EATING IN IRIOMOTE: UEHARA

Laugh La Garden: Long-running 2nd-floor establishment serving specialities like *kamameshi* (clay-pot rice) with *inoshishi* (wild boar); English menu. *11.30am-2pm & 6.30-9pm Fri-Wed* ¥¥

Tamago: Mum-and-dad *shokudō* (inexpensive restaurant) packed with locals. Hand-drawn menu with English translations; cash only. *11am-2pm & 6-7.30pm Mon-Fri* ¥

Umanchu: Fresh juices made from local pineapple and guava; the owner hunts *inoshishi*, sometimes served here, including as sashimi. Irregular hours. *11am-6pm* ¥

Tropical Dining Jeener: Contemporary Okinawan fusion incorporating local fish, produce and boar, plus creative cocktails and *awamori*. *11.30am-2pm & 5-9pm Thu-Tue* ¥¥

You'll get back onto the boat for a stop at another reef, where you'll see thriving gardens of table and branching corals, including splashes of the blue corals for which the Yaeyamas' Sekisei Lagoon is known. Cruise around with various damselfish, rainbows of parrotfish and triggerfish, and look out for moray eels and the occasional black-banded sea krait (venomous but not aggressive).

Barasu snorkelling trips can easily be done as a half-day adventure from Ishigaki.

Multisensory Natural History

Visiting Iriomote Wildlife Conservation Centre

If you have any interest in Iriomote's natural history, be sure to check out the **Iriomote Wildlife Conservation Centre** (*iwcc.jp; free*), which had a brilliant makeover in 2022. Any old-timey taxidermy you see here integrates seamlessly with the multisensory and interactive exhibits that introduce visitors to the varied ecosystems of Iriomote's land and sea.

Remove your shoes at the *genkan* (entrance) and don borrowed slippers, then enjoy the room-sized mural that curves into the main exhibition room. The immersive mural is dense with gorgeous, lifelike depictions of the birds, lizards, marine life and mammals that inhabit Iriomote, identified by their Japanese and Latin names. Informative videos, recordings of frog calls, specimens of island geology and explanatory graphics complement the continuous mural. Almost all of the interpretive signage is translated into English. The room's centrepiece features the **Iriomote wildcat**, a Special Natural Monument of Japan. Kids will love going on a virtual ride-along with a roaming *yamaneko* via collar cam or pressing the button that releases a whiff of *eau de yamaneko* urine.

One room is devoted to detailing conservation initiatives to protect island wildlife, including controls on domestic cat populations and road infrastructure to aid safe wildlife crossings; there's even a driving simulator that tests your reflexes if something runs across the road. Having just celebrated its 30th year, the renovated conservation centre is a marvellous intro to wild Iriomote.

Glimpse Indigenous Culture

Cultural walk and talk

Learning about indigenous Yaeyama culture from a reliable, English-speaking source can be challenging to arrange, but

---

🍴 EATING ON IRIOMOTE: ELSEWHERE ON THE ISLAND

Komi Dining Umikaze: Cosy Yaeyama soba spot in Komi village using local ingredients. Look for the flag on the road south of the conservation centre. *11am-3.30pm Fri-Wed* ¥

Nakayukui: Cute cafe for a post-beach bagel with lox, or cheesecake with an iced coffee. Sea views from the terrace when not unbearably hot outside. *1-6pm Mon-Sat* ¥

Ichitaka: Friendly *izakaya* with an English menu and English-speaking servers. Call to reserve; free pickup and drop-off around Uehara. *5-11pm* ¥¥

Hook: Run by a fisherman, this *izakaya* features fresh seafood and sea views. Some English-speaking staff; reservations recommended. *6-11pm Fri-Wed* ¥¥

IRIOMOTE-ISHIGAKI NATIONAL PARK

Spanning multiple Yaeyama Islands, including its namesakes, **Iriomote-Ishigaki National Park** (*www.env.go.jp*) was established in 1972. The park covers both terrestrial and marine zones in this subtropical archipelago, such as the islands' coastal wetlands and mangrove forests, which represent vital carbon sinks. On Iriomote, the park protects the ecosystems of unique endemic species like the Iriomote cat (p223), the Ryūkyū serpent eagle (crested serpent eagle) and the Sakishima grass lizard, whose endangered populations are limited to Yaeyama-rettō. Offshore, over 360 species of coral make up its large coral communities that support dense marine biodiversity. Japan's southernmost national park protects not only this ecological splendour but also the intangible assets of the islands' traditional human culture.

on Iriomote it takes the form of an easy amble with Karola Mech of **Cultural Walk** (*cultural-walk.com; per person from ¥7900*).

Having first visited the island in 2016 and become fascinated by Iriomote culture, the Poland-born artist settled in the village of **Hoshidate** in 2020. She developed connections with local *tsukasa* (priestesses), who allowed her to witness and document traditional rituals and ceremonies. As a member of the *kōminkan* (community cultural centre), and having shown deep interest in and sensitivity toward indigenous culture, Karola has been entrusted with a foreigner's rare and limited access to it.

Walks with Karola are physically undemanding, highly informative and culturally respectful – you will view *utaki* but never enter them, and visit a public traditional house and view significant sites. She details some of the cultural traditions shared with her, including folklore and customs, and can speak on it from the perspective of a foreigner living as a part of the community. Chatting over traditional *nikkei* (Japanese cinnamon) tea and *kokutō* after the walk is also part of the relaxed experience.

Though visitors are not allowed to observe any ceremonies, they are welcome to attend festivals like **Hōnensai** (the rice harvest festival; July) and **Shichi** (festival of gratitude for a bountiful harvest; late October). Keep in mind that observing these special occasions requires the utmost respect.

Remote Beaches & Real-Life Magic

Star sand, sunsets and solitude

You don't have to travel far from Uehara port to find one of the most delightful wonders of the Yaeyamas. Only on

Hoshizuna-ho-hama

certain islands does star sand (*hoshizuna*; p215) wash up, and even then it only appears on particular beaches. Though Taketomi-jima is famous for its star-sand beach, Iriomote's **Hoshizuna-no-hama** is also a hunting ground for these specks of magic.

If you don't mind riding uphill, rent a bike for the 10-minute ride to Hoshizuna Beach – there's a parking lot and cafe with a shop renting snorkelling gear and selling souvenirs. It also sells tiny glass vials if you do collect a bit of sand. The vial size is a great measurement of how much to take so that you can leave more for others to enjoy. The water is shallow, rocky and protected, making it ideal for small kids or those who aren't confident swimmers to put on a mask and snorkel and explore the marine life.

Continue around the 'hook' of Iriomote's northern tip and you'll come to **Tsuki-ga-hama** (Tudumari-no-hama), a long crescent of white-sand beach near Hoshino Resort. It's lovely stretch for a beach walk, and its west-facing shore makes it Iriomote's top spot to watch the sunset.

To get more remote, take the scenic drive to **Shirahama port** and catch one of the handful of daily **ferries** (*funaukikaiun .wixsite.com/top-jp; adult/child return ¥960/490*) to the isolated village of **Funauki** at the southwestern end of the island, accessible only by ferry. From Funauki it's a few minutes' stroll to tranquil **Ida-no-hama**, the most gorgeous beach on the island. The village has several little places to eat and is a window on quiet island life.

PHANTOM BLOSSOMS

Like little fallen stars floating on Iriomote's slow-moving waters, *sagaribana* are a seasonal delight to behold between mid-June and mid-July. These long shoots of hanging buds only bloom in the night, their white and pink firework-like blossoms dropping off at dawn.

You may spot the puffs of white in the foliage as you stroll around at night, though some tour companies offer night hikes expressly to view these phantasmic flowers and take in their delicate fragrance. Others offer pre-dawn paddles to experience the flowers falling as daylight breaks. But during the day in *sagaribana* season you'll see these sparks of beauty scattered around trails and floating amid the mangrove roots.

Beyond Iriomote

Iriomote's magic extends beyond its own shores, where you and water buffaloes can (almost) walk on water to nearby islands.

Places

Hatoma Island p226

GETTING AROUND

Anei Kankō (p218) and Yaeyama Kankō (p218) each run two **ferries** *(adult/child return ¥5170/2600)* per day to Hatoma on their way to and from Uehara port on Iriomote – one to Hatoma in the morning and one back to Ishigaki in the afternoon. Ferries may be cancelled in the event of strong north winds. Once you're on Hatoma, which has an area of less than 1 sq km, walking is the way to go. Bikes are also available for rent.

For nature lovers, Iriomote's jungle, waterways, wild beaches and coral reefs offer endless diversions, as do its remote offshore islands. The greatest appeal for most visitors is the superb clarity of the water for diving and snorkelling – dive shops organise trips to Hatoma and around Iriomote from Ishigaki. Boat tours also bring visitors to Aragusuku (locally known as Panari), which is actually a pair of islands called Kamiji and Shimoji that become one at low tide, connected by a traversable coral shoal. While walking the disappearing shoal is novel, the perennial attraction is underwater. For something completely different, you can even take a water buffalo–cart ride to Yubu Island, where the sea separating it from Iriomote is shallow enough to wade across.

Hatoma Island

TIME FROM IRIOMOTE: **15MIN**

Small isle, sweet reef

Taking up less than 1 sq km, tiny Hatoma Island (鳩間島; Hatoma-jima) is not on most visitors' radar, unless they happen to be divers or hardcore snorkellers. Some of the island's most gorgeous underwater coral gardens are not for the inexperienced, with strong currents and deeper reefs that require strong swimming and freediving skills. But at other sites, it's safe even for children to snorkel, searching for sea turtles and marvelling at the rainbow of fish busy foraging in the layers of table and branching corals.

Book in advance for all-inclusive day trips with **Hatoma Island World** *(hatoma.co.jp/snorkel; snorkelling trips ¥16,800/13,200 adult/child)*. Trips from Ishigaki have a two-person minimum, and rates include roundtrip ferry fare, lunch and all gear rental. English-speaking staff are available, with tours running from late March through October. Conditions of each day determine which reef sites they'll hit, but the day includes a lunch stop on Hatoma with a bit of time for exploring on land.

If you do happen to be both an experienced freediver and a Japanese speaker, contact Kawamitsu Manabu of **Ray Reef** *(rayreef.com)*, who offers one-day boat tours *(¥13,000)* to Hatoma and Barasu (p222) from Uehara.

Reef, Hatoma Island

Wander and wade

Though Hatoma lies about 15 minutes from Uehara port, only one morning ferry from Ishigaki stops there on the way to Iriomote, and one afternoon ferry stops on the return to Ishigaki on a daily basis. But you may be able to hitch a ride on a snorkelling vessel from Uehara port if you'd like to visit on a day trip.

Once on the island, you don't even need a bike to explore the entirety of Hatoma. It is decidedly not a destination for anyone needing a lot of external stimulation, but if you like the idea of tranquility and the visual feast of blue-green gradient seas, the trees of Hatoma Nakamori (the island's interior forest) and views of verdant, intriguing Iriomote, this island is for you. Walking will get you all over the island in about an hour, but of course you'll want to linger for some swimming at greenery-clad **Yara Beach** or snorkelling off of **Shimanaka Beach**. Consider staying overnight for a deeper sense of peace.

FOUNDATIONAL CORAL

From the precisely laid blocks of Shuri Castle's imposing walls to the more organically stacked garden walls surrounding traditional Yaeyama homes, Ryūkyū limestone figures prominently in Okinawan architecture. This native stone varies in age and density according to its location, but its general provenance is from ancient coral reefs.

The Yaeyama Islands are a product of coral uplift, in which reefs as old as 600,000 years were pushed above the surface of the sea over millennia of tectonic activity. The limestone, composed of calcium carbonate from Pleistocene-era coral reefs, makes up the caves, beachfront cliffs and mushroom-shaped offshore rocks characteristic of these islands. It's not unusual to see fossils of molluscs and corals embedded in Ryūkyū limestone – beautiful, commonplace works of geological art.

Hateruma Island

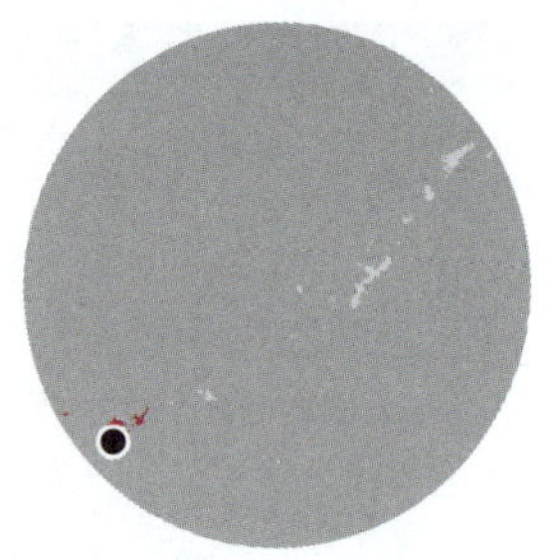

BROWN SUGAR | WHITE SAND | SOUTHERNMOST JAPAN

GETTING AROUND

Anei Kankō (p218) runs three high-speed daily ferries *(adult/child return ¥8750/4390)* to and from Hateruma and Ishigaki. About 30m up the road from the Hateruma port parking lot, you can rent two-wheeled transportation at **Oceans** *(bicycle/e-bike/motorbike per day ¥1200/2200/3300).* The no-nonsense proprietor only sets up shop in conjunction with ferry arrivals and departures, so if you drop off your bike much earlier, don't forget to leave the bike-lock keys with the bike.

Hateruma Island (波照間島; Hateruma-jima) is as far south as you can practically go in Japan – the next stop is the Philippines. Yet a surprising number of visitors make their way down here, which you'll realise as you join the queue for rental bikes. You can easily find solitude and remoteness if you go your own way. Stop to read the signposts along the ring road and follow what catches your curiosity: the sugar refinery, paths to untouted beaches and goats grazing terraced fields. Nishihama is not the only appealing slice of sand on this peaceful island (though it's the only one where swimming is allowed). Blue-tailed skinks and hermit crabs in hodgepodge shells will scatter at your feet as you make your way through jungle tunnels to semi-secret shores. Do your share as you depart by picking up plastic bottles, buoys and other flotsam to keep these southern beaches clean.

Cycling Under the Southern Cross

Slow travel in sugar-cane country

Crossing the open ocean down to Hateruma can get a little choppy, but it's smooth sailing once you're there. The high-speed ferry takes roughly 1½ hours from Ishigaki, so catch the first boat out and the last boat back to squeeze the most out of your day trip – or stay overnight to enjoy the remote quiet and spectacular stargazing. If you visit between late December and mid-June, you can see the Southern Cross.

The island's ring road is fairly flat, and you can cover it by bike in a couple of hours. Head east from the port, peering into the former **Ryūkyū Kingdom tax collection site** on the way uphill. Though not much exists besides the remains of Ryūkyū limestone stairs and walls, it may interest the curious to detour to the **Shimotabaru Castle ruins**, where jungle greenery grows over the structures from the kingdom's Gusuku Period (12th to 13th centuries).

Continue to Hateruma's eastern end past the airstrip, turning south along the main road to the domed **Hateruma**

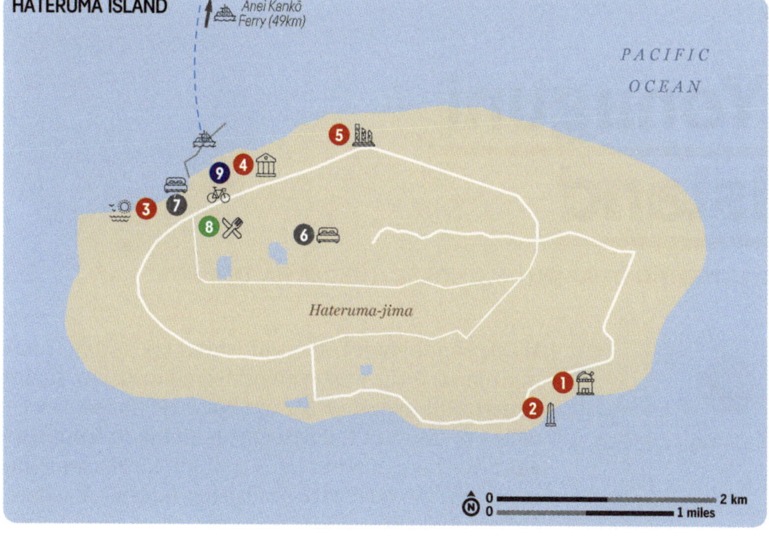

SIGHTS

1 Hateruma Observatory
2 Japan's Southernmost Point
3 Nishihama
4 Ryūkyū Kingdom Tax Collection Site
5 Shimotabaru Castle Ruins

SLEEPING

6 Manya
7 Pension Sainantan

EATING

8 Parlor Minpika

TRANSPORT

9 Oceans

Observatory, which is closed and in disrepair but makes an atmospheric photo op, as do the island's manhole covers depicting it. Another 500m west will bring you to Hateruma's top sight: the **southernmost point of Japan**. The sharp limestone outcropping beyond the monument leads to jagged drop-offs and surf crashing against the bluffs, so take care if picking your way across.

After enjoying ocean breezes at this southerly spot, pedal onward to the northwestern side of the island and the popular sandy beach at **Nishihama** to while away the rest of your afternoon. Head to the foliage backing the beach for some shade. You'll find toilets and showers here, so you can rinse off and change before boarding your ferry back.

If you've got time, end with a supremely refreshing brown-sugar shaved ice (¥600) topped with a splash of condensed milk and a sprinkle of *kinako* (roasted soybean flour) in the garden setting of **Parlor Minpika**, open 1.30pm to 4pm.

☑ TOP TIP

Clever are the crows of Hateruma, who know that unattended bike baskets often contain picnic goodies. Seriously lock down your snacks, as the dexterous crows are adept at unpacking. Visitors are required to pack their own trash off-island, so make sure the crows can't scatter your wrappers to the wind.

Yonaguni Island

WESTERNMOST JAPAN | WILD HORSES | UNDERWATER RUINS

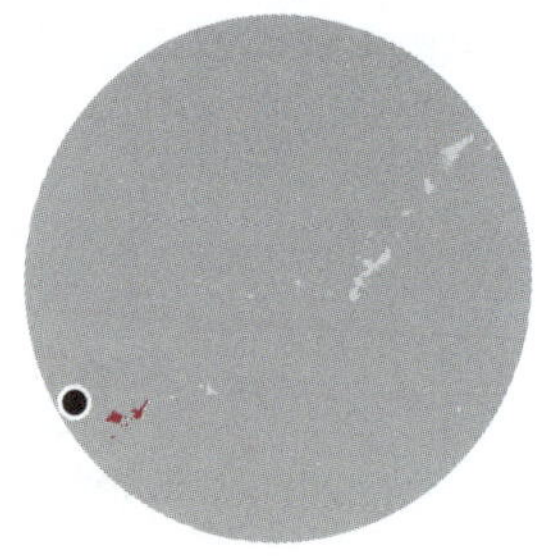

GETTING AROUND

To explore the entire island in a day, you'll need to rent a car, motorbike or e-bike. Reserve in advance, especially in high season, as of course the island has a finite number of vehicles. Last-minute travellers can try their luck at **SSK Rent-a-Car** *(yonaguni-okinawa. com/rentacar; cars from ¥4000/half-day),* across the road from the airport. You may wind up with a vintage, no-AC beater like I did, but it got me around the island and back in solid condition.

☑ TOP TIP

Keep to the speed limit, especially around corners and bends in the road, as you may unexpectedly share the two-lane coastal road with roaming ponies.

Wild, windblown Yonaguni Island (与那国島; Yonaguni-jima) is the westernmost island in Japan, sitting a mere 110km east of Taiwan but 2000km southwest of Tokyo. Most of the passengers flying in from Ishigaki live here, having left for practical reasons like receiving medical care or visiting family off-island. Others make up a visitor population of curious specialists – experienced divers coming to explore the intriguing underwater rock formations that some believe are ancient ruins or alien architecture (or both), equine lovers wishing to ride island ponies on isolated beaches or lepidopterists seeking a glimpse of the Atlas moth (its wingspan is up to 24cm). But other travellers venture out to Japan's western tip to simply see what there is to see in this faraway land. Yonaguni's geographical isolation and rugged landscape ensure its cultural integrity and feeling of unbridled uniqueness.

A Day in the Far West

Windswept cliffs, wild horses and massive moths

Yonaguni feels about as far-flung from mainland Japan as you can get. Its rugged coastline rises dramatically from the sea, punctuated by sharp offshore rock formations, and its landscape is buffeted by winds.

Driving west from the airport, start with lunch in **Kubura**, the fishing port where you may see boats coming in with their hauls. You can sample some of the local billfish catch with a delicious bowl of Yonaguni soba at family-run **Uminchu** *(soba from ¥1200),* open for lunch Tuesday through Saturday. Continue along the coast to turn off toward **Irizaki**, the westernmost point in Japan, and climb the hill to the stone monument marking the spot. If it's a clear day you may be able to see Taiwan from here. The shelter across the path has a tiled map showing Yonaguni's location and the cardinal directions.

Swing around to the island's south side, where you may encounter free-roaming **Yonaguni ponies** in warm shades of

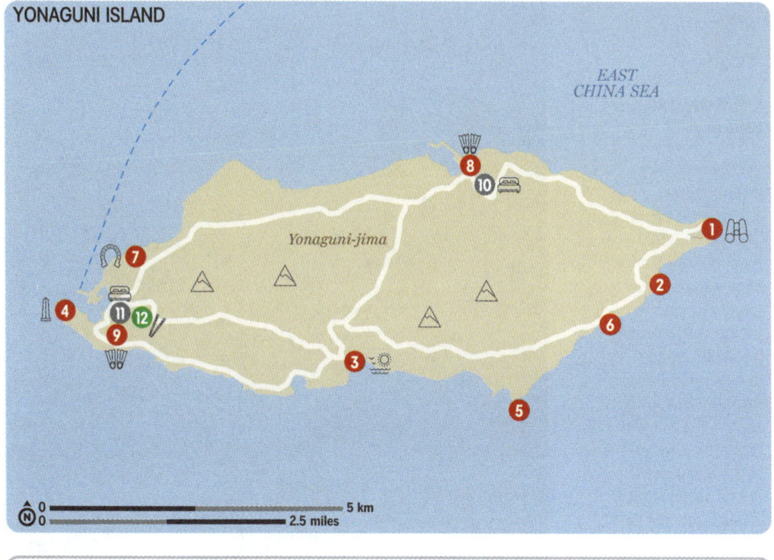

SIGHTS
1 Cape Agarizaki Lighthouse
2 Gunkan-iwa
3 Higawa-hama
4 Irizaki
5 Kaitei Iseki
6 Tachigami-iwa

ACTIVITIES
7 Chimanma Hiroba

8 Sou Wes
9 Yonaguni Diving Service

SLEEPING
10 Minshuku Sakihara-sō
11 Minshuku Yoshimaru-sō

EATING
12 Uminchu

cocoa and cinnamon. Stop at the pleasant, wide crescent of sandy **Higawa-hama**; find bathrooms at the parking area. Of interest to nostalgic fans of the early-aughts TV series *Dr Coto's Clinic*, the little house above the beach played the doctor's office in the show.

Detour into the highlands to poke around for fallen Atlas moths, and return to the coast to stop at the overlooks at Yonaguni's emblematic obelisk **Tategami-Iwa** (also called Tachigami-iwa), **Gunkan-iwa** (Battleship Rock) and onward to walk down to **Cape Agarizaki Lighthouse** at the island's eastern point.

Returning along the northern coast, you'll drop down into the town of **Sonai**, where minuscule pockets of sandy beach appear along the windy road, some amid the cemetery plots in this beautiful sector of the island. Pick up a bottle of **hanazake awamori** (60-proof firewater made only in Yonaguni) at the airport on your way to departure.

Ancient Underwater Architecture

Curious undersea geology

Yonaguni's intrigue isn't limited to land: its mystery only deepens beneath the surface of the sea. The Kuroshio Current flowing past the island carries warmer tropical waters and rich biodiversity northward, and divers travel here for the

YONAGUNI UMA

The petite Yonaguni *uma* (Yonaguni horse) resembles other Ryūkyū island horse species with its short stature and sturdy build. Because of its size, standing as tall as 120cm at the withers, it's technically classified as a pony. Whatever the name, these gentle horses were traditionally used as agricultural animals.

Some ranches, such as **Chimanma Hiroba** (chimanmahiroba.com; *2hr beach ride per two people ¥20,000)* offer the chance to meet and ride these sweet, well-cared-for beasts.

EYES ON DARK SKIES

In 2018 Dark Sky International designated Iriomote-Ishigaki National Park (p224) a Dark Sky Park, the first place in Japan to be recognised as such. Because Japan is so densely populated, this remote southern sector of Okinawa Prefecture is one of the few places to stargaze without urban light pollution.

Of course, dark skies aren't confined to the park borders – once you get away from urban centres you can find remote spots for stargazing even on Okinawa-hontō. But here in the far south, wilderness-thick Iriomote is a wonderful place to take in the Milky Way. And while Hateruma doesn't make the Southern Cross its whole personality, the chance to see the constellation is certainly an underrated selling point for overnighting on Japan's southernmost island.

Kaitei Iseki

excitement of seeing schooling hammerheads, whale sharks and large pelagic fish like tuna and swordfish.

Even more fascinating are the terraced, temple-like rock formations known as **Kaitei Iseki** (海底遺跡; Yonaguni Monument) that some claim are too geometrical to have formed naturally. Pointing to details that appear to be deliberately architectural or artistic, some divers who have visited the monument believe that they are ruins built by an ancient human civilisation. If you've got the diving credentials, you can judge for yourself – at the very least, exploring the unique geology makes for a wonder-sparking dive.

Because of the strong currents, Yonaguni's dive sites are for experienced divers only. But even non-divers can get a look at the underwater monument from a glass-bottomed boat. **Sou Wes** (*yonaguni.jp; adult/child ¥7000/4000*), founded by divemaster Aratake Kihachirō, who discovered the 'ruins' in 1986, runs boat trips to the monument; tours may be cancelled when ocean conditions are too rough. **Yonaguni Diving Service** (*yonaguniyds.com; boat dives from ¥15,950*) is another trusted dive outfit, family run by two generations of experienced divers since 1978.

Places We Love to Stay

¥ Budget ¥¥ Midrange ¥¥¥ Top End

Ishigaki
MAP p208

Iriwa ¥ Tucked away in a Kabira neighbourhood with a spacious garden area, the bright private rooms and dorms here share bathrooms and large, relaxed common space.

Hotel Cucule ¥¥ Blocks from the port, the minimalist Hotel Cucule is on Ishigaki's main street. Beyond the central locale, it offers a rooftop deck and a good breakfast.

Hotel Patina ¥¥ A rare family-run eco-conscious hotel in Ishigaki city, not 10 minutes' walk from the port, with laundry, great Japanese breakfast, wood-floored rooms and self-serve *awamori* happy hour.

Lulaliya B&B ¥¥ Kind, helpful, English-speaking staff enhance the experience at this bright, convenient guesthouse in Kabira. Amenities include drinking water, laundry and snorkel rentals. Breakfast available for ¥1500.

Tsundara Beach Retreat ¥¥¥ This spacious, self-contained, thoughtfully appointed private cottage occupies a tranquil garden setting above an isolated beach in Nosoko – a true retreat. Two-night minimum.

Taketomi Island

Takana Ryokan ¥ The longest-running ryokan on Taketomi offers dorms and private rooms. If you have trouble navigating its ancient website, ask a Japanese speaker to help you book.

Taketomijima Akaneya ¥¥¥ Splurge for a romantic overnight on Taketomi in one of the two suites that blend traditional style with modern comfort; book breakfast separately.

Kohama Island

Pana Pana ¥ Soak up peace and quiet sunsets at the very western end of Kohama in this simple guesthouse. English-speaking owner Araki-san offers breakfast for ¥1000.

Sanctuary Kohama Retreat ¥ Steps from the beach and a 10-minute walk from the port, this clean hostel has dorm beds and private rooms, and offers SUP yoga and night tours.

Iriomote Island
MAP p220

Guesthouse Nesou ¥ This peaceful, spotless guesthouse has shared kitchen, garden deck and lovely energy and is 20 seconds from Nakano Beach; book up to three months in advance.

Irumote-sō ¥ A longtime favourite, this tranquil pension in a garden setting is run by the friendly and helpful Seki-san; book ahead for meals and free port pickup.

Villa Hirugi ¥ This friendly, homey, light-filled guesthouse has one Japanese-style room; the rest have balconies, all have en-suite bathrooms, and simple breakfasts are included.

Kanpira-sō ¥ A two-minute walk from Uehara ferry port, this *minshuku* has rooms with private and shared bathrooms,

and lots of island info printed in English, though not much English is spoken.

Guesthouse Shima Otoya ¥ In Ōhara, airy, bright dorms and wood-floored rooms all share bathrooms; reserve free pickup from Ōhara port.

Villa Unarizaki ¥¥¥ This hotel's large, grassy lawn has hammocks and chairs for enjoying the amazing bay views. Each room has a small terrace, and buffet breakfast is included.

Hateruma Island
MAP p229

Manya ¥ Reserve by phone and book breakfast with your stay at this friendly *minshuku* in the village. No English spoken; port transfers included.

Pension Sainantan ¥¥ All the bright standard and Japanese-style rooms have sweeping ocean views and include breakfast and dinner. Reserve by phone only. Not much English is spoken, but it's very welcoming.

Yonaguni Island
MAP p231

Minshuku Yoshimaru-sō ¥ Has a couple of ensuite rooms, mostly tatami dorm rooms for men and women, and a *sentō* (public bath) in cooler seasons; diving guests only from 1 December to mid-May.

Minshuku Sakihara-sō ¥ Small, Japanese-style tatami rooms with shared bathrooms in the village of Sonai. Reserve a free airport shuttle in advance; very friendly, but no English spoken.

*Researched by
Manami Okazaki
and Craig McLachlan*

Amami Islands

ABUNDANT NATURE AND EXCEPTIONAL BIODIVERSITY

With pristine beaches, primeval forests and wildlife diversity like no other, it's no wonder sustainability is a high priority in the Amami Islands.

The archipelago that makes up the Amami Islands (奄美群島) sprawls over 200km southwest of Kyūshū to Okinawa. The largest and most visited island is Amami-Ōshima, but Tokunoshima, Kakeromajima, Yoron-tō, Kikaijima and Okinoerabu-jima have plenty of their own delights. The islands are verdant sanctuaries that support an abundance of life. Unique corals, flora and fauna, including rare endemic species, are found in disproportionate levels across the archipelago. Most visitor experiences on Amami are ecotourism related, so it's important to come prepared to interact responsibly with the islands' natural gifts. From its status as a UNESCO World Natural Heritage Site to local surfers advocating for less development, environmental protection is highly valued here. Amami will delight independent travellers who seek meaningful encounters with nature and want to appreciate symbiotic ecosystems at work.

Travelling the archipelago offers a view of lifestyles that prioritise the protection of nature over development. At the same time, the story of Amami-Ōshima is also one of survival. Colonised by the Ryūkyū Kingdom in the 15th century, becoming the Satsuma domain of Japan in 1609 and then being occupied by the US after WWII, Amami-Ōshima only reverted to Japan in 1953. All these periods left an indelible mark on the culture. Each practice, ritual and custom is interwoven with stories of adversity, struggle and survival.

THE MAIN AREAS

NAZE CITY AND CENTRAL AMAMI
The capital and surrounding bays.
p244

NORTH-SIDE AMAMI
Cerulean waters and stunning beaches.
p248

SOUTH-SIDE AMAMI
Undisturbed wilderness.
p252

KAKEROMAJIMA
Accessible day trip with pristine beaches.
p255

For places to stay in Amami Islands, see p273

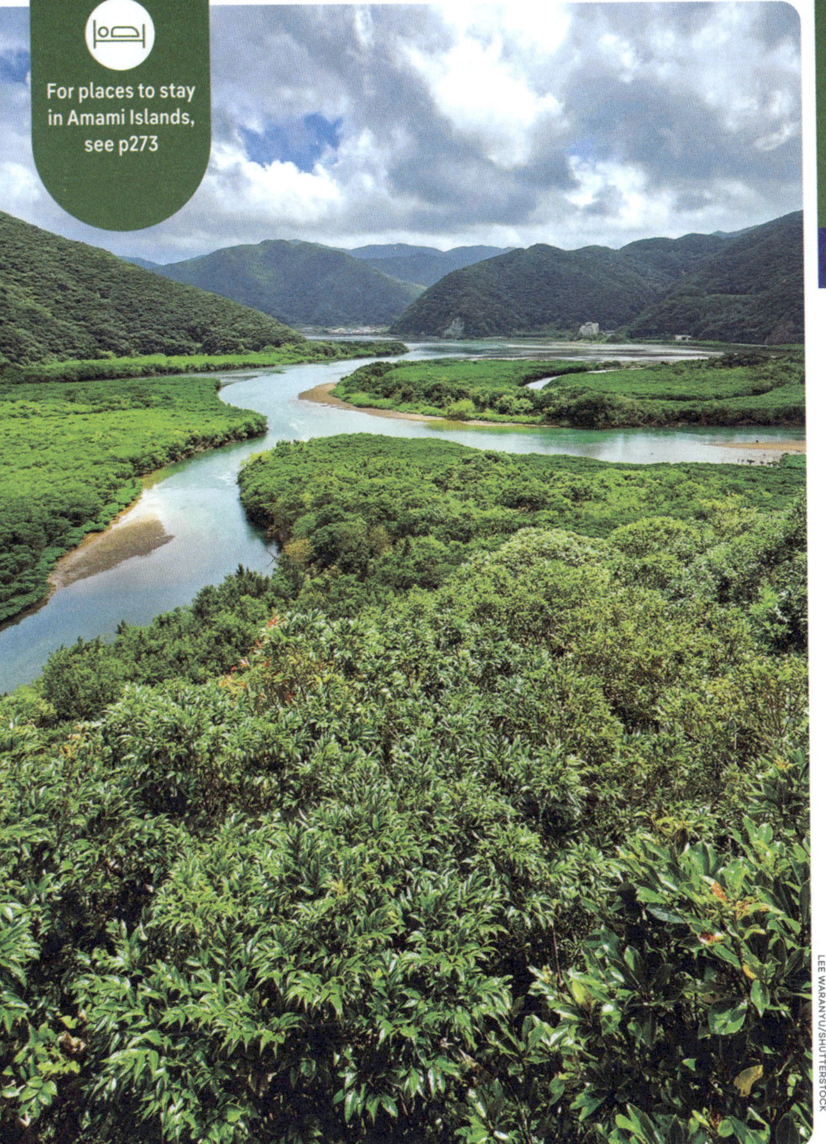

LEE WARANYU/SHUTTERSTOCK

Left: Amami tip-nosed frog (p246); Above: Kuroshio no Mori Mangrove Park (p252)

KIKAIJIMA
An island made of coral.
p257

TOKUNOSHIMA
Island of longevity, fertility and 'bovine sumo'. **p259**

OKINOERABU-JIMA
Caves, rock formations and Erabu lilies.
p264

YORON-TŌ
Gorgeous getaway with a 'phantom beach'.
p268

Find Your Way

Naze on Amami-Ōshima is the ferry hub for the chain of islands. The buses exist to serve locals but are very few in number.

EAST
CHINA SEA

Naze City & Central Amami, p244

Naze City is where the island's dinner options and cafes are concentrated. *Izakaya* (pubs) and folk music bars liven things up at night.

Iōtorishima

Tokunoshima, p259

Boasts two record holders for world's oldest person, Japan's highest total fertility rate, and a passion for *tōgyū*, a kind of 'bovine sumo'.

Amagi-dake

Tokunoshima

Amagi-chō

Inokawa-dake

Inutabu-dake

AMAMI ISLANDS

Tokunoshima-ch

Isen-chō

Okinoerabu-jima, p264

Raised coral atoll known for its limestone caves, rugged coastline and large, white trumpet-shaped Erabu lilies that bloom in April and May.

Koshiyama Wadomari-chō

Okinoerabu-jima

China-chō

Yoron-tō, p268

Shaped like a large angelfish, Yoron-tō features white-sand beaches, stunning colours within its surrounding reef and a famous 'phantom beach'.

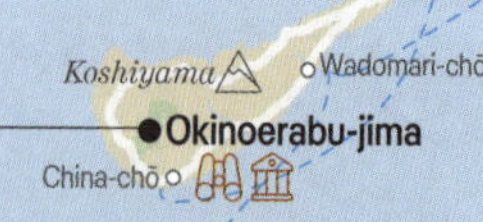

Yoron-chō Yoron-tō

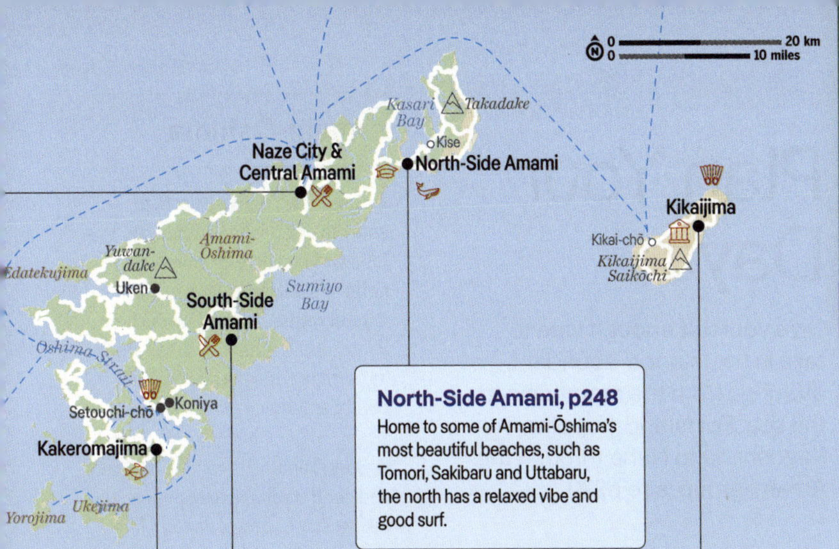

North-Side Amami, p248

Home to some of Amami-Ōshima's most beautiful beaches, such as Tomori, Sakibaru and Uttabaru, the north has a relaxed vibe and good surf.

South-Side Amami, p252

The less-developed south side has lush subtropical forests and mangroves. Setouchi port has great seafood eateries and dive operators.

Kikaijima, p257

Made of coral reefs that have been rising for the last 100,000 years, Kikaijima has stunning beaches. Even the picturesque village walls are made of coral.

Kakeromajima, p255

Easily accessible by ferry from Amami-Ōshima, and with pristine beaches for snorkelling, Kakeromajima has seen very little human intervention.

CAR

The only practical way to get to many of Amami's beaches and attractions is to rent your own car. Even popular beaches have no public transport. There are many car-rental agencies across Amami-Ōshima, and even the remote islands have one or two.

TAXI

Taxis turn up in a timely manner in Naze City, but they're sparse elsewhere. While pricey, they're a lifesaver on extremely hot days. Kakeromajima has no taxi service.

FERRY

The main port for interisland travel is Naze port, for the ferry that connects Amami-Ōshima, Kagoshima, and Naha on Okinawa Main Island. Koniya port serves the small ferry that goes to Kakeromajima.

Plan Your Days

Give yourself enough time to take in the islands' abundant offerings from the mountains to the sea. For island-hopping from Kagoshima to Naha through the Amami group, see p270.

Amami Aizome Study Group (p256)

MANAMI OKAZAKI/LONELY PLANET

Amami-Ōshima

● Spend two days up north to enjoy the exquisite beaches, go for a surf or a dive, or simply do nothing at all except enjoy the crystal waters. Ultimately the best things about Amami-Ōshima are its cerulean oceans and unspoilt coral gardens.

● Spend another two days in Naze and central Amami to experience the artistry of one of Japan's finest dyeing and weaving techniques at the **Oshima Tsumugi Village** (p251); canoe in the **mangrove forest** (p252) and eat plenty of delicious local cuisine, which runs the gamut from seafood to local classic *keihan* (chicken rice).

● After dark, go on a must-do night tour of **Kinsakubaru Old-Growth Forest** (p246) to see just how many of Amami's nocturnal creatures make this forest their home.

Seasonal Highlights

Subtropical Amami-Ōshima is known for its mild weather. Plan carefully if you intend to visit during typhoon season in August and early September.

JANUARY

Winter in Amami is ideal for hiking and exploring shadeless areas such as the **Miyakozaki Peninsula** (p244) without the humidity of summer.

FEBRUARY

Amami-Ōshima is one of the first places in Japan to see cherry blossoms as the deep-pink local *hikanzakura* puts on a show.

MARCH

Springtime has good weather, blossoming *sharinbai* and good birdwatching opportunities.

South Amami & Kakeromajima

● Go for a dive from the south-side port of **Setouchi** (p252) and enjoy the sites between Kakeromajima and Amami, where you can meander through tunnels, light cathedrals and healthy corals. The table corals here are teeming with life, and the region has plenty of dives to suit all skill levels.

● Stay in Setouchi, make the 25-minute ferry trip to tranquil little **Kakeromajima** (p255) first thing in the morning and spend a full day exploring by bike. There are snorkelling beaches devoid of people, lush subtropical jungle areas and ginormous banyan trees. The island's **fishing tours** (p255) have something for everyone from beginners to pros, or if craft is more your thing, arrange a visit to indigo workshop **Aizome Study Group** (p256).

Kikaijima

● A compact island that can be circled in a few hours, Kikaijima makes a satisfying day trip. Take the ferry from Naze, which takes two hours and arrives at 8.30pm.

● Spend the next day at the magnificent **Sugira Beach** (p258) and see some of Japan's most beautiful villages with their charming coral walls. Visit the **archaeology museum** (p258), where some artefacts date back 8000 years. Outside the museum you may want to cool off in the natural pool fed by stream water.

● Make time to drive along the magical **Butterfly Road** (p257), where dozens of varieties of the island's butterfly species dance and flutter ahead of you.

● Be sure to get to bed early: the ferry back to Naze leaves at 5am.

JULY
As Japan enters summertime, temperatures start to rise. This is the perfect month for diving.

AUGUST
Summer comes alive with festivals such as Amami and Setouchi, featuring fireworks, traditional dance and folk songs. It's also typhoon season.

SEPTEMBER
The summer peak tapers off, but autumn with its harvest festivals is a beautiful time to visit the islands.

DECEMBER
Whale-watching season begins as humpbacks migrate to Amami-Ōshima.

HELP ME PICK:

Amami-Ōshima Diving

Amami-Ōshima's waters are dense with life, and the average visibility is an astonishing 20m. Marine biologist and diver Giovanni Masucci says, 'It's a coral-dominated ecosystem, with temperate species migrating from the north while subtropical species migrate from the south. It's a mix of ecosystems that are meeting there and coexist or compete.' This means you can expect a rare combination of algae, seagrass and over 220 species of coral, as well as fish, turtles and sharks.

Where to dive if you love...

Landscapes and nudibranchs

Central Amami-Ōshima has a number of operators.

East China Sea side The waters northwest of the island might seem like enclosed bays, but they're actually open-ocean dive points. Divers can explore rich landscapes that include dramatic drop-offs and picturesque underwater caves. Faster currents mean there are larger fish here, such as snappers, and even rays.

Garden eels

Central Pacific side Great for a winter dive, this side of the island is home to turtles and is a paradise for nudibranchs.

To learn how to dive

North Amami-Ōshima The East China Sea side of the island has many shallow places that have no current, so beginners can enjoy their first dives from beach entry points. The surrounding seas have flounder, clownfish, butterfly fish, lionfish, garden eels and Gilbert's cardinalfish in abundance, and the clarity and stillness of the water make conditions ideal for learning.

All local operators offer dive licence courses.

Spectacular variety

Ōshima Strait With several inlets and coves, the strait has many calm spots to dive. There are also strong tidal currents, resulting in superb clarity. Points also have larger fish such as bluefin tuna and amberjacks. Most sites offer rare goby species, red sea bream and moray eels, and Shirahama dive site has mandarin fish. The ethereal coral spawning in June after the full moon resembles a blizzard of pink atoms.

Kohollo Dive Located in Setouchi, this operator is recommended and one of the few services on the south side of the island.

Beautiful landscapes and remote island vibes

Between Amami-Ōshima and Kakeroma The dive sites between these islands are brimming with life amid dramatic underwater geography and drop-offs. White-tip sharks, bluefin tuna and spotted rays can be seen, as well as orange-striped shrimp goby, anemones, damselfish and double-lined fusilier. Fantastical sandy landscapes are dotted with abundant table corals.

Most of the Setouchi dive operators head out this way, but you can also dive off Kakeroma and enjoy the seclusion of the island.

Amami-Ōshima reef

HOW TO

When to go Diving takes place all year round in Amami-Oshima. Winter temps average 19°C, and in the main diving season temperature averages range from 23°C in March to 29°C in August.

Wetsuits The warm Kuroshio currents surrounding the Amami Islands mean that a 3mm or shorty wetsuit in summer and a 6.5mm in spring is sufficient.

What to bring Take a towel, a change of clothes and flip-flops for the boat. Sunscreen is a must during summer in particular. Most dive operators also send you photos and logbook information via Japanese messaging app LINE.

Licence Several operators offer dive licence courses for beginners. Since most sites are quite shallow, open water certification is generally sufficient.

Marine Crop Circles

People from all over the world come to dive off Katetsu village in Setouchi for one particular reason: to check out the adorable Amami *hoshizorafugu* (Amami night sky pufferfish). Discovered only in 2011 and registered as a new species a few years later, in 2014, the fish are 15cm long and have a spangle of spots on their back that resemble a sky full of stars. Though exciting for scientists, a brand new fish species might not be reason enough for national news coverage. However, the pufferfish received a lot of attention for their proclivity to make circular depressions in the sand, which were initially dubbed 'crop circles' – or 'mystery circles', as it wasn't obvious who the artist was. During the spawning season from mid-March to July, the male pufferfish makes 2m-wide sand circles and then beckons his love interest inside. When mating, the female hovers in the middle of the geometric installation. Once the eggs are laid, it is up to the male to guard them for a week. Scientists have discovered that the more ridges the sand depressions have, the higher the fish's dating success rate. Dive operators including Kohollo lead tours off Katetsu to witness the intriguing circles and their delightful architects.

HELP ME PICK:

Saunas & Bathhouses

Japan is going through a massive sauna boom, with hip bathhouses popping up across its cities. Amami-Ōshima has taken advantage of the trend to offer a wide range of experiences where you can sit, steam and get those pores open. Options range from wooden barrel saunas to no-frills bathhouses to designer hotels. While some saunas are attached to resorts, many are independent companies. Choosing one of these has the added attraction of supporting a local business.

Where to go if you love...

Maximum tranquility

Ryūkyū Villas (*ryukyuvilla .jp*) At this set of completely secluded mini cabins (p273) in Tatsugo, the resort rooms are adorned with artworks by local craftspeople and creators.

The complex has two **private barrel saunas** that you can hire even if you're not staying overnight. One offers ocean views and backs onto the rainforest. The other is next to a yard and is perfect for small gatherings. The saunas are built on a platform, and the cold plunge bath is infused with *geto* oil.

Excellent facilities

Hanahana Beach Resort (*amamihanahana.com*) The main resort (p273) resembles a water theme park, but the sauna section, attached to the resort's Amami Onsen Yamato, is inside entirely private cabins.

The **barrel sauna** has an excellent wood-fired stove. There's a tatami resting area and an outdoor cold bath.

There's also a **private onsen** at which visitors can experience the rare combination of sauna and hot spring.

The sunset views are stunning. Visitors can order food from the **restaurant** and eat it in the cabin, making it ideal for families.

First-time sauna

Hoco Rasha Sauna (*greenhill -amami.com/sauna*) Visitors can hire this affordable tent sauna for two-hour slots. The sauna uses a wood-fired stove.

It has the advantage of being located near one of Amami-Ōshima's premier beaches, Tebiro (p248), and is adjacent

to Pension Green Hill, which is popular with **surfers**. The plunge bath is basically a portable bath tub.

This place is perfect for beginners because the staff give a presentation on the benefits of sauna.

Super local

Furei no Yu (*0997-63-2299*) This local *sento* (bathhouse) in Amami-Ōshima is well patronised by locals coming in to cap off their day. *Sentos* are an important part of the mostly working-class community and offer a third space where anyone can go and enjoy social interaction.

The bathhouse offers international visitors the opportunity to hear the **local dialect** spoken as the mostly elderly locals engage in conversations with friends.

Fureai no Yu has a small cold plunge pool, a toasty sauna and a public bath.

Barrel saunas, Ryūkyū Villas

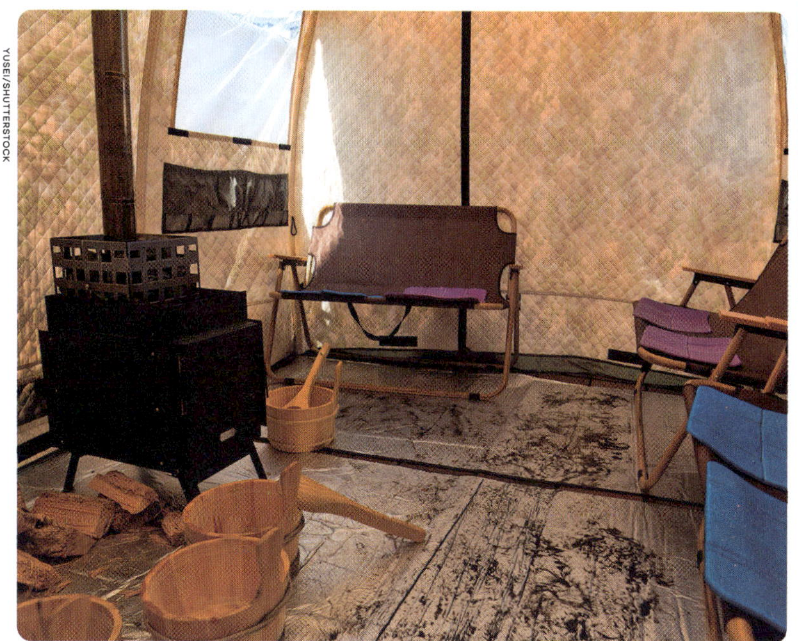

Tent sauna

HOW TO

Do as the locals do and try an Olloppo, a popular drink for sauna fans. It's a mix of Oranamin C vitamin drink and Pocari Sweat sports drink.

It's most common to do three sets of the following: steam in the sauna for 10 to 15 minutes, plunge into the cold bath and then rest outside.

Time your visit for sunset and enjoy your rest time while you watch the changing colours of the sky.

Tent saunas might seem very simple, but they usually use wood-fired stoves and offer an exceptional experience.

Revel in Nature

Saunas are a low-impact way of enjoying Amami-Ōshima's beautiful natural environment. The outdoor soak and rest period offers you ample time to contemplate your surroundings, including the island's vast skies, unobstructed by infrastructure or light pollution. Spectacular sunsets and stargazing enhance the sauna experience.

Steam baths were built within Buddhist temples from the Nara period, and the custom continued until the Edo era, when hot-water baths became more common. Developed by Olympic shooting team member Ujitoki Konomi, the first sauna was built in Tokyo's Ginza district in 1957. When the Finnish Olympic team brought their own sauna to the Tokyo Olympics in 1964 it sparked a boom in saunas, but they were usually attached to cheap capsule hotels and gyms for men. Indeed many saunas still cater to men only.

In the 1990s saunas started to appear in *sentos* and super-*sentos* (similar to spa theme parks). The current boom is part of the wellness trend. Resort facilities come with all the bells and whistles, but tent saunas are usually run by local hipsters – and it must be said that tent saunas' wood-fired stoves guarantee a great-quality sweat. Saunas inside *sento* facilities offer the ultimate local experience.

Naze City & Central Amami

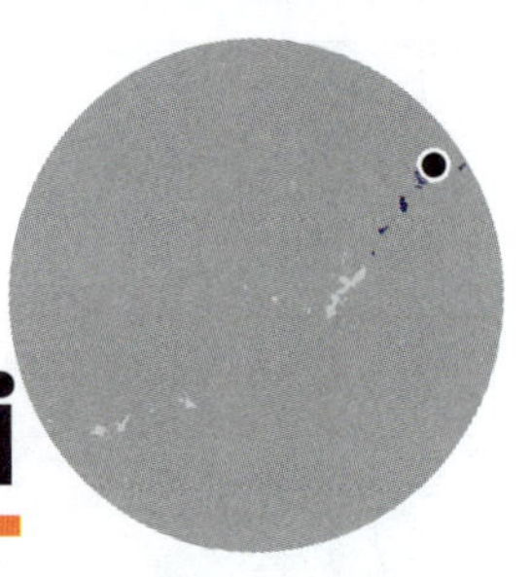

BEACHES | LUSH FORESTS | SHŌCHŪ

GETTING AROUND

You won't need a car in Naze itself. The city is tiny and easily walkable, and many tours pick guests up from their hotels. To get around the island, it's best to hire a car. The only rental agency in Naze is **Amami Lucky Rentacar**); most other car rentals (Budget, TIMES and Orix) are at **Amami Airport**.

Naze City isn't a city so much as a collection of buildings around a port that most of the interisland ferries use. What it does have are resources that are hard to find in the rest of the island, including excellent cafes and night-time restaurants. The large majority of the accommodation is clustered here, it's a transport hub, and the availability of excellent coffee at numerous cafes makes it a convenient base. Additionally most of the tour companies have their offices here or offer pickups from Naze. In the evening the lights come on at the tiny *izakaya* (pubs) as they get ready to serve local delicacies and copious sugar *shōchū* (alcohol). Amami City Museum is a good starting point to gain an overview of the island's traditional culture and ecology and the legacy of colonisation. Naze is also close to beaches such as the palm-tree-lined, white-sand Ōhama Seaside Park.

Beach Life

Small city, world-class beaches

The white-sand shores of Amami offer undisturbed time with pristine nature devoid of the bus tourists and protective concrete tetrapods characteristic of beaches in the rest of Japan. Most beaches have simple facilities such as a toilet and shower (sometimes just a hose), but there are usually no lifeguards.

A seven-minute taxi ride from Naze is **Asani Beach**, where eating options include Rashikurasu Cafe (p246), specialising in fermented food, and **Kingston Ramen** with its mammoth toppings. Around 20 minutes' drive from Naze, palm-lined **Ōhama Seaside Park** boasts aquamarine water. The park is next to little **Amami Marine Aquarium** *(ohama. marutani-amami.com; adult/child ¥700/400)*, worth a visit to appreciate the bounty of life around the island. The **Miyakozaki Peninsula**, a 1.4km hike away over grassy hills, offers expansive views. Cool off at the neighbouring **Kuninao Beach** with its bucolic, rural-town atmosphere.

☑ **TOP TIP**

Have an unforgettable dinner at Natsukashaya (p247), which prepares sumptuous home-cooked traditional Amami food and serves it in bamboo baskets.

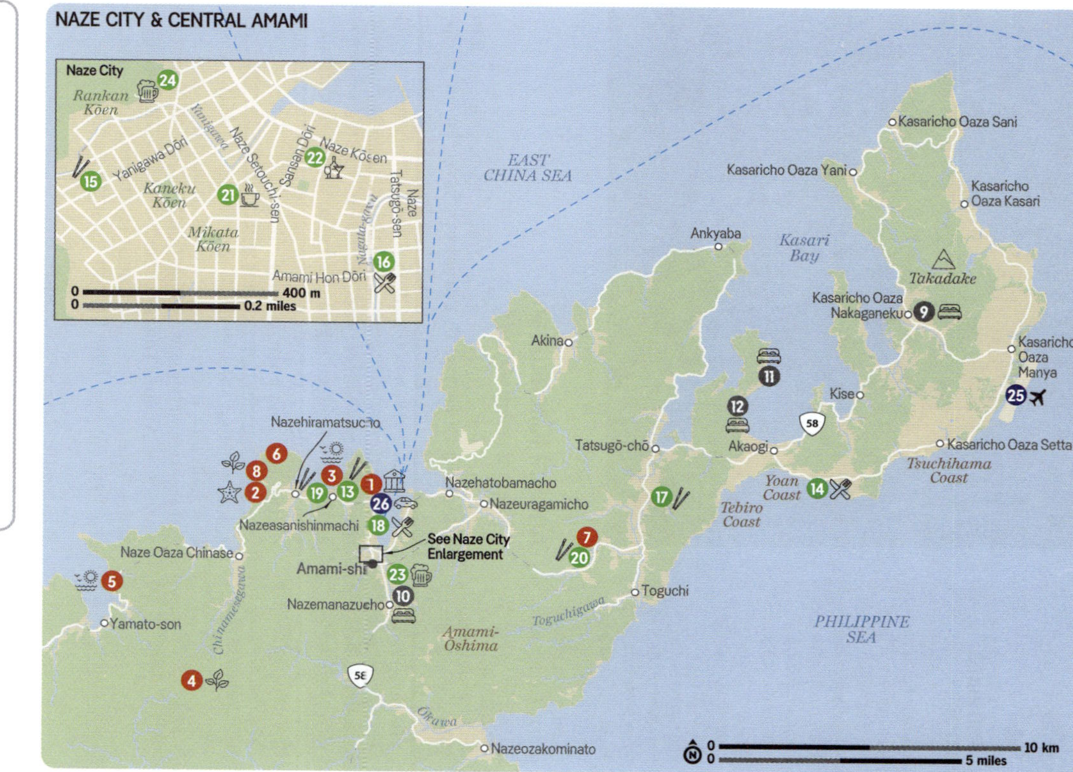

SIGHTS
1 Amami City Museum
2 Amami Marine Aquarium
3 Asani Beach
4 Kinsakubaru Old-Growth Forest
5 Kuninao Beach
6 Miyakozaki Peninsula
7 Mizuma Brown Sugar Factory
8 Ōhama Seaside Park
SLEEPING
9 Denpaku Hotel Akagina
10 Guest House An
11 Miru
12 Ryūkyū Villas
EATING
13 Kingston Ramen
14 Kulukulu
15 Natsukashaya
16 Nomad
17 Oguchi Unagi
18 Oliver's Café
19 Rashikurasu Cafe
20 Shimatofu-ya
DRINKING
21 By the Tree Coffee
22 Itwu Maajin
23 Nishihira Shuzo
24 Tomita Shuzo
TRANSPORT
25 Amami Airport
26 Amami Lucky Rentacar
NAZE CITY & CENTRAL AMAMI
Naze City
Rankan Kōen
Yanigawa Dōri
Yanigawa
Kaneku Kōen
Mikata Kōen
Naze Setouchi-sen
Sansan Dōri
Naze Kōen
Naze Tatsugō-sen
Nagatagawa
Amami Hon Dōri
400 m
0.2 miles
EAST CHINA SEA
Kasaricho Oaza Sani
Kasaricho Oaza Yani
Kasaricho Oaza Kasari
Ankyaba
Kasari Bay
Takadake
Kasaricho Oaza Nakaganeku
Kasaricho Oaza Manya
Akina
Kise
Tatsugō-chō
Akaogi
Kasaricho Oaza Setta
Tsuchihama Coast
Yoan Coast
Tebiro Coast
Nazehiramatsuchō
Nazehatobamacho
Nazeuragamicho
Nazeasanishinmachi
Amami-shi
See Naze City Enlargement
Naze Oaza Chinase
Nazemanazucho
Yamato-son
Chinameseguwa
Amami-Oshima
Toguchi
Toguchigawa
Ōkawa
Nazeozakominato
PHILIPPINE SEA
58
5E
10 km
5 miles

SUMO RINGS GALORE

A sumo ring can be seen in every village – in fact Amami has 140 of them, more than any other region in Japan. Sumo is ingrained into local kids, and it's part of community identity and local pride. The region has a history of producing many professional wrestlers, including the 46th *yokozuna* (grand champion in sumo), Asashio Tarō.

Folk harvest festivals that take place from August to December often feature sumo rituals, and newborn babies wearing sumo aprons are placed in the ring in hopes they will have a healthy childhood. The sumo *jinku* folk song performance sees wrestlers singing and dancing. The first day of the Setouchi Minato festival in early August has kids' matches all day.

Ancient Kinsakubaru

A forest teeming with life

Deep in the mountains of central Amami-Ōshima, **Kinsakubaru Old-Growth Forest** is a haven for native species such as the spider monkey tree fern, which has existed here for more than 300 million years. Entry is only possible with a registered guide, who will take you through dense subtropical forests to meet endemic species like the Amami jay and whistling green pigeon, and even the odd *habu* (viper). Tours usually go for two hours on flat terrain under a canopy of tree ferns that filter the sunlight.

On a 4WD **night tour**, a guide will take you along the forest roads, wielding a flashlight to spot Amami rabbits, Ryūkyū long-haired rats, Ryūkyū scops owls, Amami tip-nosed frogs and the Amami Ishikawa's frog. Don't forget to look up at the starry skies. **Amami Tours** (*amamitours.com*), **GANSO night tours** (*nitetour.jp/en*) and **Amami Nature Guide** (*amaminatureguide.com*) have English-speaking staff.

Amami's Sugar Shōchū

Sweet, powerful elixir

About half of Amami-Ōshima is devoted to producing the distinctive, caramelly local variety of sugar. About 20 minutes'

EATING AROUND NAZE: BEST CAFES

By the Tree Coffee: Roastery and hip cafe in the middle of Naze. Stylish interior and spot-on coffee. *7.30am-7pm* ¥

Oliver's Café: Regular meals are available, but don't miss the decadent seasonal fruit parfaits with crème brûlée, cream and jelly layers. *11am-3pm* ¥

Rashikurasu Cafe: (らしくラス) Delicious fermented food and sweets near Asani Beach. *11am-5pm Mon-Fri* ¥

Nomad: Curries, frappes and lattes are served in a laid-back space. *hours vary* ¥

Whistling green pigeon

A BIODIVERSITY HOTBED

Aside from the tidal flats and coral reefs surrounding the islands, 80% of Amami is covered in forest. The island has Japan's largest evergreen broad-leafed forest and Japan's second-largest mangrove forest, and both support a wide range of species. An astonishing 49.8% of Japan's bird species, 38.5% of its inland water fish and 22.2% of its reptiles can be found on Amami-Ōshima, despite the island's diminutive size of 712 sq km. Many species that have become extinct elsewhere in Japan still flourish here because they have adapted to environmental changes and there are no predators on the island to threaten their survival. These factors, coupled with Amami's subtropical climate, have created a mix of conditions ideal for life to thrive.

drive from Naze, you can visit **Mizuma Brown Sugar Factory** (*mizumakokutou.com*) to see the production process and purchase some sugar to take home.

Amami *kokuto shōchū* (sugar alcohol) can only be made on the islands using its aromatic sugar and malted rice. Most of the 26 distilleries on Amami-Ōshima offer tasting tours, including **Tomita Shuzo** (*kokuto-ryugu.co.jp/tomitashuzojo; tours ¥1000*). Also in Naze is **Nishihira Shuzo** (*nishihira-shuzo.com*), where **Amami Tours** (*amamitours.com*) guide John Cantu works as a producer. Cantu leads *kokuto shōchū* tours where you'll gain an insider perspective. He says, '*Kokuto shōchū* is regionally exclusive, like Chardonnay. But I liken it to Japan's mezcal, as it used to have a bad name, but now people love it because the ingredients are really high quality.' Experience *shima-uta* folk music while downing a glass of *kokuto shōchū* at **Itwu Maajin** (島料理 itwu~まぁじん~), which has live shows from 7pm, or folk-music *izakaya* Kazumi (p254). Expect a lot of drunken dancing.

EATING IN AMAMI: BEST LOCAL EATS

Natsukashaya: Courses from grilled lobster to sashimi to pork dishes are served in private rooms in a traditional house. *6.30-11pm* ¥¥¥

Shimatofu-ya: Set lunches with a wide array of tofu dishes, soups and side dishes, all freshly made in the factory next door. *10am-6pm Mon-Sun* ¥¥

Kulukulu: Beachside Italian food using many Amami-Ōshima ingredients: passionfruit, seaweed (in spaghetti) and locally caught fish. *11.30am-2pm & 6-10pm Wed-Mon* ¥¥

Ogachi Unagi: (大勝 うなぎ) Nothing beats the summer heat like delicious, fluffy *unagi* (eel) on rice. This store has been going over 45 years. *10.30am-3pm Mon-Sun & 5-8pm Sat & Sun* ¥¥

North-Side Amami

BEACHES | TROPICAL NIHONGA | MUD DYEING

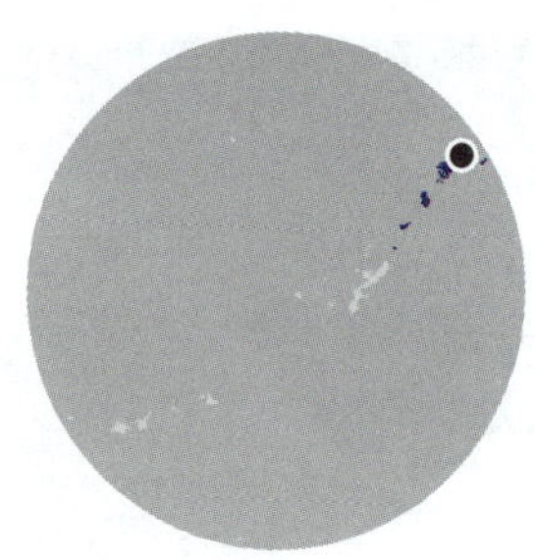

GETTING AROUND

Around 10 car-rental companies are based near the airport; they'll pick you up from the car park across the road from the terminal. Book your car in advance online if you're visiting in summer. Local buses are unreliable.

Fine beaches are the jewel in Amami-Ōshima's crown. On the island's north side, every nook of every peninsula cradles a patch of sand alongside shimmering, otherworldly blues. Sakibaru, Uttabaru and Kurasaki are some of the world-class beaches on the East China Sea side. While most of the beaches in Amami are quite still, which makes them ideal for people who want a leisurely dip, there are also famous surf spots like Tebiro, with surf schools catering to everyone from beginners to advanced surfers. There are a number of dive shops in the north as well, offering everything from whale-watching tours to dive-certification courses.

The region is no slouch when it comes to cultural attractions, either. The Tanaka Isson Memorial Museum is a thoughtful homage to a local artist, and Ōshima Tsumugi Village is a vast open-air museum devoted to Ōshima *tsumugi* textiles.

Surf's Up!

The north side's finest breaks

Amami-Ōshima has breaks of all descriptions, and high swells on the Pacific-facing side. In 2011 the World Surfing Championship was held at **Tebiro**. Local surfers such as Yusei Ikariyama (p311), who runs **Can.nen Surf** (*cannensurf.amamin .jp)*, are also advocates for ecological preservation.

A Painter of Nature

The vivid work of Isson Tanaka

Brimming with vivid sago palms, red Amami jays and lush tropical scenes, Isson Tanaka's work is a distinctive type of Rimpa painting (a school of art that often references nature and literature). Showing a clear love of the island's subtropical world, in particular its endemic birds, Tanaka's pieces have a documentary-like realism. When he was 50, Tanaka moved to

☑ TOP TIP

Take advantage of Japan's sauna craze (p242): Ryūkyū Villas (p273) has two of the best private saunas in the country, with spectacular views.

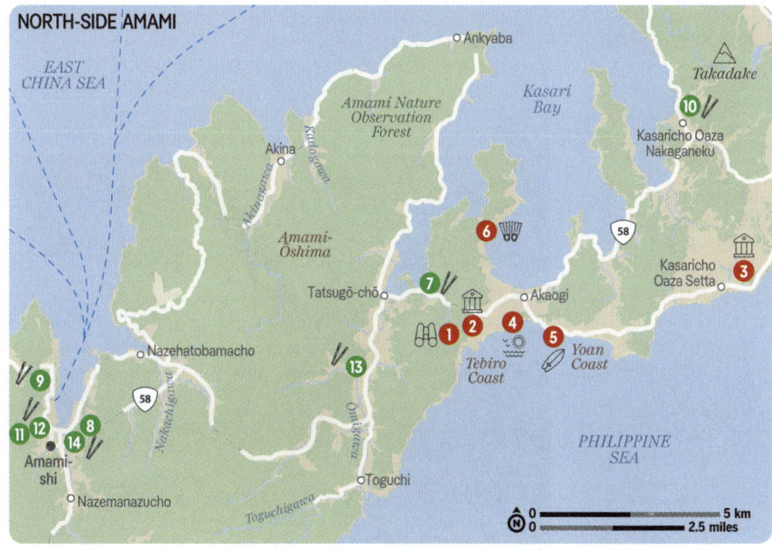

SIGHTS
1 2 Ocean Viewpoint
2 Ōshima Tsumugi Village
3 Tanaka Isson Memorial Museum
4 Tebiro Beach

ACTIVITIES
5 Can.nen Surf
6 Native Sea Amami

EATING
7 Hisakura
8 Meshiya Wakitamaru
9 Minami Sushi
10 Minatoya Amami Chicken Rice
11 Nagomi
12 Nominchu
13 Tecchan
14 Torishin

Amami-Ōshima, where he lived in a simple hut. He received acclaim only posthumously. The **Tanaka Isson Memorial Museum** (*amamipark.com/isson; adult/child ¥410/290*), whose charming architecture resembles Amami storehouses, is an impressive homage to his oeuvre.

Watch Frolicking Whales

Snorkel near a whale nursery

Humpback whales calve and tend to their young in the warm waters around Amami-Ōshima from December to March. Whale-watching tours, such as those run by **Native Sea Amami** (*amami-diving.com*) and Kohollo (p240), visit various

EATING ON THE NORTH SIDE: SEAFOOD SPOTS

Nagomi: The restaurant looks like someone's apartment, but it's popular with locals, with generous sashimi bowls and ¥1000 lunch sets. *11am-9pm Tue-Sun* ¥

Minami Sushi: Intimate sushi restaurant close to the ferry pier with affordable soba and sushi roll sets. The soba is strongly flavoured. *10am-10pm* ¥

Meshiya Wakitamaru: *Shokudō*-style all-round eatery with sushi and sashimi bowls and rice and miso soup sets. *11am-3pm & 5-9pm* ¥

Nominchu: *Izakaya* open from the afternoon serving local fish caught that day. *3-11pm* ¥¥

SPIRITUAL AMAMI

Hisayuki 'Char' Tsuchiya, surfer and photographer
I first came here for surf magazine assignments and relocated after the 2011 Tohoku disaster. Amami is full of sacred and spiritual spots. The surfing is varied, with rivers and many beaches, not just reef surfing. I go to the beaches of Tebiro (p248) and **Kusuku** a lot. It's less crowded than Okinawa, there's more nature, and it feels more local. Everyone knows each other and there are village gatherings, but its liveable and people are kind and accepting. There's respect for the elderly, and you can participate in the community. It's not necessarily about comfort, but it just feels right. Some people aren't suited to Amami and leave quickly, but the ones who are stay long term.

Humpback whale (p249)

points around the island. Once a pod is sighted, you'll get into the water with your snorkel. Be ready for more than a dozen attempts. Early in the season you may catch whales singing courtship songs. In the Amami Islands, marine (and land) tours must meet high sustainability standards.

EATING ON THE NORTH SIDE: BEST KEIHAN

Minatoya Amami Chicken Rice: The *keihan* soup is rich, and there are other chicken dishes on the menu. *11.30am-2pm* ¥¥

Hisakura: A large and famous *keihan* restaurant that uses chickens from the owner's farm as well as organic citrus and papaya. *11am-4pm* ¥¥

Tecchan: Instead of rice, this restaurant serves a ramen version of *keihan*. *3-11pm Tue-Sun* ¥

Torishin: Much-loved local eatery with *keihan*, *keihan* ramen, and pork and papaya bowls. *11am-2pm & 5-9pm Thu-Tue* ¥

TOSHIKI MAEDA/SHUTTERSTOCK

Ōshima Tsumugi Village

One of the world's most complex textile production processes, Ōshima *tsumugi* is a laborious silk-dyeing-and-weaving method that is used to create luxurious textiles that have a distinctive texture. The Ōshima Tsumugi Village offers visitors the opportunity to witness these fabrics being made using this natural dye technique. It's breathtaking to witness the skill required to create this cloth.

Ōshima *tsumugi* weaving

History of Tsumugi

Masahito Hara, an Ōshima *tsumugi* artisan, says, 'It's speculated that the influence of Bali's ikat came in via Okinawa. Miyako and Ishigaki islands have the influence of ikat and Javanese *sarasa*, and when they entered Okinawa, they became a new style. We use silk, as the ability to farm cocoons was here, and in Miyako they use hemp.' According to the museum, analysis of old textiles shows that advanced weaving techniques were in use even before the island came under Satsuma rule. It's thought that they date back at least 1500 years.

Making Tsumugi

Ōshima *tsumugi* textiles have an unusual lustre from the iron-rich rice-field-mud and tree-sap dyes. The thread is dyed up to 100 times and then woven into intricate patterns such as the chequered *ichimatsu*. It takes weavers a day to weave just 7cm of cloth; to make a full bolt of cloth can take up to a year. The symbols are usually things from Amami culture such as sago palms and a basket to ladle rice and beans.

At Ōshima Tsumugi Village you can try your hand at dyeing your own T-shirts with indigo or mud.

TOP TIPS

● Eight minutes' drive away, the **2 Ocean Viewpoint** (2つの海が見える丘) observation deck offers a spectacular view of both sides of the island.

PRACTICALITIES

● tumugi.co.jp
● 9am–5pm
● adult/child ¥550/220

South-Side Amami

LOCAL ATMOSPHERE | MANGROVES | DIVING

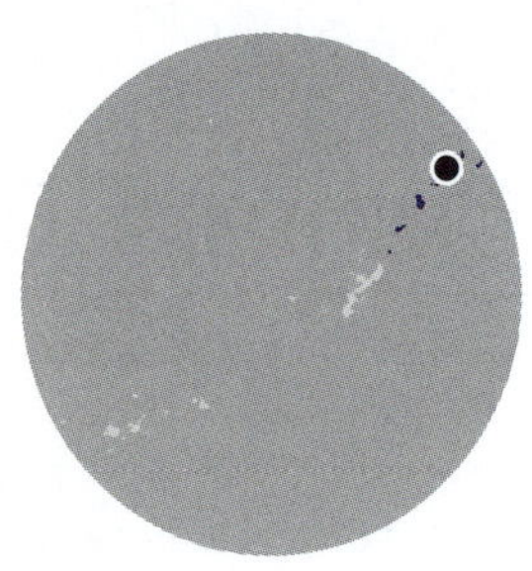

GETTING AROUND

If you're planning to explore this remote part of the island, collect a rental car from Naze or the airport before heading south.

The south of the island, covered in forests and mangroves, is significantly less developed than Naze and the north – to the degree that the locals call it wild. The dense mangrove forests offer a tranquil way to interact with another complex ecosystem that is quite different to the ocean. The closest thing resembling a city is Setouchi, a port town that has many seafood restaurants and a few dive operators for the stellar south-side sites.

As early as the Meiji era, Setouchi was a military fortress, and it remains an important strategic site; don't be surprised to see warships in the bay. Now a WWII memorial, Nishikomi Observatory Site Park was built in 1940. A fortress and ammunitions storage unit, it was made so that it could be entirely camouflaged. The site is also worth a visit for its spectacular views of the Amami Strait.

Yamato Bay

Village life and serene coves

Tranquil Yamato Bay, on the island's China Sea side, has many idyllic small beaches. A rare example of an architectural style distinct to Amami-Ōshima, the timber **Boregura** granary storehouses are five raised-floor huts that were constructed without using nails. Nearby, the **Amami Wildlife Conservation Centre** (*kyushu.env.go.jp/okinawa/awcc; free*) highlights the island's ecological activities.

Kuroshio no Mori Mangrove Forest

Japan's second-largest virgin mangrove forest

You can join a canoe tour through the 70-hectare **Kuroshio no Mori Mangrove Park**, or its **Mangrove Observatory** has a sprawling view of the point where the Yakugachi and Sumiyo rivers meet. With a guide, you can walk the mudflats barefoot at low tide, admiring the diverse ecosystems and the mangroves' aerial roots. Next to the forest, the **Amami-Ōshima**

If you're diving in the region, there's no need to get your own car, as food options are concentrated in Setouchi and dive companies will pick you up.

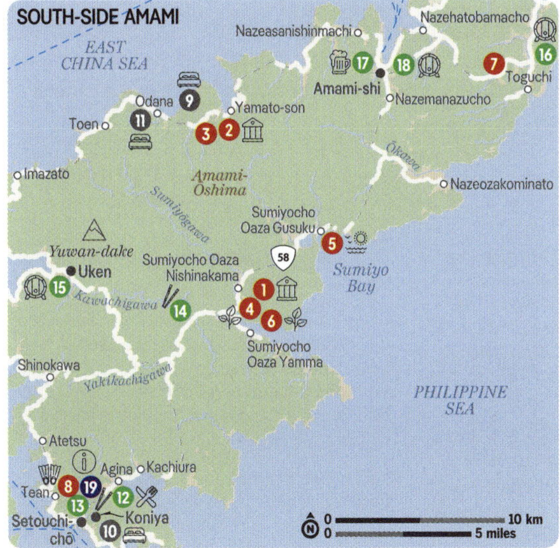

World Heritage Conservation Centre (*amami-whcc.jp/en; free*) has dioramas and explanations in English. Stop at nearby **Motoi Farm Farmers Market** (*motoinouen.com*) for fresh-squeezed *tankan* citrus juice.

Sail Away

Freedom to explore on a vintage yacht

Don't miss a trip on the **Indigo Amami** (*indigoamami.com; full/half day ¥80,000/ ¥60,000*), a 1960s Japanese-made wooden yacht owned by local surfer and photographer Char (and his beagle, Jiro; p250). Sail the turquoise waters around South Amami and swim and snorkel off islands devoid of people. The stargazing tours are breathtakingly beautiful. Pickup is around **Atetsu Post Office**, South Amami.

EATING & DRINKING IN THE SOUTH: OUR PICKS

Chiru Chiru Cafe: Wooden shack serving curries and ¥1000 lunch plates. Also has seasonal drinks such as plum and guava juice. *11am-3pm Fri-Sun* ¥

Shimazakana Amami: (島魚 あま海) Basically a fish shop with tables and chairs inside, serving delectable ¥600 seafood bowls and fresh tuna. *9am-6.30pm Mon-Sat* ¥

Kamitaka: (神鷹) Popular lunch and late-night *izakaya* in Koniya. Fresh-caught-fish lunch sets are ¥880. Spectacular dinner sashimi platters. ¥

Spice Mafia: Curry joint in Setouchi that uses local ingredients such as plum, pork and ginger. *11am-3pm & 6-8.30pm Fri-Wed* ¥

Amami-Ōshima Kaiun Shuzo: Constantly experimenting, it's known for its *shōchū*, called Lento. In Uken. *by appointment* ¥¥

Tomita Shuzo: Established in 1951, this place uses traditional earthenware pots, which adds to the flavour (p247). *by appointment* ¥¥

Machida Shuzo: Tatsugo distillery whose *shōchū*, Sato no Akebono, is made using vacuum distillation. *by appointment* ¥¥

Yayoi Shochu: Distillery in Naze City run by a fourth-generation owner; its *shōchū* is sweet and gentle with an impressive aroma. *by appointment* ¥¥

AMAMI'S DISTINCT CULTURE BY CAR

Discover Amami-Ōshima's unique cuisine, history, crafts and wildlife – it's more than an 'unknown Okinawa'.

START	END	LENGTH
Cycad groves	Naze City	80km; 2hr

Spend a day touring places that will give you some insight into Amami-Ōshima's unique identity. Start at the **1** **cycad groves** on the Ankyaba peninsula. Cycads, also called sago palms, are used to make *nari miso,* and their poisonous fruit can be processed in a special way to produce edible flour.

Amami is known for its goat dishes, and you'll see goats all around the island. Drive 20 minutes via Tatsugo to **2** **Soleil Farm** to try its delectable goat-milk soft serve. Next, drive 15 minutes west to the **3** **Mizuma Brown Sugar Factory** (p247) and take a morning tour. A five-minute drive away is **4** **Yumeori no Sato** (夢おりの郷), an Ōshima *tsumugi* textiles atelier where you can

try on a kimono and also have a go at dyeing and weaving.

Drive 45 minutes along the East China Sea side of the island to the **5** **Boregura** (p252) traditional granary storehouses. Close by are the **6** **Amami Wildlife Conservation Centre** (p252) and Quru Guru, a conservation facility and museum dedicated to the Amami rabbit.

Backtrack along the coast to Naze to enjoy traditional dishes and experience evocative *shimauta* music at intimate *izakaya* **7** **Kazumi**. You could leave the car at Naze overnight, try some of the island's sugar *shōchū* (p246) and join in the merrymaking.

Kakeromajima

SNORKELLING | AMAMI INDIGO | FERRY TAXI

Imagine a place without a convenience store, a supermarket or fast food. Phone reception is sporadic, and almost all the beaches are devoid of people, so you feel as though you're on your own private island. Welcome to Kakeromajima. Travelling from edge to edge takes around an hour by car, but if you have the time and energy, this is a delightful place to cycle (and, handily, the main road around the island's circumference is flat). From May to June, be sure to head down south to see the 300-year-old diego trees beside Shodon Nagahama beach wearing their jaunty red blooms. This is Okinawa's prefectural flower (even though the trees aren't native to Japan). The calm waters at Saneku Beach and Shiba, north of Seso ferry port, make for perfect conditions if you're keen to do some snorkelling or stand-up paddleboarding; guesthouses such as Nanryu have equipment for rent.

Fishing Kakeromajima

Gifts from the ocean

Fishing is popular across Amami-Ōshima, but Kakeromajima provides the perfect environment to enjoy connecting with nature and soak up the serenity of casting and waiting. There are several operators on Amami-Ōshima's south shore at Koniya and Setouchi and on Kakeromajima, all of whom travel around the islands in between Kakeroma and Amami-Ōshima and beyond to look for amberjack, tuna, sea bream, grouper, barracuda and trevally. There's ideal fishing for everyone, from beginners and families with kids to pros who are into big catch and deep-sea fishing. Stay in a house rental (p273) with a kitchen so you can cook up your catch later. **With Dio** (*withdio-amami.com*) welcomes beginners, and **Hideaway** (*hideaway-kakeroma.com*) also caters to experienced fishing enthusiasts and offers full charter tours. Both do pickups at Koniya.

GETTING AROUND

Seso port has bikes for hire. Lacking in traffic, the roads are perfect for cruising around on a bike. It's easier to take a rental car from Amami-Ōshima with you on the ferry, but if you'd prefer to rent one when you arrive, there are agencies on the island with a few older cars.

☑ **TOP TIP**

Get a water taxi, essentially a fishing boat, from Setouchi pier on Amami-Ōshima to Seso and enjoy the open-air ride.

AMAMI INDIGO

The *aizome* dye technique uses the fermented leaves of the indigo plant. It was an essential part of Ryūkyū culture going back to the 15th century, and in Amami its use as a medicinal plant was first recorded in 1829. It became extinct with the introduction of chemical dyes in the Meiji period. 'Later, during the Shōwa era, there was one man who revived it, but he has since passed away, so we are reviving it from scratch,' says Junichi Mizutani of the Amami Aizen Study Group. 'It's hard to cultivate and the plant can't handle direct sunlight. It doesn't produce seeds, so we use cuttings. In the old days before nets existed, people planted them under banana leaves for shade.'

Ryūkyū Blues

Learn about indigo dyeing

In Amuro village, the **Amami Aizome Study Group** (*amamiai.com/en*) keeps the culture of Amami *ai* (Amami indigo) alive. Rika and Junichi Mizutani outline the trials and tribulations of growing and harvesting the plant in their backyard and give visitors the opportunity to try their hand at dyeing fabrics. As Rika explains, the local indigo is extremely high in dye compounds, so it produces a particularly lovely hue. Attending the workshop is also an opportunity to experience a slice of village life in a small island community.

EATING ON KAKEROMAJIMA: QUICK BITES

Yui Yui: Beachside eatery with set lunches and boar curry. It's about a minute's walk from Saneki beach. *11am–5pm Sat & Sun* ¥

Tazuki: Noodle shack close to Seso ferry port with soba and pork, and rice bowls. *11.30am–2pm Tue–Sat* ¥

Isshinan Soba: (一心庵) An incredibly pleasant combination of delicious soba and crystal-clear waters in front of your table. Open weekends only. *11am–2pm Sat & Sun* ¥

Mokka: Small eatery by the bay at Nishi Amuro using local ingredients and wild greens. *11.30am–2.30pm & 6.30–11pm Mon & Wed–Sat* ¥

Kikaijima

SNORKELLING | BEAUTIFUL VILLAGES | FERRY ADVENTURE

Made of elevated coral, Kikaijima (喜界島) is a tiny island lying 25km east of Amami-Ōshima. It's a treasure trove of archaeological artefacts, some of which date back 8000 years, which suggests the island was inhabited in prehistoric times. Records suggest there were resistance forces in Kikaijima during the period of Ryūkyū colonisation. Under Satsuma rule, Kikaijima was a site of intense, forced sugar production, the legacy of which can be seen at the Sugar Road, which cuts through the cane fields in Nagamine town. During WWII the island became a strategic military site, but nowadays it feels as though time has stopped. Local villages – among them lovely Aden, which has been recognised by nonprofit the Most Beautiful Villages of Japan – have wooden houses adorned with coral stone walls. Drive around the island's compact 50km circumference, taking in the beautiful natural surroundings and sprawling banyan trees.

Butterfly Road

A magical path

No visit to Kikaijima is complete without a drive along **Butterfly Road**, marked on maps in Aden district. As its name suggests, the road is a haven for butterflies, in particular the chestnut tiger. Embarking on this drive is like entering a multicoloured blizzard, with butterflies in every direction. Drive slowly to avoid damaging them. Kikaijima has no mountains, unlike Amami-Ōshima, so it doesn't have such a variety of wildlife, but at least 30 butterfly species make the island their home. It's said in animistic lore that these fluttering beauties have mystical powers of reincarnation and eternal life. Triangles are thought have spiritual significance, so the shape of their wings is believed to be sacred.

GETTING AROUND

Getting to Kikaijima is an adventure in itself. The **A-Line Ferry** departs Amami-Ōshima at 6.20pm and arrives two hours later at Kikaijima after dark. To get around, you'll need to hire a car at one of the rental places close to the ferry port or bring a car with you on the ferry. One road follows the perimeter of the island and leads to most of the best spots.

☑ TOP TIP

On this island made of coral, snorkelling at one of the many beaches is a must.

KIKAIJIMA ARCHAEOLOGY

Souoku Takada, manager of the **Kikai Archaeological Operations Center**

Kikaijima has a lot of historical significance, and when you dig, artefacts appear in abundance, especially Jōmon period items. The oldest is 8000 years old, but generally they're around 2500 to 3000 years old. The alkaline soil and coral-based limestone mean bones don't dissolve easily, so even small fish bones have been preserved. If archaeological sites are found anywhere in the country, the items must be documented, so there's a large volume of material to investigate. We unearth pottery but also animal bones, such as those from a dugong that were used as necklaces and ornaments. There are also items from the Heian, Kamakura and Muromachi periods. In particular, numerous Muromachi tea wares have been found on Kikaijima.

● SIGHTS
1 Butterfly Road
2 Hawaii Beach
3 Kikai Archaeological Operations Centre
4 Sugira Beach

● SLEEPING
5 Seaside Magic Villa
6 Villa Kikai
7 Youth Hostel Kikai

● EATING
8 Appare

9 Jubei
10 Shima Soba Daruma

● DRINKING & NIGHTLIFE
11 Waratto

Coral Wonderland

Snorkel pristine waters

It's no surprise that the snorkelling on this coral island is stellar. As bonuses, the surrounding ocean is pristine, with excellent visibility, and there are many beaches with protected lagoons, meaning the water is still. **Sugira Beach** is behind the airport, so you can see planes take off while you're there. It has a clear lagoon teeming with life such as angelfish and boxfish. **Hawaii Beach** has no facilities and is a completely natural area with incredible corals. Note there's no sand here – you walk down into a limestone inlet and enter the water, where you can snorkel amid lush coral gardens.

EATING ON KIKAIJIMA

Shima Soba Daruma: Ryūkyū-style soba with pork and heavy use of sesame, the local speciality. *11am-8pm Thu-Sun* ¥

Appare: (天晴) *Izakaya* next to the airport with local eats such as goat dishes and sashimi. *5-10pm Tue-Sun* ¥¥

Jubei: Hearty set meals with various local dishes, fresh sashimi, soba and *keihan. 11.30am-2pm & 6-11pm Wed-Mon* ¥¥

Waratto: (笑っと) *Izakaya* with excellent seafood from sashimi to clams, plus standard *izakaya* fare like fried chicken. *5.30-11.30pm Tue-Sun* ¥¥

Tokunoshima

WORLD HERITAGE | BOVINE SUMŌ | ROCK FORMATIONS

Tokunoshima (徳之島), population 26,000, is not sure which of its list of accomplishments makes it the proudest: two Guinness World Record holders for the world's oldest person, Japan's highest total fertility rate, birthplace of legendary sumo *yokozuna* Asashio Tarō III, or its mountains and rainforests becoming World Heritage listed in 2021. That's quite a résumé, though rather than dwelling on their island's achievements, the locals seem much more focused on whose bull is going to be grand champion in the next *tōgyū* tournament, a local version of bovine sumo. Drive around southern and eastern parts of the island after 5pm and you'll see huge bulls being led along roads and beaches as part of their fitness-training program. This island is totally transfixed by *tōgyū*. The ferry port of Kametoku and the main town of Kametsu are in the southeast, while the airport is on reclaimed land in the northwest of the island.

Enraptured by Tōgyū

Sumo wrestling for bulls

Tōgyū has been the island's focus for some 500 years; indeed, its mascot is a *tōgyū* bull. In this 'bovine sumo', the bulls are pitted against each other, locking horns, with the goal of pushing the opponent out of the 'ring' or causing them to run away. This is nothing like European bullfighting, which pits human against bull and usually ends with the animal's death. On Tokunoshima, the 800–1000kg bulls are much loved and cared for by their owners.

There are three big tournaments in January, May and October, and while there's prize money, it's minimal when compared with the costs of keeping and training the bulls; on the island, it's all about pride. Bulls are ranked and given inspiring 'ring names'. There's even a **Tōgyū Shintō Shrine** at which to pray for good luck. If you're here out of tournament season, you can still visit the **Nakusamikan Arena** to see where it all takes place.

WORLD HERITAGE TOKUNOSHIMA

Tokunoshima is part of the bulkily named 'Amami-Ōshima Island, Tokunoshima Island, Northern part of Okinawa Island, and Iriomote Island' UNESCO World Natural Heritage Site, which was registered in 2021 to become the fifth such site in Japan. The islands were recognised for their unique subtropical rainforests, diverse species and influence from the Kuroshio Current (p28). On Tokunoshima, those diverse species include the Amami rabbit and Tokunoshima spiny rat. The impressive **Tokunoshima World Heritage Centre** (*tokunoshima-whcc. com; free*), open Wednesday to Monday, has excellent visual displays and explanation boards, and is well worth a visit. It's in the north, at the eastern end of the cross-island road. It doubles as a Michi-no-eki roadside rest stop, with a restaurant and souvenir shop.

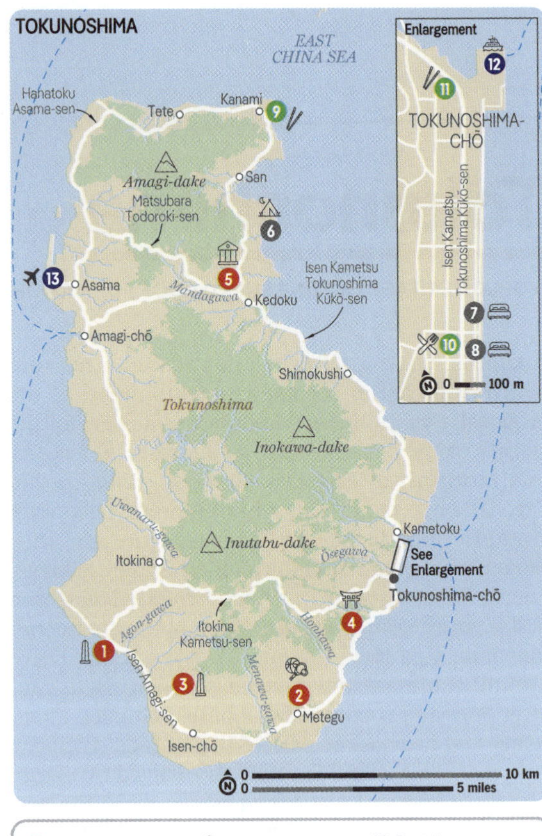

● **SIGHTS**	● **SLEEPING**	10 Dontaku
1 Kamata Hongo Monument	6 Aze Prince Beach Camping Ground	11 Izumiya
2 Nakusamikan Arena	7 Hotel Grand Ocean Resort	see 5 Michi-no-eki Restaurant
3 Shigechiyo Izumi Statue	8 Hotel Lexton Tokushima	● **TRANSPORT**
4 Tōgyū Shintō Shrine	● **EATING**	12 Kametoku Port
5 Tokunoshima World Heritage Centre	9 Blue-mail	13 Tokunoshima Airport

When I asked about tōgyū *at the tourist office, the manager whipped out his smartphone to show me and my wife photos of his own two bulls! –* **Craig McLachlan**, Lonely Planet writer

Island of Longevity & Babies

Two Guinness World Record holders!

This dot in the ocean has had not one but two Guinness World Record holders for world's oldest person. **Shigechiyo Izumi** got the big prize in 1979, then lived another seven years to reach 120 years and 237 days. **Kamata Hongo** became the

Shigechiyo Izumi

world's oldest person in 1999 and lived to 116 years and 45 days. Visit the bronze **Shigechiyo Izumi statue** in the island's southwest, where Izumi lived, then drive a tad west to find the small roadside **Kamata Hongo monument**.

Tokunoshima had Japan's highest total fertility rate of 2.25 (the number of children a woman has in her lifetime) in 2024. Unfortunately, the island's population is nonetheless declining, as young people are leaving for opportunities on the mainland.

EATING ON TOKUNOSHIMA

Dontaku: Shimizu-san has been running his friendly little *shōchū* bar, a block back from the main street, for 35 years. *5.30-11.30pm Tue-Sat* ¥¥

Blue-mail: In the island's northeastern corner at Kanamisaki, Blue-mail pulls in locals. Spot whales frolicking offshore from the window-side tables. *11am-2pm & 6-9pm Fri-Wed* ¥¥

Izumiya: Fuel up while waiting for your ferry at this popular soba noodle spot across from the Kametoku terminal. *11am-2pm & 5-8pm Thu-Tue* ¥

Michi-no-eki Restaurant: Good lunch spot at the World Heritage Centre in the north; simple, tasty fare plus farm produce for sale. *11am-2pm Thu-Tue* ¥

Driving Around Tokunoshima

Pick up a rental car at the Kametoku ferry terminal and prepare for a fun drive anticlockwise around the circumference of Tokunoshima, with the opportunity to stop whenever you see something interesting. The island is known for its intriguing rock formations, both on land and out to sea, and you'll spot plenty of them from the road. Drive carefully, and whatever you do, don't bowl over a protected Amami rabbit!

❶ Statue of Asashio Tarō III

There are only 75 names on the list of *yoko-zuna*, the highest rank in Japanese sumo, and in 1959 Tokunoshima-born Asashio Tarō III reached that legendary status. His impressive statue is just north of the ferry terminal.

The Drive: Carry on north up the coast to where the road turns inland.

❷ Tokunoshima World Heritage Centre

This very informative **visitor centre** (p260) was built after the island and rainforests achieved World Heritage status in 2021. To really get into the central mountains and rainforests you'll need to organise a local guide; do that here.

The Drive: Continue north on Rte 629 up to the island's northeastern tip.

❸ Kanamisaki Views

Walk through the famous Cycad Tunnel, where giant cycad trees, said to be over 400 years old, converge over the trail. Views from the cape's observation platform are exceptional; don't miss spotting Tonbura Rocks, way out to sea.

アラシオ, CC BY-SA 4.0, VIA WIKIMEDIA COMMONS ©

Mushiroze

The Drive: Continue west, along the northern coast.

4 Mushiroze

Huge slabs of granite at unusual angles, right by the waves, are easy to enjoy and explore thanks to a viewing platform and concreted trails.

The Drive: Turn south, down the west coast, passing the airport and the township of Amagi. Keep your eyes open for interesting side trips such as to Innojōfuta, with eroded coral rock, and the aptly named Glasses Rock.

5 Inutabu-misaki

This western cape presents beautiful coastal views, and the chance to spot whales from February to April; the WWII Yamato Battleship Monument is here.

The Drive: Turn southeast, then off the main road, towards the mountains.

6 Shigechiyo Izumi Statue

Guinness World Record holder for world's oldest person, Izumi was known for his long beard. He lived to 120 years and 237 days and is honoured with this impressive statue (p261).

The Drive: Back on the main road, head east along the southern part of the island.

7 Nakusamikan Arena

Stop here to see where the biggest *tōgyū* events are held (p259); there are often bulls here, even if it isn't tournament season. Take a look around the back.

The Drive: Carry on around the coast, heading back to Kametoku. Before town, keep your eyes open for the Tōgyū Shintō shrine on the left and Gorilla Rock in the sea.

Okinoerabu-jima

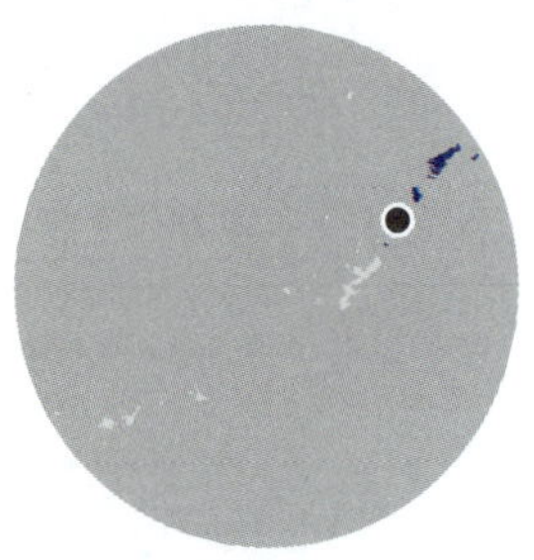

LIMESTONE CAVERNS | FLOWERS GALORE | SPECTACULAR COASTLINE

GETTING AROUND

Wadomari, the ferry port, is in the east and China township is in the southwest. The island is long and hilly but has excellent roads and the efficient **Okinoerabu Bus** *(okinoerabubus. org)*. Consider renting a small car or an e-bike, especially if you're thinking of circumnavigating the island. **Island Cycles** *(island-cycles.com/ island-cycles)* is based in Wadomari.

A raised coral island to the southwest of Tokunoshima, Okinoerabu-jima (沖永良部島), with a population of 13,000, is about 20km long and shaped like the Nike swoosh. It has a high point of 246m at its hilly western end. The island is known for its flowers, intriguing land formations and over 300 caves, but it's well off the beaten track for international visitors. Throughout its history, Okinoerabu-jima's remoteness saw it used as a settlement for political prisoners, including members of the Ryūkyū royal family. The legendary samurai Saigō Takamori was exiled here for 19 months in the early 1860s for rebellion. Don't let these stories put you off, though, as Okinoerabu-jima is a very inviting island, living off the production of sugar cane, potatoes and flowers, along with a healthy dose of domestic visitors. Turn up when the flowers are blooming from mid-April and you may not want to leave.

Underground Okinoerabu-jima

Shōryūdō, the island's easily accessed cave

Of some 300 identified caves on the island, only four are accessible, and for three of those you'll need a guide (ask at Erabu Coco). Easily accessed, however, is the remarkable **Shōryūdō** (昇竜洞; *chinatyo-syoryudo.com; adult/child ¥1100/550*) cave system, 600m of which is open Wednesday to Monday. You'll need wheels to get there. From the car park, descend to the visitor centre and cave entrance, borrow a walking stick, then walk mostly downhill on a formed trail. There's no guide, but it's easy to follow your nose. Colourful lights illuminate interesting stalactites, stalagmites and rock formations, and there's occasional music.

☑ **TOP TIP**

Drop in to **Erabu Coco** *(okinoerabujima.info)*, the excellent tourist information centre, cafe and souvenir shop near China township in the west.

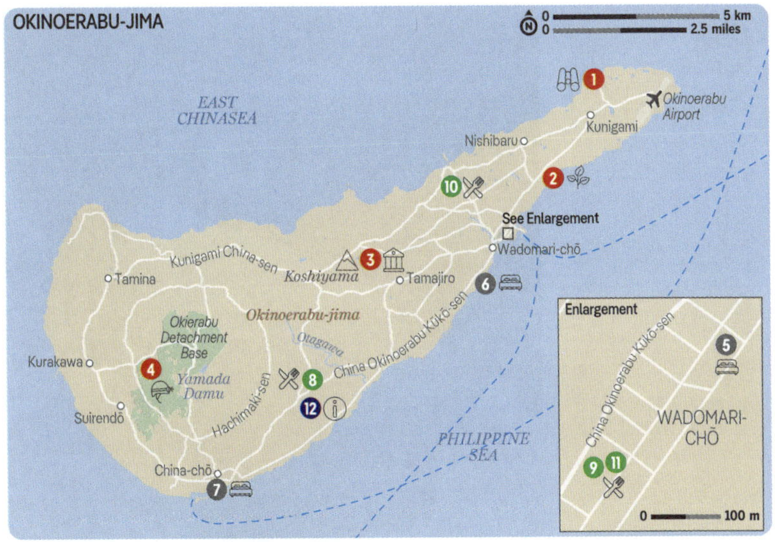

SIGHTS
1 Fūcha
2 Kaisashi Beach Park
3 Shiryōkan

ACTIVITIES
4 Shōryūdō

SLEEPING
5 Hotel Seaworld

6 LOG INN tarasso
7 Okierabu Floral Hotel

EATING
8 Diner Paru
9 Dontsuki

10 Saigo Shokudō
11 Shokuzaiya En

INFORMATION
12 Erabu Coco

Geyser-Like Eruptions on Windy Days

Blowhole at the eastern end

You'll want transport to get to **Fūcha** (フーチャ; *okinoerabujima .info/spot/1001)*. Spiky limestone formations line the coast in both directions, and a concreted trail leads down to a blowhole and a partly eroded cave open to the sea. At high tide and on windy days, the sea erupts to soak onlookers. Water can spout to around 10m, and apparently up to 50m in a typhoon. Even on a calm, sunny day, this is a great place to visit as you can gaze down into the blowhole – note there are no guardrails. Wander to the end of the trail to spot sea turtles swimming right beneath you.

 **EATING & DRINKING ON OKINOERABU-JIMA: OUR PICKS**

Dontsuki: Funky little *izakaya* down near the port; squeeze a squawking chicken to call your server. *6pm-midnight Tue-Sun* ¥¥

Shokuzaiya En: Popular locals spot near the port with open tables and private enclosed rooms; excellent *izakaya* fare. *6-10.30pm Tue-Sun* ¥¥

Diner Paru: Opposite information centre Erabu Coco, this relaxed little place serves tasty set meals. *11am-2pm & 6.30-9pm Mon-Sat* ¥

Saigo Shokudō: Enjoy the freshest fish and seafood going at Saigo, on the north coast near the small port at Inobe. *11.30am-2pm & 6-10pm Mon-Sat* ¥¥¥

ERABU LILIES

Okinoerabu-jima is renowned for large, white trumpet-shaped Erabu lilies that bloom from mid-April to May and are absolutely spectacular. Wild lilies were transplanted to farm fields for cultivation on the advice of a visiting Englishman in the late 1890s. These days, bulbs are cultivated and, along with cut flowers, sent to the Japanese mainland and overseas as a major earner for the island. The Erabu lily was introduced to Europe in the early 1900s, becoming known as the Easter lily, an alternative to the Madonna lily for Christian events. An excellent place to see them is at **Kaisashi Beach Park**, 2km northeast of Wadomari port. Don't miss the display of lily varieties at the Wadomari Town History & Folklore Museum.

Fūcha (p265)

Find Out More at the Shiryōkan

History and folklore museum

This excellent little **museum** (和泊町歴史民俗資料館; *okino erabujima.info/spot/1010; adult/child ¥200/100)* is well worth making the effort to get to, though it's pretty much out in the middle of nowhere; you'll want wheels to get here (note it's closed Wednesday). Peruse stunning island photographs, brilliant displays on island life and culture, and an excellent lily exhibition. Outside is a small collection of old local buildings that have been relocated on-site.

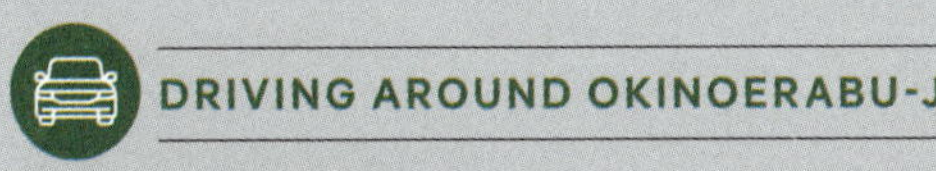

DRIVING AROUND OKINOERABU-JIMA

Get yourself a rental car and drive around this fascinating island to see everything it has to offer.

START	END	LENGTH
Wadomari	Wadomari	50km; 4–5hr

From ❶ **Wadomari**, head northeast, up the coast. Even if it's not flower season, stop at ❷ **Kaisashi Beach Park** to enjoy a stroll and views from atop a small observation tower. A bit further up the road, look for signage to the ❸ **'Best Banyan in Japan'**. It's in the grounds of Kunigami Elementary School, and while there's no denying it's a beauty, you may question the requirements to be anointed Japan's best banyan. It's only a short drive to ❹ **Fūcha** (p265) on the northern coast, an enthralling blowhole that you shouldn't miss. Spot sea turtles from the end of the trail.

Turn west along the northern coast's main road. Make sure to stop at ❺ **Wadomari Town History & Folklore Museum** for some local culture, then drive to ❻ **Tamina-misaki**, the cape at the island's northwestern tip. There's a nice short walk with lovely coastal views here. It's time to head underground, so drive to ❼ **Shōryūdō** (p264) and explore the amazing cave system. Head back down to the main road, then drive through ❽ **China township**. Stop for a coffee at ❾ **Erabu Coco** (p264), the island's tourist information centre that doubles as a friendly cafe, before carrying on northeast through agricultural fields to complete your island circumnavigation in Wadomari.

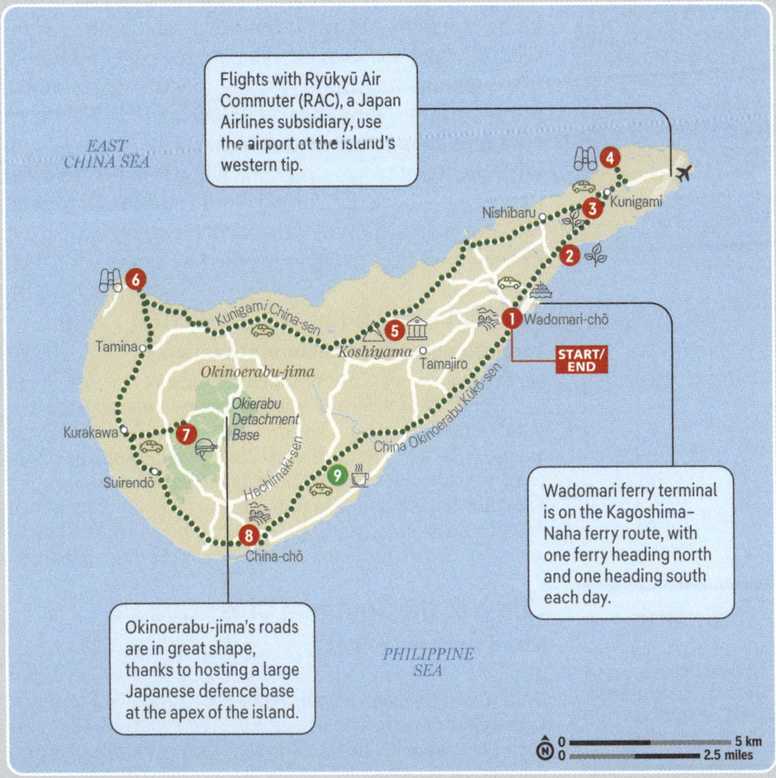

Yoron-tō

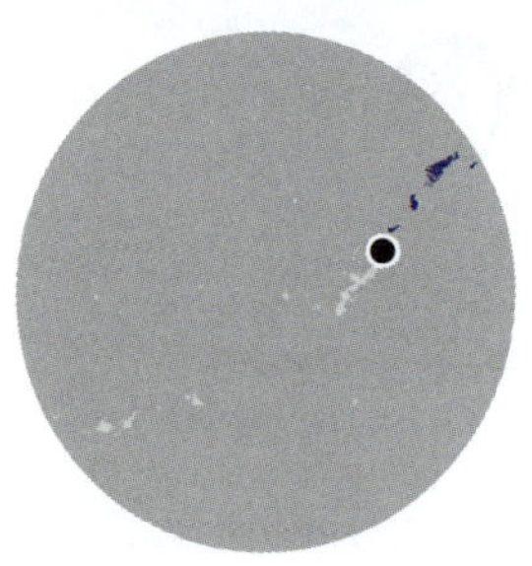

GORGEOUS BEACHES | WARM WATERS | LOCAL CULTURE

GETTING AROUND

Visitors arrive by ferry (p270) or **plane** *(rac-okinawa.com)* from Naha or Kagoshima. It takes an hour or so to drive around the island, two to three hours by bike. Accommodation is scattered around Yoron, but once you're away from Chabana, eating options are limited. Rental cars, motorbikes and bicycles are available.

Shaped like a huge angelfish, Yoron-tō (与論島) is the southernmost of the Amami Islands and Kagoshima-ken. On a good day, Okinawa main island's northern tip, Hedo-misaki, is clearly visible 23km to the south-west. A small island, Yoron-tō has a circumference of only 24km, a high point of 97m and a population of 5000. Surrounded by coral reef, it has a reputation as a tropical paradise, with some 60 white-sand beaches and great waters for marine sports. The island has its own version of the 'communication drink', *Yoron-kempō*, which involves introducing yourself and imbibing copious amounts of locally made sugar *shōchū*, often ruining plans for the following day. The ferry port and airport are at the western tip of the island, with the main town, Chabana, a few kilometres away to the east. Check out Yoron Island Tourism *(yorontou.info)* for info and images that will have you transfixed by turquoise hues of water inside the surrounding reef.

The 'Phantom Beach': Yurigahama
Yoron-tō's best-known natural attraction

On the eastern coast, the **Ōganeku-kaigan** (大金久海岸) is a spectacular 2km stretch of white-sand beach mostly backed by parkland. The highlight, however, is 500m offshore, where the 'phantom beach', **Yurigahama** (百合ヶ浜), appears and disappears with the tides. Check the Yurigahama Beach Appearance Forecast Calendar on yorontou.info, turn up at the suggested best time and cross your fingers. Small boats shuttle beachgoers out to Yurigahama whenever it makes an appearance.

Climb to the Southern Cross Centre
Island views and culture

At N 27° 22', Yoron-tō is the most northerly point in Japan from which you can view the Southern Cross. The **Southern Cross Centre** *(yorontou.info; adult/child ¥400/200)* sits at the island's high point, almost 100m above sea level, with captivating 360-degree views. The centre has excellent displays on the

☑ **TOP TIP**

No buses or taxis meet port and airport arrivals, so pre-book a taxi or rental car, or talk to your accommodation about a pickup.

SIGHTS
1 Southern Cross Centre
2 Yoron Minzoku-mura
3 Yurigahama

SLEEPING
4 Pricia Resort
5 Shiomi-sō
6 Yurigahama Campsite & Cottages

EATING
7 Blue Coral Reef
8 Ōganeku Sushi
9 Taito Sushi

DRINKING & NIGHTLIFE
10 Yoron Seaside Garden

TRANSPORT
11 Yoron Airport
12 Yoron Ferry Port

WHY I LOVE YORON-TŌ

Craig McLachlan, Lonely Planet writer
This is a very special spot with a real sense of community. My wife, Yuriko, and I were pedalling around in paradise when I was overjoyed to hear something that has largely disappeared from most parts of regional Japan. At noon, loudspeakers around the island cranked up with tropical Yoron island music, then announced to everyone working in their fields that it was lunchtime. Later, at 5pm, that same music over the loudspeakers was followed by an announcement thanking everyone for their hard work, saying that it was time to go home, and telling workers to be careful of children playing roadside – and not to drink and drive!

island's history, culture and natural environment. The friendly tourist office is next door, as is the island's main shrine and the ruins of Yoron castle, half-built by the Hokuzan King of Ryūkyū in the early 1400s. An e-bike is recommended for riding up here.

Explore Yoron Folk Village

Local culture up close and personal

Run by the Kiku family, **Yoron Minzoku-mura** (与論民俗村; *yoronminzokumura.com; adult/child ¥500/300)* is a lovely little outdoor museum. Among coral walls sprouting colourful flowers are thatched-roof houses and work buildings relocated from around the island. Prebook to take part in hands-on Yoron experiences such as dyeing cloth using the juices of local plants. A great souvenir shop sells crafts, clothing and Yoron specialities such as pickled papaya.

BEST EATING & DRINKING ON YORON-TŌ

Blue Coral Reef: Try *mozuku soba* (noodles with seaweed in the dough) while looking out over gorgeous Paradise Beach. *11am-3pm ¥*

Taito Sushi: Excellent location in Chabana looking west over the commercial fishing port; as fresh as it gets. *11am-9pm Tue-Sun ¥¥*

Ōganeku Sushi: Top sushi out east with a character owner; opening hours are based on whether he has fresh fish or not. Takeout too. *¥¥*

Yoron Seaside Garden: Entry and drink for ¥600 at this gorgeous tropical garden looking east over the turquoise lagoon. *hours vary ¥*

RICHARD CUMMINS/ALAMY

A-Line ferry

Island-Hopping

Didn't know you could go island-hopping in Japan? The ferry route between Kagoshima and Naha is one of the world's great boat journeys, linking Kyūshū and Okinawa via the string of subtropical Amami Islands, well off the nation's regular tourist trail. There's one ferry in each direction every day, meaning you can hop on and off wherever you like.

DON'T MISS
Kagoshima City
Amami-Ōshima
Tokunoshima
Okinoerabu-jima
Yoron-tō
Motobu
Naha

The Ferries

Don't expect luxury: these are interisland ferries for which delivering freight, the lifeblood of the islands, is the primary purpose. In return they move agricultural products from the islands to market. Taking islanders to and from the various islands to Kagoshima and Naha comes next, and carting tourists, especially non-Japanese-speaking ones, is a bit of an afterthought.

There are two ferry companies operating on alternate days: **Marix Line** and **A-Line** (Marue Ferry). They both run to the

PRACTICALITIES

● marixline.com & aline-ferry.com ● one ferry daily in each direction
● year-round

same schedules and charge the same amount, so it doesn't really matter which one you ride with. The ferries have outside viewing decks and a variety of styles of sleeping room. The cheapest ticket gets you a sleeping mat, pillow and blanket on the floor of a large room that may have 50 to 60 such spots.

The Journey

It's a 25-hour ferry journey between Kagoshima and Naha, with stops at four islands along the way: Amami-Ōshima, Tokunoshima, Okinoerabu-jima and Yoron-tō. Each day there's one ferry heading south (Kagoshima to Naha) and one ferry heading north (Naha to Kagoshima). Each of the islands has its own personality. There's not a lot of English spoken out this way, so you're going to have to make an effort with language on this adventure, but expect it to be very satisfying.

Outside of the Japanese holiday seasons – Golden Week (late April to early May) and the summer break (20 July to the end of August) – you can pretty much turn up an hour before a sailing and get the cheapest ticket to ride to the next island. You'll want to prebook a spot in Japanese holiday periods.

If you like planning ahead you can prebook all your ferry rides and accommodation on each island. If you're into total flexibility and will be travelling at quiet times, you're free to do as you please.

When to Go

While there are daily ferries year-round, if you're after some beach time, everything has warmed by mid-April. Summer can be extremely hot and humid, and the weather cools down again by mid-November.

Keep in mind that June to October is typhoon season in Japan and typhoons can play havoc with ferry schedules. It's pretty much the luck of the draw during these months, so think of it as part of the adventure and try to build a bit of flexibility into your schedule.

Taking Your Own Wheels

You can take a car, moped or bicycle (for a fee) with you on the ferry between any of the islands, but in this case it pays to make a booking. Also, be aware that one-way rental-car return fees will be exorbitant if you take a car on the ferry from Kagoshima to Naha or vice versa; it's much more cost-effective to get a rental vehicle for as long as you need it on each of the islands.

This island-hopping trip is excellent for backpackers and bike-packers. Taking along a bike is a great option, and all the islands have camping areas.

PEDALLING AROUND YORON-TŌ

Rent a bike and cycle clockwise around the 24km circumference of the island, stopping along the way wherever you feel like it.

START	END	LENGTH
Chabana	Chabana	24km; 3–4hr

Pick up a regular or e-bike at **1** **Yoron Rental Cars** *(yoron-rentalcars.sakura.ne.jp)* in Chabana, have a look around town, then head north; the ocean will be on your left the whole way. There's no set route – just keep left and close to the sea. Pass the **2** **Yoron Millet Vinegar Factory**, with earthenware pots of vinegar filling the fields. Carry on up and around the coast, biking through agricultural fields and exploring small beaches as you go. At the **3** **Minata Coast** spot kayakers and SUP tours in the protected waters inside the island. Take a break at **4** **Yoron Seaside Garden** (p269) to enjoy a drink and the views.

Back on your bike, cycle south along the **5** **Ōkanegu-kaigan**, stopping for a swim at the beach. In the southeastern corner of the island, stop at **6** **Yoron Folk Village** (p269) for some local culture before turning west for the climb up to the **7** **Southern Cross Centre** (p268). While you could coast down the hill back into Chabana from here, aim further west to drop into the **8** **ferry port** (p268). It's a short ride to **9** **Paradise Beach**, an absolute stunner; enjoy a swim and try a local speciality, *mozuku soba*, at Blue Coral Reef restaurant. Ride under the airport runway, then back into Chabana to return your bike.

Places We Love to Stay

¥ Budget ¥¥ Midrange ¥¥¥ Top End

Amami-Ōshima

MAP p245, p253

Minima House ¥ Tiny container unit in Setouchi that fits one comfortably and two at a squeeze. The price is right for budget travellers.

Guest House An (ゲストハウス 奄ん) ¥ Conveniently located house in Naze with single rooms for rent; shared kitchen and bathroom facilities.

Yamato Inn ¥ You can rent snorkel sets at this delightful 60-year-old wooden house in a hamlet about two minutes' walk from the beach.

Hanahana Beach Resort ¥¥ While there's a theme-park feel to this place, it's convenient for families with kids. Pools, saunas, onsen and restaurants on-site.

Denpaku Hotel Akagina ¥¥¥ This smart, architecturally designed modern hotel has traditional appeal. Located not far from the airport, it's a great base for short stays.

Miru ¥¥¥ Luxury villa with beachside private cottages with pools or baths on the veranda. The beach is right in front of the cottages.

Ryūkyū Villas ¥¥¥ Two luxurious villas with private saunas in a secluded mountainside setting. Each villa displays work by local artists.

Kakeromajima

MAP p256

Nanryu ¥ Inside the small village community Nishi Amuro, this is one of the few guesthouses where you can rent just a room, as opposed to the whole house.

Denpaku Umimiru-yane-no-yado ¥¥ At Sukumo beach, this is an affordable option in a traditional wooden house.

Guest House Yui (ゲストハウ ス結) ¥¥¥ An entire beachfront house at the stunning Saneku beach. Sleeps seven guests.

Kikaijima

MAP p258

Youth Hostel Kikai ¥ Dorm-style youth hostel in a great location.

Seaside Magic ¥¥ Rent an entire traditional wooden island house by the coast. Huge tatami rooms and excellent sound system. The garden is also lovely.

Villa Kikai ¥¥ Stylish, contemporary interiors accentuate these private beachside units with a lovely view.

Tokunoshima

MAP p260

Aze Prince Beach Camping Ground ¥ This fine little campground has showers, nice grassy campsites and a trail down to a pretty, secluded beach.

Hotel Lexton Tokushima ¥¥ The best option on the main street through Kametsu, this updated place is within walking distance of the ferry terminal.

Hotel Grand Ocean Resort ¥¥ Convenient in the main street of Kametsu, this hotel is big and dated; easy walk from the ferry terminal.

Okinoerabu-jima

MAP p265

Hotel Seaworld ¥¥ Just a short walk from the ferry terminal in Wadomari, this simple place also has rental cars at a decent price.

Okierabu Floral Hotel ¥¥ This big hotel overlooking the China port area in the west is the island's best, with good rooms and facilities.

LOG INN tarasso ¥¥ Nice wooden-walled rooms about 1km southwest of central Wadomari town; well priced but a tad inconvenient.

Yoron-tō

MAP p269

Shiomi-sō ¥ This guesthouse in central Chabana has been around for decades and is a budget favourite; Japanese-style rooms and shared bathroom.

Yurigahama Campsite & Cottages ¥¥ Just back from the beach on the Ōkanegu-kaigan; chill out here for a few days or a week.

Pricia Resort ¥¥¥ The most upmarket accommodation on the island, it feels as though it belongs on Yoron's sister island of Mykonos, Greece; lots of amenities right next to the airport runway.

おきなわ屋
おきなわ屋
日本全国発送!!
送料一ケ所一律
1,300円

TOOLKIT

The chapters in this section cover the most important topics you'll need to know about in Okinawa. They're full of nuts-and-bolts information and valuable insights to help you understand and navigate Okinawa and get the most out of your trip.

Arriving
p276

Getting Around
p277

Money
p278

Accommodation
p279

Family Travel
p280

Health & Safe
Travel
p281

Food, Drink
& Nightlife
p282

Responsible
Travel
p284

LGBTIQ+
Travellers
p286

Accessible
Travel
p287

Island
Languages
p288

Nuts & Bolts
p289

Language
p290

Arriving

Naha (OKA) airport services 30 domestic destinations;and connects to international routes via Tokyo, Seoul, Hong Kong, Shanghai and Taipei, with flights to a further seven cities in China and Taiwan. Other island air hubs are Ishigaki (ISG), Miyako (MMY) and Amami (ASJ). International ferries no longer sail into Naha, but mainland ferries do; see p270.

Visas

International visitors require a valid visa to enter Japan and clear customs and immigration on arrival into Naha. Subject to approval, get 90-day tourist e-visas at *mofa. go.jp*.

SIM Cards

e-SIM apps like **Saily** and **Nomad** are stress-free and great value: both use KDDI's network for the islands' best coverage. Otherwise, buy data SIMs at the airport or *konbini*s.

Clothing

Pack light! Even in winter, it's rarely cold. Summer days are hot and sweaty: temps rarely fall below 30°C. In-room laundry facilities mean you can wash-and-wear, and Naha is a shopper's paradise.

Language

The decades-long US military presence has made many Okinawans confident communicators in English. Bilingual signs are common. **DeepL Translate** is shockingly good if your Japanese isn't.

Transferring from the Airport

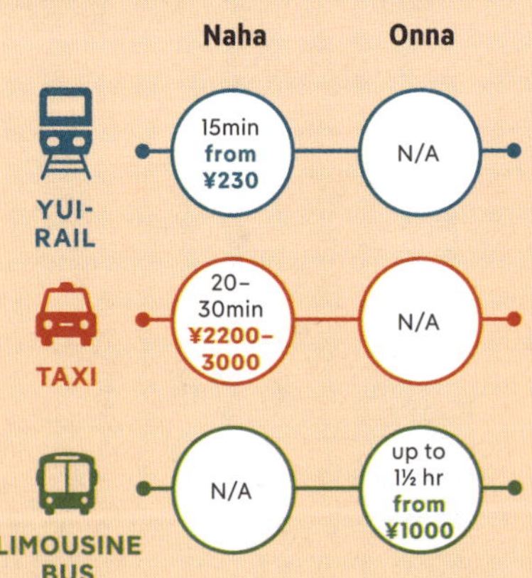

ACCESS ALL AREAS

Japan Airlines' **Japan Explorer Pass** and ANA's **Discover Japan** air passes are both great value to foreign tourists holding an international ticket to Japan, keen on exploring the islands.

Each pass offers up to eight discounted flights anywhere on that airline's domestic network, costing around $US55–120 per flight sector. Changes aren't permitted and tickets are nonrefundable.

JAL's **Japan Explorer Pass** has the added benefit of free Wi-Fi and a 2 × 23kg baggage allowance on all flights, and is valid on all JAC interisland routes.

The **Discover Japan** pass doesn't, and isn't, but ANA's network has more routes Japan-wide.

Getting Around

Proper exploration of Okinawa-hontō, Ishigaki and Miyako-jima requires wheels: not necessary if you're only visiting Naha (ride Yui, the monorail), smaller islands (rent bikes), or plan on never leaving your resort.

TRAVEL COSTS

Car hire:
from ¥4500 per day

Petrol:
¥160/L

Toll: (Naha–Nago)
¥1610

Zamami Ferry
¥4990 return

Car Rental

Countless local agencies compete with the big names in the lucrative islands car-rental game. Many agencies offer support in English. Some don't. Use **Kayak** (*kayak.com*) and **Klook** (*klook.com*) to find deals: rates rise as inventory drops. Book ahead.Compare conditions between agencies and find out if your credit card/travel insurance lowers the deductible. Check for: corporate rates, CDW inclusion, if a deposit is required and if debit cards are accepted; and for good car-karma, rent an EV.

Driving on Okinawa-hontō

Okinawa's railways were destroyed during WWII and never rebuilt, making motor vehicles the main mode of mass transport (a car-to-people ratio of 3:4). Every day, thousands of tourists (who are unfamiliar with driving on the left) hit the roads and the Okinawa not-so-Expressway: silliness ensues, accidents happen and things can move very, very slowly. But what's the rush, anyway?

TIP

Flights to Oki from ¥4000? Try: **Peach**, **Solaseed** and **Skymark**!

DRIVING ESSENTIALS

Drive on the left.

An International Driving Permit is required to rent a vehicle.

Beware twisty, narrow streets.

Speed limit: 40/80km/h (city/hwy).

.03

Blood-alcohol limit: 0.03.

Local Buses

Making sense of where you are, where you're going and how to use the islands' public buses can be a bit tricky if you don't speak Japanese. Less so in Naha, where there's a shiny bus terminal and a vast network with transfers to Yui-Rail (*kotsu-okinawa.org/en*).

Ferries

Interisland ferries operate out of Naha, Motobu, Nakijin and Nanjō (Okinawa-hontō) from Naze (Amami-Ōshima), and from Miyako and Ishigaki to islands in their chain. But there are no ferries to Miyako or Ishigaki from anywhere outside the Miyakos and the Yaeyamas – you must fly.

Island-hops

Figuring how to get between the 53 islands of the four groups can be a complex process involving ferries, flights, chartering boats or light aircraft, bridge crossings, open ocean swims, growing wings or mastering teleportation. The tourism officer at your destination always knows best.

Money

CURRENCY: YEN (¥)

Cash or Card?

Visa and Mastercard are widely accepted but often attract a minimum spend or surcharge. Cash remains king in more remote villages. Even in Naha, some supermarkets and ferry operators are cash-only; keep some on hand for unexpected situations.

Pay by Phone

Contactless phone-pay systems like Apple Pay and Google Pay don't always work in Japan. Although you might tap to pay at most *konbinis* without incident, this won't always be the case everywhere you shop. Avoid potential embarrassment by always keeping cash and your physical cards on hand.

ATMs

Withdraw cash from credit/debit cards with the Visa or MasterCard symbol at post offices and convenience store ATMs. Transactions in yen usually nets a better rate.

Tipping

Tipping is not required in Japanese culture. In Okinawa, with so many Americans around, it's optional. Follow your instinct.

HOW MUCH FOR A...

Yui-Rail day-pass
**¥800/400
(adult/child)**

Beach parking
**¥600/3000
per hr/day**

Junglia entry
**¥8000/5400
(adult/child)**

Spa treatment
¥22,000+

Save on Hotels

Room rates fluctuate according to demand. Last-minute deals can be found if you watch the trends, but when the islands are hopping (indicated by unusually high rates) it's best to book ahead. Use multiple apps like **Trivago** and **Vio** to find the best deals.

REUSE & RECYCLE: SHOPPING

Shop at secondhand stores, done as only the Japanese can do. Decades of American influence catering to *gaijin* (foreigner) tastes and sizes has made Okinawa Japan's thrift-shopping capital.

TAX & DUTY FREE

Okinawa is a shopper's paradise. Naha's **T Galleria by DFS** (p64) is one of Japan's largest urban duty-free malls. **Duty-free** shops, usually only in airports, waive duties and reciprocal taxes on liquor, tobacco and merchandise to lower the sell price, but it doesn't mean duty-free is always cheaper: caveat emptor. **Tax-free** shopping is when retailers (everywhere) absolve you of Japan's 10% consumption tax for purchases over ¥5000 upon presentation of your passport and tourist (only) visa.

Accommodation

Hotels

Business in Okinawa's well-established hotel sector is booming. Throughout Okinawa-hontō, on Ishigaki-, Miyako- and Kume-jima and on little Amami-Ōshima, visitors are spoiled for choice. From small hostels to behemoth builds with hundreds of rooms and with offerings from all the big brands, for backpackers, big spenders and families, there's a hotel for every taste and budget.

Beach Resorts

You'll find a wide range of luxury beach resorts, as well as family-friendly resorts and smaller boutique resorts geared towards the lucrative honeymoon market on Okinawa-hontō, around Onna and the Motobu peninsula, and on Ishigaki and Miyako-jima. Both Kume-jima and Amami-Ōshima offer a more low-key island resort experience.

Guesthouses & Inns

If you're seeking some degree of cultural exchange or more opportunities to interact with your hosts and fellow guests, family-run *minshuku* (Japanese guesthouses) and ryokan (traditional Japanese inns) offer island hospitality in a relaxed environment with varying degrees of comfort and amenity, and some include meals. You'll find them everywhere, especially on the smaller islands, and on Ishigaki and Miyako-jima.

Apartments

In the last decade, an abundance of low-cost studio-style apartments with small kitchens, laundry facilities and small balconies have sprung up in Naha and the islands' larger cities, providing an alternative to the business-hotel format popular throughout Japan. Often with a car space, they're great value for transits and short stays.

HOW MUCH FOR A NIGHT IN...

Naha studio
¥7000

Luxury Airbnb
¥45,000+

Beach resort
¥35,000+

Cottages & Camping

Amami-Ōshima has some divine options for beachside camping, but if you love the great outdoors and being among nature, there are campgrounds and simple hut-style cottage accommodation available far and wide across the archipelago, with the highest concentration on Okinawa-hontō. And if you're a little bit fancy, never fear: there are plenty of glampsites here too!

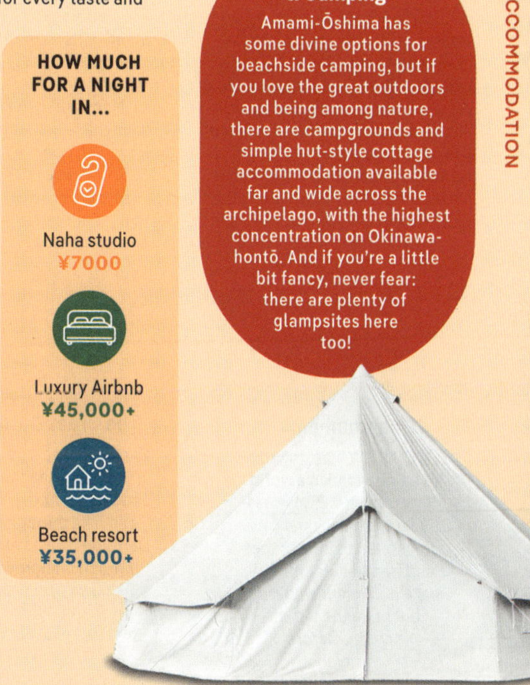

TO AIRBNB OR NOT TO AIRBNB...

Some of the islands' most fabulous accommodation is owned privately and rented on Airbnb – from rustic cottages and luxe beachfront pads with private plunge pools, to penthouses with amazing views and a large inventory of apartments of varying styles and sizes, in Naha and the major cities. Properties are sometimes listed on multiple platforms, with lower cleaning and admin fees. Sharing with family or friends can help bring the sometimes staggering cost of those really incredible listings to within reach. Remember: always check the most recent reviews first!

Family Travel

With cheap airfares and a huge range of fun, family-oriented experiences, Okinawa-hontō gives you some compelling reasons to add it to your Japan adventure – not to mention warm, friendly people and their unique history, culture and environment.

Culture for Kids

Getting hands-on with Ryūkyū traditional crafts and culture is a great way to educate and inspire kids. You can take a pottery class or make a *shiisaa* (traditional guardian lion statue), try your hand at *bingata* (Okinawan resist dyeing), sail a wooden *sabani* boat, romp around castle ruins, ride horses along the beach, meet a karate master... and that's just before lunch!

Theme Parks

It's not a stretch to say that for an island of its size, Okinawa is top-heavy with family-friendly attractions, activities and theme parks. Many are in the Motobu/Nakijin area, including Junglia (p137), which opened its doors in 2025. Life-size animatronic dinosaurs promise to make any dinosaur-mad munchkin's dreams come true.

Taketomi-jima

Taketomi is a time-trip back to a tiny island in a world of its own, just 15 minutes by ferry from Ishigaki. Its atmospheric streetscapes and period authenticity make it a winner with kids, but prise them from screens *before* arrival.

The Great Outdoors

All of Okinawa's designated swimming beaches have lifeguards. Active families can hike through World Heritage forests and kayak through mangroves, but Okinawa's resorts have perfected 'Kids Clubs' if you'd rather just relax.

OKINAWA-HONTŌ FOR FAMILIES

Good feels follow you from the moment you ride Yui (the monorail) from the airport. Compared to Honshū, getting around Okinawa-hontō and connecting with locals is easy. Rent wheels and explore at your own pace, taking the chance to unwind and experience a Japan many don't see. With the money you saved on airfares, splurge on a beach house in Motobu, an area packed with family fun, sea, sand and sunshine. Travel north for spiritual hikes, stargazing and to connect with Ryūkyū culture, then sample Naha's delights for a night or two, before heading home, hearts full, bags bursting and kids inspired for life.

Health & Safe Travel

TYPHOONS

May–October is typhoon season. Though most storms aren't severe, strong winds and heavy rains can last days, causing minor damage and cancelling flights and ferries. Stay forewarned: install **Windy** on your phone.

Quakes & Tsunamis

You may hear 'Okinawa doesn't get big quakes' and 'the reefs protect us from tsunamis'. Neither is true. A large earthquake and/or tsunami could strike any time. If you feel strong shaking or hear tsunami sirens, head immediately to higher ground or the 3rd floor of a reinforced concrete building.

Snakes & Marine Stingers

The venom of Okinawa's endemic viper habu and the stinging toxins of *habu kurage* (box jellyfish) are both potent and extremely painful, capable of causing paralysis and cardiac arrest. Deaths are uncommon, but hospitalisations do occur. Swim in netted areas, and wear covered shoes when walking in long grass. Don't be paranoid. Be aware.

ESSENTIAL APPS

Stay safe: download the **NHK News and Disaster Info** and **NERV Disaster Prevention** apps, and activate alerts.

BEACH SAFETY SIGNAL FLAGS

Emergency Evacuation
Evacuate from the water in the case of emergencies such as tsunamis.

Swimming Area
Swim in the safe zone between the two flags.

No Swimming
Current conditions make it too dangerous to swim.

Caution
Waves and currents are higher and stronger than usual; stay where you can stand.

Safe to Swim
Conditions are safe to swim and enjoy the sea.

Sick or Injured?

City hospitals – invariably staffed with kind, compassionate professionals – provide 24-hour care. You cannot be refused treatment for not having insurance, but for any medical treatment you'll have to foot the bill and apply for reimbursement when you get home. Be sure to buy travel insurance predeparture.

CRIME

Okinawa has low crime by world standards, but incidences of theft and sexual assault are higher than in mainland Japan. Cases involving sexual violence against local women by US military personnel have caused public outcry. It's less likely you'll experience crime here than at home, but when travelling anywhere unfamiliar, always keep your passport safe and stay aware of your surroundings.

Food, Drink & Nightlife

When to Eat

Breakfast (7–9am) might include rice, miso soup, Spam *onigiri* (yes!), *nattō* or *yushi tōfu*, *umi budō* (sea grapes), bread, pastries, juice, tea or coffee.

Lunch (noon–1.30pm) Many restaurants stop serving by 2.30pm. Okinawans tend not to linger over lunch.

Dinner (5.30–8pm) Fewer options in small towns. Not so in Naha, with plenty of choice and lively *izakaya* open till late.

Where to Eat

Izakaya Japanese-style pubs serving small plates to go with sake or beer; open 5pm to late.

Sushi-ya Counter joints (both casual and fancy) specialising in sushi (raw fish on rice).

Shokudō Inexpensive venues that serve set meals of home-cooked classics; open for lunch and dinner.

Kissaten Coffee shops; 'morning sets' include coffee, toast and a hard-boiled egg, before 11am.

Convenience stores Aka *konbini*; ubiquitous 24-hour snack emporiums.

Family restaurants Often open 24 hours, with big cross-genre menus.

MENU DECODER

Gōyā champurū Pork and gourd stir-fry

Shikuwasā A sour citrus fruit rich in nobiletin

Umi budō (海ぶどう) Sea grapes – a kind of seaweed

Okinawa-soba (沖縄そば) Thick noodles in pork broth

Yaeyama-soba (八重山そば) Soba with pork, bean sprouts and scallions

Taco Rice Tex-Mex and cheese on boiled rice

Mimigā Sliced pig's ears in vinegar

Rafutē Sweet, ginger-soy stewed pork

Ikasumi-jiru (イカスミ汁) Black squid-ink soup with pork

Teishoku (定食) A set meal, including rice, *miso-shiru* and pickles

Nomi-hōdai (飲み放題) All-you-can-drink (usually for two hours)

Awamori (泡盛) Okinawan rice liquor

Habu-shu (ハブ酒) Snake sake, infused with viper (whole snake!)

HOW TO… Eat Like a Local

Master using *o-hashi* (chopsticks) but never stick them upright in a bowl of rice, pass food to another pair of *hashi*, or stab food with them; these are actions reminiscent of Japanese funeral rites.

When serving yourself from a shared dish, flip the chopsticks around and use the back end to pick up the food and place it in your bowl, to prevent the spread of germs.

Lunch is one of Japan's great bargains, but restaurants can only offer cheap lunch deals because they anticipate high turnover.

Knowing this, locals don't linger at lunchtime, nor should you, unless you're somewhere special paying for the privilege.

Slurping noodles is not considered rude; it's how you're meant to eat them: briskly, sucking in cool air with the soft noodle and hot broth.

It's mildly offensive to walk and eat, unless eating ice cream. Don't do it.

FROM LEFT: SUNABESYOU/SHUTTERSTOCK, FIM RACHANON/SHUTTERSTOCK

HOW MUCH FOR A...

bowl of Okinawa soba
¥800–1200

soft-serve ice cream
¥200

Spam onigiri
¥350

katsu teishoku ranchi (pork cutlet lunch set)
¥1050

pitcher of Orion beer
¥400

can of Orion beer
¥230

cold Calpis soda (600ml)
¥180

steak dinner
¥1000–2500

HOW TO...

Dine with Confidence

You're welcomed with an enthusiastic *'men-sō-re-!'* and then asked how many are in your party: *'nan-mei sama?'*. Indicate the number with your fingers, as Japanese sometimes do. You may be asked if you prefer, or will be directed to, a: *zashiki* (low table on *tatami*), *tēburu* (table) or *kauntā* (counter) and presented with an *o-shibori* (hot towel), tea or water and a menu.

For an English menu, ask: *'eigo no menū arimasu ka?'*

Restaurants sometimes offer *o-makase* (chef's choice) sets, but most menus are *o-konomi* (as you like/à la carte).

Impress your hosts before you taste anything, by saying *'i-ta-da-ki-ma-su'* (lit: 'I'm about to receive') to express your gratitude and anticipation for the meal.

After service, a bill is placed discreetly on your table. If it isn't, catch your server's eye with *'sumimasen'* (excuse me) and then, *'o-kaikei o kudasai'*: 'the bill, please'. To split it, ask: *'betsu betsu de, onegaishimasu'*.

Payment is usually settled at the counter, not the table. Most restaurants now accept cards. Some do not. To save everyone great discomfort, be sure to always carry cash – for when you miss that huge '現金のみ! Cash only!' sign on the front door.

Cultural Awareness: Thanking Your Host

When leaving somewhere you've been served food, it will delight the chef if you call out *'gochisō-sama deshita!'* ('it was a feast!'), bowing briskly as you exit.

ADVENTUROUS DINING: RYŪKYŪ CUISINE

The Japanese are food-obsessed and the people of Okinawa are possibly even more so. Their diet – heavy on seafood (raw and cooked), pork (every part of the animal), *imo* (a kind of potato) and other root vegetables, tofu, miso and seaweed – is one of the reasons the country set a 2025 record for having 100,000 centenarians, many from Miyako.

At the lively, up-early fish markets (魚市場; *uo-ichiba*) you can get mouthwatering sushi and sashimi, *kaisen-don* (seafood rice bowl) and *ikasumi-jiru* (squid's ink soup). You might be able to find *tako-yaki* (octopus balls), *dango* (soft, rice-flour balls) or try *nattō* (partially fermented soybeans, which may be an acquired taste). *Nattō* is secretly how the Japanese judge a *gaijin's* toughness!

Awamori, Okinawa's version of sake, is made by fermenting rice with *koji* (a kind of mould) and distilling it into a potent liquor. It won't take long before you'll come across a bottle of *habu-shu*, which is a type of *awamori* infused with the juices of a deceased but deadly viper in the bottle as it ferments. Awful to look at but extremely smooth to the taste, it's believed to have medicial and pain-relieving properties.

So...how adventurous are you?

Responsible Travel

Climate Change & Travel

It's impossible to ignore the impact we have when travelling; Lonely Planet urges all travellers to engage with their travel carbon footprint, which will mainly come from air travel. While there often isn't an alternative, travellers can look to minimise the number of flights they take, opt for newer aircrafts and use cleaner ground transport, such as trains. One proposed solution – purchasing carbon offsets – unfortunately does not cancel out the impact of individual flights. While most destinations will depend on air travel for the foreseeable future, for now, pursuing ground-based travel where possible is the best course of action.

The **UN Carbon footprint calculator** shows how flying impacts a household's emissions.

The **ICAO's carbon emissions calculator** allows visitors to analyse the CO_2 generated by point-to-point journeys.

Connect with the Ryūkyū Spirit

Walk beneath sacred peaks in World Heritage Yambaru National Park with ASMUI Spiritual Hikes. In Nanjō, visit Sefaa-utaki and pay your respects to the gods, then experience the calm simplicity of Kudaka-jima, said to be the birthplace of the Ryūkyū people.

Leave No Trace

It's a huge bugbear to the Japanese that visitors from overseas don't properly dispose of their rubbish. As a rule of thumb, where bins aren't provided, take your rubbish back to your accommodation, separate it correctly and dispose of it there.

Kijokasho – the Ōgimi Creative Hub

Meet the friendly folks at Kijokasho – the Ōgimi Creative Hub, which was once the Kijoka Primary School (p148) – to experience what sustainability can actually mean, and get ideas on how to inspire the repurposing of unused spaces in your community.

National Parks epitomise responsible travel. Iriomote-Ishigaki NPs International Dark Sky Park and Okinawa-hontō's World Heritage Yambaru NP are living examples of what matters.

Tuna species are threatened by overfishing, while chemicals found in sunscreen poison precious coral reefs: eat sustainably and use earth-friendly products.

RESPECT THE RULES

Rules are not made to be broken in Japan. Visitors breaking them, such as walking across a pedestrian crossing when the walk light is red, will be frowned upon, even in more-laidback Okinawa.

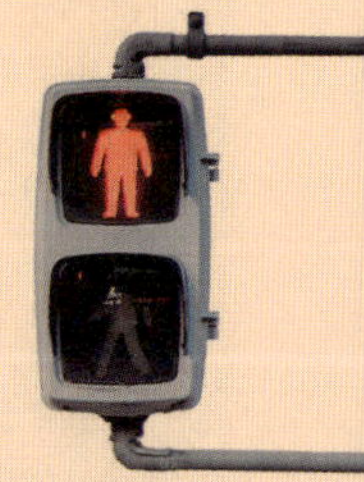

GO GREENER – RENT AN EV

Unfortunately, car rental is something you'll likely need on your travels, but it only costs a little extra to rent a hybrid or fully electric car, and charging points are now commonplace. It might even save you money in the end.

Say No to 'Fukuro'

It will take generations to breed out the Japanese obsession with wrapping and/or placing individual items in separate plastic bags – more reason why we must all politely refuse them at the register. Say *'fukuro wa irimasen'* ('I don't need a bag') or simply *'fukuro iranai'*, unless you absolutely do.

Check out Okinawa's amazing secondhand stores *as well as* the big malls, and help to build a circular economy.

Snorkel in the Zamami Islands (p166), dive in the Yaeyamas (p206) or kayak the Hija mangroves to better understand biodiversity.

Care for Coral

Like many worldwide, Okinawa's delicate coral reefs are at risk of coral bleaching and other damage. Use reef-safe sunscreen and take care not to trample or touch living corals.

Veggie Vitality

Absorb some of what drives Okinawa's famous longevity by sampling the vibrant local produce, like *beni imo*, *shikuwasa*, and *goya*. Try the bounty at **Gajimaru** (p119) and **Emi no Mise** (p149).

Your Own O-Hashi

Japan uses around 24 billion pairs of *waribashi* (disposable chopsticks) every year: around 185 *hashi* per person. Do your bit: buy an ornate set of proper reusable *o-hashi* to carry with you.

RESOURCES

eia-international.org
Learn what species are endangered and how to protect them.

darksky.org
Combatting light pollution, worldwide.

endemicgarden.jp/en
Responsible touring in World Heritage Yambaru National Park.

LGBTIQ+ Travellers

In Japan you can be yourself or be who you want to become, without fear of discrimination. In Okinawa, things are a lot more laidback – folks don't really think about what others do, or care. Here, it's all about building supportive communities: Okinawa is for *everyone!*

No Same-Sex Marriage

As of 2025, Japan is the only G7 country without legal protection for same-sex unions.

Japan has been governed by the conservative Liberal Democratic Party (LDP), almost continuously, since 1955. With the rise of the right-wing Sanseito Party, which has become the fourth-largest political party in Japan in mid-2025, things aren't getting any less conservative!

There's a growing gulf between the LDP and public opinion on gender-related issues; the most recent opinion polls show about 70% of the Japanese public support same-sex marriage, but only 11% of lawmakers within the LDP favour legalising it.

PARTNERSHIP RECOGNITION

In Japan, sexual activities between same-sex people are not restricted in any way by law, other than the age of consent, set at 16 in 2023, and no Buddhist and Shintō doctrine exists that denounces homosexuality. No national laws protect same-sex marriage, but over 500 municipalities and 31 prefectures, including Naha City and Okinawa Prefecture, have 'partnership oath' systems, recognising same-sex partnerships.

Statistics

While 9% of Japanese identify as members of the LGBTIQ+ community (according to a 2020 national survey), as of 2025 two out of the 713 members of the Japanese legislature (the Diet) were openly LGBTIQ+.

KEEP PDAS AT A MINIMUM

Mainland Japanese, regardless of their sexual orientation, don't typically engage in displays of affection in public. It's possible you'll see handholding now and then, but probably won't see couples smooching, and definitely not necking voraciously. Things are more laid-back in Okinawa, but the basic programming still underpins society. Be discreet.

RAINBOW OF INFORMATION

Rainbow Night Out (*rainbownightout.jp*) compiles the most up-to-date list of the 40 or so places you can meet LGBTIQ+ folks in Okinawa. Note that if you're anything other than gay on the spectrum of sexual diversity, you're not exactly spoiled for choice. More establishments outwardly cater to gay boys than to gay girls. In most instances, though, everyone is welcome and the vibe is fun and inclusive.

Oki-Pride

Since 2013, Pink Dot Okinawa (*pinkdot-okinawa.com*) holds a Pride Parade in downtown Naha, featuring a march, panel discussions, and live music. The parade is typically held in autumn.

Accessible Travel

Okinawa works hard to provide equity for people with accessibility needs. While Okinawa doesn't have the same design challenges as space-hungry mainland Japan, it doesn't have the same infrastructure budget either.

Transport

Naha's Yui-Rail has elevators, ramps and accessible toilets. Key bus routes in Naha, Ishigaki and Miyako are wheelchair accessible, but smaller routes mightn't be. Book accessible taxis in advance.

Airport

Accessible Japan has detailed information on Japan's major international airports. In general, all have electric-cart pickups, guided assistance to/from flights, wheelchairs available, accessible toilets and parking for those with disabilities.

Accommodation

All major hotels have accessible rooms on their inventory. For Airbnb and private apartments, contact the provider directly to determine the level of accessibility.

RESOURCES

The Japanese term for accessibility is *bariafurii* (barrier free; バリアフリー).

Accessible Japan *(accessible-japan. com)* is the most comprehensive resource on accessibility infrastructure in Japan, and features detailed lists of accessible hotels, attractions and tours, and an online forum (Tabifolk).

Japan Accessible Tourism Center *(japan-accessible. com)*: accessible tourism listings, by city.

Barrier Free Okinawa *(barifuri-okinawa.org)* operates a Tourist Information Centre and maintains a facilities database.

EATING

If you're unable to use chopsticks, bring with you whatever utensils you need. Smaller restaurants may not have the space for a wheelchair, but there are plenty of good, accessible options across the islands.

Toilet Facilities

Multipurpose toilets with grab rails, accessible sinks and emergency buttons are available in most public buildings, department stores, larger supermarkets, some parks, at Yui-Rail and bus stations, and highway rest areas.

WHEELCHAIRS

If you're deciding on whether to travel with a motorised or a manual wheelchair, consider taking the smaller, more compact one, as it's more likely to fit into smaller restaurants, shops and attractions.

Places of Interest

Most popular sights are now accessible – staff will always try to assist where they can. Major attractions such as Shuri-jō, Churaumi Aquarium, and Ryūkyū-mura have free wheelchair lending.

Island Languages

Kokugo (国語; standard Japanese) is the only official language of modern Okinawa, but before 1879 when Japan invaded the Ryūkyūs, hundreds of languages were spoken in the kingdom. In 2009 UNESCO declared the Ryūkyūan languages were 'severely or critically endangered'. Today, only a handful remain. Learn more about the world's endangered languages and why we should protect them, at endangeredlanguages.com.

Japanese (日本語; Nihongo)

Unlike some other Asian languages, spoken Japanese has no tones. The vowels 'ā' (ahh), 'ē' (ehh), 'ū' (ooh) and 'ō' (aww) are held twice as long as a regular vowel. Its sounds cross over to English, making spoken Japanese easier for most *gaijin* than the written language.

The Ryūkyūan Languages

Ryūkyūan languages are not simply dialects of *kokugo*, as each subgroup is linguistically distinct; and, within each, further variations exist. Following are some words and phrases from each of Ryūkyūan-language family members, and the English translation. To demonstrate the distinct differences between group members (not just dialectical variations in structure or pronunciation), we've listed how to say 'hello' and 'thank you very much', in each language for comparison.

Okinawa (沖縄口; Uchinaguchi)

Hello ハイサイ *haisai*
Thank you very much にふぇーでーびる *nifeedeebiru*
Meeting makes us family イチャリバチョーデー *icharibachōdē*

Someone who loves to eat, a gourmet ガチマヤー *gachimayaa*
Important human connections ユイマール *yuimāru*
Welcome to Okinawa! メンソーレ沖縄 *mensōre Okinawa*

Yaeyama (八重山物言; Yaimamuni)

Hello くよーなーら *kuyōnāra*
Thank you very much すーうんがむ *suu ungamu*

Miyako (宮古口; Myākufutsu)

Hello ンミャーチ *nmyaachi* ('welcome')
Thank you very much タンディガタンディ *tandigatandi*

Amami-Ryūkyūan (島口; Shimayumuta)

Hello うがみしょうらん *ugamishōran*
Thank you very much オブクリダリョン *obukuridaryon*

Yonaguni-Ryūkyūan (与那国物言; Dunanmunui)

Hello すーうんがむ *suu ungamu*
Thank you very much フガラッサ *fugarassa*

Nuts & Bolts

OPENING HOURS

May vary seasonally, especially on remote islands, but generally:

Banks 9am to 3pm (some to 5pm) Monday to Friday

Bars 6pm to closing (varies)

Cafes 7am to 10pm (some to midnight)

Department stores 10am to 8pm (some to 10pm)

Post offices 9am to 5pm Monday to Friday

Restaurants lunch 11.30am to 2pm; dinner 6pm to 10pm

News Media

Ryūkyū Shinpo *(english.ryukyushimpo.jp)*: Since 1893
Okinawa Times *(okinawatimes.co.jp)*: Okinawan *Japan Times* affiliate
Stars and Stripes *(okinawa.stripes.com)*: Military and expat community news

GOOD TO KNOW

Time Zone
GMT +9

Country Calling Code
(+81)

Emergency Number
110

Population
1.3 million

Weights & Measures

Okinawa uses the metric system.

Smoking

Smoking is not allowed outside designated areas. Can be strictly enforced.

Electricity
100V/50Hz

Type A
120V/60Hz

PUBLIC HOLIDAYS

New Year's Day 1 January

Coming-of-Age Day 2nd Monday in January

National Foundation Day 11 February

Emperor's Birthday 23 February

Spring Equinox Day 20 or 21 March

Shōwa Day 29 April

Constitution Day 3 May

Green Day 4 May

Children's Day 5 May

Marine Day 3rd Monday in July

Mountain Day 11 August

Respect for the Aged Day 3rd Monday in September

Autumn Equinox Day 22 or 23 September

Sports Day 2nd Monday in October

Culture Day 3 November

Labour Thanksgiving Day 23 November

 # Language

You can have a fantastic time in Japan's major cities without speaking Japanese, but even just a few phrases will help you make friends, attract smiles and advice from locals, and ensure you have a rich and rewarding travel experience.

Basics

Hello
こんにちは
kon·ni·chi·wa

Goodbye
さようなら
sa·yō·na·ra

Yes
はい
hai

No
いいえ
ī·e

Please (general request)
お願いします
onegai shimasu

Please give/bring me...
...を下さい
o ku·da·sai

Please (when offering)
どうぞ
dō·zo

Thank you
ありがとう
a·ri·ga·tō

Excuse me (to get attention)
すみません
su·mi·ma·sen

Sorry
ごめんなさい
go·men·na·sai

What's your name?
お名前は何ですか?
o·na·ma·e wa nan desu ka

My name is ...
私の名前は … です
wa·ta·shi no na·ma·e wa ... desu

How are you?
お元気ですか?
o·gen·ki desu ka

Fine. And you?
はい、元気です。 あなたは?
hai, gen·ki desu a·na·ta wa

Do you speak English?
英語が話せますか?
eigo ga ha·na·se·masu ka

I don't understand.
わかりません
wa·ka·ri·ma·sen

Does anyone speak English?
どなたか英語を 話せますか?
do·na·ta ka eigo o ha·na·se·masu ka

Directions

Where's the ... ?
…はどこですか?
... wa do·ko desu ka

What's the address?
住所は何ですか?
jū·sho wa nan desu ka

Could you please write it down?
書いてくれませんか?
kai·te ku·re·ma·sen ka

Can you show me (on the map)?
(地図で)教えて くれませんか?
(chi·zu de) o·shi·e·te ku·re·ma·sen ka

Signs

Entrance	入口
Exit	出口
Open	営業中/開館
Closed	閉店/閉館
Information	インフォメーション
Danger	危険
Toilets	トイレ
Women	女
Men	男

Emergencies

Help!
たすけて!
tasukete

Go away!
離れろ!
ha·na·re·ro

Call the police!
警察を呼んで!
kē·sa·tsu o yon·de

Call a doctor!
医者を呼んで!
i·sha o yon·de

I'm ill.
私は病気です
wa·ta·shi wa byō·ki desu

NUMBERS

1	一 *i·chi*
2	二 *ni*
3	三 *san*
4	四 *shi/yon*
5	五 *go*
6	六 *ro·ku*
7	七 *shi·chi/na·na*
8	八 *ha·chi*
9	九 *ku/kyū*
10	十 *jū*

PRONUNCIATION TIPS

Japanese pronunciation is not considered difficult for English speakers. Unlike some other Asian languages, it has no tones and most of its sounds are also found in English.

Vowels

Vowels in Japanese can be either short or long. The long ones should be held twice as long as the short ones and are represented with a macron (horizontal line) on top of them.

Consonants

Most consonant sounds are pretty close to their English counterparts. Pronounce the double consonants with a slight pause between them, as this can change the meaning.

10 Phrases to Sound Like a Local

All good? – Daijōbu?
Really? – Maji?
Awesome! – Sugoi!
Uncool! – Dasai!
Cute! – Kawaii!
Ridiculous! – Yabai!
Annoying – Uzai
The worst! – Saitei!
Sneaky! – Zurui!
That's funny! – Ukeru!

Three Phrases to Learn Before You Go

What's the local speciality?
ji·mo·to·ryō·ri wa na·ni ga a·ri·masu ka
Throughout Japan most areas have a speciality dish and locals usually love to talk about food.

Can you recommend any local tourist attractions?
ji·mo·to no kan·kō su·pot·to o o su·su·me shi·masu ka
Locals will be happy to recommend places for you to visit, and often will go out of their way to tell you the best way to get there and how to enjoy it to the fullest.

How do I get to…?
…e wa dō i·ke·ba ī desu ka
Finding a place can be difficult in Japan. Addresses usually give an area, not a street; practise asking directions.

READING & WRITING JAPANESE

Written Japanese is actually a combination of three different scripts. The first, kanji, consists of ideographic characters. The other two, hiragana and katakana, are syllabic scripts – each character represents a syllable.

Kanji

Kanji (漢字) are ideographs (symbols that each represent a concept, idea or thing as well as pronunciation, rather than a word or set of words) borrowed from Chinese, eg 本 (hon) for 'book', 娘 (mu·su·me) for 'daughter' and 日本語 (ni·hon·go) for 'Japanese language'. Each kanji may be made up of anything from one to over 20 strokes written in a particular order. Some kanji characters have two or more ways of being pronounced depending on the context. For example, the kanji 水 is pronounced *mi·zu* when it means 'water', but *su·i* when it's part of another word like 水筒 (pronounced *su·i·tō*) for 'water bottle'.

There are over 2000 kanji in use in modern Japanese, of which 1945 are considered essential for everyday use.

Hiragana

Hiragana (ひらがな) is used to represent particles and grammatical endings particular to Japanese. Hiragana characters are placed alongside the ideographic characters – one single Japanese word can contain both scripts. There are 46 basic hiragana characters, each representing a particular syllable. They can be combined to represent over 100 different syllables.

Katakana

Each hiragana character also has a katakana equivalent. Katakana (カタカナ) are used to represent recent borrowings from other languages, especially English. They're also used to write foreign names – you might want to figure out how to write your own name in Japanese.

STORYBOOK

STORYBOOK

Our writers delve deep into different aspects of Okinawan life

A History of Okinawa & the Southwest Islands in 15 Places

The history of Okinawa runs as deep as its turquoise waters.

Rie Miyoshi

p294

Meet the Okinawans

Tolerance and the nurturing of diverse customs are an integral part of Okinawan culture.

Saya Tanahara

p298

Ryūkyū Mingei: Resistance & Survival

Since the genesis of the mingei movement, Okinawa has been a focal point for folk craft and culture.

Manami Okazaki

p300

Karate: From Okinawa with Love

The martial art with global appeal, karate's roots lie in the unique cultural stew of the Ryūkyū Kingdom.

Helen A Langford-Matsui

p304

The Okinawan Table

For centuries Okinawans have enjoyed a long, healthy life. Their secret? The colourful, nutrient-packed Okinawan diet.

Rie Miyoshi

p308

Where Nature Rules

Amami-Ōshima offers abundant opportunities to learn about sustainability and ecological conservation.

Manami Okazaki

p311

Niya Thiya Cave (p139), Ie Island

A HISTORY OF OKINAWA & THE SOUTHWEST ISLANDS IN
15 PLACES

The history of Okinawa runs as deep as its turquoise waters. From prehistoric settlements and the rivalries of the Sanzan period to the Ryūkyū Kingdom's maritime legacy and the devastation of WWII, Okinawa and its neighbouring islands blend centuries of culture, resilience and tragedy with tropical beaches, charming villages and captivating traditions. By Rie Miyoshi

OKINAWA MAY BE famous for its relaxing resorts and crystal-clear waters, but the archipelago's postcard-worthy vistas belie its turbulent history. In the 14th century the main island was divided into three rival polities during the Sanzan period: Hokuzan, Chuzan and Nanzan. Chuzan ultimately unified the islands, establishing the Ryūkyū Kingdom (1429–1879), a maritime trading power linking Japan, China and Southeast Asia. This left a lasting mark that is still visible today in coral limestone-walled castles, vibrant traditions and unique cuisine across Okinawa and neighbouring archipelagos such as the Amami, Miyako and Yaeyama Islands.

The 20th century brought tragedy. The 1945 Battle of Okinawa between US and Japanese forces claimed around 200,000 lives – including those of roughly 90,000 civilians, about a quarter of the island's non-military population. Many perished during the US invasion or from starvation, while others, following Japanese military orders, hid in caves and took their own lives.

Today Okinawa balances history and modernity: enigmatic castle ruins and sacred sites coexist with oceanside attractions and contemporary island culture. Whether you're lounging on the sand or diving into history, Okinawa has something for you, including a glimpse of what some call Japan's very own lost city of Atlantis.

1. Yonaguni Monument
DIVING IN JAPAN'S ATLANTIS
One of the ocean's greatest archaeological mysteries lies off the coast of Yonaguni, Japan's westernmost island and the most remote of Okinawa's inhabited islands. Discovered by a diver in 1986, this massive underwater stone formation resembles terraces, steps and pyramids, leading some to believe it's the remains of an ancient civilisation predating recorded history. Others insist it's a natural formation shaped by tectonic forces. Found in shallow waters but subject to strong currents, it's best suited to experienced divers. Divers can see hammerhead sharks patrolling this monument between November and April.
For more on Yonaguni, see p234.

2. Amami City Museum
PALAEOLITHIC ARTEFACTS
Sitting between Kyūshū and Okinawa, the Amami Islands have a history shaped by trade, exile and survival. Archaeological finds, including shell mounds, pottery and stone tools, reveal human settlement dat-

ing back to the Palaeolithic period and the transition to the Jomon period. See these ancient finds at the Amami City Museum on Amami-Ōshima, as well as village dioramas and everyday items from the Ryūkyū Kingdom and Satsuma domain, established in the 17th century, that shaped Amami's culture, language, people and cuisine. The island also served as the place of exile for Saigō Takamori, the famed 'last samurai', during the final years of the Tokugawa shogunate.

For more on the Amami City Museum, see p244.

3. Ōshima Tsumugi Village

LIVING SILK-WEAVING TRADITION

Set amid lush subtropical gardens, this 'village' on Amami-Ōshima invites visitors to witness and experience the island's famed silk-weaving tradition. Originating over 1300 years ago, Ōshima *tsumugi* is a high-class silk pongee (a thin, plain-weave fabric) naturally dyed in the island's iron-rich mud, which gives its black threads a distinctive sheen. Once favoured by samu-

rai and now prized for ceremonial kimonos and obis (belts), the craft flourished through the early 20th century. Watch artisans at work, try weaving or dyeing, and stroll through gardens alive with hibiscus, butterflies and birdsong.

For more on Ōshima Tsumugi Village, see p251.

4. Nakijin-jō Ruins

FORTRESS OF HISTORY

Perched on a hill on the Motobu Peninsula in northern Okinawa, Nakijin Castle was built in the late 1200s and served as the seat of the Hokuzan Kingdom during the Sanzan period. In 1416 Chuzan king Sho Hashi captured the castle, unifying the island and becoming the first ruler of the Ryūkyū Kingdom. The castle then became a residence for Ryūkyūan government officials. Today the Nakijin Village History and Culture Centre, beside the castle ruins, displays artefacts and exhibits on local life. Among the highlights are Chinese pottery pieces from the early Ming dynasty, a testament to the Ryūkyū Kingdom's flourishing trade across Asia.

For more on Nakijin, see p137.

5. Taketomi Island

TIMELESS OKINAWAN CHARM

A 10-minute ferry ride from Ishigaki, this quaint island is a living example of Ryūkyūan architecture, with coral-lined lanes, red-tiled roofs, and stone walls draped in bougainvillea. Taketomi retains deep cultural roots expressed through songs, crafts and festivals. Visitors can explore the island by bicycle or water buffalo cart, relax on the famous star sand of Kaiji Beach, or visit the folk museum to learn about island life. Most accommodation is in cosy guesthouses and family-run *minshuku*, but there's also a luxury resort on the island's eastern side.

For more on Taketomi, see p218.

6. Ōgimi Village

HOME OF CENTENARIANS

Tucked away in the northern part of Okinawa's main island, this village has gained international attention for its remarkably long-lived residents: many thrive well into their 80s, 90s and even 100s. It's part of Okinawa's reputation as a 'Blue Zone' – a

Nakijin-jō (p137)

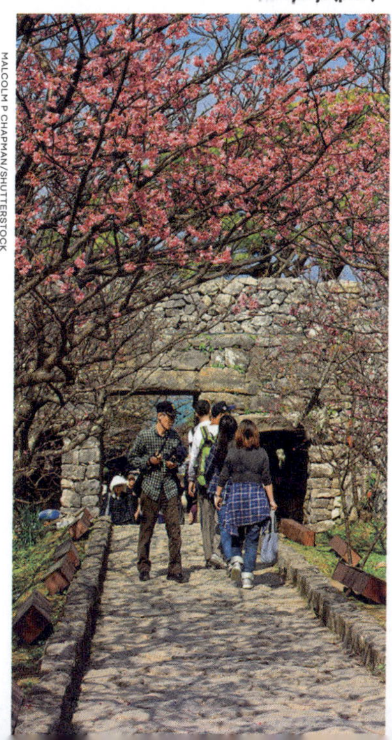

region known for exceptional longevity. The close-knit community celebrates traditional weaving, cuisine, agriculture and festivals deeply rooted in Ryūkyūan culture. Stroll quiet lanes, visit small museums celebrating folk crafts, or sample local produce such as *goya* (bitter melon) and *beni imo* (purple sweet potato), both said to promote healthy ageing. For a taste of homestyle Okinawan cooking, book ahead at beloved local restaurant Emi no Mise.

For more on Ogimi, see p148.

7. Shuri-jō
HEART OF THE RYŪKYŪ KINGDOM

Okinawa's biggest castle was the political and cultural heart of the Ryūkyū Kingdom; it showcased a blend of Japanese and Chinese architecture. Vivid vermilion walls, curved tiled roofs and ornate golden details mark the restored sections, while stone walls and gates hint at the castle's former grandeur. Although the castle was sadly destroyed by fire in 2019, visitors can still explore the restored sections and on-site museum. Shuri-jō is expected to be fully rebuilt in 2026.

For more on Shuri-jō, see p65.

8. Tamaudun Mausoleum
ROYAL RESTING PLACE

Just a two-minute walk from Shuri-jō, Tamaudun is the royal tomb of the Ryūkyū Kingdom's third king, Sho Shin. Built in 1501, the stone structure, with its austere grey walls, traditional tiled roof and symmetrical design, reflects Ryūkyūan reverence for ancestors. The mausoleum features three stone chambers: left for kings and queens, right for princes and princesses, and a central chamber for recently deceased bodies awaiting the bone-cleaning ritual. The entry fee includes access to a small museum where visitors can view photos of the mausoleum and models showing what lies behind the closed chambers.

For more on Tamaudun Mausoleum, see p66.

9. Harimizu Utaki
AN ISLAND'S SACRED ORIGINS

This sacred site is said to mark the mythological creation of Miyako Island, where the Heavenly Emperor sent the deities Koitsuno and Koitama to cultivate the land and populate it. According to legend, Koitsuno and Koitama nurtured the land and bore its first inhabitants. Centuries later, Koitsuno is believed to have reincarnated as a serpent at Harimizu Utaki, fathering children with a local woman; the children went on to become Miyako's guardian deities. The *utaki* features weathered stone altars, ancient trees and natural rock formations. Touring the site typically takes 30 minutes.

For more on Harimizu Utaki, see p179.

10. Sonai & Hoshidate Villages
HIDDEN TRADITIONS IN THE JUNGLE

Located on the northwestern coast of Iriomote Island, Sonai and Hoshidate offer a glimpse into Ryūkyūan life that you can experience on a half-day tour. Sonai, the island's oldest village, is said to have existed since the 14th century. Explore historic shrines and thatched-roof homes, learn about edible plants and snack on sugar cane before moving on to the spiritual Hoshidate with its village rites and opportunities to sip herbal tea prepared by a shaman. Home to the elusive Iriomote wildcat, Iriomote is a 45- to 50-minute ferry ride from Ishigaki Island and is popular with outdoor enthusiasts for its waterfalls and mist-shrouded jungles.

For more on Sonai and Hoshidate, see p235 and p228.

11. Peace Memorial Park
STORIES OF SURVIVAL

Overlooking the ocean, this peaceful park located on the southern coast of Okinawa's main island commemorates the lives lost during the 1945 Battle of Okinawa, one of WWII's bloodiest conflicts and one of the largest amphibious operations in history. The park honours both civilian and military dead, with solemn monuments, stone memorials and the poignant Cornerstone of Peace engraved with thousands of names. The on-site Okinawa Prefectural Peace Memorial Museum offers detailed exhibits, including photographs, personal artefacts, and displays recounting the battle's devastation and survivors' stories.

For more on the Peace Memorial Park, see p80.

Makishi Public Market (p52), Naha

12. Former Japanese Navy Underground Headquarters

SUBTERRANEAN WWII HISTORY

Located near Naha, this labyrinthine site is where Rear Admiral Minoru Ota and his forces made a desperate last stand during the Battle of Okinawa. As the Japanese defence collapsed, Ota sent a famous telegram praising the Okinawan people's efforts before he and his men died by suicide. Opened to the public in 1970, the bunker serves as a solemn reminder of war's futility. Visitors can explore narrow tunnels and the operations room and reflect on the heavy human cost of the battle.

For more on the Former Japanese Navy Underground Headquarters, see p77.

13. Niya Thiya Cave

A SHELTER FOR 1000 PEOPLE

Near Ie Island's southern coast, Niya Thiya Cave, also known as Sen-nin Gama (Cave of 1000 People), served as an air-raid shelter during the Battle of Okinawa, shielding approximately 1000 islanders, with reportedly no casualties. The cave also houses a sacred stone called Bijiru-ishi; it's said that women who pray while holding it will be blessed with a child. Ie Island, a compact 23-sq-km outcrop, is 30 minutes by ferry from Okinawa's Motobu Port. It's mostly flat farmland, dominated by Mt Gusuku. Visitors can reach the cave by bicycle (rentals are available), enjoying a scenic journey there through rice fields and villages.

For more on Niya Thiya Cave, see p139.

14. Makishi Public Market

OKINAWA'S FOOD SCENE

Located in the heart of bustling Naha, this market has been a hub of Okinawan commerce since it opened in the 1950s, growing out of the black market that thrived in the chaotic years following WWII. Known as the 'kitchen of Okinawa', Makishi is a lively blend of stalls selling fresh seafood, tropical fruit, produce and traditional ingredients. It's an engaging window on Okinawa's culinary culture. Visitors can wander the narrow aisles, sample delicacies including *goya*, *beni imo*, pork and fresh *sashimi*, or pick up souvenirs and handmade crafts. The 2nd floor is a prime spot to enjoy a local meal.

For more on Makishi Public Market, see p52.

15. American Village

A SLICE OF AMERICA IN JAPAN

About 40 minutes from Naha airport, this destination with its kitschy charm attracts Americana enthusiasts and American expats who miss home. It was developed in the early '90s on a former US military base, embodying a fusion of Okinawan and American cultures. Stroll along the aptly named Sunset Walk to catch spectacular sunsets and soak up the resort-town atmosphere with plenty of shopping, dining and entertainment options. Daily street performances and live music add to the energy. Highlights include Depot Island, a waterfront mall with more than 100 shops, and Dragon Palace Arcade.

For more on the American Village, see p102.

MEET THE OKINAWANS

Tolerance and the nurturing of diverse customs are an integral part of Okinawan culture. Expect a warm welcome, but always remember that traditions are highly valued here. SAYA TANAHARA introduces her people.

ON THE ONE hand, Okinawa is shaped by democratic protest against and resistance to the central Japanese government and the US military presence after WWII. Okinawans have a reputation for pursuing the right of self-determination over our own land. On the other hand, the supplies and food culture the US bases brought in their wake supported impoverished local dining tables after the war and became essential elements of modern Okinawan cuisine. Yet we are proud to call ourselves Uchinānchu (Okinawan). It's a powerful aspect of our identity.

Strong community bonds unite the large Uchinānchu diaspora. Okinawa Prefecture has hosted overseas Okinawan descendants, including immigrants, at gatherings every five years since 1990. This sense of community is reflected in the Okinawan phrase *ichariba chōdē* (loosely, 'meeting makes us family'). This phrase expresses the islands' spirit of deep humanity, a mindset that values friendship and the traditional mutual aid that is deeply rooted in Okinawan society.

The indigenous practices of our mixed culture have been influenced by those of China and mainland Japan. Traditions centre local deities through priestesses called *noro,* who have existed since the era of the Ryūkyū Kingdom (1429 to 1872). It's said that in ancient times the fire god Hinukan gave fire to the *noro* in every village to create a village hearth, stipulating that every family should light their own hearths from that fire. Fire is believed to protect the house and its occupants, and many Okinawan homes to this day have a small shrine to Hinukan in their kitchens. The family memorial altar called a *tōtōme* (a Ryūkyūan term meaning ancestor) is extremely important for ancestral worship rites. Traditionally, it is passed on to the eldest son or to male relatives. The distinctive family tomb is often shaped like a turtle shell *(kamekōbaka),* which symbolises a return to the mother's womb.

Belief in the enduring family structure is an important part of our culture. In spring we celebrate *shīmī,* in which families gather in the family tomb and share layered box meals featuring festive red and white fish cakes while honouring our ancestors. The practice is named after the Quingming festival, which originated in China. In summer the family welcomes the spirits of ancestors at home for three days. In some areas youth groups perform *eisā* (a vigorous and splendid Buddhist chant dance) at that time to pay respect to ancestors. Beyond the traditional O-Bon festival (a Buddhist observance honouring ancestral spirits), there are opportunities to see *eisā* performances throughout the year, such as at September's Okinawa All-Island Eisā Festival. It's cherished by many as a summer tradition. The dancers' dynamic movements to soul-stirring rhythms have an unforgettable, powerful impact and will make your heart race.

Okinawan Stats

Japan reclaimed Okinawa from the US in 1972. The prefecture's population stands at 1.468 million, and its birth rate has been the highest in Japan for 40 years. The Okinawan diaspora consists of approximately 420,000 people and spans five continents.

Pictured clockwise from top left: *Eisa* (Buddhist chant dance) performer; *Noro; Sanshin* player; *Shīmī* gathering

FAMILY MATTERS

I was born and raised in Urasoe, on the border of the central and southern part of Okinawa-hontō. I grew up with 13 cousins from my mother's and father's sides of the family. Ancestor worship gatherings are some of my best childhood memories. The women prepared the meals and the men welcomed the visitors. My cousins and I gathered and played all day until sunset. After I graduated from college, I lived in the US for a few years. Okinawans carry on our legacy always, no matter how far away we go or how long we have been gone. After my children were born, my father sang Okinawan folk songs to them and my mother taught me how to make Okinawan food. It was a necessary comfort to me to feel a sense of home, and it was important that my children should know their identity. Now I am back on the island, maintaining the blend of cultures for our family.

RYŪKYŪ MINGEI:
RESISTANCE & SURVIVAL

Since the genesis of the *mingei* movement, Okinawa has been a focal point for folk craft and culture. By Manami Okazaki

WHILE MOST PEOPLE think of beaches when they think of Okinawa, it is also one of the most important sites for *mingei* (folk craft), and the islands are dense with artisan studios, from pottery and woodworking to textiles. *Mingei* are often related to the folk customs of the region and imbued with talismanic and protective qualities.

The Landscape of Textiles

It is a blazing hot day in the middle of summer; we are on a field in Miyako Island where several women are cutting nettlelike ramie plants, while others are stripping the fibres. It's difficult to believe this process will end up with *Miyako-jōfu*, some of the most sumptuous, complex textiles in Japan. The production process is entirely by hand, from the planting of the trees to the making of the threads and the dyeing with Ryūkyū indigo; but it is the weave technique that is so complex: only eight bolts of cloth were produced in 2024. The work requires perseverance, dedication and a complete reverence to the process, rather than just the product.

'When you hold the textiles up to the light, because the threads are made by hand there is an imperfect beauty,' says *Miyako-jōfu* artisan Miyuki Urasaki. 'I call this the fabric's "landscape". The emotional state of the artisan is also reflected in the work, whether they are jubilant, angry, sleepy; all those moods are reflected subtly in the texture of the threads. That is why Miyako-jōfu is so endearing: it reflects real life.'

Mingei is connected to nature, in that the materials are usually obtained from the surrounding environment and, to a degree, the aesthetic of the wares is determined by natural resources, such as the available plants.

Mingei Movement Roots

Mingei are vernacular wares characterised by a simple aesthetic that reflects the beauty of the mundane. The concept of '*mingei*' was initiated by philosopher Yanagi Soetsu in the 1920s as a backlash to a time of industrialisation, which brought about rapid decline in traditional life. His musing created a movement that included activists, educators and designers. While Soetsu was rather idealistic, collecting aesthetically pleasing works and putting intellectual values on items that he thought 'ought to exist', he brought wider appreciation to Japan's folk craft and his stance during the time of mass production, and factory-made wares were nothing short of radical.

STORYBOOK

Yanagi once said, 'Asides from Kyoto, I have never visited another place where the woven and dyed fabrics are comparable to Okinawa.' Since the genesis of the *mingei* movement, its founders (as well as prominent folklorists of the time, such as Kunio Yanagita) found inspiration in Okinawan folk culture, and advocated for Ryūkyū people's cultural rights. Famed potters Kawai Kanjiro and Shoji Hamada were moved by the Ryūkyū interpretations of Korean pottery and went to study in Okinawa. Similarly, designer and textile artisan Serizawa Keisuke went to Okinawa to train in *bingata* dye technique. In 1939, the collective produced a film, *Ryūkyū no Mingei*, which was the first documentation of pottery that can be viewed at the excellent Okinawa Prefectural Archives. This, in turn, according to researcher George H Kerr, marked a 'local cultural renaissance'.

Resist Dyes

The broader political situation saw the Ryūkyū Kingdom annexed in 1879, with the inhabitants reclassified as Japanese. Even while they were forced to assimilate, there was widespread discrimination against Okinawans, and they were seen as a second-class minority. According to scholar Kim Brandt, the nullification of culture saw campaigns that were driven by a mono-ethnic vision, and at several elementary schools in Naha, 'any child caught speaking Okinawan was forced to wear a placard of disgrace until he or she discovered another child guilty of the same transgression'.

Every aspect of Ryūkyū *mingei* is interwoven with tales of cultural survival. Shoko Yamashiro of Gusuku Bingata, a *bingata* textiles atelier in Naha, explains that the history of the dye technique reflects the hardships Ryūkyū people overcame, and that Okinawan identity is 'different to mainland Japanese'. Yamashiro explains that the natural environment, like the vivid sky and strong sun, affects the colors she uses and she references local flowers like hibiscus and Queen of the Night cactus in the work. 'The people's brightness is shown in the *bingata*. When you look at it, your heart becomes richer. The colours are vibrant and healing.'

Aside from the forced assimilation, the Battle of Okinawa in 1945 was among the deadliest, with around one-third of the civilian population dying and much of the cultural artefacts destroyed. Post-WWII, *bingata* artisans used found bullet casing for the line work in the textiles, while pigments were taken from the American GI wives' lipstick, as resources were scarce. This situation was reflected in many craft trades; similarly, glass factories were destroyed postwar, so Ryūkyū glass artisans had to use soda bottles that the US military discarded.

Yuken Teruya, an Okinawan artist now based in Berlin, uses *bingata* dyeing in his kimonos and fabrics, and his symbols of resistance are even more blatant. The colours are traditional *bingata* hues, but he modifies the designs to include former US President Obama's face, US jet fighters and parachutes, as well as Okinawan land-rights protestors, which are only visible upon close inspection of the details. Using these conflicting elements, Teruya alludes to the complicated geopolitical history.

Multicultural Chanpurū

Ryūkyū *mingei* has the sensibilities of various cultures – owing to Okinawa's geographic proximity and trade with China, Taiwan, Korea and Southeast Asia – giving it a distinct aesthetic. One of the most ubiquitous forms of *mingei* in Okinawa is pottery known as *yachimun*, the history of which started with Korean potters in the Satsuma domain who were invited to Naha in 1616. While *yachimun* usually takes the form of tableware as well as vessels for alcohol, one of the main uses of pottery is to make *shisa*, the lion-dog icon of Okinawa imported from China around the 14th century. These mythical guardians are seen at entrance gates to houses and establishments across Okinawa.

Naotoshi Kinjō is a pottery artisan based in Miyako Island, the youngest of the Kinjō pottery lineage that starts with Jirō Kinjō, Okinawa's first Living National Treasure. Kinjō plates and cups are instantly recognisable; the dense and solid forms are adorned with vivid sea life painted in broad brushstrokes. Naotoshi Kinjō explains, 'The motifs we use, like the fish, are auspicious symbols which represent fertility, while peonies symbolise prosperity. I have a background in design, so I focus on composition, and combine traditional craft with contemporary sensibilities'.

'During the Ryūkyū Kingdom era, around 400 years ago, the king began gathering artisans in Tsuboya. This was the genesis of Yachimun pottery, where my lineage has its roots. Around the time of Okinawa's return to Japan, post American occupation, the climbing kilns they used were banned in Naha, so Jirō Kinjō moved to Yomitan Village in 1972. That is how Yachimun village started'.

'Okinawan pottery tends to be vibrant, even though Okinawa was historically poor,' Naotoshi Kinjō adds. 'Some say it was to make even everyday items more aesthetic. Okinawa has a *Chanpurū* (mix) culture, combining different elements and influences, and I think that's what makes Okinawan craftsmanship unique.'

Survival Has Meaning

One of the most endearing and ubiquitous folk crafts is *kokeshi*, the simple wooden dolls that originate from the Tōhoku region. Ryūkyū Miyarabi *kokeshi* resemble traditional Okinawan dancers, wearing *hanagasa* hats painted in red to represent the hibiscus flower and blue to represent the ocean. They are made in Naha at a facility called Taiki, which employs people with disabilities. The popularity of *kokeshi* among tourists provides an important income stream to its residents, and the creation of souvenirs has always been a part of the *mingei* story.

For artisans nowadays, a driving force for their work is connected to *ikigai* (life purpose) and cultural preservation, rather than pure economics. Miyuki Urasaki says, 'We are desperately trying to pass down the skills of those that came before us. It is heritage that has lasted hundreds of years, so we can't let it end here. There are very few artisans that can weave textiles this fine. We can't let elements like the design, colours and technique disappear over time.'

Similarly, along the coast in northern Naha in Kijoka, there are small plots of land filled with *bashō* plants, a banana-like plantain that is used for food and medicine. From this plant's fibres, *bashō-fu* (a delicate, light fabric) is woven: it is ideal for Okinawa's hot climate. Mieko Taira, an artisan and representative at the Bashōfu Kaikan, explains while tending to the precious trees that the key to good-quality textiles is good-quality plants, and the entire process starts from the planting of the *bashō* seeds to the weaving, and takes three years.

Mieko Taira sees this production as the antithesis of fast fashion, where an entire ensemble can be bought for cheap so they can be thrown away after one use. 'With *bashō-fu*, the cloth is made by hand, with a lot of passion. You can't describe it with words, it is a feeling – I don't even want to throw away one thread.'

ONE OF THE MAIN USES OF POTTERY IS TO MAKE SHISA, THE LION-DOG ICON OF OKINAWA IMPORTED FROM CHINA AROUND THE 14TH CENTURY. THESE MYTHICAL GUARDIANS ARE SEEN AT ENTRANCE GATES TO HOUSES AND ESTABLISHMENTS ACROSS OKINAWA.

Shisa **statue**

MANAMI OKAZAKI/LONELY PLANET

KARATE:
FROM OKINAWA WITH LOVE

The martial art with global appeal, karate is often called Japanese, but that's a misconception; its roots lie in the unique cultural stew of the Ryūkyū Kingdom, an area known today as Okinawa. By Helen A Langford-Matsui

OKINAWA IS SMALL but mighty. Making up 0.6% of Japan's landmass and, as of 2024, just 1.18% of its population, it has managed to play an outsized role in Japan's international influence. Karate is one of the country's best-known cultural exports, with celebrity practitioners and starring roles in Hollywood movies and streaming shows. For years 'karate' was the catch-all term for Asian martial arts, regardless of country of origin. And today millions of *dōgi*-clad children make their way to karate class on every inhabited continent. Karate has even been practised in Antarctica, if only on a small scale.

What makes karate's infiltration of the international imagination even more incredible is the fact that karate – as we know it today, at least – isn't even particularly old. In fact the term 'karate', with its meaning of 'empty hand', was only officially adopted in Okinawa in 1936. The competition side of karate, too, is relatively new, with the first organised competition only occurring in 1957, roughly 64 years before its debut as a medal sport at the delayed Tokyo Olympics in August 2021. But while modern karate is a recent phenomenon, its foundations – from its roots to its defining principles of courtesy, respect and cultivation of character – stretch back centuries to at least the days of the Ryūkyū Kingdom in the 14th century.

To jump back to those *dōgi*-clad children, in the late 1980s and early '90s I was one of them. My dojo practised Gōjū-ryū, considered one of Okinawan karate's major styles, and like those of many dojos, its walls were adorned with portraits of revered teachers from the Gōjū-ryū lineage. Occasionally our sensei would regale us with stories of karate masters fending off attackers with their bare hands or weapons fashioned from workaday implements. These stories enthralled me, setting my imagination on fire as I dreamed of karate masters taking down assailants surrounded by scenery inspired by an old calendar of Okinawan landscapes that I had: dense mangroves crisscrossed by waterways; vibrant hibiscus blossoms against blue skies; turquoise seas and white-sand beaches.

I've since learned that the history of karate is shrouded in mystery, and fanciful myths often take the place of facts. But within the history that we do know lie enough adventure and complexity to render the legends superfluous. Karate is fascinating enough without the folklore.

Secret Defensive Arts of the Upper Class

In his 1975 book *Karate-dō: My Way of Life*, Funakoshi Gichin, one of karate's most

STORYBOOK

famous masters and advocates, wrote, 'Inasmuch as there is virtually no written material on the early history of karate, we do not know who invented and developed it, nor even, for that matter, where it originated and evolved'. Tales handed down through generations, he said, 'tend to be imaginative and probably inaccurate'. An example is the oft-cited fallacy that karate was the creation of Ryūkyūan peasants.

The truth is quite the opposite. Okinawa's historical martial arts were the domain of the upper classes, including nobles, aristocrats and *samurē* (Okinawan samurai). These socially elite practitioners trained in *tī* (also *te*), a traditional form of self-defence passed down from father to son or from master to student in secret, and later in *tōdī* (also *tōde*), a fusion of Chinese boxing and traditional Okinawan martial arts.

Some might be surprised to learn of a Chinese connection, but Okinawa's ties to China run long and deep: for centuries, the Ryūkyū Kingdom was a trading hub, welcoming merchant ships from China and Southeast Asia. Ryūkyū also paid a tribute to China's Ming and Qing dynasties for over 500 years, during which time economic ties and cultural exchange enriched China's empires and the Ryūkyū Kingdom. Along with the purposeful introduction of diplomatic and scholarly knowledge, Chinese envoys and migrants brought with them their own martial arts, which mingled with local practices. Ryūkyūans, too, were known to travel to China with the clear intention of training with Chinese martial arts masters. This China connection was once crystal clear: both *tōdī* and karate – in a former orthography at least – use a character meaning 'Tang' or 'China'. Combined with *tī* or *te*, meaning 'hand', karate's former names translated as 'Chinese hand'.

When as a soon-to-be graduate I started searching for a job in Okinawa to support my recently reignited karate aspirations, I knew none of this. All I knew – unlike a surprising 65% of Japanese living outside Okinawa – was that karate came from Okinawa, and that's where I should go. Unfortunately, jobs in Okinawa at the time were scarce, so off to the Japanese mainland I went.

Karate Comes Out of the Shadows

There are all sorts of karate dojos in mainland Japan. This has been true since soon after karate was introduced there in the 1920s. Some of these dojos teach Japanese styles of karate, like *kyokushin*, which, while sharing varying levels of similarity with Okinawan karate, were born on the mainland by Japanese practitioners; other mainland dojos teach Okinawan styles. My dojo was the latter: it taught Okinawan karate, albeit with Japanese influences. I remember walking in for the first time and being surprised to see faces I recognised hanging on the wall – those same masters revered at my childhood dojo in Canada occupied a place of honour in my Tokyo dojo too.

Karate's steady march from covert martial art of the Ryūkyū Kingdom to mainstream martial art and sport practised by approximately 130 million people across more than 193 countries began in the late 19th century, when Japan annexed the Ryūkyū Kingdom, turning it into Okinawa Prefecture. While the post-annexation environment meant that karate could be practised in the open, it didn't immediately capture the imagination of the general public. That didn't happen until karate was introduced into the Okinawan curriculum in the first years of the 20th century.

Within a few decades some of karate's most skilled masters were teaching karate on the mainland, while Okinawan karate was also being spread abroad by Okinawan emigrants. Several Okinawan masters also made trips abroad – or emigrated themselves – to give karate demonstrations in Taiwan (a territory of Japan at the time), Hawaii and Brazil. The spread of karate continued in the post-WWII years, with American service members taking home skills honed during tours of duty.

This karate, however, was distinct from that practised in the days of secrecy – a simplified, less dangerous version, adjusted by karate masters like Itosu Ankō and, later, Funakoshi, to better match the abilities of children and, more generally, the average person. In his 1975 book, Funakoshi stated that the 'karate that high school students practise today is not the same karate that was practised even as recently as ten years ago, and it is a long way indeed from the karate that I learned when I was a child in Okinawa'. Some practitioners lament this fact, but as Funakoshi noted in the same book, 'Times change, the world changes, and obviously the martial arts must change, too.'

While karate's techniques may have had their lethality downgraded, karate's core philosophy and allure have remained the same. As the chief of the Okinawa Karate Information Centre (OKIC) explained to me, 'Its appeal lies not only in physical strength, but also in its deep emphasis on courtesy and respect, as well as in the cultivation of character through rigorous training of both body and mind'.

I couldn't agree more; I most certainly wouldn't be who I am without the training, physical and mental, that I received at dojos teaching Okinawan karate.

Karate in Modern-Day Okinawa

Itosu and Funakoshi, both considered fathers of modern karate, were on to something with their drive to make karate more accessible to everyday people. Today karate is enjoyed by millions worldwide. In Okinawa Prefecture, roughly 400 dojos serve approximately 6000 practitioners. Beyond dojos, karate is deeply integrated into Okinawan life, with the martial art enjoying intangible cultural asset status in the prefecture and karate demonstrations part of sports days and athletic festivals at schools from daycare through to high school. Cultural events, too, include karate, with Okinawa's Karate Day – celebrated on 25 October since 2005 – involving a variety of karate-centric events.

Funakoshi Gichin (p304)

The Okinawa prefectural government is also seeking to have Okinawan karate inscribed on the UNESCO Intangible Cultural Heritage list. The hope, says OKIC's chief, is to 'increase global recognition of Okinawa karate's value – not only among karate practitioners, but among people everywhere – while also fostering greater awareness and momentum for its preservation and transmission'.

Karate is alive. It lives in multiple styles and it changes by dojo, by teacher and by generation in subtle and not-so-subtle ways. It awakens the imaginations of its practitioners and expands their perception of the possible, all while strengthening their bodies and spirits. That it began in secrecy on a small island in the Western Pacific and now inspires practitioners worldwide while remaining an important part of its homeland's culture is a profound testament to its timeless teachings.

THE OKINAWAN TABLE

For centuries Okinawans have enjoyed a long, healthy life on their tropical island. Their secret? The colourful, nutrient-packed Okinawan diet. By Rie Miyoshi

WALK THROUGH ŌGIMI village in northern Okinawa and you'll see locals tending their gardens, chatting with neighbours and enjoying a friendly game of gateball (a cross between golf and croquet). The surprising part? Many of them are well over 80. Beyond its tropical beaches, Okinawa is a designated Blue Zone – home to one of the highest concentrations of centenarians in the world, where people don't just live longer but also better. Researchers point to the Okinawan diet, a way of eating grounded in simplicity, seasonality and the strength of community.

A Heritage of Longevity

The Okinawan diet is a philosophy and cultural identity. For centuries islanders relied on limited resources and practised moderation, following the Confucian-inspired *hara hachi bu,* which means eating until you're 80% full. Even after the islands were annexed, the local cuisine remained rooted in the Chinese principle of *ishoku dogen,* which links good health to eating high-quality, seasonal ingredients.

Okinawans also prioritise communal meals, as *moai* (lifelong social bonds) reduce stress. Physical activity, whether it's gardening, walking or dancing, complements a nutritious diet of whole foods that protect against heart disease, diabetes and cancer.

Signature Dishes

An Okinawan spread is packed with vegetables and island-grown superfoods. What makes these dishes healthy isn't just the ingredients but the balance: plenty of vegetables, fruit and seaweed with moderate amounts of protein, mainly pork.

Unlike mainland Japan, where rice was the dominant staple, Okinawans historically relied on *imo* (potatoes and yams). In recent years the vibrant, purple-fleshed *beni-imo* (Okinawan sweet potato) has become a major ingredient and provides slow-release carbs and antioxidants.

Goya champurū is a popular dish of *goya* (bitter melon) stir-fried with tofu, egg and pork or tuna. It has become a symbol of Okinawan resilience, as *goya* grows easily in hot, humid weather and has nourished families during times of hardship. *Goya* is rich in vitamin C, antioxidants and compounds that help regulate blood sugar, support digestion and boost immunity.

Hechima (sponge gourd) is used as a bath sponge elsewhere in the world, but in Okinawa the young, tender vegetable is eaten as a summer food. Because it's high in water, *hechima* is hydrating and cooling.

STORYBOOK

It has a mild, slightly sweet flavour and a soft texture when cooked, similar to zucchini or eggplant. *Hechima* is usually stir-fried, simmered with miso or bonito stock, or added to clear soups.

Other side dishes include *shima dofu*, a firm tofu that's higher in protein and minerals than regular tofu. Mineral and fibre-rich seaweed like *mozuku* is packed with anti-inflammatory compounds, while *konbu* and *hijiki* are stewed with vegetables or added to soups for calcium, iron and iodine. *Umi budo* (sea grapes) are tiny green clusters of seaweed that pop with a salty, ocean-fresh burst. Packed with minerals, antioxidants and fibre, they're often served chilled with ponzu citrus sauce.

Hearty dishes include Okinawa soba (wheat noodles in clear pork or bonito-based broth topped with green onions and fish cake) and *rafute* (pork belly braised in soy, brown sugar and a local liquor called *awamori*).

Preserving the Ryūkyūan Diet

While the Okinawan diet has drawn international acclaim, the reality in Okinawa today tells a different story. 'The traditional Okinawan diet changed drastically after WWII, when the US military established bases here,' explains Yukie Miyaguni, a traditional Chinese medicine (TCM) practitioner and Okinawan diet chef. 'Most cuisines evolve gradually, but Okinawa's food culture shifted almost overnight.'

American foods quickly captured local curiosity, and traditional dishes were replaced. As fewer people cooked at home, knowledge of Okinawan recipes began to fade. Working as a hospital nutritionist, Miyaguni saw the health consequences firsthand.

'There was a stark contrast,' she recalls. 'Near the US bases people craved French fries with gravy and coffee. In the countryside the elderly still preferred traditional dishes.' The difference showed up in their health too. Obesity and lifestyle-related diseases like high cholesterol were more common near the bases, while rural elders often displayed the old wisdom of 'food as medicine'. For Miyaguni, the link between diet and wellbeing was undeniable.

Her research revealed deep parallels between Okinawan cuisine and TCM philosophy, particularly the idea that food and medicine share the same origin. This inspired her to open a cooking school in Uruma, an hour north of Okinawa's capital, Naha. Her classes begin with an introduction to the traditional Okinawan diet. She then assesses participants' skin, tongue and energy levels before recommending tailored foods. Finally, she teaches authentic recipes that students can recreate at home.

Miyaguni also works to dispel a popular myth. 'People think the Okinawan diet is mostly vegetarian, but pork has always been central,' she says, pointing to her treasured copy of *Gozen Honzo*, an 1832 diet therapy guide written by Tokashiki Pechin Tsukan, physician to the king of the Ryūkyū Kingdom. The book describes over 300 ingredients, from grains and vegetables to meat and fish, and details their medicinal uses and ideal combinations.

In Okinawan cooking, pork is carefully prepared; first, it's boiled for over an hour to remove harmful fats while preserving collagen-rich ones, then simmered in soups, stir-fried or broiled. Nothing goes to waste: lard, blood and every cut of the pig is used. 'Everything but the oink!' Miyaguni laughs. 'But the key is balance – pairing the meat with plenty of vegetables and other nourishing ingredients.'

Where to Eat the Okinawan Diet

Naha's Makishi district was once a hub of Asian trade, and at the bustling Makishi Public Market (p52) visitors can still browse everything from colourful fish and tropical fruits to Okinawan staples. The surrounding alleys tempt passersby with ready-to-eat treats such as fresh tempura, steamed cakes and even refreshing *goya* juice. On the 2nd floor, eateries serve homestyle Okinawan cooking.

About an hour north of Naha is Onna no Eki Nakayukui Market, one of Okinawa's most popular roadside stops, as you can sample the island's flavours on the go. It showcases local produce and gourmet treats, with fruit and vegetable stands overflowing with seasonal bounty like mangoes, dragonfruit and pineapples in summer and *atemoya* (sugar apple) and island citrus in winter.

WHERE NATURE RULES

Amami-Ōshima offers abundant opportunities to not only experience nature, but also learn about sustainability and ecological conservation. By Manami Okazaki

MANY OF THE tourist sites and activities – such as surfing, diving, and canoeing – take place within complex ecosystems where one can immerse oneself in nature. However, rather than exploitation, the focus is on sustainability, and relationships between human and nature. Most of the Amami museums are devoted to educating visitors about environmental conservation.

Human & Nature Symbiosis

Driving around Amami-Ōshima for the first time feels like a revelation. In a country where the coast is lined with seawalls and overwhelmed with concrete tetrapods, the sight of verdant mountains dropping down to pristine beaches is exceptional.

Amami's landscape is teeming with life, as dense forest habitats dominate the island. Approximately five million years ago, Amami-Ōshima was separated from the Eurasian continent and became an island, which led to geographic isolation. This led to high biodiversity of species that have evolved over time, like the abundant Amami rabbit and Amami spiny rat that have become extinct on the mainland. In fact, there are numerous endemic species thriving on the island, such as the Lidth's jay, Ryukyu woodpecker, Amami thrush, and Amami Ishikawa's frog that can be seen on ecotours around the island.

QuruGuru is an Amami-rabbit-conservation research facility, where visitors can observe their rehabilitation efforts nursing injured rabbits. Taisei Shiraishi from QuruGuru explains, 'The Amami rabbit is only found on Amami and Tokunoshima Islands because there were no natural carnivorous predators, and the high mountains allowed for their survival even when sea levels rose.'

The abundance of Amami's nature is largely due to this isolation, coupled with the basic fact that the locals – from tour guides to surfers – are conscious of its importance. Photographer and researcher at the Amami Museum, Tatsuya Hiragi, says: 'In 2017, the Amami Islands were designated as Japan's 34th National Park and a new concept called "environmental culture" was introduced. While the conventional idea behind national parks focused solely on conservation, the Amami Islands became the first to incorporate a model that emphasises cultural aspects, where the people live closely connected with nature, adapting to seasonal changes and continuing a lifestyle that benefits from the sea and mountains.'

Local surfer and environmental activist Yusei Ikariyama (and owner of Can. nen Surf School) is part of a community of

STORYBOOK

around 300 surfers, some in their seventies, who are blessed with being on an island with reef breaks – a rarity for Japan. For Ikariyama, the experience of surfing is holistic, not just whether the waves are good or not. 'The ocean is so clear and beautiful, even the smaller waves are enjoyable because the overall experience is of such high quality.' He explains: 'The view from the ocean is devoid of man-made structures, so it's a great environment for surfing.'

He points out that the appeal of Amami is just as much the people as the nature: 'The fact that Amami has preserved its ecosystem is because the people didn't overdevelop it, unlike in Okinawa. Locals have prioritised a tradition of living alongside nature over business. That is why cultural events are so valued here; the sense of community is incredibly strong. It is a culture that relies on the environment.'

Fragile Ecosystems

The importance of conscious tourism is paramount with an isolated and fragile ecosystem. In recent years, the question of how humans and the environment should coexist became a point of contention with the invasion of non-native plants and animals, and infrastructure that is harmful to wildlife. Tatsuya Hiragi explains: 'another issue is poaching. Amami-Ōshima is home to many rare and endemic species protected by law and local regulations. In recent years, there have been many incidents where these species were illegally taken off the island.' Naturally, as a photographer, Hiragi wants tourists to enjoy 'observing or photographing wildlife, rather than capturing and taking them'.

Marine biologist and environmental activist Giovanni Masucci agrees that forests are extremely sensitive environments. 'Even if you keep the majority of the surface area natural, sometimes just cutting through a forest can create fragmentation and disturb species migration,' Masucci says. 'Unless it is wildlife that can fly, roadkill is a big problem, not just in Amami but Okinawa and Iriomote Islands.'

Masucci sees a need for pragmatic environmental advocacy that emphasises benefits to humans as well. 'Amami is relatively underdeveloped, but on the brink of becoming developed; but how? First of all, you need to put a price on the natural benefits and make it economically viable. if you have tourism that's based on consumption and shopping malls, they won't care about the coastline, so tourism should be steered towards the beauty of nature. Protected areas and national parks are helpful, but without solid management, generally local people won't be invested in it. An economy where nature brings money will make them feel that nature is worth protecting.'

Local Eco-Guides

Amami-Ōshima once had a thriving forestry industry, which means that a lot of what covers the island is secondary forest. Given that protecting the remaining primeval forests has become a priority ever since, many areas are only accessible with a registered eco-guide. New Zealand native, John Cantu is an Amami-Ōshima eco-guide at Amami Tours and explains that in order to receive an 'eco-guide' licence, the process is quite the ordeal. 'One needs to be living on the island for two years prior to starting a two-year course, armed with a deep knowledge of nature. Only after a year of experience guiding does one get licensed,' says Cantu. 'I think it's important to keep up the quality of guides in order to protect the natural world – that is Amami's future. If it's not looked after, then future generations won't have a natural world to present. It's a balance.'

Yusei Ikariyama says, 'If you look at just the scenery, tourists will miss the depth of the Amami experience, which encapsulates the lifestyle, culture and values of local people. Tourists and locals can work together to preserve and enhance the island. Even for experienced surfers, they will benefit a lot from going out with a guide who knows the culture.

'The reason I love diving and surfing is that they allow me to completely disconnect from phones and emails; it is just you and your thoughts. I think Amami allows people to feel something extraordinary and that becomes more valuable the more we preserve nature. That's the real meaning of "Amami's legacy".'

Kinsakubaru Old-Growth Forest (p246)

INDEX

Map Pages **000**

Map Pages **000**

walking 39, see also hiking
walking tours
    Hirara 179, **179**
    Iriomote Island 223-4
    Naha 55, **55**
    Nanjō 86, **86**
waterfalls
    Pinaisāra waterfall 219, 222
weather 28-9

weights 289
whale watching
    Amami-Ōshima 249-50
    Tokashiki-jima 169
    Tomarin 60-1
wildlife 39, *see also individual species*
wildlife watching 37
    Iriomote Wildlife Conservation Centre 223
    Yambaru National Park 144-6
WWII sites 80-1

Yachimun no Sato 110-11
Yaeyama Islands 26-7, 200-33, **202-3**
    itineraries 204-5
    navigation 202-3
    travel seasons 204-5
    travel within 202
Yambaru National Park 23, 144-7, **145**

Yomitan 107-9, 123, **108**
Yonaguni Island 27, 230-2, 233, **231**
Yonaguni *uma* 231
Yonaha-Maehama 24
Yoron-tō 21, 268-9, 272, 273, **269**, **272**

Zamami-jima 23, 166-8, 171, **167**

'In Okinawa, I'm confronted with the irony of researching folk culture by day, and at night scarfing massive quantities of culinary wonders like taco rice, root beer and Blue Seal ice cream (p102).'

MANAMI OKAZAKI

'Sitting on the sand at Yoron-tō's offshore 'phantom beach', Yurigahama (p268), which appears and disappears with the tides.'

CRAIG MCLACHLAN

Mapping data sources:
© Lonely Planet
© OpenStreetMap http://openstreetmap.org/copyright

THIS BOOK

Destination Editor
Selena Hoy

Coordinating Editor
Sarah Bailey

Cartographer
Alison Lyall

Production Editor
Kathryn Rowan

Image Researcher
Fabrice Robin

Assisting Editors
Michelle Bennett, Jennifer McCann, Karyn Noble, Charlotte Orr, Maja Vatrić

Cover Researcher
Daisy Korpics

Thanks Chris Lee-Ack, Wayne Murphy

Paper in this book is certified against the Forest Stewardship Council™ standards. FSC™ promotes environmentally responsible, socially beneficial and economically viable management of the world's forests.

Published by Lonely Planet Global Limited
CRN 554153
1st edition – July 2026
ISBN 978 1 83758 820 6
© Lonely Planet 2026 Photographs © as indicated 2026
10 9 8 7 6 5 4 3 2 1
Printed in Malaysia